Cultural Sociology in Practice

P9-EAX-688

21ST-CENTURY SOCIOLOGY

SERIES EDITOR: Steven Seidman, State University of New York at Albany

The *21st-Century Sociology* series provides instructors and students with key texts in sociology that speak with a distinct sociological voice and offer thoughtful and original perspectives. The texts reflect current discussions in and beyond sociology, avoiding standard textbook definitions to engage students in critical thinking and new ideas. Prominent scholars in various fields of social inquiry combine theoretical perspectives with the latest research to present accessible syntheses for students as we move further into the new millennium amidst rapid social change.

CULTURAL SOCIOLOGY IN PRACTICE

LAURA DESFOR EDLES

Blackwell Publishing

© 2002 by Laura Desfor Edles

BLACKWELL PUBLISHING
350 Main Street, Malden, MA 02148-5020, USA
9600 Garsington Road, Oxford OX4 2DQ, UK
550 Swanston Street, Carlton, Victoria 3053, Australia

The right of Laura Desfor Edles to be identified as the Author of this Work has been
asserted in accordance with the UK Copyright, Designs, and Patents Act 1988.

All rights reserved. No part of this publication may be reproduced, stored in a retrieval
system, or transmitted, in any form or by any means, electronic, mechanical, photocopying,
recording or otherwise, except as permitted by the UK Copyright, Designs, and Patents Act
1988, without the prior permission of the publisher.

First published 2002 by Blackwell Publishing Ltd

4   2008

Library of Congress Cataloging-in-Publication Data

Edles, Laura Desfor.
    Cultural sociology in practice
    p.   cm. — (21st-century sociology)
    ISBN 978-0-631-21089-4 (alk. paper) — ISBN 978-0-631-21090-0 (pb. : alk. paper)
    1. Sociology. 2. Culture. I. Series.

HM585 .E37 2001
306 — dc21

                                              2001025206

A catalogue record for this title is available from the British Library.

Set in 10 on 12 pt Photina
by Ace Filmsetting Ltd, Frome, Somerset

The publisher's policy is to use permanent paper from mills that operate a sustainable
forestry policy, and which has been manufactured from pulp processed using acid-free and
elementary chlorine-free practices. Furthermore, the publisher ensures that the text paper
and cover board used have met acceptable environmental accreditation standards.

For further information on
Blackwell Publishing, visit our website:
www.blackwellpublishing.com

Contents

Figures and Tables

Figures

Tables

Acknowledgments

This book is dedicated to Professor Jeffrey C. Alexander, and the "Culture Club" reading groups at UCLA, past and present (as well as "culture groups" everywhere). Although I feel like I've "always" been interested in "culture," my understanding of what culture is and how culture works really began to take shape at UCLA in the 1980s. I had spent a year in Spain on the University of California Education Abroad Program in 1980–1. I was fascinated by Spanish (and Basque and Catalan) language/s, music, dance, festivals, religion, public life – but also by the tremendous *political* changes in Spain. When I began graduate school in 1982, I was intent on explaining the relationship between "culture structures" and "social structures" sociologically. Jeff Alexander guided me in this quest. I was deeply influenced also by other students in the "Culture Club," whose intellectual journeys seemed to parallel mine. Moreover, the Culture Group provided a supportive environment for becoming a "culturalist" at a time when being a "culturalist" was still viewed suspiciously. How far cultural sociology has come in twenty years!

In Spring 2000, the UCLA Culture Group again helped me by reading several chapters of this book. I am tremendously grateful to Jeff and his students for their comments and suggestions. I hope this book will be read and enjoyed by many more students of culture at various stages of their careers, my own students included.

I owe a special thanks to my department chair at California State University, Northridge, Jane Prather, for her friendship and support as I finished this book. I am also indebted to my new colleague and friend, Scott Appelrouth, who, despite being a recently relocated assistant professor in the first year of his first tenure-track job (and the father of two toddlers) took time away from his own work to carefully read and comment on this entire book. In the last several years, I have benefitted also from conversations with and/or comments from colleagues throughout the United

States, most importantly, Bill Gibson, Ron Jacobs, Anne Kane, Paul Lichterman, Eric Rambo, Lynn Rapaport, Lyn Spillman, and Rhys Williams.

I was very fortunate to have had the support of my former department chairs at the University of Hawai'i, Manoa, Eldon Wegner, and Kiyoshi Ikeda. I thank too the students and faculty in the University of Hawai'i and East/West Center International Cultural Studies Certificate program, particularly Geoffrey White, for allowing me to share my work with them. My research assistant, Ida Yoshinaga, performed all sorts of tasks outside her official job description, for which I am very grateful. David Johnson and Miriam Stark were wonderful former colleagues, who are now simply "friends."

At Blackwell, I thank Steve Seidman for his expertise, comments and support. I am also grateful to Susan Rabinowitz, who got this project going, Ken Provencher, who helped it stay on track, and Juanita Bullough, who saw it through to the end. This book is much better because of them.

This book was written during a rather difficult transitional period in my life – the consequences of a "dual-career" family situation. I am grateful for the love and support of my husband, Mike, as well as the strength and patience of our children Benny and Ellie. As *ipso facto*, involuntary students of culture, this book is also written for them.

L. D. E.

Introduction: What is Culture, and How Does Culture Work?

"Culture" is one of sociology's most interesting and widely used concepts. "Culture" is central to the humanities, the social sciences, and the fine and performing arts, where it is understood in a variety of ways. "Culture" is also used colloquially in everyday life, where it takes on a myriad of meanings. But while the tremendous range of definitions and usage makes the concept interesting, this same multiplicity of meanings makes culture confusing and ambiguous. In this book, we seek to sort out the concept of culture. This project is at once theoretical, methodological, and empirical. In the ensuing chapters, we seek to explain: what is culture and how does culture work? How do we identify and "measure" the basic elements of culture? How and why does understanding culture enhance our view of the world? In other words, how and why does culture matter?

Three Usages of "Culture"

Despite the plethora of meanings of the term "culture," by and large, these definitions can be divided into three groups. "Culture" can be used to refer to (1) humanistic refinement and elite artistic activities (classical ballet, opera); (2) an entire way of life of a people or group (e.g., as seen in *National Geographic*); or (3) systems or patterns of shared symbols. These categories can be understood respectively, as aesthetic, ethnographic, and symbolic definitions of culture.

Aesthetic (or humanistic) definitions of culture — culture as "high culture"

One of the most common uses of the term "culture" comes from the same root as "cultivation," as in agriculture; it means the "cultivation of the human mind and sensibility" (Griswold 1994, p. 7; see also Eagleton 2000, p. 1). In this sense, "culture" can be used as a noun to refer to "the best and most important or glorious achievements of a people or civilization" (e.g,. classical ballet, opera, Shakespeare); or "culture" can be used as an adjective to refer to aesthetic sensibility, i.e., emotional or intellectual sensitivity to art and beauty (e.g., to become "cultured," a "cultured" person). The relationship between culture as a noun (the elite arts) and culture as an adjective (aesthetic sensibility) is that it is thought that through the experience and "appreciation" of classic aesthetic form (ballet, opera, literature, art) that aesthetic sensibility is acquired.

The importance of the humanistic definition of culture is that the arts and aesthetic sensibility are what makes human groups distinctive. Debates may rage as to whether or not and to what extent nonhuman animals have "emotions" and use "language"; but there is no question that only human activity is mired in such vibrant, complex, abstract, varied aesthetic forms. So far as we know, only humans seek to create "art" for the sole purpose of self-expression. So far as we know, only humans are moved to tears by *fictional* books and films.

Nevertheless, there are two conceptual problems with the aesthetic definition of culture. First, the problem with defining culture as aesthetic sensibility, sophistication, or refinement is that this is taken to refer to a quality in *individuals*, but, as we will see, culture is a *collective* phenomenon. Culture, by definition, is shared; there is no such thing as "individual" culture. Secondly, the problem with defining culture as "the best that has been thought and said in the world" is that this conceptualization is elitist. It is part and parcel of a "high culture"/"low culture" dichotomy in which only select cultural forms are seen as "genuine." Conversely, the opposite of "high culture" is deemed "low culture" (or "mass culture," "folk culture," or "popular culture"). Such cultural products are understood as less "sophisticated" or "refined" – or relatively superficial, or even base – forms of expression. This high culture/low culture dichotomy implies that there is a relatively "objective" degree of sensibility apparent in every cultural work, such that some cultural works are clearly distinguishable as "better" than others. But in fact, why one category or genre of art is "high" and another "low" is primarily a sociological rather than an aesthetic issue; the classification of art as "high" or "low," or "popular" or "folk," revolves around socioeconomic and sociocultural, far more than *aesthetic*, standards and conditions.

Consider, for instance, the example of jazz – often heralded as the United

States' most important native musical form. While there are obviously many styles and genres of jazz, technically, intellectually, and emotionally, jazz is "sophisticated." In terms of its complexity, sensibility, and historical role, surely jazz qualifies as (high) "culture."

But of course, jazz first developed in the United States around the turn of the century out of West African musical traditions and African American folk music. Though jazz also reflects the vocabulary and structures of European classical and popular music, it is most distinctive for its West African traits: vocal styles that include great freedom of vocal color, a tradition of improvisation, call-and-response patterns, and rhythmic complexity – both syncopation of individual melodic lines and counterpunctuated rhythms played by different members of an ensemble.[1]

The point is, jazz did not become (high) "culture" when the music itself became more sophisticated or complex; the exact same characteristics that make jazz "sophisticated" are also apparent in its earlier, more "popular" or "folk" forms. Rather, jazz became *recognized* as "high" culture only after it was legitimated in the early twentieth century by white cultural elites (although, significantly, even today some people think of *only* classical music – not jazz – as "high" culture).[2] Specifically, the first jazz band record was not recorded by American blacks; it was recorded in 1917 by a group of white New Orleans musicians called The Original Dixieland Jazz Band. This record created a sensation in Europe and the United States, and gradually – especially after classically trained white musicians (such as George Gershwin and Aaron Copland) turned their attention to jazz – jazz became respected as a "true," elite art form (Appelrouth 1999).[3]

In sum, the difference between the "field hollers" sung by unschooled African Americans as they picked cotton in the nineteenth century and the "jazz" performed at the Lincoln Center for the Performing Arts today is not so much aesthetic, but socioeconomic and symbolic: each genre reflects distinct locations in hierarchical class and status systems. Indeed, the very idea that (high) culture is the "most important or glorious achievements of a people or civilization" should alert us to the fact that this is a *social* and *cultural* and not an aesthetic classification.

Yet this is not to say that "high culture" is simply a reflection of socioeconomic phenomena. As we will see, to say that culture or art simply *reflects* economics is not a very *cultural* argument or interpretation. Nor am I saying that all culture has the "same" artistic merit, creativity, etc. That the high culture/low culture dichotomy is false and elitist does not mean all artistic expression is of equal quality or value, nor that all people in society have equal access to "culture" (see Bourdieu 1984). There is good "popular" art, and bad "popular" art, and good classical music and bad classical music, etc. (though, obviously, in deeming art "good" or "bad" one must be clear as to the criteria one is using as a yardstick).

ETHNOGRAPHIC DEFINITIONS OF CULTURE — CULTURE AS AN ENTIRE
WAY OF LIFE

In contrast to the narrow definition of culture as aesthetic (and generally
elite) sensibility is the broad, anthropological definition of culture as "that
complex whole which includes knowledge, belief, art, morals, law, custom and any other capabilities and habits acquired by man as a member
of society" (Tylor 1958 [1871], p. 1; Griswold 1994, p. 8). This expansive
definition of culture has been preponderant in the social sciences since
first enunciated by the anthropologist E. B. Tylor in the late nineteenth
century. The advantage of this definition of culture is, first, that it circumvents the ethnocentrism and elitism of the aesthetic definition of culture;
and second, that it underscores that "culture" is not "above and beyond,"
but part and parcel of, the everyday world (Griswold 1994, p. 8). For
cultural anthropologists (as well as others) who utilize this conceptualization
of culture, culture is all-encompassing and all-pervasive. Culture is at the
heart of human existence.[4]

Yet, as E. P. Thompson has pointed out, the problem with the ethnographic definition of culture is that "any theory of culture must include
the concept of the dialectical interaction between culture and something
that is *not* culture" (Hall 1980 [1973], p. 62). The broad, ethnographic
definition inflates "culture" to mean all that is produced by human groups,
to include all elements of social life – anything that is not biological or
evolutionary. In other words, while the definition of culture as aesthetic
sensibility is too narrow and does not link "culture" and "society" enough,
the ethnographic definition of culture as "an entire way of life" is too
broad; it links "culture" and "society" too much. There is no way to
distinguish the cultural realm from *other* dimensions of society. There is a
complete *fusion* of the *social* and the *cultural* realms.

One of the most unfortunate consequences of the ethnographic
overinflation of "culture" (or the fusion of the culture and social structure) is that it has periodically spurred anthropologists and sociologists to
abandon the concept of culture altogether. This trend began in the 1930s,
when the eminent anthropologist Alfred Radcliffe-Brown set his sights on
explaining "social structures" (such as kinship) rather than "culture,"
because while "culture" denotes only a "vague abstraction," "social structure" denotes "networks of actually existing social relations," which can
be revealed by "direct observation."[5] For Radcliffe-Brown, anthropology
was a *scientific* discipline parallel to the physical and biological sciences;
thus, anthropology had no place for abstract concepts that were hard to
measure. As he states (in Applebaum 1987, p. 122): "I conceive of social
anthropology as the theoretical natural science of human society, that is,
the investigation of social phenomena by methods essentially similar to

those used in the physical and biological sciences. I am quite willing to call the subject 'comparative sociology' if anyone so wishes." Interestingly, this focus on the *social* rather than the *cultural* realm diminishes the distinctions between human and nonhuman groups. There is only an empirical – and not a theoretical – difference between social anthropology and zoology, etc. Thus, Radcliffe-Brown maintains:

> In a hive of bees there are the relations of association of the queen, the workers and the drones. There is the association of animals in a herd, of a mother-cat and her kittens. These are social phenomena; I do not suppose that anyone will call them cultural phenomena. In anthropology, of course, we are only concerned with human beings, and in social anthropology, as I define it, what we have to investigate are the forms of association to be found amongst human beings. (p. 122)

Elsewhere he states (1957, p. 58, as cited by Kuper 1996, p. 52): "You cannot have a science of culture. You can study culture only as a characteristic of a social system . . . if you study culture, you are always studying the acts of behavior of a specific set of persons who are linked together in a social structure."

Interestingly, forty years later, structural sociologists in the United States abandoned cultural variables for much the same reason. Whereas Radcliffe-Brown and his associates replaced "culture" with social structural variables such as kinship, sociologists such as Charles Tilly (1978) and Theda Skocpol (1979) replaced subjective variables such as "solidarity" (the feeling of "oneness" with a group) with "objective" variables such as "organizational resources" and "social networks" in order to explain the rise and success of specific social movements. They argued that extant forms of social change, such as revolution, can be fully explained by focusing on *economic* and *political* factors and ignoring *cultural* conditions (see Edles 1995, 1998). Structural sociologists of the 1970s did not *deny* the existence of culture; but they considered culture *epiphenomenal* (a *consequence*, and not a *cause* of social change).[6]

Indeed, even today sociologists and cultural analysts continue to spar around the theoretical and methodological problems caused by the *subjectivity* of cultural phenomena. Yet, as we will see in this book, theoretically and methodologically, contemporary cultural analysts *are* creating new ways to get a handle on *meaning*. Even more importantly, today cultural sociologists are demonstrating *how* culture informs and thereby *shapes* very real social issues and concerns.

SYMBOLIC NOTIONS OF CULTURE — CULTURE AS SYSTEMS OF SHARED MEANING

Since the 1960s, increasing numbers of social scientists have turned away from defining culture as an "entire way of life" and moved toward defining culture as systems or patterns of *shared symbols and/or meaning* (Geertz, 1973, p. 89). This is the definition of culture adopted in this book. Cultural systems (or symbolic systems, or systems of meaning) include highly organized and formalized systems of meaning, such as religion, as well as relatively mundane, taken-for-granted webs of signification integral to daily life (e.g., knowing whether or not to bring a gift to the home of a friend, or whether or not to take off one's shoes when entering the house), as well as highly organized but also open symbolic systems, such as language and fashion.

Thus, significantly, the symbolic definition of culture coincides with the humanistic/aesthetic definition of culture discussed previously in that art *is* a type of symbolic phenomenon. The relationship between "art" and symbolic phenomena in general is that art is simply a particularly *effective* symbol; "art" combines "economy of statement with richness of expression" (Jaeger and Selznick 1964, p. 664, as cited by Gilmore 1992, pp. 408–9). However, in contrast to the aesthetic definition of "culture" (which limits culture to *only* the "arts"), the symbolic definition of culture includes *all* symbolic phenomena (not just art), i.e., language, religion, fashion, etc.

Yet, in contrast to the aesthetic definition of culture, the symbolic definition of culture underscores that culture is collective and *shared*. Like the ethnographic definition of culture, the symbolic definition of culture emphasizes that cultural systems are historically linked to specific social groups at specific moments, and intertwined in complex ways with other societal dimensions. The *collective* nature of culture is most evident in *language*, which is, as indicated previously, one of the most fundamental systems of meaning. (*Webster's Dictionary* defines language as "the words, pronunciation, and methods of combining them used and understood by a considerable community . . . a systematic means of signs, gestures, marks, or especially articulate vocal sound.")[7]

In my view, the symbolic definition of culture is most useful in conjunction with the more general notion that societies are composed of three analytically (but not empirically) distinct parts: the (1) economic, (2) political, and (3) cultural realms.[8] Specifically, all societies have some sort of *economic* system/s, or means through which goods and services are produced and distributed. Common economic systems include "capitalism" (in which land and labor are bought and sold by private individuals), "bartering" (the exchange of goods/services without the intermediary of money), and "reciprocation" ("turn-taking" systems, such as barn-raisings and gift exchanges, e.g., I give you a gift on your birthday, and you give me one on mine). Secondly, every society has some sort of *political* system/s (e.g., dictatorship, theocracy, monarchy, democracy), or ways in which *power* is distributed (or not distributed) and decisions are made. For instance, since the 1990s, we have seen a rapid decline in socialist regimes, and a rise in more formally *democratic* political systems (see Edles 1995, 1998).[9] Finally, every society has *cultural* (or *symbolic*) systems through which people "make sense" of the world. These "webs of signification" (Geertz 1973, p. 5) provide a nonmaterial or metaphysical structure; they represent a level of organization that patterns action as surely as structures of a more visible kind (Alexander and Smith 1993, p. 156).

As we will see further in the next chapter, one of the central ways that cultural systems are *structured* is into the "sacred" and the "profane." In this basic symbolic dichotomy the "sacred" is that which is "holy" and "good"; the sacred is *set apart* from everyday life, it is respected and revered. While the symbolic opposite of the "sacred" is the "profane," that which is evil, or bad. The "profane" is typically the violation of the sacred. The sacred and the profane are most readily apparent in the religious realm (e.g., God and Satan; the Ten Commandments, etc.), however, this basic symbolic dichotomy underlies all kinds of cultural systems as well.

Thus, for instance, the "high culture"/"low culture" dichotomy at the heart of the aesthetic definition of culture discussed previously imbues "high culture" with the qualities of the sacred (the good and revered); and "low culture" (including "popular culture" or "mass culture") with the qualities of its symbolic opposite, the profane (the bad or common). According to this symbolization, "high culture" is *pure, precious*, and *good*; thus, "high culture" must be set apart and away from both "low culture" and the everyday world. The sacrality of "high culture" is reflected and reaffirmed in the great cultural institutions of the world (museums, libraries, theatres) through such architectural features as grand entrances and high ceilings, and through norms and rituals that inspire awe and silence (Griswold 1994, p. 7). It is precisely this *sacrality* that gives "high culture" the imposing mantle of religious authority (Eagleton 2000, p. 2). "High culture" must be carefully guarded and preserved – because it is in "danger" of being "lost," debilitated, wiped out, or *overrun* by (profane) popular or mass cultural forms.[10]

The problem with the symbolic definition of culture is that it erroneously implies that culture is *only* symbolic. This is why, as we will see in chapters 6 and 7, contemporary theorists such as Pierre Bourdieu and the late Michel Foucault introduce provocative new concepts – e.g., "habitus" and "discourse" – that pointedly *integrate* social/cultural and political/economic realms. These analysts demonstrate that culture is continuously embodied, *practiced*, and reproduced, i.e., that it does not simply "exist" in abstract forms. However, whether one uses new terms and concepts (e.g., *habitus*, discourse), or the symbolic definition of culture (as I do in this book), the point is that "culture" and "social structure" are only analytically, and never empirically, distinct. There are intricate systems of meaning about production and distribution (e.g., consumerism, reciprocation), and there are complex notions of authority and power (e.g., ideology). Thus, while certain areas of social practice (e.g., the arts, religion) are more overtly symbolic than others (e.g., the economy), there is nothing inherently noncultural about utilitarian activities. All collective social practices are potentially symbolic and therefore potentially cultural (Gilmore 1992, p. 409). In sum, as Alexander (1998) states:

> Every action, no matter how instrumental and reflexive vis-à-vis its external environments, is imbedded in a horizon of meaning (an internal environment) in relationship to which it can be neither instrumental nor reflexive. Every institution, no matter how technical, coercive, or seemingly impersonal, can only be effective if related to patterned sets of symbols that instruct it to become so and to an audience that "reads" it in a technical, coercive, and impersonal way. For this reason, every specialized subfield of sociology must have a cultural dimension; if not, the very workings of action arenas and institutional fields will never be fully understood.

The Example of Colonialism

Consider, for instance, the issue of colonialism/imperialism.[11] Colonialism is typically considered an *economic* phenomenon. Historically, whether it was procuring new spices in the Orient, or land or gold and silver in the Americas, the explicit goal of the European and American expansionist movements of the last several centuries was (and is) often economic or material gain.This is precisely the type of motivation that Marx and Engels so eloquently discussed in *The Communist Manifesto:* "the need of a constantly expanding market for its products chases the bourgeoisie over the whole surface of the globe. It must nestle everywhere, settle everywhere, establish connections everywhere" (Marx and Engels 1970 [1848], p. 474; see also Lenin 1917).

But as Marx and Engels also realized, imperialism/colonialism is, and has always been, an overtly *political* issue – the goal is/was not simply the extraction/production/distribution of resources/goods, but also the quest for new territory, more power and greater strategic advantage. This is what is represented by placing the flag of the "old" world on the "new" one (whether it be in Latin America or on the moon).[12] It is a *political* statement that *this* territory belongs to *this* nation. In terms of strategic advantage, the case of the Hawaiian islands is a relatively recent example in this regard. Hawai'i was particularly attractive to the United States not only because of the islands' natural resources, but because of its location in the middle of the Pacific Ocean, literally halfway to Asia.

There is no question that colonialism/imperialism *is* a politico-economic issue. Nevertheless, important cultural questions remain. For instance, what if we find out that colonialism is *not* politically or economically advantageous for the colonizing country? Fieldhouse (1973) points out that especially after the 1880s, colonies often became a tremendous economic and political burden. The point here is not the empirical one as to why a particular country "keeps" or relinquishes its colonies, or why it overlooks "short-term" losses, in anticipation of "long-term" gains. The point is that colonialism "makes sense" *only* in relation to specific economic, political, or ideological goals; and these goals are rooted in specific systems of meaning.

Put in another way, colonialism came about in a specific *cultural* as well as *political* and *economic* context; in order to understand colonialism, we must also understand these systems of meaning. Obviously, the systems of meaning in fifteenth-century Europe or twentieth-century America are varied and complex. Nevertheless, historically, there have been two central cultural lynchpins of colonization. The first is what is generally called "manifest destiny," i.e., the very idea that it was good, and morally right – indeed, inevitable – for Europeans to go out and "tame" or exploit the globe. The racialized version of "manifest destiny" is a type of white supremacy in which whites have the right, destiny, or "burden" of bringing order and "civilization" to, and ruling, the world. Thus, for instance, a colonial planter in Hawai'i in the 1880s proclaims:

> Europe was given to the white man, America to the red man, Asia to the yellow man and Africa to the black man. And with the slight exceptions the white man is the only one that has ventured beyond the "bounds of his habitations". He has over run Europe, and crossing the Atlantic westward has taken possession of America, and is "monarch of all he surveys" from Cape Horn to Behring's [sic] Strait. He has stepped across the Pacific Ocean, leaving the imprint of his enterprising foot upon the various islands of the sea; he has taken possession of Australia and India, with their countless thousands; he has gone to Africa, and this time to stay . . . . The coming of the white man to Africa means government, enterprise, agriculture, commerce, churches, schools, law and order. It will be better for the colored man of India and Australia that the white man rules, and it is better here that the white man should rule. (Daws 1968, p. 213)[13]

The second cultural lynchpin of colonization was Christianity, specifically Christian evangelism, the very idea that Christians had not only the right – but the duty – to propagate and disseminate their religion. Thus for instance, the Philippines became predominantly Catholic instead of Muslim in the sixteenth century because after the Spaniards' early, disappointing search for spices and gold, Spanish colonizers turned single-mindedly to evangelism (Wurfel 1988, p. 4).

That is not to say that "missionaries" were guided by "Christianity" and "politicians" by strategic advantage; historically, political, economic, and cultural motivations were complex and intertwined.[14] Rather, the point is that Christian evangelism and manifest destiny helped define and affirm the very notion of colonialism from the beginning.[15] Christian evangelism and manifest destiny/white supremacy were vital systems of shared meaning that were part and parcel of geographical expansion. The purpose of cultural analysis is to systematically sort out and explain precisely these types of symbolic systems, i.e., the exact nature and impact of systems of symbols/meaning.

In sum, while Radcliffe-Brown set his sights on *ignoring* cultural (and only exploring *social structural*) phenomena, here I follow Geertz (1973, p. 30), who first maintained that we cannot expect to understand human societies without exploring the symbolic (or cultural) realm. As Geertz (1973, p. 30) states, "To look at the symbolic dimensions of social action – art, religion, ideology, science, law, morality, common sense – is not to turn away from the existential dilemmas of life for some empyrean realm of de-emotionalized forms; it is to plunge into the midst of them."

Cultural Sociology vs. Cultural Studies

But of course, there is not *one* "cultural sociology" either. Cultural sociologists are inspired by a wide variety of theoretical and methodological traditions and orientations, both "classical" (e.g., Weber, Durkheim, Gramsci, Mead, Du Bois), and contemporary (e.g., Bourdieu, Foucault, Baudrillard).

To step back a bit: sociology first emerged as a discipline in the late 1800s as a "*science* of society." As we have seen, the anthropologist Radcliffe-Brown sought to explain human societies scientifically. In a parallel way, the founding scholars of sociology, most importantly Max Weber and Emile Durkheim, sought to replace utopian visions with objective, value-neutral, and empirically controlled social explanations (Seidman 1994, p. 11).[16] As Rabinow and Sullivan (1979, p. 1) state:

> As long as there has been a social science, the expectation has been that it would turn from its humanistic infancy to the maturity of hard science, thereby leaving behind its dependence on value, judgement, and individual insight. The dream of modern Western man to be freed from his passions, his unconscious, his history, and his traditions through the liberating use of reason has been the deepest theme of contemporary social science thought.

However, since the 1980s, "interpretive" social scientists, such as Rabinow and Sullivan (1979) and Seidman (1994), have pointed out that replacing the contextual understandings of everyday life with context-free categories is neither possible nor desirable. These analysts emphatically refute the claim that one can somehow reduce the complex world of signification to the products of a self-consciousness in the traditional philosophical sense. Rather, they maintain that "interpretation begins from the postulate that the web of meaning constitutes human existence to such an extent that it cannot ever be meaningfully reduced to constitutively prior speech acts, dyadic relations, or any predefined elements" (Rabinow and Sullivan 1979, p. 5). In short, in accordance with Geertz (1973) and Alexander (1998), these analysts concur that sociology *must* have a cultural dimension.

At the same time that new "interpretive" social scientific perspectives have come to the fore, a new interdisciplinary field called "cultural studies" has emerged. In its most strict sense, cultural studies refers to a tradition that emerged in Britain during the 1960s and 1970s. Often called "British cultural studies," this type of cultural studies can be traced to the founding of the Birmingham Centre for Contemporary Cultural Studies in 1964 as a research grouping within the English Department at the University of Birmingham in the UK. The first director of the center (now called the Birmingham Department of Cultural Studies) was a professor of English, Richard Hoggart, but the second director was Stuart Hall, who though trained as a literature scholar, later took up a Chair in Sociology at the Open University in England. British cultural studies blends seminal work by European structuralists, such as Lévi-Strauss and Barthes, with the work of certain European Marxists, most importantly Antonio Gramsci and Louis Althusser (Turner 1996 [1990], p. 3) (although cultural studies tends to draw on theory informally and "unsystematically," and/or implicitly, rather than explicitly).

In a broader sense, cultural studies refers to any type of work on the relationship between *culture* and *society*. In this sense, cultural studies includes both literary "essays" about culture and society that fall well within the traditional boundaries of the humanities (e.g., Toni Morrison); and more theoretically and methodological grounded works on culture that fall well within the traditional boundaries of sociology (e.g., Joshua Gamson, Stuart Hall). In this broader sense, "cultural studies" is practiced by linguists, geographers, essayists, historians, sociologists, anthropologists, and political scientists, among others.

Nevertheless, as indicated previously, I am not at all arguing that we should *abandon* sociology in favor of "cultural studies." On the contrary, the point is that the subject of culture falls well *within* traditional sociological boundaries; sociology must, in a sense, get *back* to its roots – for sociology was founded as a discipline with an emphasis on locating and identifying systems of shared meaning. In other words, the founding scholars of sociology sought *methodical, empirical* ways of uncovering "social facts" – but they never lost sight of the *existence* and *significance* of human subjectivity. The European classical social theorists "aimed to furnish a sociohistorical account of the making-of-the subject and to expose a social and political unconsciousness in the movement of individuals, societies, and histories" (Seidman 1997, p. 47). In this book, I seek to bring this focus into the present. The idea is to use a methodical, albeit *interpretive*, approach to uncover what the philosopher Wilhelm Dilthey called "human-social-historical-reality" (see chapter 7). Put in another way, Seidman (1997, p. 55) challenges sociologists to dare to see what social knowledge would look like "if we abandon or seriously rethink a modern Enlightenment framework, if we no longer fetishize the Real." The purpose of this book is to help actualize Seidman's challenge.

Cultural Sociology vs. Sociology of Culture

Yet there is another important theoretical and empirical split in the sociological study of culture. This is the split between those who focus on the organizational, bureaucratic, economic, political, and social processes behind the *production* of cultural objects; and those who focus on the *content* and *meaning* of cultural objects themselves. For Berezin (1994, p. 15), cultural sociology is a "fissured terrain," characterized by an uncomfortable split between explanatory methods whose goal it is to explain social processes [sociology of culture], and interpretive methods where the objective is to interpret a wide range of materials in order to identify what might be described as an underlying *Gestalt* [cultural sociology]).

Specifically, since the 1970s, sociologists working within what is now known as the "production of culture" perspective – most importantly, Peterson (1976; 1978), Powell (1978), Becker (1982), and Fine (1992) – have been exploring the *social organization* of "culture" (in the more "artistic" sense of the term). These analysts focus on the "complex apparatus" between cultural creators and consumers (Peterson, 1978, p. 295). This apparatus includes:

> facilities for production and distribution; marketing techniques such as advertising, coopting mass media, or targeting; and the creation of situations that bring potential cultural consumers in contact with cultural objects. Placing racks of paperbacks in a supermarket, signing a new singer with a record company, legwork done before and after a Billy Graham rally, organizing a blockbuster museum exhibit, getting publicity for a new trend in fashion – all of these activities are grist for the production-of-culture mill. (Griswold 1994, p. 71)

Production of culture analysts set their sights on exploring the often *mundane* dimensions of cultural production, including focus on the *reward structure* in artistic production; *gatekeeping* and *decision chains*; and the *careers* of artworkers.

For instance, in his seminal work which helped define the "production of culture" approach, Richard Peterson (1976, 1978) showed the impact of market changes on country music. Peterson showed that after the emergence and dominance of Elvis Presley in the 1950s, country singers banded together to form the Country Music Association (CMA) in order to preserve "country" music. The CMA was in large part responsible for a proliferation of "country" music radio stations in the 1960s. However, ironically, country stations sought to broaden their market by reaching beyond traditional country music fans. Thus, the country stations turned from "country radio" to "modern country radio," i.e., they began to resemble the "top 40" stations, featuring the country songs that sounded most like rock. The result was not simply that country music became less and less distinguishable from other popular music; but, most importantly, that certain genres of country music (e.g., old singing styles such as "cowboy music") dropped out of the marketplace altogether. Traditionalists formed a new organization, called the Association of Country Entertainers, to fight the "dilution" of the country sound; but the problem was that record companies and radio stations preferred "crossover" music. Musicians and singers felt compelled to develop a "crossover" strategy in order to "make it" as musicians. There was little incentive for individual musicians and singers to develop and/or maintain a traditional "country" style. Thus, Peterson explains the emergence of a new genre of music – country rock – by focusing not on *meaning* at all, but by focusing on *organizational* and *market* concerns.

Theoretically and methodologically, the production of culture perspective falls well within the rubric of mainstream sociology. As Peterson (1994, p. 165) points out, "many of the early researchers in the [culture of production] perspective had been trained in the sociology of organizations, industry, and occupations and brought their skills in the analysis of material production to the field of symbol production." The culture of production perspective simply applies organizational sociology to a new arena. It provocatively demonstrates exactly how political, economic, and social elements – most importantly, market structure and bureaucratic structure – impact the "cultural" realm.

Of course, from an *interpretive* point of view, this is precisely the "problem" with the production of culture approach. It focuses on the *production* of culture, rather than cultural objects themselves. It does not purport to explain the "statement" itself, to uncover *what* cultural objects/ statements *mean*. Thus, for instance, Peterson is not interested in why consumers, especially urban consumers, *liked* "country-rock" music; he does not discuss the fact that Elvis imitated urban "black" styles, thereby creating a new "white," working-class, macho sexuality, and that this *fusion* of "white" and "black," and "urban" and "country," was exciting and aesthetically pleasing.[17]

However, the point here is that while, clearly, market forces must not be ignored, at the same time, symbolic forces should not be dismissed either. In other words, "sociology of culture" and "cultural sociology" are *distinct* ways to approach cultural objects, but there is no reason why these two approaches cannot be brought together. Indeed, the central premise of this book is that cultural sociologists can and must uncover the underlying *Gestalt* of culture, without ignoring the critical organizational parameters of cultural production. This point is illustrated in figure 1.1, which presents a *continuum* of types of cultural analysis. At the "interpretive," humanities end of the spectrum are Toni Morrison and George Lipsitz, who, as we will see in chapter 4, provide insightful self-reflective essays and provocative, intuitive analyses of such phenomena as the O. J. Simpson trial. At the "positivistic" "social scientific" end of the continuum is Richard Peterson, whose work on the *production* of culture fits well within the sociology of organizations.[18] At the heart of cultural sociology are analysts like James W. Gibson (1994), Joshua Gamson (1998), Sharon Hays (1996), and Darnell Hunt (1999) – all of whom readily acknowledge the organizational and bureaucratic parameters behind the *production* of culture, but at the same time, also use systematic discourse analysis, ethnography, interviews, and/or social history to sort out the complexities of the cultural realm. It is this *comprehensive* type of cultural sociology that I emphasize in this book (see chapter 7).

Table 1.1 summarizes the fundamental theoretical and methodological differences between cultural studies and cultural sociology (and the sociology of culture). Cultural studies relies primarily on self-reflective essays and unsystematic (or ad hoc) literary or discursive analysis; while cultural sociology relies on the *systematic* analysis of data, albeit within an interpretive tradition. The very term "cultural sociology" reflects that we're

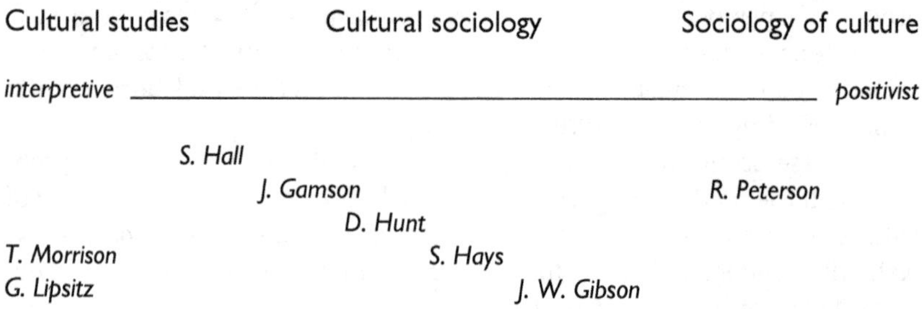

Cultural studies	Cultural sociology	Sociology of culture
interpretive ———————————————————————————— *positivist*		
	S. Hall	
	J. Gamson	*R. Peterson*
	D. Hunt	
T. Morrison	*S. Hays*	
G. Lipsitz	*J. W. Gibson*	

Note: Approximate position of exemplary cultural analysts featured in this book.

Figure 1.1   A continuum of cultural studies, cultural sociology, and the sociology of culture

Table 1.1 Distinguishing characteristics of cultural studies, the sociology of culture, and cultural sociology

Subdiscipline	Disciplinary home	Theoretical stance	Methodological stance	Empirical focus	Exemplary authors (featured in this book)
Cultural studies	Interdisciplinary (but primarily humanities, especially English)	Atheoretical or implicit/ad hoc theory (especially critical/cultural Marxist, structural, or postmodern)	Unsystematic (ad hoc) (e.g., self-reflective essays, unmethodical discourse analysis)	Meaning of cultural objects	G. Lipsitz T. Morrison S. Hall*
Sociology of culture	Sociology	Explicitly theoretical (especially organizational/ Weberian or critical/ cultural Marxist)	Systematic	Production of cultural objects	R. Peterson
Cultural sociology	Sociology	Explicitly theoretical (neo-Durkheimian, neo-Weberian, critical/cultural Marxist, or postmodern)	Systematic	Meaning of cultural objects	S. Hays D. Hunt J. Gamson J. W. Gibson S. Hall*

* Stuart Hall is a cultural sociologist who helped found (British) cultural studies. His work is explicitly theoretical, but methodologically unsystematic (or amethodological).

talking about a particular *type* of *sociological* analysis – one that blends the basic premises of sociology with the insights of the recent "cultural turn."

Outline of the Book

We begin our systematic exploration of the theoretical, empirical, and methodological quagmires and nuances of culture in the next chapter by focusing on one of the fundamental culture structures in all societies: religion. As Durkheim and Weber first pointed out (and Gramsci also underscored), understanding *religion* is important because it illuminates how *systems of meaning* (or culture in the symbolic sense) work in general. The basic elements of religion – values, rituals, doctrine, symbols, and the binary opposition between the *sacred* and the *profane*– are fundamental *cultural* categories that move far beyond the world of the "Church."

In chapter 3, we focus on one of the most important arenas for the creation and dissemination of meaning in modern societies: *the media*. Today we take for granted the extent to which our world is *mediated*, i.e., the extent to which we conceive of and act in the world via television, movies, radio, newspapers, computers, etc. We explore "the media" and "popular culture" in chapter 3 because so much of "popular culture" is *mediated* (most obviously, television). Indeed, this is one of the fundamental characteristics of modern (as well as postmodern) culture – that it is mediated.

In chapter 4, we explore one of the most pivotal and volatile categories of meaning within American society today: *race*. We will see that race is an independent criterion for vertical hierarchy in the United States (Bonilla-Silva 1997, p. 475). Race is a core *symbolic code*, or system of meaning. We will analyze racial categories (as well as class and gender categories) historically and semiotically, in order to shed light on how race in the United States *came* to take on a "life of its own." In addition, we will also see how racial and other symbolic codes were central in one of our most effervescent recent media events: the O. J. Simpson spectacle.

In the second part of this book, we explore qualitative *methods* for studying culture and society. We focus especially on naturalist ethnography and ethnomethodology in chapter 5; textual/discourse analysis and audience/reception research in chapter 6; and "comprehensive" cultural sociology in chapter 7. We will see that traditional field research (ethnography) focuses on "culture" in the ethnographic sense (i.e., the "entire way of life" of a specific social group); while discourse/textual analysis focuses on"culture" in the *symbolic* sense of the term. We conclude the book by calling for a *comprehensive* cultural sociology – one that illuminates the complex workings of culture and social structures without ignoring individual agency and interpretation.

IMPORTANT CONCEPTS INTRODUCED IN THIS CHAPTER

- Culture
- Cultural studies
- Cultural sociology
- Production of culture perspective
- Colonialism
- Imperialism

STUDY QUESTIONS

1   Discuss the relationship between being "cultured" (i.e., "sophisticated" or "refined," as in a "cultured person"), and the "high culture"/"low culture" dichotomy. Do, for instance, classical music and opera *do* something for the individual that "popular" cultural forms (such as heavy metal music and hip hop) do *not*? Discuss three different ways that you have experienced "high culture" and "low culture."

2   Have you ever heard of "culture shock"? Have you ever experienced it? If so, describe it. What is "shocking" about culture shock? Is it just "extreme difference"? Why should finding out "differences" (no matter how extreme) or finding out "things you didn't know" be so *shocking*? Is there something else involved? If so, what is it?

3   There are many excellent movies on the relationship between "art" and "culture." One of my favorites is *Basquiat*, about the New York "graffiti artist" of the same name. View this film (preferably twice), and discuss: (a) the relationship between Basquiat's life and work and the "high culture"/ "low culture" (or "pop culture") dichotomy; and (b) the relationship between art and "high society" (as portrayed in the film).

Suggested Further Reading

Berezin, Mabel. 1994. "Fissured Terrain: Methodological Approaches and Research Styles in Culture and Politics," in Crane, ed., *The Sociology of Culture*.

Crane, Diana, ed. 1994. *The Sociology of Culture*. Oxford: Blackwell.

Gray, Herman. 1997. "Jazz Tradition, Institutional Formation, and Cultural Practice: The Canon and the Street as Frameworks for Oppositional Black Cultural Politics," in Long, ed., *From Sociology to Cultural Studies*.

Griswold, Wendy. 1994. *Cultures and Societies in a Changing World*. Thousand Oaks, CA: Pine Forge.

Long, Elizabeth, ed. 1997. *From Sociology to Cultural Studies*. Cambridge, MA: Blackwell.

Peterson, Richard. 1994. "Culture Studies Through the Production Perspective: Progress and Prospects," in Crane, ed., *The Sociology of Culture*.

Seidman, Steve. 1997. "Relativizing Sociology: The Challenge of Cultural Studies," in Long, ed., *From Sociology to Cultural Studies*.

Smith, Philip, ed. 1998. *The New American Cultural Sociology*. Cambridge: Cambridge University Press.

Williams, Raymond. 1977. *Marxism and Literature*. Oxford: Oxford University Press.

Notes

1   "Jazz," *Microsoft® Encarta® 98 Encyclopedia*. © 1993–7 Microsoft Corporation; Appelrouth 1999.

2   Analysts such as Gray (1997) might argue that the legitimation of jazz has been far more recent – i.e., the inauguration of the Jazz Program at the Lincoln Center for the Performing Arts in 1991. Appelrouth (1999) points out two other defining moments in the historical legitimation of jazz: (1) Dizzy Gillespie's tour of the Middle East and Latin America under the auspices of the State Department in 1956; and (2) the adoption of Congressional Resolution 57, which suggested, among other things, that "jazz is hereby designated as a rare and valuable national American treasure to which we devote our attention, support, and resources to make certain it is preserved, understood, and promulgated" (Berliner 1994, p. 759).

3   The opposite is true as well: some of our most celebrated types of "high" culture – e.g., eighteenth-century European opera – were "popular culture" in their day. Shakespeare was popular melodrama in 1850, but classical high culture by 1920. See Levine (1988).

4   Sadly, there are a few cases of children raised in extreme isolation that demonstrate this point. In a now classic article, Kingsley Davis (1947) discusses the case of "Anna," a girl raised in extreme isolation. Anna apparently received only enough care to keep her alive; she had no instruction or friendly attention. When Anna was discovered at six years of age (she died at ten), she had "no glimmering of speech, absolutely no ability to walk, no sense of gesture, not the least capacity to feed herself even when the food was put in front of her," and she "failed to grasp nearly the whole world of cultural meanings." Indeed, Anna was so apathetic that "it was hard to tell whether or not she could hear," although later tests found her hearing to be perfectly normal.

5   A. R. Radcliffe-Brown, Presidential Address to the Royal Anthropological Institute, reprinted in Applebaum 1987, pp. 121–35.

6   Significantly, the structuralist approaches dominant in sociology in the 1970s (e.g., Skocpol 1979; Tilly 1978) were themselves a reaction to the functionalist "value analysis" popular in the 1950s and 1960s, which grossly ignored or underemphasized structural concerns. Value analysts (not only sociologists, but political scientists, and social psychologists as well) used surveys and questionnaires to identify and measure "values" and "root beliefs" – which they

assumed stood for "culture." They conducted extensive empirical research, much of it comparative (e.g., cross-national surveys of "religiosity," "political attitudes," etc.) in order to explain the role of "culture" in a wide variety of social phenomena, e.g., differences in national development and stability (see, for instance, Pye and Verba 1965; Lipset 1963). See Edles (1998) for a brief critique of functionalist political cultural analysis. See also Ragin and Becker (1992), who point out that value analysts erroneously assumed that objects of investigation were similar enough and separate enough to permit treating them as comparable instances of the same general phenomena.

7 *Webster's Seventh New Collegiate Dictionary* (Springfield, MA: G. & C. Merriam), 1967, p. 474.

8 The notion of the "relative autonomy" of political, economic and cultural realms comes from Poulantzas (1982), who borrowed from Parsons (1951). Poulantzas first argued that the ideological and political levels in a society are partially autonomous to (i.e, are not mere expressions of) the economic level. (As will be discussed shortly, while the Marxist term "ideology" contains specific connotations of power, it is essentially comparable to the more general term "culture.") By "analytically" and not "empirically" distinct I mean that, in the "real" world the social, cultural, economic, and political realms are inevitably entwined. There are cultural dimensions to "economic" phenomena, and vice versa, etc.

9 By "democratic" system, I mean systems in which there is (1) a real possibility of partisan alternation in office, and (2) a real possibility of reversible policy changes resulting from alternation in office, and (3) effective civilian control over the military (see Przeworski 1991; Edles 1995).

10 Of course, language also reflects the basic symbolic dichotomy of the "sacred" and "profane." "Bad" words (profanity) are precisely those that violate core religious or moral codes (taking the "Lord's name in vain"; the "f-word") or what we consider bodily filth.

11 "Colonialism" and "imperialism" are often used synonymously, but generally colonialism refers specifically to the Western expansionist movements which began in the 1400s, while "imperialism" is commonly used to refer to various types of capitalist domination of the periphery, e.g., multinational corporations (Borgatta and Borgatta 1992, p. 881). To be sure, analysts such as Said (1993) distinguish "imperialism" from "colonialism" in a different way. For Said (1993, p. 9), "The term 'imperialism' means the practice, the theory, and the attitudes of a dominating metropolitan center ruling a distant territory; 'colonialism' which is almost always a consequence of imperialism is the implanting of settlements on distant territory."

12 Interestingly, the actual planting of an American flag on the moon on July 20, 1969 did not technically "do" anything – for according to the 1967 "Treaty on Principles Governing the Activities of the States in the Exploration and Use of Outer Space including the Moon and Other Celestial Bodies," territory in outer space is not subject to national acquisition. Nevertheless, this act was extremely provocative and important: the image of staking an American flag on the moon symbolized and reaffirmed – it meant (and for many still means) – American supremacy, "manifest destiny," etc. In short,

this extraordinary symbolic act did not "do" anything "politically" in a technical, material sense; but it did do quite a lot "politically" in the ideological sense of the term.

13 As Bonilla-Silva (1997, p. 473) points out, the major problem with orthodox Marxist analyses of colonialism is that they have not been able to accept the fact that after the expansion of European capitalism into the New World, racism "acquired a life of its own"; "the subjects who were racialized as belonging to the superior race, whether or not they were members of the dominant class, became zealous defenders of the racial order." This is why, as postcolonial cultural Marxists such as Fanon (1968 [1963], p. 210) and Trask (1999 [1993]) point out, a pivotal part of decolonization is to "remake the image" and "rewrite the history," i.e., to reconstruct the discourse, of formerly colonized people.

14 For instance, in the Philippines, the (Spanish) governor general had appointive powers over the church, while the archbishop had the status of lieutenant governor and sat on numerous boards and council duties (Wurfel 1988, p. 4). While in Hawai'i, as Daws (1968) points out, the Christian missionaries said they came in peace, but they were quite prepared for war. And one generation later, the missionaries' children became powerful capitalist elites.

15 Of course, colonizers used Christian evangelism and manifest destiny to rationalize, justify and/or carry out political and economic goals. My point here is simply that – contrary to the mainstream position – there was more to it than this. In theoretical terms, most analysts implicitly or explicitly suggest that culture is "epiphenomenal," i.e., that culture does not explain the "causes" of colonialism. Thus, for instance, the entry on "imperialism/ colonialism" in the *Encyclopedia of Sociology* (Borgatta and Borgatta 1992, pp. 881–4) makes no mention of Christian evangelism or manifest destiny or racism or any other cultural elements at all. Colonialism is explained as a function of the rise of new markets and luxury goods, the need to invest outside the domestic economy, or international economic relations – i.e., the classic economic explanations of Lenin (1917), Baran and Sweezy (1966), Frank (1967), and Wallerstein (1974); and Schumpter's (1951) classic political (rather than economic) explanation.

16 However, as Seidman (1994, p. 11) points out, despite their emphasis on sociological methods, "social facts" and "value-free" sociology, Weber and Durkheim were "no less inspired and informed by moral and political commitments" than were their predecessors, though they did tend to bury their moral commitments in the language of empirical science.

17 As will be discussed in chapter 4, I use quotation marks for "race words" such as "black" and "white" to signify that these are *social* categories of perception and experience, but not biologically or physiologically tenable ones.

18 "Positivism" refers to a tradition in which objective "truths" are held to be attainable strictly through "scientific" methods and observations. Positivists believe that, like natural scientists, social scientists can infer general laws from observed regularities, the goal being not only to explain, but to predict (Baert 1998, p. 5).

PART ONE

Culture and Society

CHAPTER TWO

Religion and Ideology: Systems of Meaning in the Modern (and Postmodern) World

By all accounts, the United States is the most religious of the major Western, industrial countries (Hoover and Wagner 1997, p. 7; Gallup and Lindsay 1999, p. 119). Over 90 percent of Americans believe in God, and 70 percent in an afterlife; on a typical Sunday, about 40 percent of the nation participates in some form of worship (Gallup and Lindsay 1999; Davis and Smith 1991, as cited by Warner 1993, p. 1046). By contrast, in England, only about one in ten (10 percent) participate in some form of religious services, and the most religious country in Europe – the Republic of Ireland – reports levels of religious service attendance at about two thirds of those of the United States (Szaz 1993, p. 23; Hoover and Wagner, 1997, p. 7). Visitors are often astonished by the popular public display of religion in the United States – i.e., bumper stickers, license plates, and billboards that proclaim "God is Number One" or "Jesus is My Best Friend" (Szaz 1993, p. 23). Clearly, one of the most important systems of meaning in the United States is *religion*.[1]

Interestingly, in the late nineteenth century, many prominent social scientists anticipated not a resurgence but a *decline* in religion in American society. Max Weber, one of sociology's "founding fathers," maintained that the establishment of highly rational bureaucracies would mean that the structures of society would be sustained by bureaucratic rather than religious legitimation. The demands for efficiency, productivity, predictability, rational calculability, and control over the environment would promote a secular public culture (Seidman 1990, p. 224). Other social scientists expected increasing religious pluralism, as well as the expansion of *science* as a means for explaining the world, to result in a *decline* in religious affiliation. Their thinking was that exposure to both scientific explanations and attitudes toward the world, and exposure to people who hold religious explanations of the world quite different from their own, might cause individuals to question and challenge the plausibility of any one tradition. Modernization would entail the growing "confidence" of the individual,

> from a creature as subordinate to his gods as he was to his political masters, to one asserting first the right to make choices in ever-expanding spheres of behavior, then insisting on the right to define reality, and finally, because the definitions arrived at by any large number of people clash, asserting relativism (what is true for you and what is true for me may be very different things) as the practical attitude. (Bruce 1995, p. 417)

As Peter Berger (1967, p. 156) put it, the fundamental problem of modern religious institutions is "how to keep going in a milieu that no longer takes for granted their definitions of reality."

However, despite modernization, despite secularization, despite increasing religious pluralism, and despite the increasing "privatization" of religion, American religion has not fallen by the wayside. On the contrary, over the course of the nineteenth and twentieth centuries, the number of churches, the range of denominations, and the proportion of the population holding membership in religious organizations in the United States have grown (Wuthnow 1988, p. 7).[2] Moreover, today fundamentalist, conservative, and orthodox denominations are growing more than (or are at least as stable as) liberal denominations (Iannaccone 1997; Roof and McKinney 1997). Thus, for instance, in the 1950s, only four of the top ten largest seminaries in the United States were evangelical institutions, but by the 1980s eight of the top ten were run by evangelicals (Wuthnow 1988, p. 192).[3] And while 40 or 50 years ago, many analysts predicted that Orthodox Judaism would die out by the twenty-first century, instead, we are now witnessing a rejuvenation of Orthodox Judaism (Davidman 1997). In addition, today religious home study and television are thriving: as part of the do-it-yourself trend, the sales of religious books have risen by 50 percent in the last ten years (Updike 1999, p. 84).

The obvious question is, how do we explain the continuing centrality of religion in our modern, "secular" society? How do we explain what Herberg (1967, p. 417) pointed out over thirty years ago: that the United States is "at once the most secular and the most religious of nations"?

On one hand, analysts such as Finke and Iannaccone (1993) take an economistic, rational choice approach to explaining the salience of religion in contemporary US society. They maintain that it is the fierce *competition* between "religious organizations" or "firms" in the United States that makes them strong: "in a competitive environment a particular religious firm will flourish only if it provides a product at least as attractive as its competitors" (p. 28). Finke and Iannaccone argue that this also explains why religious participation is greater in religiously pluralistic (like the United States), rather than in "monopoly" religious societies (e.g., "Catholic" countries such as Spain and Italy): "monopoly religious firms tend to be lazy". After all, "no single religious organization can meet the diversity of tastes always present among potential consumers," and religiously heterogenous societies are more likely to have something for everyone (Finke and Stark 1997, p. 44). In short, "free market capitalism explains why Americans are rich; free-market religion explains why Americans are church-going" (Bruce 1995, p. 417).

From a similarly economistic and rationalistic, albeit more cynical, point of view, one might suggest that the reason religion is so prevalent in the United States is because religion is *big business*. Nowhere is religion *marketed* like it is in the United States, where marketing itself is elevated to, well, a *religion*. Our multimillionaire televangelicals (television preachers), such as Oral Roberts, Billy Graham, and Jerry Falwell, who earn fame and fortune through their ministries, are the most obvious examples in this regard. Indeed, in light of the plethora of bumper stickers, angels, plastic Jesus figures, gold-plated crosses on necklaces, Christian video games and rock music, religious publishing, and even a religious theme park (Holyland USA) – where one can see the depiction of various biblical scenes and events (McGuire 1997, p. 113) – one might conclude that the reason religion is so prevalent in the United States today is because it is not *really* about religion at all. It is about the *selling* of "religion."

Yet, this brings us to the central question: *what* exactly is being marketed here? How is it that millions of Americans send millions of dollars a year to televangelicals? Why do millions of Americans choose to be "saved" every week in all different kinds of church services on their own accord? Why do Americans visit the theme parks, buy the bumper stickers, wear the gold crosses? What is the appeal of religion in the modern world? How is religion the same and different than in previous eras? How is it that demands for efficiency, productivity, predictability, rational calculability, and control over the environment seem to *coexist* with religion? We'll explore these issues (and others) in this chapter.

The Study of Religion in Sociology

The study of religion has been at the heart of sociology since it was first founded as an academic discipline in the late nineteenth century. For these early sociologists (including the secularization theorists discussed

" *'Chicken Vindaloo for the Hindu Soul' is but the tip of the*
iceberg in our initial strategy of global expansion."

Figure 2.1   Jack Zeigler, "'Chicken Vindaloo for the Hindu Soul," *The New Yorker*,
October 5, 1998. © The New Yorker Collection 1998 Jack Zeigler from
cartoonbank.com. All rights reserved.

previously), religion was central to their general conceptions of social and
cultural life (Robertson 1970, p. 7). This is most apparent in the works of
two "founding fathers" of sociology: Emile Durkheim (1858–1917) and
Max Weber (1864–1920). For both Durkheim and Weber, religion is a
basic construct of culture and society; one cannot understand a particular
society without taking a concerted look at "religion." Yet Weber and
Durkheim understood religion in fundamentally different ways. While
Durkheim's greatest contribution has been to show that religious practice
is a celebration of the reality of the social sphere (Robertson 1970, p. 15);
Weber's central project was the far more empirical one of illuminating the
historical relationship between specific worldviews – particularly religiously-
inspired ones – and the economic and political structures of the societies
in which they are located. Though they used different terms and definitions, Durkheim and Weber, as well as Marxist-inspired theorists such as
the great Italian philosopher Antonio Gramsci (discussed later), all considered religion a fundamental system of meaning, i.e., a fundamental
component of *culture* as well as society.

Ritualization, Symbolization, and the Communal Function of Religion

For many Americans, religion is a "private" issue. Many Americans say
that they have a "personal" relationship with God, but, at the same time,
they eschew participation in, and/or identification with, any specific reli-

gious organization. Yet, for Durkheim, this *seemingly* "private" view of religion is fallacious. For Durkheim, the quest for meaning is not only a psychological/spiritual, but a *social*, imperative. For Durkheim, social life is inherently religious, and religious ceremonials are celebrations of social life, such that so long as there are societies, there will be religion (Robertson 1970, p. 13).

Of course, by saying that society is inherently "religious," Durkheim is defining religion in a very broad way. "Religion" for Durkheim does not mean merely "churchly" things; rather, for him, religion is a system of *symbols and rituals*, about the *sacred*, involving a *community of believers*. This definition of religion is often called "functionalist," rather than "substantive" (McGuire 1997, p. 9). The Durkheimian definition of religion emphasizes not the *substantive* content of religion – such as institutions or doctrine (i.e., a church or synagogue; or belief in an afterlife, higher beings, etc.); rather, it emphasizes the social *function* of religion.

For Durkheim, the primary function of "religion" is social and communal. Religion encodes the system of relations of the group (Eliade and Couliano 1991, p. 2). It focuses and reaffirms the collective sentiments and ideas that hold the group together. Religious practice binds participants together in a "celebration" of the social sphere (Robertson 1970, p. 15). As Durkheim (1965 [1912]) states:

> There can be no society which does not feel the need of upholding and reaffirming at regular intervals the collective sentiments and the collective ideas which makes its unity and its personality. Now this moral remaking cannot be achieved except by the means of reunions, assemblies and meetings where the individuals, being closely united to one another, reaffirm in common their common sentiments.

This *social* and *communal* function of religion is carried out through the dual processes of *ritualization* and *symbolization*. A "ritual" is a highly routinized *act*, such as taking communion. As the name reveals, "communion" is not only a commemoration of an historical event in the life of Jesus; it is also a representation of participation in the unity ("communion") of believers (McGuire 1997, p. 187). Most interestingly, because they are *acts* (not "beliefs" or "values"), rituals can "unite" a social group *regardless* of individual differences in beliefs, strength of belief, etc. Mere *participation* in ritual acts can bind participants together.

This is why, for Durkheim, there is no basic difference between "religious" and "secular" ritual acts. "Let us pray" (an opening moment in a *religious* service) and "Let us stand for the national anthem" (an opening moment of a *baseball game*) are both *ritual acts* that bond the individual to a community of believers. In exactly the same way, for Durkheim, there is no basic difference between religious holidays, such as Passover or Christmas, and secular holidays, such as Independence Day or Thanksgiving. Both are collective celebrations of identity and community.

Thus, paradoxically, this *communal* function of religion is also readily apparent in what is the fastest growing religious organization of all today: the nondenominational Protestant *megachurch* (generally defined as churches with weekly attendance of over 2,000). While at first glance these huge, independent, entrepreneurial organizations might seem to reflect the exact opposite of communality – they might seem to reflect an anonymous, mass, alienating religious experience; in fact, "megachurches" (also known as full-service churches, seven-day-a-week churches, new tribe churches, seeker-sensitive churches, or shopping-mall churches) offer a plethora of both spiritual and secular types of reunion and activities – from bible study, to twelve-step groups, to sports teams, to Ladies Bunko Night – seven days a week (Trueheart 1996, p. 1). As Trueheart (1996, p. 1) states, the megachurch may be "the clearest approximation of community, and perhaps the most important civic structure, that a whole generation is likely to have known or likely to find anywhere in an impersonal, transient nation." The megachurch represents a reconfiguration of secular as well as religious *community*, without spires, crosses, robes, clerical collars, biblical gobbledygook, or forced solemnity; and the deliberate abandonment of centuries of "European tradition and Christian habit" (ibid.; emphasis added).

As noted above, in addition to ritual practices, there is another important means through which the communal function of religion is achieved: *symbolization*. A "symbol" is something that stands for something else. It is a *representation* that calls up collective *ideas* and *meanings*. Thus, for instance, the "cross" is a marker that symbolizes Christian spirituality, tradition, and/or community. Wearing a cross on a necklace often *means* that one is a Christian. It attaches the wearer to a specific religious community, and/or specific shared ideas (e.g., a religious tradition in which Jesus Christ is understood as the son of God, etc.). Most importantly, symbols such as the cross are capable of calling up and reaffirming shared meaning and the feeling of community *in between* ritual acts (such as religious celebrations, and weekly church services). States Durkheim (1912 [1965], p. 232), "Without symbols, social sentiments could have only a precarious existence."

As discussed briefly in the previous chapter, the most fundamental classification of symbols is into the "sacred" and the "profane." The "sacred" refers to the holy and good, that which is set apart from, and "above and beyond," the everyday world. The symbolic opposite of the sacred is the *profane*, which in the religious realm, is denoted by *evil*. The profane is often the *violation* or *pollution* of the sacred (e.g., stomping on a flag, burning a cross). From a Durkheimian perspective, burning the American flag, or singing the (sacred) national anthem in a comic (profane) manner (as Rosanne Barr did at a baseball game in San Diego several years ago), or tearing up a picture of the Pope (as Sinead O'Connor did on television) is a *profanation*, or defamation, because of what the flag/the anthem/the picture *represents*. To burn or defile the American flag/national anthem/ picture of the Pope is a profanation *because* the flag/anthem/picture are not merely a "piece of cloth"/ "piece of paper"/"song"; they are symbols of the *community/society/church* itself.

However, Durkheim ambiguously used "profane" to refer to *both* the emotionally charged realm of evil, and the *un*charged level of the every-day world, the world of the *mundane* or *routine*. Callois (1959) first sought to resolve this ambiguity by turning Durkheim's sacred/profane dichotomy into a threefold classification: the *sacred*, the *profane*, and the *routine*. According to this trichotomy, the *sacred* and *profane* are the effervescent, *emotionally charged* categories of good (sacred) and bad (profane). These effervescent, charged categories contrast with routine, mundane *signs*, which do not carry such profound symbolic weight. Thus, for instance, lighting a candle can either be a relatively *mundane* task to enhance one's dinner table, or it can be a *sacred* ritual act, as in the case of a lighting a candle of the menorah to commemorate the Feast of Lights (the Jewish holiday of Hanukkah) (McGuire 1997, p. 17). A major part of Durkheim's analysis was showing how *mundane* objects, such as lizards and plants, could take on the sacredness of the "totem" (the symbol of the tribe). His point was that there was nothing *intrinsically* sacred about these objects, but that they are invested with sacrality through social processes.

From a Durkheimian perspective, the *function* of binary opposition is that it creates symbolic *order*. Culture imposes system on the inherently untidy experience of living (J. Gamson 1998, p. 141). In other words, a central task of any culture is "separating, purifying, demarcating, and punishing transgressions," and defending classifications against the ambi-guities and anomalies to which they give rise (J. Gamson 1998, p. 141; Douglas 1966, p. 4). As Mary Douglas (1966, p. 35) states, dirt "is matter out of place . . . . Dirt is never a unique isolated event. Where there is dirt there is system."

This symbolic function is most readily apparent in Orthodox Judaism. The two tractates of the Mishnah (the compiled rabbinical interpretations of scriptural ordinances) are called, significantly, *Kilaim* ("hybrids") and *Erubin* ("mixings"), and are devoted exclusively to boundary issues (Zerubavel 1997, p. 56). The Mishnah prohibits garments made of both linen and wool; and there is such a careful dietary separation of meat and milk products, that not only separate plates, but separate kitchens are required.

Yet, symbols and rituals not only order *physical* or *material* matter (e.g., men and women, food/not food, etc.), but *time* and *space* as well. Ritual moments (e.g., "let us pray"; "let's stand for the national anthem") turn a relatively mundane moment into a *sacred* moment; while places where ritual acts regularly occur (e.g., a church, mountain, or shrine) mark out sacred space – places which compel attitudes of awe and inspiration. For example, Muslims, who pray five times daily – no matter if they're at home or work – convert a mundane space into a sacred space for praying by laying down a prayer carpet. This physical, spatial reordering helps transform profane (work) time/space into (sacred) spiritual time/space. It helps *order* and organize the world into the sacred and the profane.

However, as Douglas (1966) is quick to point out, the creation and affirmation of symbolic order is not all pervasive. Anomaly and ambiguity are stimulating. The possibility of seeing a sculpture equally well as a landscape or as a reclining nude enriches the viewers' interest in the work; aesthetic pleasure often arises from the perceiving of inarticulate forms (Douglas 1966, p.37). In other words, while the function of traditional religious prescriptions is to maintain symbolic order, the aesthetic function of language and art is to create new and provocative symbolic linkages. As we will see in the next chapter, many cultural products rely on blurring or obscuring taken-for-granted symbolic boundaries.

Thus, for instance, tabloid talk shows use transsexual and transgendered guests not simply to titillate but to "mess with" the gender categories of the audience: "what's being promoted is the kick of gender confusion, of suddenly not being able to tell the difference [between men and women]" (J. Gamson 1998, p. 156). Of course, in exactly the same way, pop stars like Madonna provocatively meld (sacred) Catholic icons (a cross, Jesus Christ), with (profane) erotica. It is a titillating *profanation* that Madonna seeks. As we will see in the next chapter, some analysts might maintain that Madonna "subverts," "opposes," or "resists" the (hegemonic) symbols of the Catholic Church by incorporating them into her videos and her personas. However, the point here is that Madonna still relies on, and in that sense works within, *Catholic* systems of meaning. The provocativeness of juxtaposing the (sacred) cross with (profane) erotica would be *lost* if we did not "know" Catholic iconography.

This gets us back to Finke and Stark's (1992) and Stark and Iannoccone's (1992) *rationalistic* thesis as to why religious practice is lower in "monopoly religious" than in "heterogenous religious" societies. Recall that Stark and Iannoccone (1992, p. 2031) find that religious participation is highest where there are a *variety* of religious groups, and lowest in societies with "monopoly" churches. Thus for instance, nowhere is Catholic practice as low as in "Catholic" societies (e.g., Spain and much of Latin America), and nowhere is Catholicism more vigorous than where Catholics make up but a small minority (ibid.).

While Finke and Starke's findings are not undisputed,[4] from a neo-Durkheimian perspective, it makes sense that "religious firms" would be visible and salient in religiously pluralistic societies. For, from a neo-Durkheimian perspective, religious firms must *work harder* to build a *shared* reality in religiously heterogeneous societies. While in monopoly religious societies the "national" religion is, by definition, *shared*; it is implicit rather than explicit; it is *taken for granted*. For instance, many years ago when I was a student in Spain (commonly deemed a "monopoly religious society"), I noticed that the primary discourse regarding religion did not revolve around whether one was a "Catholic" or not. The normative discourse regarding religion was whether one was a *practicante* or a *no practicante* – i.e., a "practicing" or "non-practicing" member of the *taken-for-granted* religion. The point is that in contrast to the terms "agnostic" or "atheist" (which involve *rejecting* or dis-identifying with Catholicism), the category *no practicante* maintains a shared Catholic identity. It allows one to be Catholic *without* practicing (or accepting the tenets of) *his/her* religion.[5]

By contrast, in heterogeneous religious societies such as the United States, religious identity is not normally fixed or assumed. Instead, it reflects the process of individualized choice. In the United States, membership in a particular religious collectivity is *culturally* appropriate (Robertson 1970, p. 182); it is *how* one establishes one's religious identity. "Religion is still a prime idiom by which Americans identify themselves" (Warner 1993, p. 1077). In other words, one can certainly be a "non-practicing" Catholic in the United States, but it is far more meaningful to establish first whether one is a "Catholic," a "Protestant," a "Jew," a "Muslim," etc., or not – and this is most readily done through group membership, through *"choosing* a religion."[6]

This same *taken-for-grantedness* of religious identity apparent in Spain is also readily apparent in other modern "monopoly religious societies," such as Israel. The term *no practicante* is similar to one of the most popular religious designations in Israel – "secular Jew." Akin to the term *no practicante*, the term "secular Jew" reflects "secularization" in a "monopoly religious society." Yet, the point is, that it also reflects a *taken-for-granted* religious identity; it reflects that no matter what the *basis* for identity actually is (e.g., "spiritual" or "ethnic"); "Jewish" identity is not *eradicated*.

To be sure, up to two-thirds of Jews in the United States are "secular Jews" too. But still, the taken-for-granted, collectivistic experience and understanding of religion, common in monopoly religious societies, contrasts tremendously with the experience and understanding of religion in heterogenous religious societies. In the case of Judaism especially, outside Israel, the hold of the "secular Jew" on his/her identity is less firm. As one secular Jew who immigrated from Israel to the United States lamented, "In Israel we don't have to go to the synagogue to show we're Jewish."

But in the United States, affiliation with a synagogue is integral in ensuring cultural as well as religious continuity.[7]

Of course, this helps explain why Reform and Conservative movements make up the majority of Jews outside of Israel, but only a minority within the Jewish state.[8] Reform and Conservative movements were born as explicit attempts to *bridge* the "modern" and "religious" worlds; they were born from the desire to *practice* Judaism, to live Judaism, without having to give in to what seemed like archaic Orthodox traditions. Interestingly, this is the same type of process that Weber so brilliantly described in *The Protestant Ethic and the Spirit of Capitalism* (to be discussed shortly). As Weber pointed out (and subsequently ignored in his writings on modern capitalist society), religious *tension* – i.e., between competing systems of meaning, or between the *religious* and the *secular* worlds – is a critical source of social change.[9] Most importantly in terms of our critique of Finke and Iannaccone and Finke and Stark, the point is that this is a complex *cultural* and *social psychological* tension – *not merely a capitalistic or market one* (though, ironically, Finke and Stark do acknowledge that religious organizations compete for the market produced by the psychological tension of the potential believer).

Ideology and Cultural Hegemony

Thus far we have seen that for Durkheim there is no such thing as an "areligious" society. Because there can be no society without *symbol, ritual,* and *beliefs* that express a collective identity, there can be no society without *religion.* However, as many sociology students know, another of sociology's "founding fathers," Karl Marx (1818–83), had a far less cheery view as to the role of religion in society than did Durkheim. For Marx (and his collaborator, Fredrich Engels), religion is not a system of meaning or body of practices that reflects the *genuine,* sacred, collective sentiments of the society as a whole (as Durkheim supposed). Rather, for Marx and Engels, religion is an *ideology* that justifies the concrete material interests of a dominant group; while religious *institutions* solidify the dominance of the upper classes and the relative subordinance of the lower classes. In sum, from a Marxist point of view, religious ideology does not merely *separate* and *order* society for sacred social purposes as Durkheim might suppose; rather, it *legitimizes* a *hierarchical* system of power.

Yet, just as Durkheim supposed that religion functions *in the same way as* other (secular) systems of meaning that carve the world into the "sacred" and "profane", Marx and Engels maintained that *all* cultural ideas (not only religious ideas) are a reflection of the *material* system of production, and hence, in the end, serve the interests of the ruling class. As Marx states:

> The ideas of the ruling class are, in every epoch, the ruling ideas: i.e., the class, which is the ruling *material* force of society is at the same time its ruling intellectual force. The class which has the means of material production at its disposal, has control at the same time of the means of mental production, so that in consequence the ideas of those who lack the means of mental production are on the whole subject to it. The ruling ideas are nothing more than the ideal expression of the dominant material relations, the dominant material relations grasped as ideas. (*The German Ideology*, 1845/6)

Certainly, it is not difficult to find evidence of *oppression* within religious institutions and doctrines. Many religions systematically grant certain prerogatives to one group at the expense of another. For instance, the Hindu caste system selectively grants certain permanent prerogatives, benefits, and responsibilities to those who have been born into a particular (Brahmin) caste, which legitimates and solidifies prevailing social hierarchies (McGuire 1997, p. 122). Similarly, the Judeo-Christian tradition (among others), has a long history of reserving central ritual and symbolic roles – most importantly, priesthood – for men. Consider, for instance, the following excerpt from St. Paul (1 Tim. 2:8–15, RSV), which is a popular theological explanation for the exclusion of women from the priesthood: "Let a woman learn in silence with all submissiveness. I permit no woman to teach or to have authority over men; she is to keep silent. For Adam was formed first, then Eve; and Adam was not deceived; but the woman was deceived and became a transgressor" (cited in McGuire 1997, p. 126). In a similar vein, one of the most notorious but longstanding aspects of Mormon theology (which is, after all, based on the "divine revelations" of a few white, male prophets)[10] – was the so-called "Negro doctrine" which prohibited black men from entering the priesthood. Whether the founder of Mormonism, Brigham Young, or his disciple, Joseph Smith, was ultimately responsible for Mormonism's "Negro doctrine" is a matter of considerable controversy; but the discriminatory policy itself is "an incontrovertible fact," not revoked until 1978, when the First Presidency of the Mormon Church announced that, "all worthy male members of the Church may be ordained to the priesthood without regard for race or color" (Hansen 1981, pp. 184–6; 198).

Yet Marx and Engels maintain not only that religious institutions and ideologies *justify* and *solidify* existing social and class hierarchies, but also that religious institutions and ideologies effectively *pacify* subordinate groups and inhibit them from seeking social change. As Marx and Engels (Bottomore, *Early Writings*, as cited by Robertson 1970, p. 158) state: "*Religious* suffering is at the same time an expression of real suffering and a *protest* against real suffering. Religion is the sigh of the oppressed creature, the sentiment of a heartless world, and the soul of soulless conditions. It is the *opium* of the people."

That religion is the "*sigh* of the oppressed creature," that it is the "*opium*" of the people, points to the high cost of religious "illusions" for Marx. Religion is a *veil* that produces *passivity* and deflects the demand for social change. In other words, while the Hindu caste system, as well as Christian refrains such as "The meek shall inherit the earth," may very well help people endure the pain of this world; the problem is that by *accepting* one's "fate," or *giving up on* reparations in this life, the *source* of this "real suffering" – the class system – goes unquestioned and unchallenged.

In sum, from a Marxist perspective, the dominant class invariably creates institutions and ideologies to justify and solidify their position of dominance. The working class adopts or internalizes these ideologies because they are the *victims* of capitalist institutions of domination. Religion and ideology are *illusions* that veil the hard reality of material production (Thompson 1984, p. 16). While in the short run, workers may seem to benefit from these *illusions* (e.g., they feel comfort and the conviction of a better life in *another* world), from a Marxist perspective, the problem is they are *duped* and *deluded*. They are oblivious to the "real" basis of their subservience – not divine ordinance, but *hierarchical, patriarchal* power relations – hence they are unable to enact social change. In one famous passage, Marx compares this *illusive* operation of ideology to the workings of a *camera obscura*, which represents the world by means of an image turned upside down, such that what we think of as "reality" is *really* an inverted life image. The *material* basis of religious systems is as obscure for believers as is "the inversion of objects on the retina."[11]

Nevertheless, Marx did not focus on the actual *process* by which ruling ideas that in fact go against workers' material interests are adopted by nonelites. Marx was far more interested in the *material* relations of production, and this is especially apparent in his later works. Thus, since the turn of the twentieth century, many writers have reworked and expanded Marx's seminal work on ideology and given it more weight. Perhaps the most important of these *cultural* Marxists is the Italian philosopher, Antonio Gramsci (1891–1937). Gramsci was not an academic, but a journalist and political activist whose achievements include founding the Italian Communist Party. He was imprisoned from 1926 until his death in 1937, and during this 11-year period, wrote most of the work for which he is now famous.

Gramsci was impressed by the tremendous power of the Catholic Church in Italy; he saw that the Catholic Church possessed not merely *political* and *economic* influence, but *cultural* or *ideological* power. Gramsci theorized that a ruling group, whether of the Left or the Right, must govern with a balance of domination and persuasion. In other words, while, like

Marx, Gramsci viewed society as utterly hierarchical, he insisted that the ruling class does not sustain itself mainly by force. Rather, according to Gramsci, society is held together by what *appears* to be the voluntary adherence to dominant ideas. Since these ideas are really part and parcel of the economic and political order, they form a "moral-political bloc." Gramsci calls the ideological domination of the masses by intellectuals "cultural hegemony." "Cultural hegemony" refers to the notion that the dominant class(es) *leads* a society through the exertion of moral and intellectual leadership. The ruling class does not simply impose a uniform conception of the world on the rest of society; instead, it articulates specific ideologies of the world that *neutralize* the opposition (Laclau, as cited by Storey 1996, p. 189). Prevailing ideas *appear* as "natural," "inevitable," or "universal" ideas, their link to material class relations obscured. Thus, subordinate classes *actively* support and subscribe to the values, ideals, objectives, and cultural meanings which ensure their domination (Storey 1993, p. 119).

Thus, for instance, from a Gramscian perspective, the *power* of televangelicals, like Jerry Falwell and Billy Graham, as well as the so-called New Christian Right (NCR), in general, is not simply that they have tremendous economic resources at their disposal. The power of the "Religious Right" is that it provides the United States with ideological (or cultural) *leadership*. The "New Christian Right" is the source of America's *moral education*. Thus, in direct contrast to analysts such as Bruce (1995), who insist that the impact of the Religious Right is in fact small, because the religious right makes up "only a small minority of the American people" (p. 157), cultural Marxists might point out that the Religious Right has an *ideological* power that far outweighs its numerical strength. Though the religious right's ideological campaigns are often met by a vehement "secular humanist" backlash, as Bruce himself states, there is also "general public sympathy for NCR values" and "conservative socio-moral positions" (pp. 159–60). Thus, for instance, feminists argue that the discourse on abortion has been steered and *dominated* by the NCR. Similarly, as we will see in chapter 3, Ansell (1997) maintains that the New Right has set the ideological agenda about race, directly impacting policy formation.

However, in contrast to Marx, whose materialistic emphasis led to the prediction that capitalism would ultimately fail because it was not *economically* viable; Gramsci borrowed from Hegel the *idealistic* notion that revolution would occur only if there was a change in *consciousness*.[12] For Gramsci, the concern with meaning is an *inseparable* dimension of every human action and every historical form of social order (Alexander 1987, p. 6; emphasis added). This accords not only a greater role to culture and ideology than Marx supposed; it accords a greater role to *intellectuals* – the elites of the cultural realm. In other words, for Hegelian Marxists, the continuity of capitalism depends on the existence of a *cultural system* which hides workers' true interests in a veil of illusion. But at the same time, the *cultural system* can come to the aid of the working class. Indeed, the role of communist intellectuals (and the communist party in general) is to *educate* workers in order to replace "false consciousness" – i.e., "the class-conditioned *unconsciousness* of one's own socio-historical and economic condition" – with "class consciousness", i.e., an awareness as to the existing system of oppression (Lukács 1968 [1922], p. 52, as cited by Ritzer 1992, p. 139).[13] This position contrasts significantly from that of Marx, for it accords relative *autonomy* to the cultural realm. Ideology does not simply *result* from the material relations of production; it can help *challenge* the material relations of production as well. In the next chapter, we will see that this *culturalist* perspective has profoundly impacted contemporary cultural studies. Today cultural Marxists emphasize both the role of the *media* in the creation and maintenance of cultural hegemony, and how the working class *resists* ideological hegemony as well.

Rationalism and Worldview: Weber's Historical Approach to Religion

In contrast to both Durkheim and Marx, another of sociology's "founding fathers," Max Weber (1864–1920) emphasized the *historical* relationship between religion, culture, and society. In contrast to both Marx and Durkheim (neither of whom set their sights on explaining how and why any particular religious system prevails over any other at any particular historical moment), Weber sought to show how *particular* cultural orientations, value systems, or "worldviews" are rooted in and impact the social world. He attempted to sort out "the practical impulses for action which are found in the psychological and pragmatic contexts of religions" (Weber 1974 [1946], p. 267). Moreover, in contrast to both Durkheim and Marx (but in conjunction with recent poststructuralists), Weber emphasized the tremendous *ironies* in social history, and how it is often the unforeseen combination of conditions that results in social change.

Above all, Weber sought to explain the extraordinary *rationalism* that permeated all realms of Western life – from the sciences (such as astronomy, geometry, mechanics and physics, biology) to political thought and jurisprudence; to the arts (such as architecture, music, and printing); and most importantly, modern, European-American capitalism. For Weber, Western *rationalism* refers to a preoccupation with routines and procedures, with predictability and order, with a search for ever-increasing efficiency (Bruce 1996, pp. 47–8).[14] Weber sought to "deconstruct"

Western rationalism by comparing it to the type of rationalism found in "oriental" religions.[15] Thus Weber wrote comprehensive analyses of the five major religions of the world: Confucianism, Hinduism, Buddhism, Christianity, and Islam; and he began but did not finish a study of Judaism.[16]

Yet Weber did not simply set out to *describe* different religious worldviews. Rather, he sought to demonstrate the complex, historical relationship between economics and religion. In other words, in contrast to Marx (as well as conservative economists such as Adam Smith, whose famous "invisible hand" theory of laissez-faire capitalism appeared in *Wealth of Nations*), who assumed that capitalism evolved "naturally" or "inevitably" from previous economic systems, Weber argued that some of the features of capitalism in its modern, Western form were so markedly different from what had gone before that they needed to be explained by finding the source of the new attitudes and patterns of behavior (Bruce 1996, p. 11).

In one of the most provocative and influential books in sociology, *The Protestant Ethic and the Spirit of Capitalism* (first published in 1904–5), Weber shows that the extraordinary *rationalism* at the heart of Western capitalism was related to the extraordinary *rationalism* at the heart of Protestantism. In other words, he maintains that the features that were integral to making a good capitalist were related to those that made a good Protestant. He investigates how the unique Protestant approach to the world was integral to the historical institutionalization of modern Western *capitalism*.[17] Specifically, Weber noted that modern Western capitalism required methodical production, a disciplined workforce, and reinvestment of capital. In *The Protestant Ethic*, he showed how this extraordinarily *rationalistic attitude* or approach to the world (which he called the capitalist "spirit") sprang from the *methodical individualization* of religion incumbent from the Protestant Reformation.

To briefly explain: the most important innovation of the Protestant Reformation was the rejection of the institution of religious professionals (Bruce 1996, p. 13). Before the Protestant Reformation, most societies had a religious division of labor: the majority of the population went about their daily business while religious belief and practice were left to a small handful of professionals and virtuosi, who placated the gods either on behalf of the whole society or on behalf of those who paid them for these services. But the Protestant Reformers rejected this practice. Martin Luther insisted that every man be his own monk, that we all have a constant obligation to live moral and religious lives. In particular, he argued against the idea that religious merit and salvation could be transferred from one person to another, and especially that paying a priest to say Masses for your soul would guarantee you a spot in heaven (Bruce 1996, pp. 15–16).[18]

In addition, the Protestant Reformation changed the meaning of *work* in the Western world. Whereas in medieval Catholicism, work had been part of the mundane world (except for priests and nuns), Luther's Reformation abolished the monasteries, and turned ordinary occupations into religious "callings." The idea was that one's *work* as well as *everything else one does in everyday life* should be a glorification of God. The duty of the religious believer is to live a godly life in every respect, every moment of the day. Religious faith and practice should not be reserved either for merely the clergy, or for merely an hour on Sundays.

Most interestingly, Weber argues that one of the practical *unintended* outcomes of this new *individualization* of religious practice was the *accumulation of capital*. Puritans worked hard, but they did not indulge themselves. They did not "waste" their hard-earned money on idle play or "luxury" goods, for that would reflect sloth, rather than the glorification of God. Protestant Reformers were anxious not to sin because there was no way of buying forgiveness. Thus, rather than spend their earnings, committed Puritans began to plough their profits back into business expansion. Of course, this brought even more economic success – and *voilá*, we have the rise and dominance of modern, Western, capitalism.

Nevertheless, Weber's central point was *not* that the Protestant ethic *caused* the emergence and growth of Western capitalism itself. Protestantism alone was not "sufficient" for producing this profound economic change. Rather, Weber argued that the capitalist "spirit" worked alongside and became intertwined with other important structural and social conditions – e.g., a rationalized financial system, good communications and transport, technologies for the extraction of raw materials, law and order, and a number of peculiar advantages (such as an equitable climate) – that resulted in the dominance of Western capitalism. Hence, Weber's most important *culturalist* point is that the Protestant Reformation affirmed specific attitudes and behaviors (most importantly, *individualism*) that were related to the capitalist *spirit* (or culture), and without this deep capitalist *spirit* (or culture), modern Western capitalism itself (as an economic structure) might have been stillborn.

However, Weber concluded *The Protestant Ethic* with a most controversial thesis. He maintained that once the capitalist system was underway, the *structure* of capitalism itself rendered both the Protestant *ethic* and the capitalist *spirit* obsolete. Modern, Western capitalism became an *"iron cage."* "The Puritan wanted to work in a calling; we are forced to do so." Like it or not, the momentum of capitalism carries us along with it. We scramble for success not to assure ourselves of salvation, but merely to keep from falling to the bottom of the class structure (Collins 1996, p. xiv). Weber (as cited by Collins 1996, p. iv) states "in the United States, the pursuit of wealth, stripped of its religious and ethical meaning, tends to become associated with purely mundane passions, which often actually give it the character of sport."

This brings us back to the *secularization* thesis, with which we began this chapter. Weber imagined that the most dynamic phase in the development of Western culture was from roughly the sixteenth to the mid-nineteenth century: "Western societies created modern science, free-market capitalism, the inner-directed individualism exemplified by the Puritan and political democratic structures such as rule of law, constitutionalism, civil rights, and parliamentary government" (Seidman 1994, p. 77). However, Weber insisted that successive waves of rationalization would undermine liberal, individualistic society. "In particular, the spread of bureaucracy and its utilitarian, status-oriented culture to all modern institutions fashioned a society of other-directed, spiritually bland, and apolitical individuals ruled by a soulless bureaucracy" (ibid.). In sum, Weber argued that the *methodical individualism* that emerged from the Protestant Reformation would be overtaken by the processes of *bureaucratization* and *secularization*. The result would be a *dearth* of subjectivity and meaning, a dehumanizing focus on formal rationality at the expense of ethical and moral concerns.

To be sure, it sometimes seems as if not only the "Protestant ethic" but morality itself has been wiped out. Many Americans today feel "trapped" (or at least hemmed in) by the economic imperatives of their lives. And certainly it sometimes seems as if – in direct contrast to the ethical self-denial and frugality of the Puritans – the "bottom line" really is, as the bumper sticker proclaims, that "the one who dies with the most toys wins." Ironically, as Schmidt (1995) points out, even "religious" holidays, such as Christmas and Easter, seem to be "consecrations of consumption rather than spirituality" today. As he (1995, p. 10) states:

> Between the gift-seeking of individuals and the profit-making of merchants, between the rationalistic calculation of individuals and the hard-bitten secularism of business, the fundamental religious meanings of Christmas and Easter seem to be lost in a sea of goods. It seems as if the integrative, unifying powers of festivity have been lost in the impersonal world of malls and the private, fragmented dreams of consumers . . . . Spiritual, nonmaterialistic, and eternal verities are thought to be seriously subverted in a consumer culture enthralled by abundance, self-gratification, and novelty.

Yet perhaps the contemporary period is more complex than Weber foresaw.[19] For instance, Tiryakian (1996, p. 102) maintains that there are in fact three fundamental "metacultures" at the heart of modernity: "Christian," "Gnostic" (seeking salvation though "divine knowledge" of the hidden truths of the universe), and "Chthonic" (pagan). "These metacultures,

"I can't imagine why we didn't think of this before."

Figure 2.2   Gahan Wilson, "Big Bunny," *The New Yorker*, April 17, 2000. © The New Yorker Collection 2000 Gahan Wilson from cartoonbank.com. All rights reserved.

and their principal agents, are interactive in the public arenas; they compete for space, for adherents and for institutions. They are forcibly interactive and to some extent interpenetrating (since human agents are exposed to elements of all three) in different ways at different periods" (Tiryakian 1996, p. 102).[20]

Indeed, perhaps, as Hannah Arendt (1958) first maintained, rather than *eradicate* subjectivity, modernization *fortifies* the need for explanations and strategies with which to deal with suffering, injustice, alienation, and anonymity. For Arendt (as cited by Wuthnow 1998, p. 138), "a noticeable increase in superstition and gullibility" is invariably a sign of "alienation from the world." This might explain why "from upstart sects to controversial cults" the United States has continually been the breeding ground for new faiths and new approaches to faith (Finke and Iannaccone 1993, p. 28); it might explain why religious "outsiders" – e.g., Catholics, Jews, Mormons, fundamentalists, ethnic or race-based religious groups, and a host of smaller sectarian communities – have always energized the American religious scene (Moore 1986, as cited by Stein 1999, p. 22). It also might explain the vitality of American evangelicalism, which, according to C. Smith (1998, p. 89) "*thrives* on distinction, engagement, tension, conflict, and threat. Without these, evangelicalism would lose its identity and purpose and grow languid and aimless." In conjunction with Arendt, C. Smith (1998, p. 112) maintains that "modernity can actually *increase* religion's appeal, by creating social conditions which intensify the kinds of felt needs and desires that religion is especially well-positioned to satisfy." Smith rejects Weber's image of modern society as an "iron cage." Rather, for Smith (1998, p. 111–12) modern society is more akin to "a large coral reef ecosystem, teeming with an abundance of complex and varied life forms which occupy well-suited niches in mutual coexistence." He asks: "Does this not better depict the sociocultural character of New York City, for example, than representations which suggest uniformity and homogenization?" Of course, this gets us back to the central observation with which we began this chapter: the United States is *at once* the most "secular" and the most "religious" of nations.

Put in another way, while Weber eloquently and magnificently demonstrated the *interpenetration* of religious and secular realms in explaining the emergence and dominance of rational capitalism in Western society in *The Protestant Ethic*, he eradicated this complex dialectic in explaining the contemporary period. In part, this error may have been a function of both pessimism and ethnocentrism: Weber seems to have "projected the worst features of Germany onto humanity's future" (Seidman 1994, p. 78).[21]

Yet interestingly, had Weber continued his multidimensional historical project into the contemporary period, he might have found the persistence of traces of the "Protestant ethic" and the capitalist "spirit" in new guises. For instance, he might have noted (as Hansen did much later) that Mormonism (or the Church of the Latter-Day Saints) is built on the exact same cultural (or symbolic) linking of *work* and *prosperity* with *salvation* that Weber believed led to the success of both rational capitalism and Protestantism in the late sixteenth century. Indeed, Hansen (1981, p. 82) maintains that Mormonism might very well be "the most typically American theology yet formulated." In the next section, we explore Mormonism from a *cultural* perspective in more detail.

The Church of the Latter-Day Saints

The Church of the Latter-Day Saints (commonly referred to as the Mormon Church) is undoubtedly the most powerful and influential of American-born religions. In the last 150 years, Mormonism has grown from a small, vilified American sect to a global, multi-*billion*-dollar enterprise. One of the fastest growing creeds anywhere, the Mormon Church currently has over ten million members worldwide. It has churches in 161 different countries, and it dedicates some 600 new buildings per year. The evangelical success of the Mormons is rivaled only by their economic success: current assets total some $30 billion (Van Biema 1997, p. 50). Indeed, the Mormon Church is so successful that if it were a corporation, it would be about halfway down on the Fortune 500 list (a little below

Union Carbide and the Paine Webber Group, but bigger than Nike and the GAP).[22] The Church's president and current prophet, Gordon Hinkley, is currently engaged in massive foreign construction, spending billions of dollars to erect 350 church-size meeting houses and 15 Cathedral-size temples, a year.

Mormonism was officially born on September 21, 1823, when Joseph Smith was visited by a heavenly messenger. The messenger told Smith where to look for a book written on gold plates, which Smith proceeded to find and "translate" into the Book of Mormon (see Hansen 1981, ch. 1). The original plates themselves, written in "Reformed Egyptian," were mysteriously taken up again to heaven (Van Biema 1997).

By the 1840s, Smith's small band of followers had expanded to some 30,000 souls, who were chastised and persecuted as dangerous radicals. Mormonism was reviled for a number of reasons, but among the most "blasphemous" of Mormon practices were "ancestralism" (Mormons believed in preexistent spirits and performed vicarious baptisms for the deceased) and "plural marriage" (polygamy). Joseph Smith first instituted polygamy in the 1830s (after receiving a divine revelation condoning it); but even at the time, polygamy was viewed by some of Smith's followers as merely a justification for Smith's sexual transgressions (Hansen 1981, p. 166).[23]

Fleeing persecution, Smith and his followers left upstate New York and wound up in Kirtland, Missouri. But their settlement in Kirtland was short-lived, as they were expelled under threat of the Governor's extermination order. The sect then made its way to Commerce, Illinois, on the banks of the Mississippi River, where they founded their "dream city, which they renamed Nauvoo (Hebrew for "a beautiful place"). But in the middle of winter 1846, the Mormons were run out of Nauvoo and began a 1,000-mile trek westward, derided by nonbelievers as absurd as their faith (Van Biema 1997, p. 1). Led not by Smith (who had been assassinated) but Smith's successor, Brigham Young, some 10,000 Mormons found their way to Utah, which is the still the center of Mormonism today (Barlow 1999, p. 146).

Today one of the most interesting empirical sites to explore Mormonism is the Polynesian Cultural Center (PCC), in La'ie Hawai'i which is owned and operated by the Mormon Church. The Polynesian Cultural Center, created in 1963, is one of Hawai'i 's most popular, paid tourist attractions, entertaining about one million customers annually. Its annual revenues total some $40 million. The PCC pioneered a brand of tourist attraction in Hawai'i now known as "cultural" or "ethnic" tourism (Webb 1994, p. 195). This type of tourist industry draws on travelers' interest in native dwellings, ceremonies, foods, and the like.

How did this Mormon tourist attraction come to be? Interestingly, it began with Mormon *evangelicalism* and Western *expansionism* – and the Mormon emphasis on material prosperity. Specifically, as indicated previously, one of the most intriguing aspects of Mormonism (especially from a Weberian point of view) is that the founders of Mormonism encouraged its adherents to prosper materially to build God's kingdom. The Mormons sought to set up the *material* kingdom of Zion on earth, and they fully expected worldly prosperity as part of their covenant with God (Webb 1994, p. 197–8). The Book of Mormon expressly warrants the pursuit of material prosperity to build God's kingdom as part of one's spiritual progress: "After ye have obtained a hope in Christ ye shall obtain riches, if ye seek them; and ye will seek them for the intent to do good" (Jacob 2:18-19, as cited by Webb 1994, p. 198). Geographic isolation and social exclusion no doubt also spurred Brigham Young to proclaim over 150 years ago that "the Kingdom of God cannot rise independent of Gentile nations until we produce, manufacture, and make every article of use, convenience or necessity among our people" (Van Biema 1997, p. 3).

This emphasis on material prosperity was most apparent in the expansionist Mormon economic system of the nineteenth century. Between 1850 and 1890, the church called great numbers of missionaries to perform gainful labors that were considered as sanctified as the evangelical missions. The laborers mined gold and lead, manufactured iron, raised silk, operated businesses, farmed cotton, milled textiles, and built factories as part of a deliberate plan to fulfill the Mormon's religious errand (Arrington 1958, p. 33, as cited by Webb 1994, p. 199).

This was precisely the motivation behind the Mormon Church's "purchase" of the town of La'ie, Hawai'i, in 1865. Brigham Young intended La'ie to be an "agricultural mission" to produce cotton and sugar for the vast distribution of goods that made up the early Mormon economic system (Spurrier 1978, p. 17, Britsch 1986, p. 129, as cited by Webb 1994, p. 199). However, in the mid-1900s, Hawai'i's sugar industry declined (cotton had proved fruitless from the start); and the tourist industry began to boom. In the 1960s, then president and prophet of the church, David O. McKay, made a decision to create a tourist attraction that combined audience participation, cultural activities, the feast of the *hukilau*, and the staged spectacle of the Polynesian Panorama in La'ie. Today, the 42-acre Polynesian Cultural Center, owned and operated by the Mormon Church, continues to be the economic centerpiece of the town – and the Hawaiian tourist industry.[24]

Yet La'ie is rich with stories of visions and prophecies as to its material prosperity. Mormon prophesies about the construction of both La'ie's temple (which was the first Mormon temple outside the continental United States), and the construction of the Church College (later BYU-Hawai'i) flourished (Webb 1994, p. 203). In 1955, President McKay prophesied that the town of La'ie was to become "a missionary factor, influencing not thousands, not tens of thousands, but millions of people who will come seeking to know what this town and its significance are" (cited by Webb 1994, p. 204). To the Mormons of La'ie, the PCC literally fulfills McKay's prophecy by attracting a million visitors annually (Webb 1994, p. 204).

However, the success of the Polynesian Cultural Center (and the Mormon Church in general) is not without controversy. From a Marxist perspective, the construction and operation of the Polynesian Cultural Center (and the Mormon Church in general) demonstrate how elites *use* religious ideology to perpetuate and legitimize their power (and make a lot of money). For instance, today the PCC employs approximately 700 students, mostly Mormon Polynesians, who work part-time, mostly at minimum wage, in the Center's seven "villages." However, the Center's directors and top administrators are predominantly white ecclesiastical leaders from the continental United States, appointed by church officials in Salt Lake City (many of them prophets) (Webb 1994, p. 196). Marxist-oriented critics of the PCC might also charge that it is economics (rather than religion) that drives the PCC – because the PCC serves coffee (a beverage proscribed by the Mormon Church) and showcases performers wearing costumes that are immodest by the church's strict dress code. To such critics, it seems like church elders are willing to put Mormon beliefs and values on the back burner if they interfere with the maximization of profit (ibid.).[25]

To some extent, this is the view taken by the United States' Internal Revenue Service (IRS), which, since 1974, has sought to revoke the income tax exemption granted the Polynesian Cultural Center. In a case it eventually lost, the IRS argued that since its opening, the PCC has "sublimated" its cultural preservation and educational purposes, and had "evolved into an entertainment center to the extent that its exempt status should be revoked" (Corsi 1975, p. 2, as cited by Webb 1994, p. 208). The IRS based its case on the Center's enormous marketing and advertising operations that are unparalleled among nonprofit organizations (though typical of commercial ventures). The 10-year court battle ended in the Center's favor (although the Center's restaurant and gift shop lost their tax exempt status); however, further litigation and appeals have followed, which suggests that this matter will go on for years (Webb 1994, pp. 208–9).

From a Gramscian point of view, the power of the Mormon Church derives not only from its economic achievements, but its *ideological* sway. The fact that Polynesians *voluntarily* participate in church activities, doctrines, and practices (including tithing 10 percent of one's income, paying one's way for a year abroad on a volunteer mission, and working for minimum wage at the PCC) is the most compelling aspect of cultural hegemony. Similarly, for cultural Marxists, the Polynesian Cultural Center's re-creation of seven South Pacific villages – each with ceremonial houses and brief shows – is a glaring exemplar of imperialist ideology. Seven dynamic Polynesian cultures are reduced to the role of the "sideshow," and admired as the quaint antithesis to modern Western society. Significantly, though the cultural portrayals are artificial and shallow and, according to many critics, demeaning, this brand of tourist attraction has become immensely popular in Hawai'i in the last two decades, inspiring takeoffs and replicas – but none as popular or profitable as the Polynesian Cultural Center (Webb 1994, p. 195).

Yet the Gramscian assumption of "false consciousness" is problematic. For if we simply deem subjects' (e.g., Mormon Polynesians') experience "false" because it goes against their alleged, long-term, material self-interest, we have given up any semblance of subjectivity or *internal* motivation. As Easthope and McGowan (1992, p. 44) point out, a "false consciousness" that reaches far into the subject, hardly qualifies any more as in any useful sense "false." Similarly, Thompson (1984, pp. 5–6) says that we must "resist the view that ideology is pure *illusion*, an inverted or distorted image of what is 'real' . . . . Ideology is not a pale image of the social world but is part of that world, a creative and constitutive element of our social lives."

From an interpretive, Weberian point of view, the *motivation* behind the Polynesian Cultural Center (and Mormonism in general) is more complex. The *cultural attitude* at the heart of Mormonism that led to the founding of the PCC was at once profoundly "radical" and profoundly *American*: Mormonism challenged certain mainstream (Christian) beliefs and practices; but at the same time, took others – e.g., "manifest destiny," evangelicalism, and geographical expansionism – to new levels.

Specifically, Mormonism takes mainstream Jacksonian notions of social progress and individualism and raises them to heretical – even blasphemous – heights (Hansen 1981).[26] According to Mormon theology, those who have entered into the new and everlasting covenant "shall inherit thrones, kingdoms, principalities, and power, dominions all heights and depths" – and that *"then they shall be gods;"* i.e., for Mormons, the highest purpose of life is not merely salvation in the celestial kingdom, but the achievement of godhood, or "exaltation" (Hansen 1981, p. 80). This sense of immortal possibility open to humans is explicit in the Mormon assertion, "As man is, God once was; as God is, man may be" (Stein 1999, p. 25). Anyone willing to accept Mormon beliefs and practices can achieve "exaltation." As Hansen (1981, p. 83) poignantly states: "Andrew Jackson may have professed the belief that the common man could hold public office, but Joseph Smith out-Jacksoned the Jacksonians by proclaiming that the common man could become a god".

In addition, from a Weberian point of view, the success of Mormonism in the Pacific Islands might be rooted in the "elective affinity" (symbolic overlap) between Mormon and Polynesian ancestralism. Mormon notions of ancestralism and the "celestial family" mesh nicely with the widespread Polynesian belief that gods are ancestors living in another world (Eliade and Couliano 1991, p. 203). Specifically, like many Pacific Islanders, Mormons envision the family as a cohesive unit not merely here on earth but in heaven, and they perform ordinances vicariously for the dead; Mormons believe that those who die without receiving baptism and other ordinances must nevertheless receive these sacraments (Webb 1994, p. 200). This message from Joseph Smith is among Mormons' favorite scripture.

This dual Mormon and Polynesian emphasis on ancestralism is readily apparent at the Polynesian Cultural Center. Polynesians don costumes supposedly worn by their ancestors; they perform songs, dance, and simulate the lifestyles said to have been practiced centuries ago by their forebears. As Webb (1994, p. 201) maintains, though the PCC merely *models* ancient villages, "because the employees themselves are Polynesian, their role-playing is deeply personal; because they are Mormon, their attitude toward their ancestors is overlaid with religious significance and fervent intensity." As one Maori dancer (interviewed by Webb) states: "This piece of land, the building, and everything [the Maori village] belongs to our *tupuna* [ancestors], and we're upholding those principles in this latter-day. We're upholding the principles that they upheld, and this makes us feel good" (Webb 1994, p. 201). In a similar vein, a Hawai'ian Mormon student states:

> Each practice is opened and closed with prayer. Right there, it's a comfortable feeling . . . . [The instructor] will get up and give a strong testimony and the relationship with the Hawai'ian people and the Book of Mormon and with Christ. He knows a lot about Hawai'ian genealogy, and he'll just [recite] the names that go all the way back to Book of Mormon times, and we'll just get goosebumps listening to him. (Webb 1994, p. 203)

And a Maori dancer maintains:

> I could really feel the spirit of God with us today as we performed . . . . Everyone put their faith in Him. I felt as we were performing that I was actually back in the days of the ancient Maori. I felt fear as the trumpet was blown announcing strangers into our village. I felt proud of our Maori warriors as they challenged them, and I felt happiness when they made known to us that they came in peace and were welcomed into the village. I think everyone today performed at their best and really showed . . . that we are proud of our heritage and respect it. (Webb 1994, p. 205)

Most importantly, these comments reflect not only the theological but the *social* dimensions of ancestralism, i.e., the *communal* imperatives of religion that, as we saw earlier, were emphasized by Durkheim. This type of ritual not only links living members of a group together; it links the "living" and the "dead" in a common identity (see Calhoun 1993; Edles 1999). Here we find Maori dancers engaged in a *cultural* practice, which has symbolic and social, rather than strictly economic or political, motivations. This ritual reflects the *cultural* as well as the *social* construction of the self (Seidman 1994, p. 85).

However, Webb (1994) maintains that there is yet another cultural (or symbolic) link between Polynesian culture and Mormonism: a Mormon fascination with Polynesia, based on the Mormon scriptures' repeated referral to unnamed "isles of the sea." Although the scriptural "isles" remain nameless, Mormons consider them to be the Pacific Islands because of the brief story in the Book of Mormon about Hagoth the shipbuilder, who undertook a series of ocean voyages around 55 BC and never returned. Thus the Mormon church contends that "Polynesians are literally Israelites," the descendants of Hagoth and his followers.

In sum, the point is that cultural elements are multidimensional and complex. The Polynesian Cultural Center may reflect both a re-creation of the sacred origins of Polynesia, and a secular, tourist infatuation with Polynesia (among other things). As Webb (1994, p. 209) states:

> The PCC thrives as a contemporary economic mission because Mormons and tourists share a fixation for Polynesia. For the church, it is a fascination with Polynesian origins. For tourists, the popular image of a tropical island paradise peopled with beautiful "primitives," creates a powerful mystique and an invigorating tonic. The church capitalizes on this mutual fascination, but also employs the quasi-religious stature of the Center and the ethnicity of its employees to make the place successful. The tourists are grandly entertained. The employees, however, are steeped in Mormon lore and doctrines that overlay their involvement in the Center . . . . The employees are actually engaging in an approximation of a religious experience, and feel all the emotions attending such an occurrence.[27]

In addition, following Weber, we see that motivation is neither unidimensional or stagnant; the factors that propel a new religion (like Mormonism) forward in the beginning are not necessarily the same factors that sustain it later. As Hansen (1981, p. 206) maintains:

> Max Weber's Protestants . . . were tradition-minded people who had little inkling that their famous "ethic" was catapulting them headlong in the modern world. The same was true of the Mormons who, while building their anti-modern kingdom of God, developed those modern habits of initiative and self-discipline that helped dig the grave of the kingdom and ushered in a new breed of Mormon thoroughly at home in the corporate economy of America and its corollaries, political pluralism and the bourgeois family.

Conclusion

We began this chapter with conventional questions as to the role of *religion* in the United States today. We asked how pervasive formal religious systems are in the United States, and why they are more prevalent in the United States than other modern Western societies. What we found was that despite the ongoing process of *secularization*, which Weber adroitly underscored, neither "subjectivity" or "religion" is close to being "wiped out" in the United States or throughout the world. In terms of formal religion, despite the decline of certain denominations (e.g., Episcopalian, Methodist), new types of Christianity, such as Mormonism, are thriving; and belief in the afterlife is going up even as church attendance drops (Updike 1999). We are also witnessing new types of religious institutions and association, such as the huge, nondenominational "megachurch" and virtual religious groups (e.g., Christian chatrooms).

In addition, we have explored three basic theoretical approaches to religion and *culture*. First, the central contribution of Emile Durkheim, as we have seen, is the illumination of the *communal* and *social* function of religion. Durkheimians maintain that *all* systems of meaning rely on the binary opposition of the sacred and profane, and the intertwined processes of ritualization and symbolization. Second, we have seen that Max Weber sought to sort out and explain the *historical emergence* and *social psychology* behind specific worldviews. In one of the most important books in sociology, *The Protestant Ethic and the Spirit of Capitalism*, Weber explained the relationship between an extraordinary *secular*, pragmatic approach to the world (the capitalist "spirit") and the specific religious "ethic" that emerged out of the Protestant reformation. Weber showed that the "Protestant ethic" had the profound, unintended consequence of propelling the capitalist "spirit" forward, and that this interpenetration of worldviews, in conjunction with other structural conditions, helped result in the proliferation and domination of modern Western capitalism.

Finally, we have seen that the Marxist contribution to the study of religion is not only the *rationalistic* one as to the *material* links between religion, economics and politics. In addition, cultural Marxists point out that there is a *reciprocal* relationship between the ideal and material worlds; ideology shapes the material world because it shapes the very *idea* of action. Most importantly, from this point of view, cultural hegemony is maintained not only "from above," but "from below," as the lower classes participate in and reaffirm their own subordination. Nevertheless, cultural Marxists locate the origins of ideology in the ruling class (while Weber and Durkheim root culture in the basic constitution of "man," and thus at a more "autonomous" level) (Alexander 1988, pp. 2–3). In the next chapter we continue this discussion of culture and power in more detail by focusing on a central site in which systems of meaning are shaped and reshaped in the modern (and postmodern) world: the media.

IMPORTANT CONCEPTS INTRODUCED IN THIS CHAPTER

- Religion
- Secularization
- Symbol
- Ritual
- Sacred
- Profane
- Routine
- Ideology
- Cultural hegemony
- Rationalism

STUDY QUESTIONS/PROJECTS

1 Weber states: "in the United States, the pursuit of wealth, stripped of its religious and ethical meaning, tends to become associated with purely mundane passions, which often actually give it the character of sport" (Collins 1996, p. xiv). To what extent do you think this statement is true? Give at least two examples in support of, and in opposition to, this statement.

2 Write an autobiographical account of how holidays are celebrated in your family. Are your celebrations mired in consumption and consumerism? To what extent and how are secular and religious concerns melded within your family's traditions?

3 Interview five friends about their experience of holidays. Put the accounts together (you may also include your own experience, as per the previous question), and discuss religiosity, holidays, consumerism, materialism, and secularization in the United States today. Do you think materialism and spirituality conflict? Do you think "consumerism" is better understood as an oppressive *ideology* in the United States, or as simply a system of shared meaning?

4 Do an *ethnography*/participant observation of a religious group/sect (before you begin, see chapter 5, which explains this particular methodology). The great advantage of doing an ethnography of a religious group is that most temples and churches are open, i.e., anyone is free to attend services (make sure this is true before you begin your participant observation, however). The goal of your study is to grasp and articulate, as accu-

> rately as possible, the religious "world" you have entered. You can use "informants," but not in the first stages of your research. Just go, see, experience, and write down as much as you can.

Suggested Further Reading

Bellah, Robert, ed. 1973. *Emile Durkheim: On Morality and Society*. Chicago: University of Chicago Press.

Berger, Peter. 1967. *The Sacred Canopy*. Garden City, NY: Doubleday.

Bruce, Steve. 1996. *Religion in the Modern World: From Cathedrals to Cults*. New York: Oxford University Press.

Dillon, Michèle. 1999. *Catholic Identity*. Cambridge: Cambridge University Press.

Douglas, Mary. 1966. *Purity and Danger*. London: Routledge.

Dowdy, Thomas, and Patrick McNamara, eds. 1997. *Religion North American Style*, 3rd ed. New Brunswick, NJ: Rutgers University Press.

Durkheim, Emile. 1965 [1912]. *The Elementary Forms of Religious Life*. New York: Free Press.

Gallup, George, Jr., and D. Michael Lindsay. 1999. *Surveying the Religious Landscape: Trends in U.S. Beliefs*. Harrisburg, PA: Morehouse Publishing.

Gramsci, Antonio. 1971. *Selections from the Prison Notebooks*. New York: International Publishers.

Hansen, Klaus, J. 1981. *Mormonism and the American Experience*. Chicago: University of Chicago Press.

Hart, Stephen. 1996 [1992]. *What Does the Lord Require?* New Brunswick, NJ: Rutgers University Press.

Lemmen, M. M. W. 1990. *Max Weber's Sociology of Religion*. Heerlen, The Netherlands: Gooi en Sticht.

McGuire, Meredith. 1997. *Religion: the Social Context*, 4th ed. Belmont, CA: Wadsworth.

Robertson, Roland. 1970. *The Sociological Interpretation of Religion*. New York: Schocken.

Schmidt, Leigh Eric. 1995. *Consumer Rites*. Princeton, NJ: Princeton University Press.

Seidman, Steve. 1994. *Contested Knowledge*. Malden, MA: Blackwell.

Smith, Christian. 1998. *American Evangelicalism: Embattled and Thriving*. Chicago: University of Chicago Press.

Thompson, John B. 1984. *Studies in the Theory of Ideology*. Berkeley: University of California Press.

Updike, John. 1999. "The Future of Faith," *The New Yorker*, November 29, 1999, pp. 84–91.

Van Biema, David. 1997. "Kingdom Come: Salt Lake City Was Just For Starters," *Time* 150 (5) May 8 (http://www.california.com/`rpcman/TIME.HTM).

Webb, T. D. 1994. "Missionaries, Polynesians and Tourists: Mormonism and Tourism in La'ie, Hawai'i," *Social Process in Hawai'i* 35 (1994): 195–212.

Weber, Max. 1974 [1946]. "The Social Psychology of the World Religions," in *From Max Weber: Essays in Sociology*, trans and ed. H. H. Geerth and C. W. Mills. New York: Oxford University Press.

——. 1996 [1930]. *The Protestant Ethic and the Spirit of Capitalism*. Los Angeles: Roxbury.

Wuthnow, Robert. 1988. *The Restructuring of American Religion: Society and Faith Since World War II*. Princeton, NJ: Princeton University Press.

——. 1998. *After Heaven: Spirituality in America Since the 1950s*. Berkeley: University of California Press.

Notes

1   Social scientists usually measure the prevalence of religion in a given society either by focussing on the more "objective" variable, church attendance, or the more subjective variable "religiosity" (e.g., how many people say they believe in "God," etc.). However, it must be noted that even ascertaining the more "objective" of these two variables, "church attendance", is not unproblematic. Heated debates as to whether "self-reporting" (asking people whether or not they attended religious services the previous week), or church records are a more accurate measure of church attendance abound. Analysts such as Caplow (1998) and Hout and Greeley (1998) rely on self-reporting and conclude that church attendance has increased in the United States since the 1980s; while analysts such as Hadaway, Marler, and Chaves (1993, 1998) rely on church records instead of surveys, and conclude that church attendance has actually declined. Hadaway et al. maintain that the problem with self-reporting is that respondents tend to exaggerate the number of times they go to church; but Caplow (1998) and Hout and Greeley (1998), argue that church records underreport church attendance (since not everyone signs in). Most importantly for our purposes, even if we accept Hadaway et al.'s more conservative estimate – that one out of four, rather than two out of five, Americans attend services each week – the United States is still the most religious of modern industrial societies (e.g., 29 percent in the United States and 14 percent in Britain). See C. Smith (1998, ch. 2) for an insightful discussion of measuring American religious "strength."

2   Indeed, whereas about 10 percent of the population were church members at the time of the American Revolution, about 60 percent are today.

3   Evangelicalism (and its "religious cousin," fundamentalism) can be defined in different ways. However, generally, evangelicals (1) regard the Bible as the actual word of God; (2) have undergone some form of personal conversion; and (3) claim a desire to lead nonbelievers to a point of conversion (Gallup and Lindsay 1999, p. 65). This latter characteristic seems to be the most important colloquial association with "evangelicalism." C. Smith (1998, p. 242) finds that, positively or negatively, the primary characteristic most Protestants associated with "evangelical" was "actively evangelizing, taking a stand in the world for religious commitments . . . being more outspoken . . . evangelizing, preaching the Word." For more on the recent rise of evangeli-

calism in the United States, see Lippy (1999, pp. 51–3) and C. Smith (1998).

4   Bruce (1995, 1996) argues that there is more diversity in so-called "mo-
    nopoly religious" societies, and less heterogeneity in "pluralistic" religious
    societies than Stark and Iannaccone (1992) attest. For example, urban "black"
    churches in the United States do not really "compete" with rural "white"
    churches. In short, despite the actual "number" and "variety" of churches in
    the United States, the question remains, do Americans really experience a
    "plethora" of religious options, or do they find, especially given race/ethnic
    as well as geographic considerations, that their "options" are in fact as lim-
    ited as those in "monopoly" religious societies?

5   This point reminds me of one of my favorite sociology jokes, first told to me
    (as I recall) by Alfonso Pérez Agote, of the University of the Basque Country.
    A Mormon missionary is sent to the Basque Country, in northern Spain. The
    missionary goes out and begins proselytizing to a group of Basque shepherds.
    (Basques, and especially rural Basques, are known as being particularly reli-
    gious.) Suddenly, one of the shepherds interrupts the American missionary
    and says, "I don't even believe in my own religion – which is the true one –
    so why should I believe in yours?"

6   Smart (1995) points out that *choosing* a religion is a profoundly modern,
    American phenomenon. See also Rose (1999).

7   *Los Angeles Times* (April 22, 1998, p. 19).

8   Reform Judaism first emerged in the early nineteenth century, when a group
    of young, intellectual, German Jewish men sought to "modernize" Judaism
    and emancipate Jews from some of the limitations of traditional Judaism. At
    the end of the nineteenth century, the Conservative movement arose as a
    reaction to what was perceived as the "overmodernization" of Judaism by the
    Reform movement. Conservative Judaism sought to maintain the basic prac-
    tices of Judaism (Sabbath observation, the importance of Hebrew in Jewish
    life, and many of the dietary laws) without being strict observers of every
    nuance of Halacha (the code of Jewish practice). Another attempt to syn-
    chronize Judaism with modern times was begun in the United States in 1922
    by Mordecai Kaplan. Kaplan's Reconstructionist Branch sought to eliminate
    "outdated" doctrines as did Reformers, but Kaplan emphasized the main-
    tainance of many traditions for social rather than religious reasons. Of course,
    all these reforms of Judaism (or "Judaism-lites" as they have pejoratively
    been called), build too on the long-standing American tradition of individual-
    ism (see Dowdy and McNamara 1997, p. 139; and Goldscheider and
    Zuckerman 1984, p. 68, as cited by Davidman 1997, p. 141).

9   See also Dillon (1999, p. 255) who shows how American "pro-change Catho-
    lics" (e.g., gay or lesbian, feminist, or pro-choice Catholics – who are often
    disparaged as "cafeteria-style Catholics" or Protestantized Catholics) are "in-
    stitutionalizing new ways of speaking about and being Catholic, by express-
    ing what it means to be (or become) Catholic and gay, or lesbian, or an
    advocate of women's ordination, or pro-choice". As Dillon points out, "what
    makes pro-change Catholics interesting is that they try to forge a new iden-
    tity while retaining connections to a larger tradition. They chart new sym-
    bolic territory that integrates apparently incongruous identities while

maintaining links to Catholicism as a community of memory" (ibid.).

10 As Hansen (1981, pp. 29–33) points out, one of the distinctive characteristics of Mormonism is its emphasis on divine revelation. Beginning in 1823,
when the founder of Mormonism, Joseph Smith, received a divine revelation
as to where to look for a book written on gold plates, which Smith proceeded
to find and "translate" into the Book of Mormon, Smith received a series of
divine revelations which established not only the general principles of Mormonism, but the details of church organization. Thus even today, the all-
male church hierarchy still insists that their decisions are based on "divine
revelation." For instance, in 1978 when the First Presidency of the Mormon
Church finally (and unexpectedly) revoked the infamous "Negro doctrine"
prohibiting black men from the priesthood, it was explained not as merely a
policy change; but, rather, a change that had come by way of divine revelation (Hansen 1981, p. 198).

11 Marx states: "If in all ideology men and their circumstances appear upside-
down as in a camera obscura, this phenomenon arises just as much from
their historical life-process as the inversion of objects on the retina does from
their physical life-process" (*The German Ideology*, in Lemert 1993, p. 43). Interestingly, the term "camera," as well as the apparatus itself, derives from
camera obscura, which is Latin for "dark room" or "dark chamber." The
original camera obscura was a darkened room with a minute hole in one
wall. Light entering the room through this hole projected an image from the
outside on the opposite darkened wall. The image formed this way was inverted and blurry, but artists used this device, long before film was invented,
to sketch scenes projected by the "camera." Over the course of three centuries, the camera obscura evolved into a handheld box, and the pinhole was
fitted with an optical lens to sharpen the image ("Camera obscura," *Microsoft®
Encarta® 98 Encyclopedia.* © 1993–7 Microsoft Corporation.)

12 G. W. F. Hegel (1770–1831) was a German philosopher who greatly influenced Karl Marx (1818–83). Hegel is known as an idealist, i.e., he was
interested not so much in the material world, but in the spirit of societies.
Hegel believed that changes in consciousness led to material change. Benedetto
Croce (1866–1952) was an important contemporary of Gramsci, who also
reconstructed Hegelian idealism.

13 Like Gramsci, Georg Lukács (1885–1971) was a Hegelian Marxist who sought
to revive subjectivity from Marx's early work. His most important book is
History and Class Consciousness (1922).

14 Weber maintained that the better able an ethic is to bring human conduct
systematically to a conscious and enduring inward unity, the more highly
rationalized that ethic is (Lemmen 1990, p. 120). Weber used two central
interrelated "yardsticks" to judge the level of rationalization of a religion: (1)
the degree to which a particular religion is divested of magic; and (2) the
ethical relationship between the religion and the world, i.e., "the degree to
which it [the religion] has systematically unified the relation between God
and the world and therewith its own ethical relationship to the world"
(Lemmen 1990, p. 117).

15 While Weber was perhaps less "Eurocentric" than many of his contemporar-

ies, nevertheless, his dichotomization of "the Western" and "the oriental" is a binary opposition that inherently involves all sorts of theoretical, methodological, and cultural baggage, including a Western bias. See Said (1978) for a now classic critique of this type of "orientalizing."

16 However, ironically, Weber never defined his main concept. At the beginning of his discussion of the sociology of religion in *Wirtschaft und Gesellschaft* Weber said he would define "religion" at the end of his study, but he never did (Berger 1967, p. 175).

17 Weber also noted that industrial capitalism thrived not in Spain or Italy, but in parts of Germany and Holland, England and colonial American – those places where the Reformation (and especially the Calvinist part of the Reformation) had had its greatest impact (Bruce 1996, p. 13).

18 John Calvin's "predestinarianism" took this methodical individualization of religious practice even further. The Genevan Reformer believed that if God really is all powerful, he could not be placated by prayers, rosaries and offerings by anyone – whether religious professional or layperson. As Bruce (1996, pp. 15–16) states:

> Out went penance, and, for most Protestants out went confession. In came the idea that life was a ledger with a plus and a minus column and a running score at the bottom of the page. And there was no longer any magical device to alter the balance of good and bad. Each individual had to take a passionate interest in assessing his/her conduct. Many of the English Puritans kept detailed diaries in which they daily recorded evidences of their spiritual state.

But of course, "predestinarianism" is psychologically discomfiting, for one never knows whether or not one is saved.

19 Indeed, as early as 1835, Alexis de Tocqueville remarked that Anglo-American society reflected a "marvelous combination" of the spirit of religion and the spirit of freedom, two distinct elements that in other societies clashed with each other (Tiryakian 1993, p. 42).

20 Tiryakian (1996, p. 105) uses the term "chthonic" rather than the more common term "pagan" to refer to "a basic ontological affirmation of earth as the primordial locus of reality, and of the forces of life which have to be cultivated, enhanced, or placated in order to insure the reproductive processes of survival," because the term "pagan" has a derogatory connotation he wishes to avoid. By "metaculture," Tiryakian means "a set of beliefs and symbols, generated in the distant past and renewed by succeeding generations of actors" (Tiryakian 1996, p. 102).

21 German pessimism traces back to the philosopher, Arthur Schopenhauer (1788–1860), who believed that the tragedy of life arises from the nature of the will, which constantly urges the individual toward the satisfaction of successive goals, none of which can provide permanent satisfaction. Schopenhauer's philosophy of pessimism significantly influenced the German philosopher and poet, Friedrich Wilhelm Nietzsche (1844–1900). Nietzsche, best known for his infamous statement, "God is dead," believed that traditional values (represented primarily by Christianity) had lost their power in

the lives of individuals. Nietzsche valued the creative "will to power" of the heroic individual, which sets him apart from the inferior masses. However, extreme nationalists mixed the Nietzschean "superman" with a romantic glorification of the German people, resulting in a heady concept of German racial superiority that contributed to two world wars. See "Arthur Schopenhauer," and "Friedrich Wilhelm Nietzsche," *Microsoft® Encarta® 98 Encyclopedia.* © 1993–7 Microsoft Corporation.

22   *Time* (August 4, 1997, pp. 52–3); *Salt Lake City Messenger* 93 (November 1997). The Mormon Church claimed that *Time* magazine exaggerated its financial worth. However, the church did not divulge what its assets really amounted to, and unlike many other churches, the LDS Church refuses to give a financial statement to its members (*Salt Lake City Messenger* 93, November 1997).

23   Only a small proportion of Mormons in fact practiced polygamy; the "privilege of taking extra wives was pretty well monopolized by [Joseph Smith] and a few of his trusted disciples" (Ivins 1972, p. 103). According to Mormon teachings a woman could "never obtain a fullness of glory, without being married to a righteous man for time and all eternity"; thus "one of the responsibilities of those in official church positions was to try to make sure that no woman went without a husband" (ibid., pp. 108–9). Joseph Smith may have had as many as sixty wives; and his wives included at least three pairs of sisters (ibid., pp. 104–5). In response to pressures from the US government, plural marriage was outlawed in 1890 (Hansen 1981, p. 81).

24   Webb (1994, p. 199) succinctly states: "La'ie now exploits tourism for the church as it once exploited natural resources." However, the Polynesian Cultural Center was not economically profitable from the start. Rather, it turned a profit only after the church managers struck a shrewd deal with tour operators, in which the PCC returned 30 percent of profits to tour companies, in exchange for including the Center in their marketing and tour packages (Ferre 1988, as cited by Webb 1994, p. 200).

25   Marxist critics might also note that the Church spends most of its funds acquired by tithing not for charity or construction or building maintenance, but for investments (Van Biema 1997).

26   Andrew Jackson (1767–1845) was the leader of the democratic western frontier element, and the first westerner elected president of the United States (1829–37). Small farmers, laborers, and many other Americans struggling to "better themselves" looked to Jackson for leadership. "Andrew Jackson," *Microsoft® Encarta® 98 Encyclopedia.* © 1993–7 Microsoft Corporation.

27   However, Webb (1994) erroneously portrays the multivocality of the Polynesian Cultural Center individualistically rather than culturally. In other words, Webb maintains simply that "tourists" interpret the PCC one way and "workers" another, etc.; but, from a culturalist perspective, the point is that the PCC reflects multiple *discourses* that individuals tap into in a variety of ways.

CHAPTER THREE

The Media and Popular Culture

One of the most distinctive features of modern society is the extent to which our knowledge and experience of the world is *mediated*. We conceive of, and act in, this world via television, movies, radio, newspapers, and computers. Today we take for granted both the centrality of media in our everyday lives, and the near-instantaneous transmission of information. By the term "media," I mean "any extensions of the human sensory apparatus, any technologies that enable communication" (Real 1996, p. 7).

This instantaneous transmission of news is even more remarkable when one realizes that up until the 1840s, when the telegraph was invented, there was no such thing as instantaneous communication over long distances that were physically wired together. Before that, the only way to communicate across long distances was for tangible, written messages to travel physically between the two locations. This meant, for instance, that it took 44½ days for a message to travel from New York City to Cincinnati, Ohio in 1794, although with improved transportation systems the time was reduced to 19 days by 1817 (Croteau and Hoynes 1997, p. 10). This meant that up until the mid-1800s, it took five to eight months for a message to reach India from England by ship; but that by 1870, a telegram sent from London could reach Bombay in five hours (Kundnani 1998, p. 49).[1]

In addition, since Thomas Edison developed the phonograph in 1877, and Louis Lumière invented the cinematograph, which subsequently led to "moving pictures" in 1895, our "leisure time" has moved from being largely "unmediated" to being largely "mediated." Today, we flock to the movies and listen to recorded music, much more than we tell stories and sing songs. Of course, the most profound change in this regard began merely in the 1940s, with the advent of *television*. The first commercial television broadcast was in 1941. Less than ten years later, over 65 percent of American households had television sets, and television had become the most popular leisure-time activity in the United States. Today televisions are turned on in American households an average of seven hours a day. Many American households have television sets in the den, the kitchen, several bedrooms, and the garage; spatially, most family rooms are organized around the television. According to the most conservative estimates, Americans spend almost half of their available waking leisure time watching television (Kubey and Csikszentmihalyi 1990, as cited by Croteau and Hoynes 1997, p. 5). And by the time many American children start school, they will have already watched more hours of television than the total number of hours of classroom instruction they will encounter in their school careers (Lemert 1997a, p. 27).

To be sure, not all culture, or all cultural products, are technologically mediated. People still write stories and poems (with paper and pen); play musical instruments; draw, paint, and so on. Nevertheless, today there are few cultural products and leisure-time activities unaffected by the media. Thus, for instance, the recent proliferation of book groups is in part attributable to Oprah Winfrey, who started a book group on her popular television show. Similarly, the recent upsurge in golf as a youth sport is in part attributable to Tiger Woods, whose success and charm is splashed all over magazines, newspapers, and of course, television.

Traditionally, media analysts have used the term "mass media" to denote a *one-way* dissemination of information to a mass, anonymous audience, e.g., newspapers and television; while media analysts have used the term "interpersonal media" to denote a *two-way* process between specific individuals, e.g., the telephone. However, in recent years new technology – dubbed "the new media" – have collapsed this distinction. Today "mass" and "interpersonal" media are merged: one can *respond* to mass-generated messages via e-mail; set up one's own "web page" complete with personal photos and information (for a mass, anonymous audience); and engage in virtual relationships and even virtual sex, which clearly epitomizes not only the melding of "one-way" (mass) and "two-way" (interpersonal) media, but *intimacy* and "mass" communications.

In this chapter, we focus on the media not only as systems of communication, but as systems of meaning, from various theoretical perspectives. We begin with a neo-Durkheimian exploration of "media ritual events"; we then shift to a more critical discussion of the political and economic parameters of cultural production. Next, we examine two approaches that challenge some of the basic premises of mass culture theory and neo-Durkheimianism: audience/reception analysis, which underscores the complex relationship between texts and the audience/viewer/reader; and postmodernism, which is even more suspicious of *any* attempt to "fix" meaning. In this way, in this chapter we outline the *cultural* dynamics of the media and popular culture.

Media Ritual Events

One of the most remarkable features of the proliferation of the mass media in modern society is that it allows millions of people the world over to experience the same cultural products (e.g., McDonald's, Disney films, Hollywood shoot 'em ups, *Dallas*) and historical moments (e.g., moon landings, World Cup soccer, the death of Princess Diana). Mass media allow these events to be "shared," despite the fact that the people who "share" them are geographically dispersed, and often number in the millions. Indeed, one *billion* people are said to have watched the 1990 World Cup soccer match between Germany and Argentina (De Mooij and Keegan 1991, p. 4, as cited by Croteau and Hoynes 1997, p. 289).

From a neo-Durkheimian perspective, there are important parallels between mass media events such as World Cup soccer and traditional rituals (e.g., weddings, funerals, communion) in which individuals are *physically* gathered together. Whether "contests" (such as the Superbowl), "conquests" (such as the Gulf War or the moon landings), "coronations" (e.g., the marriage of Prince Charles and Princess Diana), or tragedies (e.g., the Kennedy assassination), special media events capture the attention of vast populations and elicit collective excitement, celebration, or mourning (Dayan and Katz 1988). By sharing the experience of the ritual media event, individuals are "gathered together" into a sacred space and time. For instance, Dayan and Katz (1992, p. 123 as cited by Schudson 1994, p. 38) report an Indian student's description of how his family watched Mahatma Gandhi's funeral on television: they washed and dressed "as if we were going to be physically present at the scene. My mother insisted that we wear long clothes and cover our heads as a mark of respect."

Of course, the *significance* of media ritual events is not simply that they are *shared*, but that they call up and reaffirm specific shared *symbols* and *meanings*. Media ritual events clarify and reaffirm symbolic order, the binary opposition of the sacred and profane, the good and the bad, the holy and the evil. One of the most important symbols that media ritual events call up and reaffirm is that of the *nation*. For as Benedict Anderson (1983, pp. 15–16) first pointed out and David Kertzer (1988) confirms, the nation is an "imagined community."[2] "Without rites and symbols there are no nations" (Kertzer 1988, p. 179). Thus, for instance, international contests like the Olympics unite an entire *nation* under one banner.[3] Similarly, "conquests" like the first moon landing, displace contested, domestic clashes for the momentary *national* victory of the space project. The first moon landing was a celebration of American omnipotence, "progress," and the wonders and marvels of science and technology. As Tom Hanks explains why he took to the creation of a 12-hour HBO "docudrama" about the first moon landing: "To me, the idea that there are footprints on the moon is as beautiful as the Sistine Chapel. There are periodic benchmarks in the history of mankind that are evolutionary moments and walking on the moon is one of the them."[4]

Most importantly, the *power* of the media in ritual media events lies precisely in the fact that these moments do not *seem* mediated. Television fits so intimately in our daily lives that we lose the feeling of "mediation." Thus, for instance, we "remember" the assassination of Martin Luther King; we "remember" the beating of Rodney King; we "remember" the 1998 soccer final between France and Brazil. We have vivid images in our heads of these moments, such that when asked, "Do you remember John Kennedy getting shot?," or "Do you remember the first moon landing?," we do not think to say, "Well, no, I was not there; but I remember the mediated version of the event." We say, "Yes, I was in the sixth grade. Wasn't that horrible?" (or incredible, or whatever). In these (and most) cases, *the mediated "memory" of the event and the "event" itself are one and the same.*

In addition, there is an *interruptive* power to media ritual events that compares to the *interruptive* power of traditional rituals (e.g., funerals) and moments (e.g., the Sabbath). Indeed, Dayan and Katz (1988) call mass media events the "high holidays" of contemporary life. Like traditional rituals, mass media ritual events are moments "in and out of time." Like holidays, media ritual events *interrupt* "normal time"; "regular" television programs are postponed to make room for the occasion. As Dayan and Katz (1988, p. 162) state: "this disorganization and the slight sense of chaos which accompanies it fulfill a major dramatic function: television's most powerful gesture consists precisely in interrupting the continuous flow of its own programs; in dismantling its own 'supertext.'"

This interruptive power of the media is most readily apparent in *unscripted* ritual media events, such as natural disasters (e.g., earthquakes, hurricanes), and what Liebes (1998) calls "disaster time-outs" or "disaster marathons," i.e., non-stop live broadcasting that recycles the horrors of, or "the day after," a tragic event (e.g., the monotonous, continuous coverage of John Kennedy Jr.'s fatal plane crash in 1999, or Princess Diana's fatal car crash in 1997). In these moments, only the media has the "big picture"; we *must* turn to the media to find out what is going on, what has happened. Liebes contends (1998, p.81): "Wallowing in the reality of the moment, making it fill the whole of the screen and the whole of the collective consciousness," disaster marathons operate to blur "the memory of past events, historical contexts and long term processes, connecting the present only to other disasters, equally torn from their contexts. Forgotten are past suffering and long-term alternatives."[5]

This brings us to one of the most important *sites* of media ritual events: the courtroom. The first modern media courtroom ritual event was probably the Scopes Trial of 1925 (though, to be sure, the so-called "Monkey Trial" was played out in print rather than on television). The Scopes Trial (in which a Tennessee high school biology teacher, named John Scopes, was prosecuted for having taught the theory of evolution) juxtaposed the competing ideologies of religious fundamentalism and secularism/modernism. The trial received worldwide publicity and was conducted in a circus-like atmosphere. The press dubbed it the "Monkey Trial," because according to popular belief, evolution meant that humans were descended from monkeys.[6]

Of course, in the 1990s, we witnessed a spectacular trilogy of ritual media courtroom events highlighting pivotal race/gender/class issues: the Anita Hill/Clarence Thomas hearings; the Rodney King verdict; and the most effervescent, volatile, and long-lasting "trial of the century" – the O. J. Simpson spectacle (further discussed in the next chapter). From a neo-Durkheimian point of view, courtroom conflicts are "heavily burdened with ambiguities that demand resolution." Despite (or in conjunction with) their "circus-like" atmosphere, these events call up and reaffirm "the collective ideas which map up [a society's] unity" (Dayan and Katz, 1988, p. 162), and these ideas are often explicitly reworked and/or reaffirmed in the "final verdict."

Yet this brings us to important criticisms of the neo-Durkheimian approach – criticisms that point to the *mundane* (rather than *sacred*) dimensions of cultural production and interpretation. First, neo-Marxists charge that media ritual events are not rooted in a *sacred* collective consciousness as a whole, but are *framed* by a handful of elites; most individuals are not voluntarily committed, active participants in the construction of media events, but merely passive consumers and spectators. Thus, for instance, the first moon landing was created by NASA, the US government, and the media industry. While, to be sure, no one has *complete* control over how a ritual event plays out (e.g., the 1986 Challenger explosion); NASA, the US government, and the media determined the parameters as to what would be seen (e.g., for John Glenn to plant the American flag on the moon). As McGuire (1997, p. 195) asks, "is the quality of civil religious commitment not changed when a Fourth of July celebration is an elaborately staged, professionally orchestrated spectacle, parading US technology . . . underwritten by corporate contributions, and promoted as a 'Kodak moment'" (see also Wuthnow 1994)?

In a parallel way, critical analysts point out that there are *narrative* parameters behind ritual media events (that do not necessarily emanate from the "sacred values" of the society as a whole). Ritual media events are structured texts that rely on "convention and formulae (e.g., plotting and pacing) in order to tell their stories of motive, action, and causality" (Hunt 1999, p. 28). For instance, as Lipsitz (1997a, p. 9) maintains regarding the O. J. spectacle:

> The Simpson trial became a story that was easy to sell, in part, because it seemed to replicate so perfectly the world of commercial television and its generic conventions. The athlete/actor/celebrity defendant charged with murder could have come out of *Murder, She Wrote* or *Columbo* while the details about his residence and vehicles might fit easily into segments of *Dallas, Dynasty,* or *Life Styles of the Rich and Famous.* For experienced television viewers, courtroom confrontations enacted half-remembered episodes of *L.A. Law, Perry Mason,* and *Quincy,* while the history of unheeded claims of spousal abuse evoked the concerns and conflicts often aired in the movie-of-the-week.[7]

Relatedly, production of culture analysts locate the coherence of media ritual events not in a universal collective consciousness, but in the structural parameters of the media, i.e., bureaucratic, organizational imperatives.

In short, if there is a particular theme behind and within a cultural event or product, it may *not* be a function of the sacred "collective consciousness" as a whole. Rather, it may be a function of structural dynamics, most importantly those of class and power, as neo-Marxists attest; or it may reflect more *mundane* issues of narrative/genre or bureaucracy/organization.[8]

However, as we will see later in this chapter, postmodernists and audience/reception analysts take this rejection of a sacred "collective consciousness" even further. These analysts challenge the very notion that there is a "coherence" to media products and events. They emphasize that no matter who produces (or tries to produce) media products and events, in the end, *interpretation* is up to the *individual* viewer/reader.

For instance, many Americans – "black" and "white" – came to see the short video clip of the beating of Rodney King as a reflection of African Americans' long history of racialized abuse at the hands of white authorities. Later, many people – "black" and "white" – came to view Rodney King's simple plea, "can't we all get along?," as an expression of the sacred American ideals of tolerance and pluralism. But clearly, this is not the *only* way this video clip was viewed. Some Americans did not see these clips at all; and others (mostly "white") perceived the beating of Rodney King as justified. After all, the man *did not stop* when the police asked him to stop; the police may have been a little rough, but they were just "doing their job."

Of course, as we will see in the next chapter, nowhere was *multivocality* more apparent than in the O. J. Simpson trial. As most everyone knows, Americans responded to the O. J. spectacle in different ways. In contrast to "white" Americans, many "black" Americans began to see in the O. J. media ritual event familiar images of "pogroms" and "lynchings" (rather than the "clear" case of guilt that the media projected) (see Morrison 1997, p. xii). In general, African Americans were far more skeptical and critical of the mainstream *media's* role in creating the "breaking story" than were "whites." This makes sense, given that African Americans are, in general, far more skeptical about the role of what they perceive as primarily *white* media institutions in society. In a CBS/*New York Times* poll, blacks were more than three times as likely as whites to say that the media are biased against blacks (46 percent versus 13 percent); while whites were more nearly twice as likely as blacks to view the media as racially neutral (68 percent versus 35 percent) (Hunt 1999, p. 8).

Yet the neo-Durkheimian emphasis on the sacrality and unifying power of ritual media events does not necessarily conflict with audience/reception analysts' recent emphasis on individual *agency*. Today neo-Durkheimians maintain that ritual media events are not stagnant expressions of rigid values and codes, but a *cultural space* where pivotal and volatile social issues are sorted out and in which "collective identities and solidarities . . . are forged" (Curran and Liebes 1998, p. 5). Through media ritual events, "citizens actively construct their own understanding of real and ideal civil society by filtering overarching discourses and narratives through multiple public spheres and communities" (Alexander and Jacobs 1998, p. 29). Most importantly, this public construction and narration of the social often results in social change. Thus, ritual media events, like the O. J. Simpson spectacle, are *discursive* conflicts that may "begin as ceremonies designed to celebrate and (re)affirm the status quo," [but] conflicting cultural currents . . . mitigate against any final reconciliation and even incite movements for counter-hegemonic change" (Hunt 1999, pp. 27; 44).

Consider, for instance, one of the most significant ritual moments in Olympic history: the victory ceremony for the 200-meter dash at the 1968 Mexico Games. Tommie Smith, the gold medalist, and John Carlos, the bronze medalist, turned this simple ritual act into a poignant display of the "revolt of the black athlete" (Edwards 1969). As can be seen in figure 3.1, Smith and Carlos stood on the victory stand shoeless, wearing black socks and a single black glove; Smith had a black scarf tied around his neck.[9] As the US anthem played, Smith and Carlos immediately raised their fists and bowed their heads. Later Smith explained the *meaning* of

Figure 3.1 Tommie Smith (center) and John Carlos on the victory stand at the 1968 Mexico City Olympic Games (Edwards 1969, p. 140d; Wide World Photos). Reproduced courtesy of AP/Wide World Photos.

this act: the raised gloved fist stood for the unity and power of black America; the black scarf stood for black pride; the black socks with no shoes stood for black poverty in racist America. The gesture of the bowed head was made in remembrance of the fallen warriors in the black liberation struggle – Malcolm X, Martin Luther King, and others (Edwards 1969, pp. 103–4).

Tellingly, the US Olympic Committee responded harshly and hastily to Smith and Carlos's simple symbolic act. The Committee promptly suspended Carlos and Smith from the Olympic team and gave them 48 hours to leave Mexico.[10] The Committee also warned all other US athletes, black and white, that "severe" penalties would follow any further protests. Ironically, this reactionary response simply compelled athletes who were not hitherto particularly militant (such as Bob Beamon and Ralph Boston) to follow Smith and Carlos's lead (Edwards 1969, pp. 104–5). Even more importantly, it confirmed Carlos's and Smith's place as African American heroes in the 1960s struggle for civil rights[11] – and it resulted in significant and immediate social change. It led directly to the opening of jobs hitherto closed to African Americans in the management of sports, and the formation of the Federation of Black Amateur Athletes to protect the interests and guarantee the rights of black college athletes (Edwards 1969, p. 108).

Yet, despite the ability of both participants and viewers' to "resist" hegemonic discourse, the *power* and *authority* of the media and government institutions *behind* the mass media cannot be ignored. This brings us to Marxist-inspired perspectives of the mass media and popular culture.

Mass Communication, Mass Culture, and Cultural Hegemony

The first contemporary studies of the mass media and popular culture emerged in the 1920s, when a number of German theorists (including Max Horkheimer, T. W. Adorno, Erich Fromm, Leo Lowenthal, Herbert Marcuse, and Walter Benjamin), emigrated to the United States (except Benjamin, who died fleeing the Nazis), and began to focus on American mass culture (Lazère 1987, p. 6). This group of theorists, known as the "Frankfurt school," applied Hegelian Marxism, and especially the works of Gramsci and Lukács, to *modern* society. As we saw in the last chapter, Gramsci stressed that society is held together by what *appears* to be the voluntary adherence to dominant ideas, but is really the *ideology* of the ruling elite. In Lukács's terms, the working class is doomed to a "false consciousness," i.e., a "class-conditioned *unconsciousness* of one's own socio-historical and economic condition." The Frankfurt school maintained that modern *mass culture* is the key agent of ideological hegemony in the twentieth century. The *culture industry* managed the cultural repression of the individual, having surpassed the church and challenged the family and the state (with which it has increasingly merged) as the most influential socializing force (Lazère 1987, p. 6). The culture industry has become the primary agent of *socialization* in modern society, such that what we have are not merely "culture industries" but "consciousness industries" (Enzensberger 1974), that administer "a nonspontaneous, reified, phony culture rather than the real thing" (Jay 1973, p. 216).

According to the Frankfurt school, "work" and "leisure" form a symbiotic relationship under capitalism: work dulls the senses, and the culture industry continues the process (Storey 1993, p. 105). Thus, for instance, in a most provocative essay, Theodor Adorno (1992 [1941]) portrays popular music fans trapped in the four-bar and eight-bar structure of popular songs as victims of cultural imperialism. In a similar vein, Herbert Marcuse (1964, p. 12) maintains:

> The irresistible output of the entertainment and information industry carry with them prescribed attitudes and habits, certain intellectual and emotional reactions which bind the consumers more or less pleasantly to the producers and, through the latter, to the whole. The products indoctrinate and manipulate; they promote a false consciousness . . . it becomes a way of life. It is a good way of life much better than before – and as a good way of life, it militates against qualitative change. Thus emerges a pattern of *one dimensional thought and behavior* in which ideas, aspirations, and objectives that, by their content, transcend the established universe of discourse and action are either repelled or reduced to terms of this universe.

By the 1960s, many American communications analysts had picked up the Frankfurt school's conviction about the tremendous *power* of the culture industry. But communications analysts, such as Bagdikian (1992) and Parenti (1993), emphasize the culture industry's *economic* rather than ideological pivot. From this point of view, artistic integrity and truth simply play second fiddle to the capitalist motivation for maximized return on media investment. Transnational corporations, driven by the financial rewards of production, exploit popular tastes for commercial profit (Real 1996, p. 148).

Consider, for instance, the role of the mass media in American democracy. Most Americans are familiar with the First Amendment to the United States Constitution, which guarantees, among other things, "freedom of the press." Most Americans realize that the First Amendment is critical to democracy for two reasons. First, "freedom of the press" enables citizens to have access to multiple venues of *impartial* information – which is essential for making informed, intelligent decisions about government and society; secondly, "freedom of the press" provides a pivotal democratic function by allowing journalists to serve as a "watchdog" over politicians and government. One important example in this regard is the "Watergate" scandal, first exposed by *The Washington Post*. As a media ritual event, Watergate affirmed that despite the unsavory political practices in which politicians may become involved, democracy can be "saved" and restored through the work of sharp and critical "investigative reporters."

Yet critical communications analysts emphasize that the quest for *profit* interferes with this idealized democratic function of the media in capitalist societies. Critical analysts point out that in recent years the quest for profit has motivated news agencies to decrease the number of journalists, cut back on long-term investigative reporting, use a larger percentage of wire services reports, rely on public relations video segments (reports prepared and provided free of charge by public relations firms) in television newscasts, focus on preplanned official events, and cover a limited number of institutions in a handful of big cities (Croteau and Hoynes 1997, p. 52). In addition, the profit motive has compelled news organizations to make the news less a source of critical inquiry and information, and more a form of light entertainment, combining sensationalism, violence, sex, crime, and fun (lifestyle trends, celebrity profiles, etc.). News broadcasts feature upbeat, reassuring, attractive newscasters, who rarely veer from time-tested formulas. Titillation is combined with an upbeat style, and, of course, a happy ending.

Even more importantly, critical communications analysts emphasize that there is an increasing concentration of media ownership in fewer and fewer hands, which impairs the democratic function of the media. For instance, in a comprehensive survey, Bagdikian (1992, p. 4) shows that the United States has over "25,000 media outlets, but twenty corporations control most of the business in daily newspapers, television, books, and motion pictures." He goes on to state that if "freedom of the press belongs to those who own one," as the old adage has it, that freedom seems increasingly narrow (Hall and Neitz 1993, p. 151).

Moreover, communications analysts emphasize that not only has there been a growing concentration of media ownership but also an increase in *conglomeration*, i.e., media companies have become part of much larger corporations, which in turn own a collection of other companies (Bagdikian 1992; Croteau and Hoynes 1997, p. 37). This increasing conglomeration has been both "vertical," in that large conglomerates buy up and control all aspects of production and distribution of a single type of media product (e.g., the talent agencies, production studios, theater chains, videocassette manufacturing plants, and a chain of video rental stores) so that the company can better control the entire process of creation, production, marketing and distribution of a movie; and "horizontal," i.e., as conglomerates buy up and assemble large portfolios of magazines, television stations, book publishers, record labels, etc., in order to enhance cross-promotion. Thus, for instance, Time Warner released the Blockbuster film *Batman* with the help of a prominent review in *Time* magazine and heavy promotion on Time Warner-owned Home Box Office (Miller 1990, as cited by Croteau and Hoynes 1997, p. 38).

Indeed, while "aesthetics" has never been the sole consideration in the production of culture, today production and promotion seem to be more fused than ever before. For example, every year Disney introduces a new children's movie, and, at the same time, launches a new line of spin-off products and unleashes a fervent marketing campaign. The question is, if McDonald's introduces a free toy from the latest Disney film in its children's Happy Meals at the same time that the new Disney film comes out, and this advertising campaign inspires parents and children (as well as celebrities such as Rosie O'Donnell) not only to see the latest Disney movie, but to visit McDonald's (to get the whole collection of new toys), and also to buy a whole groundswell of products (bedding, clothing, toys, lamps, backpacks, lunchboxes, stationery, videotapes, books, etc.), which in turn launches a new television show, is this a "film" (a piece of culture in the artistic sense) or simply an ad? Where does the advertisement end and the cultural product begin?

In sum, for both the Frankfurt school and critical communications analysts, "mass culture" is neither "popular" or "democratic." Whether the motivation is ideological or economic (or both), the shared assumption is that the media is a sophisticated, well-financed industry that creates and conditions the interpretation of a limited and biased array of manufactured entertainment goods. Mass culture is "administered . . . nonspontaneous, reified, and phony" (Jay 1973, p. 216, as cited by Ritzer 1992, p. 145); the "systematic moronization of children and adults alike" (Marcuse 1964, p. 63). Consumer culture helps convince oppressed groups that all is well with the world; it *legitimizes* exploitation and oppression by the ruling class, convincing the working class that they are really something quite different – acts of universal necessity (Storey 1993, p. 112). "Genuine" meaning does not exist, because it has been subverted and commodified.

Notwithstanding the *hegemony* of the media industries, it is the *passivity* behind mass media consumption that mass culture theorists as well as communications analysts find most problematic. Bagdikian (1996, p. 7) suggests that we are facing a "nightmare" of mass conformity, as a handful of high-tech corporations "already are organizing to inundate the world populations with what come to them as second nature, making maximum profits through their closely held control of the coming world cultural and informational systems." For Bagdikian, the culture industry is "organizing masses of children and adults everywhere, including in the Third World, into an electronic shopping mall devoted to the culture of wasteful and ultimately fatal use of the planet's natural resources and a diminishing of the human spirit" (ibid., p. 14). Similarly, Marcuse (1964) suggests that the subliminal message of almost all that passes for "art" is conformity and resignation (Jay 1973, p. 216).[12] This is precisely what Gramsci supposed in his conceptualization of hegemony: the interests of one powerful sector are universalized as the interests of the society in general.

THE IMPACT OF THE MEDIA ON REAL PEOPLE

In light of this dire view as to the oppressive role of mass culture in contemporary American society, it is most interesting to note that most Americans claim that they are not "influenced" by the media. "Ha!" Americans say, when discussing a particular show, genre, or advertisement. "It's *only* television. It is not *reality. So what* if there are stereotypes, etc.? This is *entertainment.*" Yet, mass culture theorists and contemporary communications analysts emphasize that even if (at the conscious level) we don't believe what the media say, the media still shapes the parameters of our experience. They are setting the agenda (Parenti 1993, p. 1). As Jhally and Lewis (1992, p. 17) maintain, the giant disclaimer that television is, after all, nothing more than "entertainment" grants TV producers an insidious form of poetic license. It grants them the enormous luxury of power without responsibility.

Morever, study after study tells us that the media *do* affect us. Whether we recognize it or not, mediated images not only help shape our view of the world – they help shape our values and our actions. For instance, while "everyone" may "know" that television exaggerates the scale of violent crime for dramatic purposes; studies consistently show that the more television we watch, the more violent we assume the world to be (Jhally and Lewis 1992, p. 17). Similarly, Jhally, Lewis, and Morgan (1991) found that the more people watched television news during the Gulf crisis of 1990–1, the more likely they were to support the US war effort – but *the less they knew about the underlying issues* (Parenti 1993, p. 22).

Of course, every so often there are sensationalist reports as to how the media allegedly *directly* impacts individual behavior. For instance, John Hinckley, Jr. shot President Ronald Reagan in 1981, apparently imitating the Robert De Niro character (Travis Bickle) in the movie *Taxi Driver.* Similarly, a half-hour after seeing Farrah Fawcett "burn" her "husband" in *The Burning Bed* on television, a Milwaukee man imitated it (albeit in reverse) by burning his estranged wife to death. And there were several dozen deaths reported from playing Russian roulette with a loaded handgun in the days immediately following the national cablecasting of such a scene in *The Deer Hunter* (Real 1996, p. 98). On a more positive note, five-year-old Kristin Joosten of Bellmore, New York, reportedly saved her two-year-old brother's life by performing a Heimlich maneuver she had learned from watching Robin Williams do the same to Pierce Brosnan's character in the film *Mrs.Doubtfire* (Real 1996, p. 99).

However, the primary impact of the media on individual behavior and consciousness is indirect, not direct. It is cumulative and relatively subconscious, for mediated images shape perception and action over time, as they are integrated into larger and more far-reaching, complex systems of meaning. Put in a different way, the notion that television is "only" entertainment supposes an a priori separation of social subjects and cultural texts. But the subjectivity that we bring with us as we sit in front of the television, listen to music, etc., derives in large part from our overall cultural knowledge, and experience (including that of the media). Our knowledge of the world is not neatly separated into "fictional" and "nonfictional" and "first-hand" and "secondhand" compartments, as the following quote from the sociologist Eviatar Zerubavel (1997, p. 90) makes clear:

> Stored in my mind are rather vivid "recollections" of my great-grandfather (who I never even met and about whom I know only indirectly from my mother's, grandmother's, and great-aunt's accounts), the Crucifixion (the way I first "saw" it in Nicholas Ray's film *The King of Kings* when I was twelve), and the first voyage around the world (the way I first envisioned it when I read Stefan Zweig's biography of Ferdinand Magellan as a teenager). I have similar "memories" of the Inca Empire, the Punic Wars, and Genghis Khan, despite the fact that I personally experienced none of them.

In sum, our knowledge of the world is a complex *blend* of personal, interpersonal, and mediated experience; there is a *social foundation* to mental action, as Zerubavel (1997) affirms (see also Worsley 1997). Most importantly, just as we tend to take the *social* basis of our knowledge for granted, we ignore the extent to which our knowledge is *mediated* as well.

What are the central "lessons" the culture industry disseminates to society? Communications analysts concur that the central lesson is simply *consumption*. Both advertising and the media in general emphasize that what really matters are distinctions based on the consumption of material goods. As Jhally (1987) states, advertising is one of the most influential mechanisms of socialization in modern society; but "we should not let its [advertising's] enormous presence in a wide variety of realms obscure what it is *really* about . . . the marketing of goods." Miller (1986) and Jhally and Lewis (1992), among others, have found that even popular, "liberal" sitcoms, such as *The Cosby Show*, are predicated not only on the American myth of social mobility, but gross *materialism* (i.e., a preoccupation with *material*, rather than *intellectual* or *spiritual* things). As Miller (in Colombo et al. 1992, p. 646) poignantly states:

> Each week, the happy Huxtables nearly vanish amid the porcelain, stainless steel, mahogany, and fabric of their lives. In every scene, each character appears in some fresh designer outfit that positively glows with newness, never to be seen a second time. And, amid all this pricey clutter, the plots and subplots, the dialogue, and even many of the individual shots reflect in

some way on consumption as a way of life: Cliff's new juicer is the subject of an entire episode; Cliff does a monologue on his son Theo's costly sweatshirt; Cliff kids daughter Rudy for wearing a dozen wooden necklaces. Each Huxtable, in fact, is hardly more than a mobile display case for his/her momentary possessions. In the show's first year, the credit sequence was a series of vivid stills presenting Cliff alongside a shiny Dodge Caravan, out of which the lesser Huxtables then emerged in shiny playclothes, as if the van were their true parent, with Cliff serving as the genial midwife to this anti-septic birth.

Moreover, as Leiss, Klein, and Jhally (1990) note, blatant materialism in the media is accompanied by increasingly *imagistic* modes of communication, i.e., there has been a shift from explicit statements of *value* (buy this car because it is very well made) to implicit values and lifestyle *images* (buy this car will because it will make *you* "cool"). Imagistic advertising is qualitatively different from nonimagistic advertising, because rather than lead us to "rationally" evaluate the "price" and "quality" of a particular product, it focuses on our *emotions*, and conscious and unconscious *desires*. Thus, imagistic advertising compels us to *organize* our world and place *value* via commercial culture products. We say, did you see this movie? Do you have this CD? Do you like rap, punk, jazz, or country-western music? Silently, we observe and order our lives using fashion (do they sport baggy pants, Armani, multiple earrings, a pierced tongue?) as well as other products (e.g., cigarettes). We come to "understand" who we (and you) are, in the same way we come to "understand" the commercial products at hand. We can "place" most every type of cultural product (and person), to know what they *mean*. Commercial products help us identify and create *interpersonal bonds* and group solidarity, and define who we are (to which group do I belong)? The result is that "not only has the world of true needs been subordinated to the world of false needs," but that "the realm of needing has become a function of the field of communication" (Kline and Leiss 1978, p. 18, as cited by Jhally 1987, p. 22).

Again, for mass culture theorists and mass communications analysts alike, it is the *passivity* behind this gross materialism that is most problematic. That who we are becomes a question of what we consume, rather than what we produce, means the world of production is left to others (Storey 1993, p. 118; Leiss, Kline, and Jhally 1990, p. 31). Most ironically, in modern consumer society, buying new things is portrayed as the *solution* to personal anxiety or tension. This is especially true in the case of women, for whom *shopping* is viewed as "therapeutic." Advice columnists recommend forlorn females to "pamper yourself" with a $50 manicure, or "go buy yourself something you want but don't really need, such as new pair of shoes." But of course, from a critical perspective *going shopping* to escape the alienation that stems from the gross *commodification* of modern society (and the subordination of women in the world of production) abets the very system we seek to escape. It is an absurdity; a very costly *illusion*. It is hardly an alternative to rebellion.

THE "NEW MEDIA" AND THE PUBLIC SPHERE

Interestingly, the recent proliferation of interactive technology can be interpreted as directly undermining the Frankfurt school assumption as to the passivity of the mass "audience" in modern (or postmodern) society. New technologies enable individuals to *choose* the messages they want to receive, *respond* to the messages they receive, and even create their own messages *vis-à-vis* the Internet, World Wide Web, and commercial computer services. In short, new technologies allow for more, and for more diverse, two-way communications, and they provide users with both more control and more choice (Croteau and Hoynes 1997, p. 283).

Consequently, today many analysts celebrate the profoundly *democratic* potential of the new media. For instance, Abramson, Arterton, and Orren (1988, as cited by Croteau and Hoynes 1997, p. 281), point out that the new media enable new forms of governance, such as the "electronic town meeting." Similarly, Scott and Kekula Crawford, who created the first Nation of Hawai'i site on the Internet, maintain that new technologies enable millions of dispersed people to recognize their common experience of colonization (Wood 1999, p. 157). "Increased connectivity counters the debilitating consequences of the geographical diaspora that is such a frequent accompaniment of colonialism" (Wood 1999, p. 155).[13] In addition, advocates point out that interactive technology enables isolated, rural residents and the disabled greater access to resources otherwise unavailable; and it enables otherwise marginalized and lower-status folks to take part in chat groups and other virtual communities without hindrance or stigma (Starr 1996).

Yet other analysts are more circumspect about the democratic and emancipatory potential of the new media. Critics point out, first, that the new interactive technologies are already becoming commercialized and commodified. Few users seek alternative political information on the Internet; on the contrary, the most widely used services are consumer services, i.e., *shopping*. From a cultural Marxist point of view, that the new media allow for the proliferation of home shopping channels and manufacturers' web pages is hardly cause for celebration. Moreover, other analysts point out that cyberspace is just as "raced," "gendered," and exploitative as traditional media – or even more so. Indeed, some analysts argue that the single most widely used service on the Internet today is not "shopping," but access to free porn.

In addition, critics argue that the educated and wealthy have greater access to computers than do the impoverished and/or uneducated; thus, the new media are just another means for distancing the rich from the poor. Nowhere is this gap more evident than in education – where a student in an affluent community in the United States is roughly twice as likely as one in a poor community to attend a school with Internet access (Starr 1996). Of course, even if more children are able to use new media through schools and libraries, they will still be at a disadvantage relative to children with access at home. According to a 1994 survey, 11 percent of families with incomes of less than $20,000 have a computer, compared to 56 percent of families with incomes above $50,000 (Montgomery 1996, pp. 70–1). Warns the Chancellor of the University of California, Santa Cruz, and her co-authors (Greenwood, Kovacs North, and Dollenmeyer 1999, p. 1049): "We have allowed a society to evolve that has education and information haves and have-nots . . . the have-nots are unlikely to be able to share in the advances expected in the next century, and they are unlikely to acquire the technological skills and scientific expertise assumed to be essential for success and prosperity."

In sum, the anticipated impacts of the new media are neither inevitable nor self-evident (Newman 1991, p. 165, as cited by Croteau and Hoynes 1997, p. 284). "The new hypermedia by themselves cannot make any-thing happen, for good, or ill" (Wood 1999, p. 164). The communications "revolution" will probably be slow, partial and full of contradictions. The real question is not what these technologies can do but how their capaci-ties intersect with other social and cultural capacities and conditions (Croteau and Hoynes 1997, p. 284). Quips the director of the Center for Communication Policy (CCP) at the University of California, Los Angeles

"It's very important that you try very hard to remember where you electronically transferred Mommy and Daddy's assets"

Figure 3.2 Michael Maslin, "Mommy and Daddy's assets," *The New Yorker*, July 24, 2000. © The New Yorker Collection 2000 Michael Maslin from cartoonbank.com. All rights reserved.

(UCLA), Jeffrey Cole: "Some of the positive aspects [of the Internet] are that it's almost impossible to regulate, good people can find each other and anybody can be a journalist. Negative sides are that it's almost impossible to regulate, bad people can find each other and anybody can be a journalist" (as cited by Gordon 1999, p. 49).

Nevertheless, that the new media have already had a significant *impact* on our culture and society is indisputable. This was made most readily apparent by a recent study by UCLA's CCP, which found that for the first time in television history, viewing among children under the age of 14 is declining. States Cole (as cited by Gordon 1999, p. 49): "For the first time in the 51 years of TV history kids are finding something more compelling than television." Furthermore, he notes: "Television is mostly about leisure and entertainment . . . [while] the Internet has already had a profound influence on work, school *and* play. It is change on the order of the Industrial Revolution or the invention of the printing press."

Audience and Resistance

American communications analysts have clearly shown that we cannot ignore the economic pivot of the culture industry. In 1992, the cable television industry reported $25 billion in revenue, up 10 percent from 1991 (Real 1996, p. 150). The broadcasting industry, both radio and television, reported income of $28.8 billion, up 4 percent from 1991. The telephone industry reported revenues of $165 billion (ibid). In 1993, the recording industry reported an 11 percent income increase to $10 billion (Hawkins 1995, as cited by Real 1996, p. 150). Also in 1993, US consumers spent $2 billion on computer software, $5 billion on video games, $5.2 billion on theatrical movies, and $13.2 billion on video movies (Meyer 1994, as cited by Real 1996, p. 150). "This thumbnail sketch of only the most prominent media industries adds up to a total of more than $250 billion income in a typical year" (Real, 1996, p. 1590). This trend is part and parcel of a larger transnational phenomenon; today, one-third of the world's private sector productive assets are owned by transnational corporations (Lipsitz 1997b, p. 236).

Yet, while mass culture theorists and communications analysts provide plenty of evidence about powerful corporations' enormous (though not exclusive) influence over cultural *production*, they provide much less evidence about processes of cultural *consumption*. Thus, since the 1980s, new culturalist perspectives have emerged which focus not so much on cultural *products* (or the production of culture), but on how these products are integrated into the lives of individuals. This type of cultural analysis is called audience/ reception studies. Audience/reception studies shifts investigation away from the moment of cultural *production*, and toward the act of *reading/viewing* texts themselves.

The very premise of exploring cultural reception directly challenges the mass culture assumption as to the hegemony of the culture industry. As Morley (1996a, p. 279) states: "the mass culture notion of passively consuming audiences is a thing of the past." In addition, audience/reception studies challenge the Durkheimian conceptualization of culture as an internally self-sufficient and *collectively given* system consisting of values, as well as the more general literary assumption that the meanings of texts are contained in the texts themselves. Audience analysts argue that meanings shift and slide, not only between individuals and social groups, but according to different contexts and situations. Above all, audience/reception analysts celebrate *agency* – the freedom of the audience to pick and choose which parts of texts to attend to, and thereby create their own meaning. Audience analysts today tend to be devoutly *anti-elitist*, celebrating "low" or "popular" cultural products (e.g., television shows, popular magazines, popular music, off-the-rack fashions), and taking the products, as well as the people who use them, *seriously*.

The theoretical underpinnings of the move toward reception is a seminal article written by Stuart Hall in 1973. In "Encoding and Decoding in the Television Discourse," Hall distinguishes multiple stages in the creation and interpretation of a text. In the first stage, producers *encode* specific meanings into a text; they have certain ideas as to what they want the text to *say*, and they try to make their meaning understood. In the second moment, the formal rules of language and discourse are "in dominance"; since texts contain symbols with multiple meanings and connotations, the text is now open to the play of polysemy, or multiple interpretation. In the third moment, the text is actually *decoded* by the audience/viewer. In this stage, the reader/viewer brings to bear both the formal rules of language and discourse *behind* the text, and the "raw material" of his/her own life and psyche. Thus, Hall demonstrates that meanings and messages are not simply "transmitted"; they are always produced – first by the encoder, and second, by the audience. There is nothing inevitable about the impact of cultural products. Encoding and decoding may not coincide. There is always the possibility of misinterpretation (Storey 1996, pp. 11–12).

One of the earliest and most influential reception studies is Janice Radway's *Reading the Romance* (1984), which has been described as "the most extensive scholarly investigation of the act of reading" (Brunsdon 1991, as cited by Storey 1996, p. 47). Like Hall, Radway distinguishes between the *encoded* and *decoded* meanings of texts, although, as she freely admits, she had no knowledge of Hall's work (or the existence of British cultural studies) when she undertook her study (1991 [1984], p. 2).

Radway found that romance reading pulls in different "political" directions depending on whether the focus is the act of reading or the narrative fantasies of the texts themselves. Focussing on the act of *reading*, she finds that "romance reading is oppositional because it allowed the women to refuse momentarily their self- abnegating social role" (p. 210). While focussing on the narrative fantasies of the texts themselves, she sees that "the romance's narrative structure embodies a simple recapitulation and recommendation of patriarchy and its consistent social practices and ideologies" (p. 210). According to Radway, it is this difference "between the meaning of the act and the meaning of the text as read" that must be brought into tight focus if we are to understand the full meaning of romance reading.

To say that Radway knew nothing of the newly emerging British cultural studies tradition when she undertook her study does not mean her work is theoretically ungrounded. On the contrary, Radway breaks new ground by borrowing extensively from the psychoanalytic feminist Nancy Chodorow in order to explain both the *appeal* and *pleasures* of romance reading. Most interestingly, Radway maintains that romantic fantasy is a form of regression in which the reader is imaginatively and emotionally transported to a time "when she was the center of a profoundly nurturant individual's attention" (p. 84). Romance reading can be viewed as a means by which women vicariously, through the hero–heroine relationship, experience the emotional succor which they themselves are expected to provide for others without adequate reciprocation for themselves in their normal day-to-day existence. Thus, Radway sees emotional benefits for women who read romances (whereas mass culture theorists see benefits only for the culture industry).

In recent years, the field of audience/reception studies has grown and spread, especially in the field of communications, and much of this new work has an explicit feminist bent. Like Radway (1984), Hobson (1982), McRobbie (1978), Ang (1990), and Press (1991) are openly *sympathetic* toward female viewers/readers; they seek to show that women are *not* simply hopeless consumerists or doormats. Thus, for instance, McRobbie (1978) argues that shopping grants women a space for autonomous self-expression, while Ang (1990) shows that soap operas provide the same function through fantasy (Storey 1993). This contrasts tremendously with the mass culture/critical approach which circumscribes the role of the audience/viewer/reader – and women in general – to *passivity*.[14] In addition, audience analysts have also made important methodological contributions to cultural sociology (which will be explored in chapter 6); Hays (1996), Hobson (1982), Liebes and Katz (1990), and Hunt (1997), among others, use in-depth interviews and/or focus groups to show *how* viewers/readers actively construct and "rework" media messages.[15]

In sum, recent cultural populists quite rightly underscore that symbols are multivocal, not univocal, and that the relationship between cultural products and their users is more complex than either mass culture theorists or neo-Durkheimians allow. Audience analysts also quite rightly challenge the *elitism* of mass culture theory which condemns the masses not only to "passivity" but to "false consciousness" (except for the intellectuals who are somehow able to "see through" false ideology).

Yet, in recent years, cultural populism has come under attack. Gitlin (1997, pp. 30–2) maintains that the shift toward audience analysis can at least in part be explained by liberal academics' eagerness to believe in "the people" (and the potential for political engagement): "how much more reassuring to detect 'resistance' saturating the pores of everyday life" than to believe that "the millions have been absorbed into the hegemonic sponge of mainstream popular culture! Perhaps they were free, or actually dissenting – even if at home, sitting on sofas." Similarly, Garnham (1997, pp. 67–8) suggests that liberal academics simply do not want to admit that "there are extremely constrained and impoverished cultural practices that contribute nothing to social change."

More seriously, Marxist-inspired analysts criticize audience/reception studies for its implicitly conservative economic stance. For Roach (1997, p. 53), cultural populists' portrayal of culture as a *site of struggle* rather than a process of domination makes "resistance" remarkably similar to the familiar pluralist conception that power is shared by many subgroups in society. Similarly, McGuigan (1997, p. 139) points out that "cultural populism has a close affinity with the ideal of the sovereign consumer in neo-classical economics, the philosophy of the free market, the currently dominant ideology throughout most of the world." While Angus (1994, p. 234) states: "It is much easier for the new pluralist apologists to celebrate the 'ingenuity of people' to use the products of mass culture in diverse ways (despite their control by increasingly fewer hands) than for critical theorists to define precisely the constraints that foreclose political alternatives."

Most importantly, for Marxist and non-Marxist critics alike, the problem with audience/reception studies is that it simply replaces the blanket denigration of popular culture characteristic of mass culture theory with a blind celebration of all that is "popular." Especially in the field of communications, the focus is not so much on how media and consumer messages and products are integrated into individuals' lives, or how media and consumer messages and products are actually read; but simply on individual "agency." There is insufficient knowledge about the life situation and beliefs of the reader, such that differences in interpretation are simply chalked up either to individual creativity and spunk, or to *structural* categories of class, gender, and ethnicity.

"I Hate Barney" and Other Symbols of "Resistance"

The theoretical and empirical problems of audience/reception analysis are most apparent in the field of communications, which routinely finds "sites of resistance" in popular culture. For instance, Lull (1995, pp. 39–40), includes the following in a list of examples of "resistance to hegemony":

- A well-known message about parenting and psychology that appears on many automobile bumper stickers in the United States "Have You Hugged Your Kid Today?" that's been reframed as "Have you Slugged your Kid Today?"
- The drive-in fast-food chain "In and Out Burger" bumper sticker becomes "In and Out urge."
- Barney, the harmless, ever-so-loveable purple dinosaur who is the star of the highest-rated public TV show for children in the United States, *Barney and Friends*, becomes a fierce object of hate. A Barney lookalike was viciously attacked in a Texas shopping mall, and an "I Hate Barney Secret Society" has formed, turning Barney's "I Love You, You Love Me" theme song into "I Hate You, You Hate Me, Let's Go Out and Kill Barney!"
- The organization Mothers Against Drunk Drivers (MADD) finds opposition from Drunks Against Mad Mothers (DAMM).

Lull (1995, pp. 39–40) considers these acts of "resistance" because they involve "reinventing institutional messages for purposes that differ greatly from their creators' intentions," or because they "reveal independence of thought and creativity."

Yet, if we "deconstruct" Lull's actual examples, we see that while these acts involve the manipulation of symbols, they are not at all "resistant." These acts reflect rather than refute dominant systems of meaning. First, changing a bumper sticker from "In and Out Burger" to "In and Out urge" can be considered an *exemplar* of capitalist hegemony; the fact that the symbols with which we "play" and "creatively" express ourselves emanate from corporate advertising is hardly reassuring. Morever, the fact is that these "subversions" might actually help fulfill corporate goals; people *respond* to sexualized messages (especially the young people who are targeted by fast-food advertising); and the fact that the name "In and Out" is ensconced, rather than completely erased, as Nike has shown, is a particularly effective marketing mechanism.

Even more problematically, Lull's examples of "resistance" reflect rather than "resist" our dominant patriarchal discourse. Rather than see "resistance" behind such slogans as "Have You Slugged Your Kid Today?," "Drunks Against Mad Mothers," and "I Hate Barney," these slogans can be understood as part and parcel of a patriarchal view of the world characterized by violence against and contempt for "pussy" things, including women, children, and gays.

Consider, for example, the "I Hate Barney" song. Lull suggests that the original "I Love Barney" song is an exemplar of collusion; while the "I Hate Barney" song is an exemplar of "resistance." Presumably, children who sing the "I Love Barney" song are dupes, while those who sing the "I Hate Barney" song are rebels.

Yet, if we look at the actual *production* of the Barney show, and how the "I Love Barney" and "I Hate Barney" songs are actually sung by children, we see an entirely different picture. *Barney and Friends* was envisioned as a *toddler* show. It was created in the late 1980s by Sheryl Leach, a young mother who wanted a simple program that would entertain her preschool children. The appalling fact is, *Barney and Friends* became a commercial success, not because of some media mogul's brilliance, but because it filled a previously untapped, and unthought-of, marketing niche – that of two- to five-year-olds. This suburban mother was right: existing children's programs (e.g., *Sesame Street*, *Mister Rogers*) were geared toward kindergarteners (four- to six-year-olds).[16]

This understanding of the *production* of "Barney" tells us a lot about the *meaning* of Barney. "Barney and Friends" was not only created as, but is understood by children as, a *baby* thing. Kindergarteners often do still like Barney, but by grade school, most children have learned to *disdain* him. Although the exact origins of the "I Hate Barney" song are, in fact, unknown, it seems safe to say that this song emerged not as a song of "resistance" (to either capitalist hegemony, or even the intentions of Barney's creators), but as a sign of *distinction*. Sung most often by five- to eight-year-old boys, the song tends to mean, "I am too *old* (and perhaps too *cool*) to like Barney." Looked at in this way, "hating" Barney is more of a developmental issue than one of "resistance." How one wields Barney (whether one "loves" him or "hates" him) is akin to riding a merry-go-round: one does it differently at different ages.[17]

Yet this is not the end of the story. For precisely because Barney is a *baby* thing, Barney is also a *feminine* thing. Barney appeals to young children because he is an effeminate, *demasculinized*, soft, cuddly, dorky, imaginary, purple dinosaur. Thus, especially for the boys who revel in this song, singing "I Hate Barney" at the top of your lungs often *means* not only "I am too old and too cool" – but "I am too *macho*" – to like Barney. From a social psychological perspective, the "I Hate Barney" song enables young boys to *separate* from their mother. As Chodorow (1978; 1974, as discussed by Ortner 1996) first pointed out, women are universally largely the earlier socializer of both boys and girls, both develop "personal identification" with her, i.e., diffuse identification with her general personality, behavior traits, values, and attitudes. A son, however, must ultimately shift to a masculine role identity, which involves building an identification with the father.

However, this is not the end of the story either. For "feminine" and *demasculinized* things are linked to sexism and misogyny – as well as homophobia – in our dominant symbolic system. This link between "hating Barney," sexism, and homophobia is most apparent on the playground, where, interestingly, the statement "I hate Barney" is often accompanied by the statement, "Barney is gay!" (although precisely what "gay" means here remains outside the scope of this discussion). Of course, this symbolic link also helps explain the "vicious attack" on the Barney lookalike in the Texas mall. Clearly, if "Barney" were simply a *baby* thing – and not also a demasculinized thing – this incident probably would not have happened. In sum, singing the "I Hate Barney" song at the top of your lungs tends to *mean* "I am not a baby!"; but it also often means, "I am not a girl!"; "I do not like girl things!"; "I am not gay!" This helps explain the popularity of the "I Hate Barney" song with early schoolage boys, though clearly, girls can and do learn to denigrate that which is seen as effeminate, corny, babyish, etc.

In sum, why is reveling in the "I Hate Barney" song any more "resistant" than reveling in the "I Love Barney" song and all that *that* song implies? From a mass culture perspective, the "I Love Barney" and "I Hate Barney" songs are both *equally* "false" (a function of the culture industry); whether we "love" him or "hate" him, we have *all* been suckered into thinking, talking, and singing about *Barney*. At the same time, from a neo-Durkheimian or discursive perspective the two Barney songs are equally "true." Whether they stem from and feed the culture industry or not, these songs are encoded in individuals' lives. Love him or hate him, Barney is as "real" (or unreal) as reality itself, because he is a sign that enables us to touch on and reflect actual human emotions and conditions. Barney enables self-expression, joy, and fun, as well as a means for reaffirming and separating social groups (e.g., peer groups), and identities; at the same time, "Barney" engenders expressions of hate and contempt because of its symbolic links with femininity, and therefore sexism, misogyny, and homophobia (or, more accurately our love–hate relationship with femininity). For better or worse, these are not "false" but *actual* or *genuine* dimensions of our culture. In less cheery, more postmodern terms, "All that remains to be done is to play with the pieces. Playing with the pieces – that is postmodern" (Baudrillard, in Gane 1993, p. 95, as cited by Ritzer, 1997, p. 98).

This brings us to a final problem in audience/reception studies: they typically involve reactions to discrete cultural products (for example,

Dallas or *Barney*), or at best a particular genre such as the soap opera. But in reality, we are dealing with a "total cultural package"; the average American is exposed, on a daily basis, to myriad forms of mass culture ranging from McDonald's golden arches to the O. J. Simpson trial. Thus, whether children "love," "hate," outgrow, or *ignore* Barney, is not a sign of resistance, because there are a whole host of *other* cultural products for children to be suckered into. Children "outgrow" loving and hating "Barney," only to "move on" to "loving" or "hating" the "X men," "Barbie," "Star Wars," etc.

Indeed, Stuart Hall himself recognized the *limits* of audience analysis; he argued that ideologies are not *hegemonically* imposed or "resisted" because culture works in a far more subtle and nuanced way. As Hall (1995, p. 19) maintains:

> Ideologies are not the product of individual consciousness or intention. Rather we formulate our intentions *within ideology*. They pre-date individuals, and form part of the determinate social formations and conditions in which individuals are born. We have to 'speak through' the ideologies which are active in our society and which provide us with the means of 'making sense' of social relations and our place in them. The transformation of ideologies is thus a collective process and practice, not an individual one. Largely, the processes work *unconsciously*, rather than by conscious intention. Ideologies produce different forms of social consciousness, rather than being produced by them. They work most effectively when we are not aware that how we formulate and construct a statement about the world is underpinned by ideological premises; when our formations seem to be simply descriptive statements about how things are (i.e., must be), or of what we can 'take-for-granted'. . . . Ideologies tend to disappear from view into the taken-for-granted 'naturalised' world of common sense.

Postmodern Musings

For some analysts, the discrepancy between the Frankfurt school's perception of an inert *mass* society, and contemporary trends, including *interactive* "new media," is easily explained: we are now in a *different* stage than the Frankfurt school described. We have moved from a *modern* to a *postmodern* situation. The culture of the modern age (modernism) has given way to the *breaking apart* of the modernist moment. Whereas "the modern world was allegedly well-organized along a linear history yielding straightforward meanings, the postmodern world is thought to be poorly organized in the absence of a clear, predictable historical future without which there are, at best, uncertain, playful, or ironic meanings" (Lemert 1997a, p. 36).

Confusingly, the term "postmodern" can be used to describe a particular historical "moment" or a particular type of theorizing (or anti-theorizing) that has emerged over the same course of time. In postmodernism (the historical moment), time–space configurations are completely changed. It is not just that new technology (the "new media") allows people closer communication with each other, creating a new kind of "global village"; but that social relations have been "lifted out" from local contexts of interaction and restructured across indefinite spans of time-space (Giddens 1990, p. 21, as cited by Rosenau 1992, p. 72).

Theoretically, whereas the Frankfurt school (as well as communications analysts) emphasized that the media replaced *reality* with *illusion*; postmodernists (the theorists – or "anti-theorists") take this notion one step further and argue that there is no clear *distinction* between "reality" and "illusion" anymore. As the eminent French postmodernist Jean Baudrillard maintains, reality has given way to the *simulation* of reality, or "hyper-reality." The dialectic between "reality" and "signs" is now in shreds, "and the real has died" (Baudrillard 1993 [1976], p. 7). "The code no longer refers back to any subjective or objective 'reality' but to its own logic" (ibid., p.127). "Determinacy is dead, indeterminacy holds sway. There has been an extermination (in the literal sense of the word) of the real of production and the real of signification" (Baudrillard 1993 [1976], p. 7). Indeed, in a series of controversial essays, Baudrillard (1995) proclaimed that the Gulf War "did not take place"; rather, what took place was a carefully scripted media event, the outcome of which was predestined from its inception. For Baudrillard, "the entire conflict was designed to be televised in real time, as it unfolded (unlike Vietnam, where reportage involved at least a 24-hour time lag and was captured on film rather than on tape), to be relayed, carefully censored and sanitized into millions of homes, as a sort of awful balletic exercise with its own codes and ritualized spectacles" (Dixon 1997, p. 54).[18]

Despite his misleadingly sensationalistic title ("The Gulf War Did Not Take Place"), the central premise of Baudrillard's essays on the Gulf War – that the reportage of the television networks inherently involves a tremendous amount of social manipulation – rings true. To a large extent, viewers saw only what the US military wished them to see: images of effortless, empiric conquest, bereft of death, suffering, or any other human dimension. Saddam Hussein emerged as a villain of extravagant, exaggerated proportions; equally inflated were American media constructs of an effortless victory (Dixon 1997, p. 54).

Nor can Baudrillard's central postmodern notion – that we are witnessing a proliferation of media genres and techniques that intentionally and explicitly fuse "fact" and "fiction" – be handily dismissed. Virtual reality and computer graphics are getting more and more "real"; the traditional distinction between textuality and reality has faded (Agger 1998, p. 140). In the film industry, "docudramas" are replacing "documentaries," and this does not include the plethora of movies only *roughly* "based on a true story" (e.g., *Titanic*) that seamlessly combine well-known historical truths with gross fiction. We are also witnessing a proliferation of "postmodern" techniques, such as using "real" news clips and footage in fictional shows (and vice versa). Thus for instance, in the 1990s science-fiction film, *Contact*, there were "real" news clips of President Clinton giving a press conference – but this "real" footage was dubbed so that Clinton was reporting on the "contact" between Jodie Foster and extraterrestrials.

Moreover, in recent years we have witnessed a shift from "fictional" cop shows (e.g., *Dragnet*) to "real" cop shows (e.g., *Cops, America's Most Wanted)* – with all their "reenactments" and "simulations"; to "live" crimes-in-action such as cop car chases and shoot-outs. The *drama* of these latter kinds of "programs" stems not only from the fact that the people/situations are *"real,"* but that the drama is supposedly not *scripted*. The idea is that no one – not even the media moguls who bring us the event – knows what will turn up in these dramas, and no one knows how they will end.[19] Of course, it is this exact same type of "unscripted" drama – complete with sex, violence, love, and rage – that we see on spontaneous, "real-live" "trash-talk" TV shows such as the infamous *Jerry Springer Show* (see J. Gamson 1998; discussed also in chapter 7), as well as recent television hybrids, such as *Big Brother* and *Survival*, which blend elements of the "new media," the traditional game show, and the soap opera, by bringing together several "real" strangers to live in a house or on an island; the strangers are viewed and "rated" and eliminated by the audience and/or each other until one is "chosen" as the "winner."

Of course, this exact same "hyperreal" *melding* of "fact" and "fantasy," "reality" and "unreality," and "unscripted" drama is also the crux of the "new media" – where *virtual reality* and simulation are the order of the day. For instance, on the Internet site voyeurdorm.com you can watch live pictures of "college women" as they go about their daily lives, 24 hours a day.[20] For merely $34 a month, subscribers can see women take showers, put on their makeup, study, sleep, and (so the advertising promises) sunbathe nude, and have lingerie parties.

To be sure, the media has long relied on a complex fusion of "fact" and fantasy. Science fiction shows, such as *Star Trek* and *The Twilight Zone*, popular since the 1950s, rely on the juxtaposition of *genuine* human, moral dilemmas and futuristic technology. Game shows have always relied on having real, live, everyday folks "come on down!" and experience a few moments of fame and possibly fortune. Radio talk shows have done the same. Indeed, even soap operas have long relied on the audience developing "relationships" with particular characters, "identifying with"

Figure 3.3 Garry Trudeau, *Doonesbury* — "the new media," *Los Angeles Times*, March 27, 2000. © 2000 G. B. Trudeau. Reprinted with permission of Universal Press Syndicate. All rights reserved.

or "relating" to them, or to the situations they face. And, as Lipsitz (1990, pp. 163–4) points out, we have always demanded "true lies" from commercial motion pictures:

> Commercial motion pictures generally do not claim to present historical truth. Even when films are set in the past, artists and audiences understand that the function of the movies is to entertain . . . . Yet . . . we require "true" lies, depictions of the past and present that are comprehensible to us and that locate our own private stories within a larger collective narrative . . . . Motion pictures could not function as an "escape" if they were merely distraction.

Similarly, celebrity sitcoms have long fused fact and fantasy, and "sense" and "nonsense" (Jhally and Lewis 1992, p. 26). In the 1960s and 1970s, *The Mary Tyler Moore Show* and *The Dick Van Dyke Show* relied on the ability of the protagonist to inject his/her *genuine* comic wit and personality into his/her television character. In the 1980s and 1990s, this same fusion between comedian and television character is seen on *The Bill Cosby Show*, *Seinfeld*, *Roesanne*, and *Ellen*. In each case, a complex fusion occurs between the "genuine" comedian/comedienne and the television character. This is most evident in the *titles* of these shows, which interestingly, use the protagonists' *real* name (or their "real" stage names) – even when the show's character uses a fictional one (e.g., "Mary Richards" on *The Mary Tyler Moore Show*; "Cliff Huxtable" on *The Cosby Show*). From this point of view, Ellen de Generes merely took this fusion to new heights when she "came out" simultaneously in "real life" as well as in character on *Ellen*.

Yet not only Hollywood pointedly blends "fact" and "fantasy" today. For instance, the Pulitzer Prize-winning historian, Edmund Morris, recently set off a cultural storm by inserting himself as a fictional character in his latest "non-fiction" book, *Dutch* (1999), a biography of Ronald Reagan. Morris also added imaginary Hollywood "scripts" detailing key moments in Reagan's development to more standard biographical passages (Getlin 1999, p. A5). According to Morris's admirers, *Dutch* sheds light on biographers' "deepest secret": that they are highly active characters in their books, making crucial choices about what to write, what to ignore, and frequently putting their own words in a subject's mouth (ibid.).[21]

In sum, whether this fusion of fact and fantasy is entirely "new" or not, our perceptions of the world *are* based on a complex blend of "reality" and "unreality." This point was brought home to me several years ago while teaching a course in ethnic studies. Students were assigned an essay in which they were to discuss how, or in what ways, the situation of African Americans had improved, stayed the same, or worsened in the United States in the last several decades. In class we had discussed the *economic*, *political*, and *cultural* realms (see introduction), focusing on such features as poverty and stratification within and between races, civil rights legislation, and the *image* of blacks, as seen, for instance, in movies and television. Yet, one student confused fiction and nonfiction in her essay, discussing the *middle-class* status of the Huxtable family (in *The Cosby Show*) – not as an image on television, but as if it were *real.*

The media's "true" lies (or false "truths") become especially important when we *have* no "firsthand" experience of "the other." For instance, for middle-class, white Americans who do not know any "real" upper-middle-class or lower-class blacks, the images on the *Cosby Show* and the evening news can be especially powerful (whether "fiction" or "nonfiction"). Similarly, images of the United States abroad are often rooted in such television shows as *Fantasy Island, Lifestyles of the Rich and Famous, The Bold and the Beautiful, Santa Barbara,* and *Dallas.* Despite the fact that these shows are clearly "entertainment" and even spoof, many non-Westerners enjoy these shows as a vicarious experience of what they see as the genuinely profane world of the Western Other (see Liebes and Katz 1990).

Yet, even if we have "real-life" experience or knowledge about a subject, we are not immune to the media's seamless fusion of fact and fantasy. In a way, it makes sense for my student to talk about the Huxtables as if they were a "real," upper-middle-class, American family. For as Miller (1986, p. 210) maintains, the show is *designed* so that we confuse "Cliff Huxtable" with "Bill Cosby." Miller maintains that Cliff Huxtable himself is "an ad, implicitly proclaiming the fairness of the American system," but that the close identification between Cliff Huxtable and Bill Cosby makes this mythology all the more powerful. Behind the fictional doctor lies a man whose real life is *also* a success story: fact and fiction here coalesce to confirm the "truth" they represent.[22]

Of course, it is precisely this same fusion of "real-life" social issues and "fictional" television characters that set off the "Murphy Brown"/"family values" debate. Recall that in 1992 Vice-President Dan Quayle caused a sensation by ranting against Candice Bergen's portrayal of single parenthood in the television character Murphy Brown. Speaking, significantly, in California shortly after the Los Angeles riots (an event that transpired as it did out of the media – i.e., the initial taping of the beating of Rodney King), Quayle bemoaned the sorry state of moral values and individual responsibility, claiming that "it doesn't help matters when prime-time TV has Murphy Brown, a character who supposedly epitomizes today's intelligent, highly paid, professional woman, mocking the importance of fathers by bearing a child alone, and calling it just another lifestyle choice" (Yang and Devroy 1992, p. 19, as cited by Walters 1995, p. 11). Yet, "in true postmodern fashion" the fantasy world of the media became fused with "real life." Quayle's comment on Murphy Brown not only set the discourse for election-year speeches and campaigns (e.g., the "family values" debate); this real-life drama went *back* and played itself out in the media, as Quayle's comment recirculated on the sitcom itself in the opening show of the next season. Moreover, Quayle went on to send the fictional son of the fictional Murphy Brown a stuffed elephant (symbol of the Republican party) and to air radio announcements for the television series, using another popular culture reference ("Not!" from *Wayne's World*) to describe his favorite show (Walters 1995, pp. 11–12).[23]

The Simulation of Experience

For Baudrillard (1988 [1983], p. 23), Disneyland is "a perfect model of all the entangled order of simulation": many parts of the world are *emulating* the standards (e.g., of hygiene and security) that Disneyland has set, but Disneyland is more authentic than "reality" precisely because it does not purport to be "real." Baudrillard's point was brought home to me on a recent visit to Disneyland. For there, in front of Snow White's castle – the same "happily-ever-after" backdrop that supplied the endings of *Cinderella, The Little Mermaid*, etc. – a "real" wedding was taking place. Behind a small cordoned-off area, a beautiful bride, in a traditional, white, beaded gown, stood in a flowered gazebo, holding hands with a handsome young groom in a tuxedo, while a minister performed the ceremony, and guests seated in folding chairs watched. Outside this area, "real-life" Disneyland-goers also watched, or tromped around as usual. As I came upon the scene and stood behind the ropes (the same ropes that would later fix our place as spectators for the evening parade), everyone was asking, "is this a *real* wedding"? (I kept thinking that Baudrillard might say, "it's real hyper-reality.")

Of course, having your wedding, reception, and honeymoon in the simulated world of Disneyland may not be that much different than the currently popular trend of having your wedding, reception, and honeymoon at a full-service resort in Hawai'i (although the wedding gazebos at Hawaiian resorts tend to be more distanced from the rank and file tourist). Indeed, the Hilton Waikoloa resort, on over 62 acres on the Big Island, sports an artificial swimming lagoon, including dolphins and tropical fish. With its restaurants, nightlife, lagoon, etc., the idea is that one can spend a week in "Hawai'i," without leaving the Hilton's own little world. But of course, Hilton's own little world is a *simulation* of Hawai'i (not "Hawai'i" – but not complete "fantasy" either), a "hyperreality" that includes not only "real" animals (dolphins and tropical fish) – but "real" natives (literally local "color") in the luaus and hula shows, and simulated native dwellings. This experience gives tourists the sense of having

witnessed "real" alternative lifestyles, without all the worries and complications of "reality" (getting lost, ripped off, etc.).

Yet merely a virtual step away from the Hawaiian "full-service resort"
is Florida's full-service *town* – i.e., Disney's own neo-traditional town of
"Celebration," which "opened" in the swamplands of Florida in 1996. In
addition to their new homes, the 1,800 pioneer inhabitants of Celebration
took possession of an instantly functioning downtown lined with palm
trees and sloping down to a manmade lake. According to the Disney
brochure, Celebration provides "the special magic of an American home-
town." Disney expects Celebration to eventually grow to a population of
20,000 (Ehrenhalt 1999, p. 8).

Of course, from an orthodox Marxist perspective, the Disneyfication of
"reality" is not "hyperreality" at all – but old-fashioned economic exploitation. Hawai'i may be a "hyperreal" paradise playground for tourists –
but for Native Hawaiian activists, such as Huanani-Kay Trask, it is an all-
too-real plundering of the environment for the benefit of all too real
transnational capitalist corporations. For Trask (1999 [1993], p. 88),
"the awful exploitative truth [about the Hawaiian tourist industry is] that
the industry is the major cause of environmental degradation, low wages,
land dispossession, and the highest cost of living in the United States."
She goes on (1999 [1993], p. 89):

> Hawai'i, like a lovely woman, is there for the taking. Those with only a little
> money get a brief encounter; those with a lot of money, like the Japanese,
> get more. The state and counties will give tax breaks, build infrastructure,
> and have the governor personally welcome tourists to ensure they keep
> coming. Just as the pimp regulates prices and guards the commodity of the
> prostitute, so the state bargains with developers for access to Hawaiian land
> and culture.

Trask (ibid.) maintains that the result for Hawaiians is that they must
either "fill up the unemployment lines, enter the military, work in the
tourist industry, or [out of economic necessity] leave Hawai'i."

Interestingly, critical postmodernists such as Lipsitz (1990, 1997a,
1997b) *combine* postmodernist musings with an acknowledgment as to
the dire politico-economic consequences of today's "hyperreality." Lipsitz
(1997b) maintains that while on one hand, transnational *culture* creates
new "connections" between people (e.g., Nike shoes are a favorite in
Brentwood, Tunisia, and Watts), transcultural *products* obscure the connections among people, places, and politics, as much as they highlight
them. Thus, no matter how "oppositional" we may believe our behavior
to be, our behavior fails to transform society because it is ultimately dependent upon false, bourgeois assumptions, definitions, and discourses. In
addition, Lipsitz (1997b) maintains that the very forces of production and

consumption most responsible for bringing the world together through common signs and symbols also generate grotesque inequities that divide people as much as ever. Thus, for instance, the young women in Indonesia who make "Air Jordan" athletic shoes receive around $1.35 per day in factories and workshops subcontracted by the Nike Corporation. At the same time, Nike pays basketball star Michael Jordan $20 million every year to endorse their brand. This means that the fee paid to Jordan for this endorsement exceeds the total wages that Nike pays to its combined workforce in all six of the factories under contract to produce the company's shoes (Barnet and Cavenagh 1994, pp. 325–9, as cited in Lipsitz 1997b, p. 237). Jordan's *fame* is more valuable to Nike than the labor of the workers who make the shoes that carry his name. Indeed, Jordan's fame is more lucrative than his work; he receives five times as much money for simply endorsing Nike shoes than he got for actually playing basketball for the Chicago Bulls.

Finally, Lipsitz points out the tremendous irony behind the *image* of these shoes that enables not only their high cost but their very production. The popularity of Nike shoes with affluent consumers rests on their association with "street" style, a "prestige from below." "Street" styles based on athletic wear are linked to graffiti writing, break dancing, and rap music; they connote a sense of "attitude," style, self-assertion, and even rebellion associated with African American inner-city culture. Yet, perhaps even more paradoxically, these shoes *do* also enjoy enormous popularity among genuinely dispossessed young people from oppressed communities. Inner-city kids are "buying themselves" in the sense that the *image* that Nike sells is based on their own lives. In addition, the shoes represent *inclusion* into the global consumer society, *and* they are symbols of a global, pan-ethnic, anti-racist, youth culture, what the African-born Parisian rapper M.C. Solaar has called the "cult of the sneaker" (Lipsitz 1994, p. 123). Yet, in the end, as Lipsitz (1997b, p. 239) points out, while low-wage women laborers in Asia and impoverished inner-city African American youths play crucial roles in creating products that circle the globe, these individuals remain where they are – in dead-end jobs and dangerous neighborhoods.

Conclusion

We began this chapter with a neo-Durkheimian exploration of the role of mass media in contemporary society. We saw that media ritual events (e.g., World Cup soccer) reaffirm shared meaning and community; they are moments "in and out of time" that elicit collective excitement, celebration, or mourning. Moreover, media ritual events clarify and rework symbolic order; they provide a *cultural space* in which complex social issues are displayed and sorted out. From a neo-Durkheimian point of view, recent technologies (the "new" media) have the potential to create entirely new types of community (e.g., virtual communities), uniting ethnic and cultural diaspora. There are new opportunities today with the rise of *global* culture.

Yet, as we have also seen, Marxist-inspired mass culture analysts take a much more *critical* view of the role of media in contemporary society. They maintain that the media is a sophisticated, well-financed industry that creates and conditions the interpretation of a limited and biased array of manufactured entertainment goods. The mass media helps create and reflect not "collective consciousness" but "false consciousness"; it benefits not "everyone," but merely culture producers. From this point of view, "global culture" is nothing more than a successful marketing campaign, wiping out individuality, self-expression, and *freedom*. Global culture means the predominance of "one McWorld tied together by communications, information, entertainment, and commerce" (Barber 1995, p. 1).

In recent years, we have seen two important responses to the inherently pessimistic and condescending mass culture theory: audience/reception studies and postmodernism. Audience/reception analysts explicitly challenge the passivity ascribed to readers/viewers by mass culture theorists. Audience/reception researchers demonstrate empirically that individuals read and view texts in creative ways – often unanticipated by culture producers. Postmodernists, however, take a different approach. They take the Frankfurt school notion as to the *illusional* nature of mass culture one step further, and assert that there *is* no reality anymore; reality has given way to the *simulation* of reality, or "hyperreality." This new "hyperreality" is most readily apparent in contemporary mediated hybrids, such as voyeudorm.com and MTV's *The Real World*. But for postmodernists, this is not just a *media industry* issue; rather, our current *condition* is one of *simulation*. In *all* dimensions of our social and cultural life, the *simulated* experience has come to be preferred to the "real."

In Part II of this book, we will see that both postmodernism and audience/reception analysis have significantly impacted cultural *methodology*. Today, culturalists commonly seek to understand the production and impact of cultural products by studying them both from the "bottom up" and the "top down." Meanwhile the postmodernist emphasis on the fluidity and plurivocity (multiple and changing meanings) of symbols has seriously challenged some of the basic premises of *doing* cultural "research." Before we turn to these methodological issues, however, we will continue our exploration of how culture works in the next chapter by focussing historically on our perception and experience of "race" in the United States.

IMPORTANT CONCEPTS INTRODUCED IN THIS CHAPTER

- Media
- "New media"
- Ritual media events
- Culture industry
- The Frankfurt school
- Mass culture theory
- Conglomeration
- Postmodernism
- "Hyperreality"
- Audience/reception studies

STUDY QUESTIONS

1. Videotape a ritual media event (e.g., the Superbowl) and/or "disaster marathon" (e.g., a live car chase). Discuss the basic symbolic parameters behind and within the event, most importantly, the "sacred" and "profane." What are the various ways you think this tape can be "seen"?

2. In 1964, Marshal McLuhan envisioned television creating a "global village," with basically positive, democratizing effects; today, many analysts celebrate the new media for the same reason. On the other hand, Bagdikian maintains that the mass media of the twenty-first century will not represent "a parliament of the people, but the organizing of masses of children and adults everywhere, including in the Third World, into an electronic shopping mall devoted to the culture of wasteful and ultimately fatal use of the planet's natural resources and a diminishing of the human spirit." Which side of this debate do you think is more right? Explain why, using concrete examples. Do you think the effects of the "new media" will be much different from that of the "old" media? If so, how?

3. Discuss the ways the new media impact you and your family *personally*. Be sure to discuss the "democratization" debate discussed previously. Do you use the new media to access new and alternative information? Or do you use the Internet mostly for shopping? How so, or why not? How do you think your personal situation is – and is not – reflective of American culture and society in general?

4. Keep a log documenting *every* single instance of your use of the media, including newspapers, radio, Internet, telephone, etc., for a week. In this log, write down exactly what you do/watch/listen to, for how long, etc. After a week, write a one- or two-page essay explaining the centrality (or lack thereof) of the media in your life. What is the longest period of time that you went "unmediated"?

Suggested Further Reading

Barber, Benjamin. 1995. *Jihad vs. McWorld.* New York: Times Books.

Bourdieu, Pierre. 1998 [1996]. *On Television.* New York: New Press.

Croteau, David, and William Hoynes. 1997. *Media/Society: Industries, Images, and Audiences.* Thousand Oaks, CA: Pine Forge.

Dayan, Daniel, and Elihu Katz. 1988. "Articulating Consensus: The Ritual and Rhetoric of Media Events," in Jeffrey C. Alexander, ed., *Durkheimian Sociology: Cultural Studies*, pp. 161–86. Cambridge: Cambridge University Press.

Ferguson, Marjorie, and Peter Golding, eds. 1997. *Cultural Studies in Question.* Thousand Oaks, CA: Sage.

Gamson, Joshua. 1998. *Freaks Talk Back: Tabloid Talk Shows and Sexual Nonconformity.* Chicago: University of Chicago Press.

Gitlin, Todd, ed. 1986. *Watching Television.* New York: Pantheon.

Hall, Stuart. 1980 [1973]. "Encoding and Decoding in the Television Discourse," in Hall et al., *Culture, Media, Language.* London: Hutchinson.

——, ed. 1997. *Representation: Cultural Representations and Signifying Practices.* London: Sage.

Hay, James, Lawrence Grossberg, and Ellen Wartella. 1996. *The Audience and Its Landscape.* Boulder, CO: Westview.

Hunt, Darnell. 1999. *O. J. Simpson Facts and Fictions.* Cambridge: Cambridge University Press.

Kundnani, Arun. 1998. "Where Do You Want To Go Today? The Rise of Info Capital," *Race and Class* (Oct. 1998): 49.

Radway, Janice. 1991 [1984]. *Reading the Romance.* Chapel Hill: University of North Carolina Press.

Real, Michael. 1996. *Exploring Media Culture.* Thousand Oaks, CA: Sage.

Solomon, Jack. 1988. *The Signs of our Time.* New York: St. Martin's Press.

Storey, John. 1998. *An Introduction to Cultural Theory and Popular Culture*, 2nd ed. London: Prentice Hall.

Notes

1   Consequently, standard clock time is a relatively modern phenomenon. Not until 1840, when railroad companies began using Greenwich time throughout Britain, was the first serious attempt made to standardize clock-time reckoning beyond the strictly local level (Zerubavel 1997, p. 109).

2   Anderson (1983) first pointed out that members of a "nation" typically do not know or even hear of most other members. Yet they conceive of themselves as co-members of the same, overridingly important unit. This imagined entity is "always conceived as a deep, horizontal comradeship" and this helps explain the willingness of millions of people to die for this imagined object, the nation (Schudson 1994, p. 26). Nevertheless, as Torpey (1998) points out, the nation is not *merely* an "imagined" community; national institutions, structures and laws (e.g., "citizenship," the "passport") have very profound unifying effects.

3 To be sure, contests such as the Olympics celebrate *international* or *global* symbols as well – for instance, "the rules of the game," as individuals or teams equally worthy of respect compete in good faith and in accordance with a shared set of rules (Dayan and Katz 1988, p. 168).

4 *Los Angeles Times* (April 2, 1998, p. E6).

5 Morrison (1997, p. xvi) concurs that in highly-charged media moments the slow, managed opinion of a democratic climate is suborned by "sudden, accelerated, sustained blasts of media messages – visual and in print – that rapidly enforce the narrative and truncate alternative opinion."

6 Specifically, Scopes was accused of having violated the Butler Act, which forbade the teaching of the theory of evolution in public schools because it contradicted the biblical account of creation. Scopes was convicted and fined $100, but his verdict was later reversed on a technicality. The Butler Act remained in the books until 1967. "ScopesTrial," *Microsoft® Encarta® 98 Encyclopedia.* © 1993–7 Microsoft Corporation.

7 However, that there are *narrative* dimensions to media ritual events is not necessarily inconsistent with the neo-Durkheimian approach. For instance, as Liebes (1998, p. 81) points out, disaster time-outs operate "according to the rules of melodrama." "Disaster has called the shots. . . . Tragedy is the emotional motor" (Liebes 1998, p. 76).

8 For instance, Griswold (1994, pp. 78–9) maintains that the popular nineteenth-century American "men outside society" literary theme was a function not of the "national" imagination, but of nineteenth century copyright laws – which mandated that American publishers had to pay royalties to native authors but not foreign ones. Griswold argues that there was always an oversupply of manuscripts and publishers wanted to maximize their profit; thus, American publishers favored English novels over American novels on popular subjects such as love and marriage, money, achievement, and middle-class life. Consequently, the American novels that *did* get published tended to deal with unusual, particularly *American* themes (e.g., *Huckleberry Finn*). According to Griswold, when the United States finally adopted international copyright in 1891, most of the thematic differences between American and English novels simply disappeared.

9 Smith and Carlos were joined on the victory stand by Peter Norman, the silver medalist from Australia, who wore the official badge of the Olympic Project for Human Rights to underscore his support of the black liberation struggle (Edwards 1969).

10 This harsh reaction was not unanticipated by Smith and Carlos. Indeed, they had been prepared to boycott the 1968 Olympics; six months before the Olympics Smith released a personal statement in which he said, in part:

> It is true that I want to participate in the Olympics and also in all of the other track meets scheduled for next year. But I also recognize the political and social implication of some black people participating for a country in which the vast majority of black people suffer from unthinkable discrimination and racism. I therefore feel that it is my obligation as a black man to do whatever is necessary, by any means necessary,

to aid my people in obtaining the freedom that we all seek. If I can open a single door that might lead in the direction of freedom for my people, then I feel that I must open that door. I am not only willing to give up an opportunity to participate in the Olympics, but I am also willing to give up my life if there is even a chance that it will serve to dramatize, much less solve, the problems faced by my people. (Edwards 1969, p. 64)

However, Smith was not praised – but barraged with criticism – for his selfless and heroic stance. For instance, Jim Murray, a (still) popular columnist of the *Los Angeles Times*, compared Smith to a "child who holds his breath to make his parents feel bad," and accused Smith of being close to Hitler in his political and social philosophy (Edwards 1969, p. 64). Most interesting, in my view, is Murray's comparison of Smith to a *"child,"* which accords with the historic infantilization and disempowerment of African American men (e.g., using the term "boy" to refer to a black man, etc. – a point that will be discussed further in the next chapter).

11 The single most important athlete to become a leader in the struggle for civil rights was undoubtedly Muhammad Ali, who was suspended from boxing and faced jail in 1968 for his refusal to regard the Vietcong as his enemy and to be inducted into the military as a draftee (Johnson and Roediger 1997, p. 204). The chair of the 1968 Olympic Committee for Human Rights, the sociologist Harry Edwards (1969, p. 89; emphasis in original), reverentially called Ali *"the saint of this revolution in sports"* – for not only did Ali stand alone at the time of his rebellion; "he lost almost everything of value to any athlete – his prestige, his income, and his title." Other notable athletes in "revolt" in 1968 include Lew Alcindor (who later adopted the name Kareem Abdul-Jabbar), Lucius Allen, and Mike Warren of UCLA's outstanding basketball team, who, despite threats to their life for their outspokenness, refused to try out for the 1968 Olympic team.

12 Marcuse's adamant advocacy of confrontational politics won him notoriety as a guru of the student movement, although it also made him an easy target for right-wing critics. In one of his most controversial essays, he (1969, as cited by Kellner 1984, pp. 281–2) called for "intolerance toward prevailing policies, attitudes, and opinions, and the extension of tolerance to policies, attitudes, and opinions which are outlawed and oppressed."

13 For instance, in 1995 the O. J. Simpson spectacle pushed the incarceration and trial of Dennis "Bumpy" Kanahele, the head of state of the Nation of Hawai'i, to the back pages of Hawai'i newspapers (which are owned by large, multinational conglomerates, and tend to rely on associated press and other wired stories)(Wood 1999, p. 153). Yet the Nation of Hawai'i site on the internet provided detailed coverage of Kanahele's arrest and trial; and even more importantly, the web site "framed" Kanahele's incarceration and trial in an entirely different way than did the mainstream press (see chapter 7 for more on "framing"). Specifically, according to the website, Kanahele was "kidnapped" at the Honolulu airport (rather than "arrested"); and Kanahele's trial was explicitly compared with the trial of Hawaiian Queen

Lili'uokalani held in 1893, thereby linking Kanahele with historic (sacred) martyrs and heroes of the Nation of Hawai'i and the US state/police/judges, etc., with the historic (profane) imperialists and colonialists in the Pacific (ibid.).

14   Unfortunately, however, much of this work is ethnocentric and/or Anglocentric, i.e., it is by and about *white* women and their white, middle-class world. The problem (and this is true of "women's studies" especially during the 1970s and early 1980s) is *not* so much that they focus on "white," middle-class subjects, but that they implicitly generalize from these subjects to *all* women.

15   Thus, as we will see in chapter 6, Liebes and Katz (1990) find that audiences from one nation interpret *Dallas* in ways strikingly similar to each other, but different from audiences of other nations; while Hunt (1997) shows the similarities and differences in how "white-raced" and "black-raced" inform-ants viewed a 17-minute video clip of the Rodney King "riot" in Los Angeles.

16   In fact, *Barney and Friends* did not have any serious competition for the "toddler" niche until the emergence of *Teletubbies* in 1998. Interestingly, with his androgynous appearance and handbag, the "gay" purple character on *Teletubbies*, "Tinky Winky," also reflects the same symbolization discussed here.

17   In a now classic essay, Erving Goffman (1961b) shows how people of differ-ent ages ride a merry-go-round differently. Preschool children fully *embrace* the "merry-go-round rider role"; they know how to play the role, and they play it with abandon. By contrast, six- to eight-year-old kids go to great lengths to *distance* themselves from the merry-go-round rider role (joking, flailing their arms, etc.). They do this in order to demonstrate that they are *beyond* the preschoolish merry-go-round rider role, i.e., to establish that this is *not* who they *really* are.

18   Not surprisingly, Baudrillard's essays prompted criticism from all sides. Left-ists were incensed by Baudrillard's seeming trivialization of the repressive Iraqi regime that divided its people and left them teetering on the brink of economic disaster (Pfohl 1997, pp. 138–9); some even compared Baudrillard to the (profane) right-wing deniers of the Holocaust – although, in profound contrast to right-wing Holocaust deniers, Baudrillard argued that "the conse-quences of what did not take place maybe as substantial as those of any historical event." In other words, Baudrillard does not deny that *something* dreadful took place in the Gulf in the winter of 1991; he simply asks, was it a war "or something far worse?" (Pfohl 1997, p. 140).

19   Ironically, however, even the "unscriptedness" of "real-live" television shows is somewhat illusive, as "unscripted" dramas are still staged and edited and do not appear in "real time."

20   Interestingly, though the site describes the women as "sexy, young, college girls," none of those interviewed for a story in the *LA Times* were in fact college students. The women earn $200–$400 a week, for working eight hours a day, including two to three hours in the chat room (*Los Angeles Times* September 16, 1999, p. E2).

21   Others are not nearly so impressed by Morris's new techniques. Historian

David Halberstam notes that Morris, who got a $3 million advance for the book, "was under a lot of pressure to deliver the Big Book, and pressure can cause an author to do strange things." While UCLA historian Joyce Appleby maintains: "this kind of book is the product of an anything goes culture, where you can write what you want and imagination is rewarded, even if it's shown to be harmful to scholarship" (Getlin 1999, p. A5). See chapter 5 for more on the current postmodern trend of collapsing the distinction between "fiction" and "nonfiction" in academia.

22   It is interesting to note how African Americans have "moved up" in the television world, from the tough (but humorous and loving) working-class homes/families of *Good Times* and *Sanford & Son* in the 1970s to the ease and luxury of the upper-middle-class Huxtables in the 1980s. However, prime-time television is still primarily "white," and the number and range of roles for non-white actors is limited. Indeed, in the last few years the number of African American protagonists on prime-time TV has declined, leading the NAACP to charge that we are witnessing a backlash against "black" television.

23   Of course, the entire Dan Quayle/"Murphy Brown" debacle was a *media ritual event*. Quayle's initial comment about the show was *broadcast* worldwide, and some analysts wonder whether Quayle's "gift" to Murphy Brown was scripted by the show's producers.

CHAPTER FOUR

Race and Representation

One of the extraordinary features of the "trial of the century" (i.e., the O. J. Simpson trial) was the adamant insistence, especially by "white" Americans, that the "race card" not be played. Especially in the early stages of the case, the demand was for jurors in particular, and Americans in general, to *ignore* race in the pursuit of *colorblind* "justice." The impetus for this demand was twofold. First, the idea was that "class" negated "race" in the O. J. trial: since the 1960s, the barriers to equality in the United States had been torn down, such that in the 1970s, even a "black" kid from the projects – like O. J. Simpson – could became a wealthy, well-loved celebrity. With his Brentwood mansion, his "white" wife, "white" friends, and "white" fans (and, indeed, as the *Pittsburgh Courier* sardonically noted, even his white Ford Bronco), it seemed to many that O. J. had "made it" not only to the top of "black society" – but to the top of "white society" as well. Thus, many thought that even if there were "remnants" of historical racism against *blacks* (e.g., excessive police brutality in "minority" communities), clearly this type of racism "did not apply" to the "race-neutral" O. J. – O. J. epitomized a "new" type of assimilated, *integrated* black American.

In addition, the demand for "colorblindness" in the O. J. case was motivated by the notion that even if there are "remnants" of racism "left" in our justice system (and nation), the only way to erase these "remnants" and truly *become* a "colorblind" society is to "Just Do It!" (as the Nike slogan proclaims). Akin to the self-help maxim that "if you want to be happy just make up your mind to be happy," akin to the American entrepreneurial "can-do" spirit, the thinking behind the race-neutral ideal is that enough is enough – just *be* "colorblind," for goodness sakes!

Yet, this demand for "colorblindness" is most remarkable in a country where "race" has had such a profound historical, institutional, and symbolic foothold. The metaphor of the "race card" presumes a social terrain *devoid* of race until the "race card" is (illegitimately) introduced. "Racism" is framed only "in terms of the formal exclusion of nonwhites, not in terms of the privileging of whiteness" (Crenshaw 1997, p. 106). In terms of the O. J. trial, "even the scripted declarations that this would not be a race case was itself a constitutive dimension of the racial dynamics of the case" (ibid., p. 112).

Most significantly, the whole notion of "colorblindness" is a *system of shared meaning* especially prominent in "*white*," but not "*black*" America today. This differential understanding of "colorblindness" reflects that "blacks" and "whites" (as well as other "racial" and/or "minority" ethnic groups) do not perceive of and experience "race" in the same way. For instance, Carr (1997, pp. 149–51), finds that 77 percent of white students surveyed said they were "colorblind when it comes to race" – while 60 percent of the black students surveyed said they were not. When asked what it meant that they were colorblind, most white students said it meant that they did not discriminate and were not prejudiced or that race means nothing to them. By contrast, the majority of African Americans said things like it is impossible to be African American and be colorblind in the United States, and many found the notion of colorblindness offensive.[1]

It is precisely this difference in perception and experience that is behind Kinder and Sanders's (1996, pp. 27–31) recent finding that the differences between public opinion about race policy (e.g., affirmative action) are much more drastic between races than those associated with class. Blauner (1989) also finds that there are two "languages" of race in the United States, one in which members of racial minorities, especially blacks, see the centrality of race in history and everyday experience, and another in which whites see race as "a peripheral, nonessential reality" (as cited by Omi and Winant 1994, pp. 70–1). Indeed, in a recent survey, 76 percent of "whites" perceived that black Americans were treated the same as whites in their local community. Only one in two blacks (49 percent) agreed (Gallup and Lindsay 1999, p. 120).

This differential perception and experience of race is striking because it begins early on and persists well into adulthood. For instance, in her study of racial identity, Holmes (1995) found that all 44 African American kindergarteners she interviewed emphasized the color of their skin when describing their self-portraits; by contrast, only 2 of the 42 European American children described themselves in terms of skin color.[2] Relatedly, in her study of "elite white men," Rhonda Levine (1998) found that when asked what it meant to be "white," many men had never thought about being "white" before. These well-educated, wealthy, and powerful men would respond with comments like, "I don't see myself as white"; or being white "doesn't mean anything"; or "I don't focus on being white." By contrast, Superior Court Judge Roosevelt F. Dorn (who is black) answered a question about "colorblind justice" by saying that it is something he had never encountered in his 27 years as a city prosecutor and judge. "Never seen it. Never heard of it. Never heard of anyone who has heard of it," he joked, as he sat in his chambers in Inglewood (Ford 1997, p. 142).

Baldwin (1985), hooks (1991), and Roediger (1998, p. 6), among others, argue that historically not only have whites tended to ignore their own racial identity – they have tended to fantasize that "black people cannot see them" (hooks 1991, p. 168, as cited by Roediger 1998, p. 6). "A vast amount of the energy that goes into what we call the Negro problem is produced by the white man's desire not to be judged by those who are not white" (Baldwin 1985, p. 333, as cited by Roediger 1998, p. 6). "Discounting and suppressing the knowledge of whiteness held by people of color was not just a byproduct of white supremacy but an imperative of racial domination" (Roediger 1998, p. 6).

In this chapter, we focus on both our historical obsession with "race" in the United States and the current preoccupation with "colorblindness." Using an interpretive, culturalist perspective, I will argue that race has taken on an independent criterion for vertical hierarchy in the United States (Bonilla-Silva 1997, p. 475). Race is an organizing principle of social relations in itself (ibid.), and has taken on a symbolic "life of its own" (Prager 1982). This culturalist approach to race and racial representation will be contrasted with two other sociological approaches to race: Wilson's classic social structural approach, which emphasizes the "declining significance of race" in America; and Bobo, Kluegel, and Smith's (1997) social psychological approach, which emphasizes the continuing significance of *racism*. In the latter portion of this chapter, we will look at the O. J. spectacle in more detail. While Crenshaw (1997, p. 113) maintains that the adamant call for "colorblindness" in the O. J. case simply demonstrates how *anemic* our dominant understanding of race really is; I will argue that this anemic understanding as to how "race" really works, also reflects a lack of understanding of the cultural realm.[3]

Defining Race and Ethnicity

Of course, we cannot get very far here without defining "race" (as well as "ethnicity"). Colloquially, the term "race" is used to refer to "obvious" physical differences between groups. But scientifically, the concept of "race" is untenable. No matter what system of classification is used – anatomical (e.g., skin color, hair texture, and body and facial shape), or physiological (e.g., metabolic rate, genetic diseases, hormonal activity, or blood characteristics), differences among individuals of the same group (or "racial type") are greater than those found between groups. Scientific efforts at racial classification have proved futile. The one thing about which biologists, geneticists, physical anthropologists, and physiologists agree is that "pure" races do not exist today (and may have never existed). Racial classification systems are by and large arbitrary (Marger 1997, p. 20).

To be sure, physical differences among people obviously do exist. There are evident differences between the "average" "black" person and "average" "white" person. But the statistical frequencies of certain characteristics should not be mistaken for actual human groupings. The popular division of the human population into three major racial groupings – Caucasoid, Mongoloid, and Negroid – ignores the huge populations that do not easily fit into this simple tripartite arrangement (e.g., East Indians with dark skin and "Caucasian" features), or groups with thoroughly mixed ancestry (e.g., most Indonesians and Mexicans). At the other extreme, the inflation of "race" to mean national origin – which was popular as late as World War II (e.g., "British" race, "Italian" race, "Jewish" race, etc.) – completely bypasses any semblance of physical or "biological" classification.

Yet, even more troubling than the scientific problems with the concept of "race" is the *racism* behind the concept of "race." From the time the concept of race first emerged, the assumption was that physical, external differences between groups reflected internal (moral, personality, intellectual) differences between groups, and that these differences were organized both biologically and *hierarchically*. Herrnstein and Murray's sensationalistic, bestselling book, *The Bell Curve*, is only the most recent example of this tradition.[4]

Due to the ambiguity, misuse, and abuse of the concept of "race," since the 1920s, many social scientists have thrown out the term altogether. Rather than focus on "race," these analysts focus on "ethnicity," which they explicitly conceptualize as a *social* rather than a *biological* phenomenon, i.e., not as "real" human essences existing outside or impervious to social and historical context. According to Weber's (1968 [1922], p. 389) classic definition, an ethnic group is one whose members "entertain a subjective belief in their common descent because of similarities of physical type or of customs or both, or because of memories of colonization and migration." Other analysts slide the race concept in as a "special" *kind* of ethnic group, e.g., "a racial group is . . . an ethnic group whose members are believed, by others if not also by themselves to be physiologically distinctive" (Alba 1992, p. 576, as cited by Marger 1997, p. 26).

Yet, the problem with replacing the study of "race" with the study of "ethnicity" is that "race" and "ethnicity" are *different* (albeit related) phenomena. In our common vernacular, "ethnically" similar people may be "racially" different, i.e., "Cubans" can be dark-skinned ("black") or light-skinned ("white"); while "racially" similar people ("black") might have completely different ethnic backgrounds (Haitian, Cuban, Senegalese). In other words, *both* race and ethnicity are critical categories of experience in modern society.[5] Next to gender, "race" and "ethnicity" are fundamental ways we *order* our experience, and organize meaning.

Moreover, the simple equation of "race" and "ethnicity" breeds the false "immigrant analogy." The equation of "ethnicity" with "race" falsely implies that the experience of racially defined minorities is completely coterminous with that of ethnically defined minorities. But there are at least two fundamental differences in the history and experience of "white" ("ethnic") and "nonwhite" ("racial") groups in the United States. First, the historical experience of racially defined minorities has included slavery, colonization, racially based exclusion, and in the case of Native Americans and Hawaiians, virtual extirpation (Omi and Winant 1994, p. 20). Secondly, historically "white" ethnics (Irish, Italian, German, etc.) *become* – the dominant group. By the second or third generation (if not before), the "not quite whites" (or "not *yet* whites") *become* simply "white" or simply "American"; their signs of difference and *marginality* (which, except for Jews, were a largely a function of their *immigrant* status) fade into the background.[6] "Italian Americans," "Irish Americans," etc., "take their place" as simply (white) "Americans."[7] By contrast, darker-skinned groups remain "dark" generationally and culturally. Tenth-generation African Americans tend to *still* be the "minority" group, even and alongside intermarriage (see Steinberg 1981).

In this chapter, I use the terms "race" and "racialization" to refer to the categorization and identification of people according to, largely, but not exclusively, skin color and other "obvious" visible characteristics. If it were not so distracting, I would put all the "race words" in this chapter in quotation marks (and will use quotation marks sporadically throughout this chapter to underscore this point) to signify that what we really mean is our *social understanding* of racial differences, i.e., "race" as a *social* – rather than a physiological – *fact*, as a category of experience and order in society. (Hunt [1997] uses a similar device: "white-raced" and "black-raced informants," etc.). Put in another way, what makes "race" recognizable across space and time is "the deeply held – though biologically untenable – schema of 'separation of human populations by some notion of stock or collective heredity of traits'" (Anthias and Yuval-Davis 1992, p. 2, as cited by Jung 1999, p. 363). Race "provides people with a deep sense of belonging to an imagined and limited community" (Jung 1999, p. 363); just because "race" is biologically untenable, we must not ignore this deep sense of belonging and the social consequences that such belonging and categorization creates. I use the term "racism" in this chapter to refer to a specific *kind* of racialized system of meaning – as discussed above, one in which (implicitly or explicitly) physical "racial" differences between groups are assumed to reflect internal (moral, personality, intellectual) differences, and that these differences are organized both biologically and *hierarchically*, i.e., racist systems of meaning suppose that on the basis of genetic inheritance, some groups are innately superior to others.

Stratification and Racialization

All complex societies are organized *hierarchically*. There are no complex societies in which wealth and privilege are distributed completely "equally"; and there are no societies in which wealth and privilege are distributed *randomly*, either. "Social stratification" is the sociological term for this hierarchical "layering" of specific social groups in society, i.e., the systems of rank ordering.

There are any number of ways societies can be stratified. Socioeconomic or *class* stratification is one of the most fundamental form of stratification. According to Marx, a social class comprises those who stand in a common position with regard to the society's productive system. The most basic division is between those who own and control the means of production and those who do not. Those who have access to the society's productive resources constitute a ruling class. Those who own no productive property, the working class, can offer only their labor in exchange for material needs (Marger 1997, p. 38).

Another basic way societies are stratified is by gender. While gender stratification is most readily apparent in traditional societies and institutions in which women are explicitly considered *inferior* to men or denied specific privileges (such as the right to vote, own property, etc.); modern industrial societies such as the United States are still highly gender-stratified. In the United States today, womens' wages are still approximately 69–72 percent of mens' salaries; women's autonomy is still routinely limited by violence and physical intimidation (i.e., domestic as well as public violence); in the public arena, the most important political and economic networks are still mens' networks, such as fraternities, country clubs, service clubs (Rotary, Lions Club), etc.

In addition, all modern pluralistic societies are stratified by race and/or ethnicity. A different *status* is placed on people according to their ethnic/racial group membership, which impacts individuals' access to resources, autonomy, and power, as well as self-image and identity. As indicated above in regard to gender, while racial/ethnic stratification is most obvious in systems of explicit, formal exclusion (e.g., the recently dismantled

Table 4.1 The income distributions of white and black families, 1970 and 1990 (1990 $; %)

	White families		Black families	
	1970	*1990*	*1970*	*1990*
Over $50,000	24.1	32.5	9.9	14.5
$35,000 to $50,000	24.1	20.8	13.9	15.0
$25,000 to $35,000	20.6	16.5	17.6	14.0
$15,000 to $25,000	16.9	16.0	24.0	19.5
Under $15,000	14.3	14.2	34.6	37.0
Median Income	$34,481	$36,915	$21,151	$21,423

Source: Hacker (1995 [1992], p. 98).

apartheid of South Africa; US slavery; Jim Crow laws; the colonization of indigenous peoples), the United States is still sharply stratified by race/ ethnicity. Indeed, as shown in table 4.1, though more African American families have made it into the upper economic tier than ever before, the economic gap between whites and blacks has *increased* since the 1970s. Of white families, 24.5 percent earned over $50,000 in 1970, but that figure jumped to 37.5 percent in 1992, while African American families in the upper income bracket increased merely from 10.2 percent to 16 percent. Moreover, while the number of white families earning less than $15,000 per year declined from 14.2 percent in 1970 to 12.3 percent in 1992, the number of African American families earning less than $15,000 increased from 34.3 percent to 38.2 percent (see Oliver and Shapiro 1995).

Nowhere were race/ethnic, gender, and class stratification and classifi- cation more readily apparent than on Hawaiian plantations around the turn of the century: plantation managers systematically paid different wage rates to workers of different nationalities and genders for the same work. For example, on one sugar plantation in Honoka'a, north of Hilo, Portuguese laborers were paid $15–$16 a month in 1885, while newly arrived Japanese were paid $9 for the same work (Okihiro 1991, p. 60, as cited by Merry 2000, p. 143); between 1915 and 1933, Filipino males were typically paid $18 to $20 a month, while Filipino women were paid $12 to $14 (Sharma 1980, p. 98, as cited by Merry 2000, p. 143). Most revealing of the mindset of this era are the labor documents which list workers in categories that merge plantation tasks with race and gender – as can be seen from the manager's report from the Ola'a Sugar Company

Table 4.2 Labor statement for a turn-of-the-century Hawaiian plantation

	1901	1902
Managment and office	11	13
Lunas[a]	34	14
Mechanics	42	18
Chinese cane cultivation contractors	21	46
Japanese cane cultivation contractors	399	577
Japanese day laborers	805	424
Japanese day women	38	6
Chinese	206	2
Portuguese	100	91
Hawaiians	20	9
Porto Ricans[b]	220	85
Porto Rican women	17	2
Other nationalities	19	7
Sundry clearing contracts	550	–

Source: Merry (2000, p. 142)
[a] Lunas = "foremen"
[b] Porto Ricans (sic) = Puerto Ricans

in 1901 and 1902 (the first few years of its operation) (table 4.2). As Merry (2000, p. 142) states:

> This curious list of employees, similar to that provided in other plantation manager's reports, blends occupation, nationality, and gender as if they all refer to the same thing ... work is so deeply understood in categories of race and gender that these identities stand in for occupational identities, just as the first three categories of occupation similarly encode a racial and gender destination of haole [white] male, although this identity is simply implicit.

Of course, since the passage of the 1964 civil rights bill, this type of blatant discrimination is no longer legal. The civil rights bill prohibited discrimination in public accommodations and employment on account of "race, color, religion or national origin." There were other tremendous changes brought about by the 1950s and 1960s civil rights movement too. In 1954, the Supreme Court outlawed the segregation of public schools. In 1968, the first black, Thurgood Marshall, was appointed to the Supreme Court. The civil rights debates that took place in the 1960s were the greatest since the debate over slavery and the Civil War more than one hundred years before (Kinder and Sanders 1996, pp. 98–100).[8]

The Declining Significance of Race vs. the Continuing Existence of Racism: Structuralist and Social-psychological Approaches to Race

However, as shown in Table 4.1 (and discussed previously), despite the civil rights movement, the *gap* between "black" and "white" wealth has not been erased; rather, it has *grown* since the 1960s. Thus, in the last few decades there has been heated public debate as to *why* African Americans continue to occupy the lowest rungs of the socioeconomic ladder in the United States.

One of the most important books impacting this discussion has been William Julius Wilson's provocatively titled *The Declining Significance of Race* (1978). In this book, Wilson argues that since the late 1960s, the "life chances" of black youths have been determined by their *class* position, not by the color of their skin. Wilson maintains that after state-enforced racial inequality was eliminated by civil rights legislation, blacks were admitted to the society-wide system of economic stratification, rather than being confined to a specific location by racial segregation (Omi and Winant 1994, p. 27). The result was a black community stratified into a small privileged "class" whose opportunities are equivalent to those of whites with similar high levels of training and skills, and a massive black "underclass" which is relegated to permanent marginality.

On one hand, Wilson's book aptly demonstrates that "racial" stratification is often a guise, or front, for *economic* stratification. In other words, Wilson underscores that what often are perceived to be racial differences between groups, are actually *class* differences; such "racial" differences between social groups disappear if we take into account *class* position. In addition, Wilson emphasizes that the movement of capital is to a large extent "colorblind"; large-scale demographic, economic, and political changes (such as suburbanization and federal housing policy) that have little to do with race *have* negatively impacted our inner cities. In sum, Wilson argues that the problems that plague our inner cities have *structural* – not "*racial*" – roots; inner-city problems *seem* like "race" problems (and, arguably, they become "race" problems) only because large minority populations live in these communities.

Nevertheless, the obvious problem with Wilson's thesis is its implied "zero-sum" foundation: "class and race are not antithetical ... 'more class' does not necessarily mean 'less race'" (Blauner 1989).That social class looms fateful in racial stratification today says nothing about *racialization*, or the potent symbolic aspects of "race."

Put in another way, "class" and "race" are not simply macro-level institutional structures, but complex *social* and *symbolic* structures, created and maintained through ritual and representation. As we will see in this chapter, race "matters" because racial discourses inform how individuals experience their world and theorize and act on their material conditions, "chang[ing] the boundary of rational behavior" (Boswell 1986, pp. 353–4, as cited by Jung 1999, p. 362).

Yet, ironically, while Wilson sought to demonstrate the importance of *class structures* (e.g., employment opportunities and the lack thereof) in the creation and maintenance of *inequality* in the United States; conservatives and the media interpreted Wilson's book as an affirmation of racial *egalitarianism*. In complete contradiction to what Wilson maintained, the "declining significance of race" was turned into a *social psychological* phenomenon, in which "making it" became a function *not* of race *or* class; but of individual characteristics (such as willpower, talent, personality, etc.). In this (mis)reading of Wilson, *The Declining Significance of Race* was coterminous with *The Cosby Show* – both demonstrating that if blacks *want* to make it, they can. Moreover, Wilson's differentiation between a small, successful black middle class, and a larger, alienated black "underclass" vicariously affirmed an emerging popular *dichotomy* between "good" (assimilated, middle-class) and "bad" (unassimilated, poor) blacks. This dichotomy is often verbalized much in the way that Joe Hicks, executive director of the Human Relations Comission, recently observed: "wherever you go, whoever you talk to . . . people want their kids educated, they want good jobs, they want affordable, clean housing, they want what everybody else wants."[9] We are all really "the same." There are "good" and "bad" blacks, just as there are "good" and "bad" whites. Some make it and some do not, but this is primarily because of their *individual* choices and situations.

In recent years, liberal social psychologists and sociologists have challenged this neo-conservative *social psychological* argument by replacing it with their own *social psychological* arguments. Social scientists such as Meertens and Pettigrew (1997), Carr (1997), Kinder and Sears (1981), Kinder and Sanders (1996), and Bobo, Kluegel, and Smith (1997) reject the notion that African Americans are themselves to blame for their place at the bottom of America's social hierarchy, by showing that while overt, blatant bigotry has sharply declined in this post-civil rights period, nevertheless, there is a new, more subtle, "laissez-faire racism" today. These analysts have conducted numerous surveys and found not the "declining significance" of race in contemporary American society, but the continuing significance of *racism*.

What is this "new racism" all about? Interestingly, implicitly or explicitly, many social psychologists and sociologists conceptualize the "new racism" as a specifically *anti-black* phenomenon. For instance, Bobo, Kluegel, and Smith (1997, p. 16) define "laissez-faire racism" as a "kinder, gentler anti-black ideology"; "laissez-faire racism involves persistent negative stereotyping of African Americans, a tendency to blame blacks themselves for the black–white gap in socioeconomic standing, and resistance to meaningful policy efforts to ameliorate US racist social conditions and institutions."[10] Bobo, Kluegel, and Smith go on to explain *why* racism still exists by arguing that in every historical period the *social-psychological* make-up of a society *follows from* its structural situation. Thus, just as there was slavery/overt racism in the plantation economy, and "Jim Crow" racism (or "separate but equal") in the "Jim Crow" era; today we have "laissez-faire racism" in this "laissez-faire" capitalist society. According to Bobo, Kluegel, and Smith (1997, pp. 21–2), "a significant segment of white America effectively condones as much black disadvantage and segregation as the legacy of historic discrimination and modern-day free market forces and informal social mechanisms can reproduce or even exacerbate."

Yet, like Wilson, Bobo et al. seamlessly fuse social structural and social psychological variables without exploring cultural phenomena. The problem is that while "a significant segment of America" undoubtedly do "condone black disadvantage" as Bobo et al. insist; this *attitude* is only a small piece of the complex, historical phenomena of *racialization*. We must take a look not merely at economic structures and individual attitudes, but the semiotics, or genealogy, of "race" in the United States.

Empirically, there are two fundamental problems that result from failing to acknowledge the cultural realm. First, both Wilson and Bobo et al. underemphasize the *continuities* in racialization over time and across historically situated institutions (e.g., slavery, Jim Crow racism, and the post-civil rights era). In addition, Wilson and Bobo et al. ignore the way that *all* subjects are racialized. They ignore that racialization is not simply the problem of "a significant segment of Americans" as *individuals* – but is part and parcel of *our* everyday life and experience. In the next section, we look at these problems in more detail.

Race: The History of an Idea[11]

Bobo et al. (1997, p. 30) maintain that "biological racism" peaked in the 1940s, when 53 percent of white Americans *publicly expressed* the opinion that blacks were less intelligent than whites. By the 1950s, this number had dropped to 20 percent. According to Bobo et al. (ibid.), "the character" of stereotypes have changed, such that "what were once viewed as categorical differences based in biology now appear to be seen as differences in degree or tendency. Furthermore, these differences in degree appear to be understood as having largely cultural roots." (By "cultural"

Bobo et al. seem to mean not "symbolic," but owing to the "way of life" of that group.)

Yet the problem here is that Bobo et al. do not explore the flip side of this phenomenon, i.e., the *continuities* in racialization over time. Specifically, they fail to see that the "old" biological racism still thrives in notions and images as to the supposed *primal* nature of blacks (e.g., of blacks as more sexual, aggressive, and passionate than whites); as well as in new ways, such as the "DNA mystique" (see Nelkin and Lindee 1995), i.e., our current preoccupation with "genetic" explanations for social ills.

First, biological racism cannot have been "wiped out" so long as we still perceive and are preoccupied with seemingly "commonsensical" notions as to the "obvious" physical or physiological differences between "blacks," "whites," "Asians," etc. These notions as to the *physical* differences between "racial" groups are most explicit in popular stereotypes, some of which superficially laud blacks, e.g., that "white men can't jump" (and black men can). This celebration of the physical prowess of the black *body* is linked to the traditional *biological* notion as to the more "primal" nature of blacks. Blacks have long been alleged to be more in tune with a primitive "soul," the elemental traits of the "primitive" other. This understanding of the black *body* represents one part of the traditional symbolic *opposition* between black "primal" *physicality* and white *civility* (i.e., white men "can't jump" because *their* attributes are rooted in innate "intelligence" and/or *civilization*). Most interestingly, this powerful, dichotomous symbolization, which is rooted in the traditional Western separation of "body" and "mind," is also part and parcel of the fundamental categories of "master" and "slave."

To be sure, today most public figures do not explicitly state, as did Al Campanis in his infamous interview with Ted Koppel, that blacks do not really "have what it takes" to be sports managers (though they supposedly make great athletes). But not only did most Americans know exactly what Campanis was talking about; many (mostly, but not only, white) also take these "proclivities" for granted (if only at a relatively unconscious level). Indeed, many (nonblack) Americans denounced the harsh reaction to Campanis's statement as an exemplar of "political correctness," arguing that, in truth, Campanis "didn't tell us anything we didn't already know." Of course, the point is that the *reason* people *understood* exactly what Campanis was talking about, was because his comments were a clear expression of the dominant US racial ideology/symbolic order.

Secondly, as Nelkin and Lindee point out in their fascinating book, *The DNA Mystique* (1995), in recent years there has been an increasing proliferation and popular acceptance of genetic explanations and genetic imagery in popular magazines and newspapers. DNA has become the new "cultural icon." On the one hand, we *are* witnessing fascinating new scientific breakthroughs in genetics today; this *is* "cutting-edge" science, and there *is* much to be learned. However, on the other hand, as Nelkin and Lindee point out, the United States has a long history in which policies have been guided by notions of heredity and natural ability. Historically, it seems that notions of heredity and natural ability are given new life at times when individual identity, family connections, and social cohesion seem threatened and the "social contract" appears in disarray.

Most importantly, while contemporary geneticists unilaterally underscore the *complex* interrelationship between "genes" and the "environment," the media *oversimplify* this research, such that, ironically, new scientific "data" about "DNA" and "genes" is seen as providing easy, technological "solutions" to complex social problems. Thus, in conjunction with our concern about racial, ethnic, and class differences, genetics as a science of difference seems to provide reliable, clear-cut ways to justify social policies on the basis of "natural" or predetermined characteristics. At a time of significant public concern about alcoholism and crime, genetics seems to provide hard and certain ways to codify what is normal or deviant – and good and evil (Nelkin and Lindee 1995, p. 16). This was precisely the niche that *The Bell Curve* filled: it provided cut-and-dried "explanations" for complex issues of race, education, affirmative action, etc.

Most interestingly, this is also precisely where the "DNA mystique" overlaps with the ideal of "colorblindness." Both provide comfort because they tell us that certain unfortunate contemporary realities (e.g., urban slums, criminality, stratification) are simply beyond our control. Both allow us to put the festering wounds of racialization and stratification out of our minds by assuring us that "certain unfortunate souls are destined to be losers . . . it permits prejudice without guilt" (Cose 1997a, p. 40).[12]

In sum, in direct contrast to Bobo et al.'s suggestion that laissez-faire racism has largely *replaced* biological notions of race, the point here is that biological notions of race – e.g., the "DNA mystique"; the "primal" nature of blacks – and laissez-faire racism (e.g., the ideology of "colorblindness") are actually intimately entwined. The DNA mystique, images as to the primal nature of blacks and colorblindness, are part and parcel of the *genealogy* (or historical sign system) of "race" in the United States.[13]

Put in another way, if we simply root "Jim Crow" racism in Jim Crow laws and "laissez-faire" racism in "laissez-faire capitalism," we portray racialization as only an institutional, and not a symbolic, process. But if we explore racialization as a *symbolic* process in and of itself (and not simply as a derivative of a particular social structure), we see the complex ways in which new ideas become embedded in old structures, and vice versa. We see the ways in which effervescent symbols and ideas evolve and change (but, in essence, remain the same) in accordance with new historical situations. The point is not that there are never any new ideas, but that we must not naively assume that complex, embedded, and historically provocative ethnic and racial *notions* will simply evaporate because we have new "structural" conditions.

Race: The History of an Idea, Part II

Where did notions as to the *innate* inferiority of blacks come from? While neo-Marxist analysts (such as Feagin 1997) locate the genesis of racism in the need to justify economic exploitation, in *White Over Black* (1968), Winthrop Jordan argues that long before the development of the institution of slavery, the English were *differentiating* themselves from "Africans" in what would become *racialized* ways. Specifically, Jordan maintains that four things struck the English who first encountered sub-Saharan Africans "face to face" in the sixteenth century; these four things would become the linchpins of modern racism. First, the English described Africans as "black" – an exaggerated term freighted with negative connotations – inaugurating a long tradition of speculation on the "causes" of such different skin color. Relatedly, to the English at the outset, the Africans appeared to be "heathens." Unlike Catholics or Muslims, they seemed to have no religion. Third, Africans appeared to be devoid of civilization, to be "savage." Finally, Africans struck the English as peculiarly lewd and libidinous, almost bestial.

According to D'Souza (1997), it is this perception of libidinousness and near-bestiality that differentiates the racialization of Africans from that of other "non-white" groups. While Europeans viewed both American Indians and Africans as hopelessly primitive and "savage," only Africans were singled out for *dehumanization*.[14] D'Souza (1997, pp. 60–1) maintains that this symbolic differentiation between Africans and Indians is based on both the different European conceptualizations of the Americas and Africa,[15] and the fact that Englishmen "discovered" black Africans as a group in the same place and at the same time that they "discovered" an animal they had never encountered before: the chimpanzee or two-legged ape, which they called an orangutan. Europeans bent on scientific classification and journalistic speculation linked the two, assuming that two-legged apes were the product of sexual intercourse between the monkey and the African. In 1690, a highly respected anatomist from the Royal Society of London named Edward Tyson dissected a chimpanzee which he mistook for a "Pygmy." Tyson maintained that the so-called pygmy occupied an intermediate position between beasts and men on the Great Chain of Being (D'Souza 1997, p. 61).[16]

Even so, historians concur that when the first Africans were brought to the New World in 1619 they were not "slaves" – but indentured servants (like most white laborers). A system of *black* bonded labor had not yet developed. "The Negroes were pushed into a society where most of the people were bond-servants and therefore to some degree unfree. Since the word *slave* had no meaning in English law, the Negro was thought of as a servant and not a slave" (Gossett 1963, p.29). White and black [laborers] "shared a condition of class exploitation and abuse: they were all unfree laborers" (Takaki 1993, p. 55). States Roediger (1999 [1991], p.24): "the many gradations of unfreedom among whites made it difficult to draw fast lines between any idealized free white worker and a pitied or scorned servile Black worker."

Of course, this failure to formally acknowledge "race" in 1619 does not mean that the white colonists were "colorblind." They were not. On the contrary, servants *were* differentiated: "blacks" were called "Negro servants," or, even more tellingly, *"perpetual"* (as opposed to "indentured") servants. Moreover, "mulattoes" were already talked about as the "spurious issue" or "abominable mixture" of two incompatible races in the early seventeenth century. For instance, in New England, a white woman married a Negro, lived with him for years, and bore him children – but she was completely ostracized by her family and by the community (Gossett 1963, pp. 30–1).

American racialization *developed* in the late seventeenth century, as discussions of the *heathenism* of Indians and slaves began to be supplemented by explicit discussion of skin *color*. Now the distinction was no longer between Christianity and heathenism ... but between white and black (Takaki 1993, pp. 59, 65). For instance, a 1667 Virginia law declared that "the conferring of baptism does not alter the condition of the person as to his bondage or freedom." In 1670, Virginia enacted a law declaring that "no negro or Indian," though baptized and free, should be allowed to purchase Christians; while another 1670 Virginia law makes no mention of "race," but specifies that "all servants not being Christians who were brought into the colony by sea were to be slaves for life" (Takaki 1993, p. 59).

To be sure, the institutionalization of a system of black slavery in the late seventeenth century had concrete political and economic motivations. Black slavery was an attempt by white landowners to circumvent the political wrath of "the "giddy multitude" of poor, landless white laborers, who were growing increasingly rebellious in the 1660s. However, the point is that the system of black slavery did not suddenly spring into existence with the realization that racism against blacks would be strategically useful. Rather, perceptions as to the absolute inferiority of Africans (whether because of their *class*, their *heathenism*, or their *race*) were part and parcel of colonial culture from the start, and these notions developed and coalesced with economic and political incentives. A system of *black* bonded labor (i.e., a racial caste system) emerged when notions as to the absolute incorrigibility of *Africans* began to merge with political and class interests.

According to Jordan (1968), the American revolution brought the ideology of racism to a head, as white males who declared themselves free and independent were forced to account for the males in their midst who were neither. "By the early 1800s the ideological building blocks that had been gathering for centuries had been assembled into the coherent conviction that blacks were innately inferior to white, and that the 'races' could never live together as equals" (Campbell and Oakes 1997, p. 149). "Blacks, free and slave . . . were stigmatized as the *antithesis* of republican citizens," the very *opposite* of "free, white labor" (Roediger 1999 [1991], p. 36).

Throughout the nineteenth century, the ideology of white supremacy became even more coherent and widespread. Scientists such as Samuel Morton "proved" that whites had a larger brain size, and were therefore superior to other races. Though the famous former slave Frederick Douglass poignantly denounced Morton's arguments as nothing more than "scientific moonshine that would connect men with monkeys," and "separate the Negro race from every intelligent nation and tribe in Africa" (Lott 1999, p. 58); whites soon took their "manifest destiny" for granted.[17] Indeed, from the 1830s until 1977, when Stephen Jay Gould reanalyzed the original data, the notion that whites had larger "cranial capacities" than blacks was widely accepted.

After the Civil War, there was the brief, egalitarian experiment of Reconstruction which was terminated ignominiously in 1877. A resurgence of racial hostility and turmoil followed. In 1896, the Supreme Court declared racial discrimination and the disenfranchisement of blacks to be constitutional. In this same decade, the number of lynchings reached extremes unequaled before (Woodward 1998, p. 14). "Whites accused black men of rape more than at any time before or since, and black men could be lynched for all manner of objectionable behavior toward white women." (ibid.) Notices of lynchings were printed in local papers, and extra cars were added to trains to accommodate spectators from miles around, sometimes thousands of them. School children might get a day off to attend a lynching (Woodward 1998, p. 16). Indeed, the last decade of the nineteenth century is said to be the most racially violent in United States history.

To be sure, the wave of racist legislation and violence in the late nineteenth and early twentieth centuries in the United States was not only "anti-black." In 1887, the reservation system was established, which gave the United States the authority to confine Indians and to "arrest" and return those who wandered away from these lands (Takaki 1993, p.

233). Between 1887 and 1934, the aggregate Indian landbase within the United States was "legally" reduced from about 138 million acres to about 48 million (Collier 1934, pp. 16–18, as cited by Jaimes 1992, p. 117); nearly 20 million of the acres remaining in Indian hands by 1934 were arid or semiarid, and thus marginal or useless for agricultural purposes (Deloria and Lytle 1983, p. 10, as cited by Jaimes 1992, p. 117). Sadly, a wave of anti-Chinese (later, anti-Asian) sentiment gripped the nation in the late nineteenth century as well. The 1882 Chinese Exclusion Act was the first law that prohibited the entry of immigrants on the basis of nationality (Takaki 1993, p. 7). It was followed by the "Gentlemen's Agreement" of 1908 and the Immigration Act of 1924, which also prohibited Asian laborers from entering the United States.[18]

Nevertheless, racialization in the United States has always revolved around a "black"/"white" binary opposition. And, from the start, this symbolic dichotomy was *gendered* as well. For instance, throughout the seventeenth, eighteenth, and nineteenth centuries, most "mulattos" were born to descendants of a white (slave owner) father and a black mother– but there was much greater social concern about sexual relations between black men and white women. Laws typically prohibited sex between white women and black men, but not the reverse.[19] In sum, there is a long tradition in United States culture of juxtaposing white female "civility" and social order with the sexuality and passion of the non-white Other (duCille 1997, p. 304). Indeed, the declared purpose of the Ku Klux Klan was the "defense of white supremacy and the inviolability of white womanhood".

In the early 1920s, "protecting white womanhood" resulted in a resurgence of racial violence. What has been called the worst "race riot" in American history, broke out in Tulsa, Oklahoma, in 1921, following the arrest of a nineteen year old black man for allegedly assaulting a seventeen-year-old white female elevator operator. Some 50 whites, and hundreds of blacks were killed, and an entire black neighborhood was burned down. A similar incident occurred in the almost all-black town of Rosewood, Florida in 1923. The entire town was burned to the ground (and never rebuilt) and at least eight people were killed in a week long "race riot" ignited by the accusation of a young white woman that she had been raped by an "unknown" black man (though there was evidence that the accusation was false). In profound understatement, the Tampa Morning Tribune editorialized that, "[The] assault of a young pure white woman by one or more Negroes . . . is a provocation which, more than any other, stirs the anger, and whets the determination to punish in every white man who reads of it."[20]

Indeed, as late as 1955, fifteen-year-old Emmett Till was brutally killed merely for having said "bye baby" to a white woman as she was leaving a rural Mississippi store.[21] More recently, albeit less dramatically, Sergeant Stacey Koon offered as justification for beating Rodney King the fear that King posed a "Mandingo" threat to a white policewoman (Fiske 1994, p. xvii, as cited by Ducille 1997, p. 304).

As we have seen, the "Negro-ape" metaphor was first promulgated by scientists in the seventeenth century. However, not only "science" – but popular culture and "the arts"— propagated and disseminated this imagery. Throughout the nineteenth and early twentieth centuries, ape images were used to represent black people in movies and minstrel songs. In the 1930s and 1940s, jazz and blues were commonly disparaged as "jungle" or "monkey" music (Lott 1999, p. 12).[22] Indeed, Lott (1999, p. 10) argues that the ape in the class Hollywood film, *King Kong* (1933) was "most certainly a black man"; thus, the juxtaposition of white female civility and social order, with the sexuality and bestiality of the non-white Other, is sometimes called the "King Kong narrative".[23]

Of course, this symbolization still exists today. For instance, when Andrea Ford, a black female reporter who covers the criminal beat for the *Los Angeles Times*, almost collided with two white police detectives at the entrance to the courthouse, she heard someone behind her singing, "Hey, hey she's a monkey", to the tune of the theme song of the old *Monkeys* television show. When Ford turned she found the two cops smirking, causing her to wonder: "If this is the way they treated me . . . how did they treat the suspects they brought to court?" (Cose 1997b, p. xvi).

Yet today imagery as to the sexuality and passion of the "non-white Other" is most readily apparent in advertising and fashion. For instance, in their content analysis of magazines, Plous and Neptune (1999) discovered that 70 percent of the advertisements that contained an animal- patterned print featured a black woman wearing the print. Gladden (1993, p. 26, as cited by Plous and Neptune 1999, p. 44) found that people associate animal prints with "sexy," "wild," and "seductive"; and they imagine that "women who wore animal prints were more sexually active than other women, less educated, lower in income, more concerned about their physical appearance, less concerned about society's problems, less supportive of the feminist movements, and more likely to be African American." Gladden (ibid.) notes that individuals in his study viewed animal-print wearers "in much the same way as they might view animals" – motivated by instincts, unintellectual, concerned foremost about their own welfare.[24]

According to the cultural anthropologist John Ogbu (1978), the prominent symbolic dichotomy between white *civility* and black *primality* creates a symbolic conflict in many extirpated communities. The symbolic problem is the equation of "white" with "mainstream," middle-class experience, e.g., "Mom, Dad, and apple-pie," Little League, etc. Within this dominant symbolic framework, becoming "middle class" means moving toward *white* realms of experience, e.g., predominantly "white" working and living situations. The result is that "making it"/"success" in "mainstream" society *blurs* racial identity; the involuntary, dispossessed minority group must "denounce" part of who they are to be successful (Ogbu 1978). Ogbu maintains that in specific contexts in which this symbolic opposition gains sway, the result is that speaking standard English, spending a lot of time studying, going to the library, carrying a backpack, or getting good grades, becomes a sign of "selling out."[25]

In short, "the very meaning of being black involves *not* being white" (Waters 1999, p. 69). This is precisely the "dilemma" of the black middle class: it is caught between "white" and "black" worlds.[26] This is also precisely why young black artists and musicians today have *appropriated* the "Negro-ape" metaphor – e.g., Da Lench Mob's *Guerrillas in the Mist* (1992) and *Planet of the Apes* (1995), and more generally, overt sexuality, misogyny, and violence (e.g., "gangsta rap"). Lott (1999, p. 12) maintains that, "appropriations [of the Negro-ape metaphor] by black artists and musicians can be seen as healthy signs of overt contestation."[27] However, as we saw in the previous chapter, we must be careful not to overestimate the extent to which popular cultural products reflect "resistance" to domination. As Bourdieu (1990, p. 155, as cited in McGuigan 1992, p. 13) maintains:

> When the dominated quest for distinction leads the dominated to affirm what distinguishes them, that is, that in the name of which they are dominated and constituted as vulgar, do we have to talk of resistance? In other words, if, in order to resist, I have no other resources than to lay claim to that in the name of which I am dominated, is this resistance?

The Other "Others": Racialization and the Model Minority Myth

Thus far we have seen that the problem with both structural and social psychological approaches to "race" is that they ignore the symbolic universe behind and within both institutions and attitudes. In so doing, they underemphasize the symbolic *continuities* in racialization over time. The second (albeit interrelated) empirical problem with these arguments is that they do not see that *all* American subjects are racialized. This is most apparent in Bobo et al.'s *definition* of "laissez-faire" racism as an exclusively "anti-black" phenomenon, just because blacks are in a unique, isolated, and socioeconomically underprivileged position. To be sure, Bobo et al. are not *interested* in studying non-black "minorities." Bobo et al. and Kinder and Sanders focus on the relation between *anti-black sentiments* and strategic advantage (an important concern). But nevertheless, the point is that, empirically, the situation of African Americans is intimately entwined with the meaning and location of "Asians," "Latinos," "whites," etc. Anti-black sentiments are linked to symbols that define all sorts of people that do not fit in Bobo et al.'s narrow "anti-black" conceptualization of "laissez-faire" racism.

Consider, for instance, the "model minority" myth. By "model minority" myth, I mean the widespread notion that "Asians" exemplify how to "make it" in American society – that "Asians" are a "model" minority, because they epitomize the importance of good values (e.g., family, school, obedience, respect, self-reliance) and hard work. Wong et al. (1998) have found that across the board, Asians, Native Americans, African Americans, and Hispanics *believe* the "model minority" myth. In a way, this should not be surprising, for indeed, being "Asian" *is* strongly linked to academic achievement (Steinberg 1996).

Yet Bobo et al.'s model of "laissez faire" racism excludes the myth of the model minority. Recall that for them, "laissez faire racism" is strictly an *anti-black* phenomenon, rooted specifically in African Americans' structural situation. This implies that the "myth of the model minority" is not laissez-faire racism, first, because it applies (at least explicitly) to "Asians" (rather than blacks); and secondly, because Asians – as a whole – are not in a situation of tremendous structural disadvantage (compared to African Americans).[28]

However, the problem with conceptualizing laissez-faire racism as a (serious) anti-black phenomenon and the model minority myth as a *separate*, relatively *trivial* "stereotype" is that anti-black sentiments and the "model minority" myth are, in fact, intimately related. Indeed, as we will shortly see, from an interpretive culturalist perspective, the "model minority myth" and "anti- black sentiments" are variations on the *same* theme. Symbolically, the model minority myth serves to underscore what is *wrong* with those who are *not* "model minorities" (mostly African Americans, but also Latinos, native Hawaiians, etc.).[29]

Specifically, the "model minority myth" first emerged in the midst of the civil rights movement, when *The U.S. News and World Report* (1966, p. 73, as cited by Nakayama 1998, pp. 181–2) wrote that "at a time when it is being proposed that hundreds of billions be spent to uplift Negroes and other minorities, the nation's 300,000 Chinese-Americans are moving ahead on their own – with no help from anyone else.[30] In other words, the *reason* that Asians were (and are) held up as the "model minority" was *precisely* because their "moving ahead" refracts back on "Negroes" and other [not model] minorities "underachievement" and lack of "discipline." Without implicit reference to the *not* "model minorities" (especially but not only "blacks"), the "model minority" myth would not make sense, it would have no symbolic impetus. In other words, the "model minority myth" explicitly situates "Asians" on the same side as – or even *ahead* of "whites" in the hierarchical, symbolic *dichotomy* between "black" "primality/physicality" (brawn/passion) and white/Asian "civility" (brains/rationality). This symbolization was explicit in Herrnstein and Murray's infamous book, *The Bell Curve* (1994), which placed "Asians" even higher than "whites" in IQ.

But dichotomous symbolic opposition has a downside not only for the *not* model minorities (e.g., African Americans), but for "model minorities." For while the "model minority" myth is most often *used* indirectly against blacks; it can also be *used* against "Asians." Specifically, the "model minority myth" involves the same type of individual invisibility, "otherness," as well as a resentment of success, that was behind turn-of-the-century anti-Asian legislation, and the internment of Japanese in World War II. It is the same resentment of "success" that has driven antisemitism as well. Thus, it should come as no surprise that with the widespread diffusion of the "model minority" myth, we have also seen an increase in "hate-crimes" against Asian Americans and Asians (Nakayama 1998, p. 179). While on one hand Asian Americans are lauded for "outwhiting the whites"; at the same time, they are *resented* and even *hated* for "outwhiting the whites." The feeling is, "how dare those Asians outwhite the *real* (white) Americans!"

Most importantly, these symbolic frameworks inform and give meaning to very real political and social debates and problems, and experience and action. For instance, the Los Angeles "riots" following the acquittal of the police officers who beat Rodney King occurred against the backdrop of escalating tensions between working- and lower-class black residents and Korean business owners in south central Los Angeles. In the same month that a camera videotaped Rodney King's beating by four white police officers, another camera captured the killing of a 15-year-old black girl named Latasha Harlins (Hunt 1997, p. 273, n. 3; see also Albelmann and Lie 1995). Harlins was shot to death by Korean liquor store owner Soon Ja Du, who accused Harlins of attempting to steal a bottle of orange juice. Black Americans were enraged when Soon Ja Du received no jail time (merely five years' probation), because the store's security videotape showed that after a brief struggle between the two, Harlins placed the bottle on the counter and turned to leave; but Soon Ja Du pulled out a handgun and shot Harlins in the back of the head (Hunt 1997, pp. 273–4, n. 3). One wonders about the role symbolization played, since Soon Ja Du so clearly *fit* the myth of the model minority (hardworking business owner), while Latasha Harlins *fit* the image of the expendable, black juvenile delinquent.

Culturalist Approaches to Race

For culturalists such as Hall (1990) and Prager (1982), race is closer to the model of *language*, rather than *biology*. Like a language, skin color is a *signifier* that carries tremendous *meaning*. These analysts follow Du Bois (1998 [1920]) who first pointed out that color, though of little meaning in and of itself, is a "badge for the social heritage of slavery, the dissemination and the insult of that experience."

Specifically, although, like Bobo et al., Hall (1990, pp. 12–13) distinguishes between more "overt" and less "overt" systems of racial exclusion, Hall explores this distinction in a more *discursive* way. Hall defines "overt" racism as the "obvious" type of bigotry, and "inferential racism" as "those apparently naturalized representations of events and situations relating to race, whether 'factual' or 'fictional', which have racist premises and propositions inscribed in them as a set of *unquestioned assumptions.*" Inferential racism "enables racist statements to be formulated without ever bringing into awareness the racist predicates on which the statements are grounded." Most importantly, this means that, in contrast to Bobo et al.'s notion that "old" notions are eradicated along with "old" structural conditions, there is a *continuum* in which what was "said" in one period, is *inferred* in another. This explains why specific symbols *transcend* various cultural, political, and social arenas, time periods, as well as "skin colors"; and why *seemingly* "dead" symbols and images are later revitalized and make a resurgence. Thus for instance, the notion of fundamental *biological* differences between "whites" and "blacks" has shifted from being at the *front* of discourse in notions of cranial capacity, etc., to the *back* of the discourse in "genetic" DNA arguments – i.e., from being "overt" to being "inferential," but the *continuity* in the discourse lies in the fact that what was *said* before is no longer *spoken* but merely *implied*. Whether explicit or implicit, both "theories" emphasize that, to some extent, white supremacy and black inferiority are "hard-wired" (a genetic "given").

Hall goes on to explain that "open or overt racism is, of course, politically dangerous as well as socially offensive . . . . But *inferential racism* is more widespread – and in many way, more insidious, because it is largely *invisible* even to those who formulate the world in its terms." He (ibid.) states:

> An example of *this* type of racist ideology is the sort of television programme which deals with some "problem" in race relations. It is probably made by a good and honest liberal broadcaster, who hopes to do some good in the world for "race relations" and who maintains a scrupulous balance and neutrality when questioning people interviewed for the programme. The

program will end with a homily on how, if only the "extremists" on *either side* would go away, "normal blacks and whites" would be better able to get on with learning to live in harmony together. Yet every word and image of such programs are impregnated with unconscious racism because they are all predicated on the unstated and unrecognized assumption that the *blacks* are the *source of the problem*.

Indeed, this type of racism *is* widespread. Consider, for instance, the following story about racism I read the other day in a column in the *Los Angeles Times*. An anguished reader (a white woman) wrote to a popular columnist about a jolting experience she had in a shoe store. While she was waiting in line to buy some shoes, she overheard a white male customer insist on a different sales clerk because he did not want the black clerk "to touch his socks." The white female reader was appalled but too shocked to speak, while the black male sales clerk did not say anything because (he said later) he thought "it wasn't worth it." "It's better to just let these things roll off your back," he said; although he also said he did not tell his wife about the incident, because he did not want to upset her.

This is exactly the type of story to which Hall refers. It is a typical "liberal" media story about race, i.e., it affirms that "racism" is "real" (*see* – there really are white racists still out there!), and that the "proper" reaction, taken by the white woman, is horror. She "did the right thing," and acted on her rage by sending a letter off to the editor.

Yet this story is coterminous with conservative ideologies as well. First, the incident is constructed as an "isolated incident." That the white woman was appalled, that the black sales clerk could "let it roll off his back," projects that *structural*, institutional racism is a thing of the past. After all, the black man did have a sales clerk job! After all, the white woman herself (as well as the majority of white customers) weren't worried about contamination! In other words, this story reflects that "real" racism – not only structural but also biological racism – is largely behind us today. This white racist customer was an historical *anomaly*. Merely 50 years

PROFANE (threat)	SACRED (reassurance)
militant black man _____	unmilitant black man
Malcolm X	Dr. Martin Luther King
common "thug"	Colin Powell
Mike Tyson/Dennis Rodman	Bill Cosby/Cliff Huxtable
post-trial O. J. Simpson	pretrial O. J. Simpson

Figure 4.1   A continuum of binary opposition in the symbolization of black men in the post-civil rights period

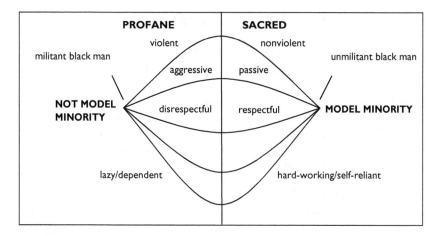

Figure 4.2 Binary opposition in the symbolization of black men in the post-civil rights period

ago, it was *normative* for whites to be concerned about *contamination;* it was simply "understood" that there must be "white" and "black" drinking fountains, bathrooms, public pools, public schools, etc.

Secondly, the "hero" in this story is the "unmilitant" black sales clerk – the *good, assimilated* black man, who does not let "minor" racial incidents disturb him. Following the footsteps of Martin Luther King, Jr. (and Bill Cosby/Cliff Huxtable), the good, assimilated, hard- working, unmilitant black man is the new white hero.[31] However, significantly, as shown in figures 4.1 and 4.2,[32] this new hero gains his symbolic impetus because he stands in symbolic opposition to those other, "bad" black men *inferred* in our dominant symbolic universe – those inner-city gang bangers, criminals, and thugs all over the TV news and in our prisons. Thus, while on the surface, the "enemy" of the story is the "bad" white racist, the other (inferred) "enemy" is the "bad" black militant or bum (definitely *not* model minority). The story affirms, once again, that if a black man *wants* to make it in this world, he can. It reflects an understanding of "racism" as:

> an historical concept, relevant only to mark the contrast between an enlightened present and a distant and unfortunate past. Within this enlightened era, not only are whites expected to adopt a "colorblind " performance, but African Americans are expected to approach the occasional discovery of racist actors or actions with cool rationality rather than with hysteria or paranoia. (Crenshaw 1997, p. 104)

British Cultural Studies and Race

In recent years, analysts within the British cultural studies tradition have expounded on Hall's conceptualization of "inferential racism," but given it more of a critical bent. For instance, analysts such as Jhally and Lewis (1992) and Ansell (1997) concur with Bobo et al. (1997) and Kinder and Sanders (1996) that today, there is a "new racism" couched within "the vocabulary of equal opportunity, colorblindness, race-neutrality and, above all, individualism and individual rights." But they explicitly link the "new racism" with the "new Right." Ansell (1997, p. 21) maintains that the new Right has "highjacked and repackaged" such words and phrases as "colorblindness" and "equality" and "opportunity," "so as to service a different agenda, this time in favor of a politics that is, albeit indirectly, exclusionary rather than inclusionary in spirit." "The new racism has become a hegemonic discourse as a function of the New Right's successful attempt to center its discourses on race and normalize it in relation to other more mainstream political discourses and popular codes" (ibid.).

Many analysts find the conservative "appropriation" of Martin Luther King as one of their own especially discomfiting. For instance, Cose (1997a) notes that in January 1996, Louisiana Governor Mike Foster signed an order banning affirmative action in agencies under his control, and, on the same day, signed a bill declaring the birthday of Martin Luther King a state holiday – and Foster *linked* these two events. States Foster, "This just says we've got to be colorblind . I do not believe I have any prejudice – never had in my opinion. I don't look at color. . . Dr. King dedicated his life to the pursuit of equality and opportunity for all Americans. He believed all men should be judged by their character, not by the color of their skin" (cited by Cose 1997, p. xii).

Of course, as Cose (1997a, pp. xii–xiii) points out, King was actually quite dismayed at white America's reluctance to take the extra steps needed to wipe out centuries of black exploitation. King fully realized, as he wrote in *Where Do We Go From Here: Chaos or Community* (1967), that "white America was ready to demand that the Negro should be spared the lash of brutality and coarse degradation, but it had never been truly committed to helping him out of poverty." As Cose hypothesizes, in terms of the current affirmative action debate, it seems most likely that King would say:

> All right, I understand why you oppose affirmative action. But tell me: what is *your* plan? What is *your* plan to crush the tragic walls separating the wealth and comfort of the outer city from the despair of the inner city? What is *your* plan to cast the slums of our cities on the junk heaps of history? What is *your* program to transform the dark yesterdays of segre-

gated education into the bright tomorrows of high-quality, integrated education?[33]

However, the notion that conservatives have simply "highjacked" civil rights imagery is problematic because it relegates the "masses" to *passivity*. As discussed in chapter two, the Gramscian notion that political elites simply "construct" ideologies for their own strategic purposes is untenable because it makes culture *epiphenomenal* (for "in the end", ideas are simply a function of class interest). To be sure, the symbol "Martin Luther King" *has* veered sharply from the actual circumstances of King's life and writing, and conservatives *have* used civil rights imagery for their own purposes. However, the civil rights imagery did not emerge out of thin air. Rather, the genius of Martin Luther King was that he *shamed* America using its *own* sacred symbols (e.g., "equality," "democracy," "progress," and "Christianity"). Martin Luther King shamed America by showing that it did not live up to its own sacred myths – most importantly, "freedom, and justice for all."[34] The civil rights movement gained the moral high ground not solely because it represented the centuries-long *black* struggle for freedom; but because it represented "the highest and noblest aspirations of white society as well" (Omi and Winant 1994, p. 100). Thus it should come as no surprise that the core symbols of the civil rights movement – e.g., "Rosa Parks," "Martin Luther King," the "I Have a Dream" speech, etc. – have been reintegrated into traditional "American" notions of "justice." It should come as no surprise that the imagery of the civil rights movement has veered sharply from the historical "reality," and taken on the qualities of American myth, to be used by the right and left alike, in our contemporary political discourse – because it was part of this discourse from the beginning.

Moreover, it is ironic that, as we saw in the last chapter, cultural analysts celebrate the "appropriation" of mainstream symbols by progressive groups, but wring their hands over the appropriation of "progressive" symbols by conservatives. Now the manipulation of symbols in new ways is not "resistance" (to liberal ideology), but symbolic "highjacking." But the point is that the manipulation and appropriation of symbols in new and old ways is a complex *cultural* process, and that this process informs and shapes the *entire spectrum* of political perception and experience.[35]

The O. J. Spectacle

As indicated previously, before it even began, and despite the adamant call for "colorblindness," the protagonists of the O. J. spectacle were raced and gendered. The central victim, Nicole Simpson, was a white woman,

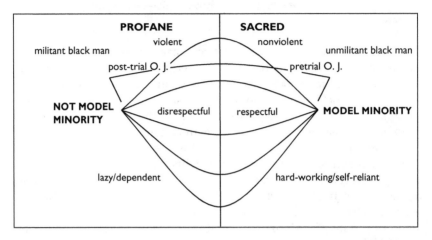

Figure 4.3 Binary opposition in the symbolization of black men in the post-civil rights period and the symbolization of O. J. Simpson

and O. J. Simpson was a black male. The other players in the drama were "raced" too: the racist white cop (Mark Furhman); the Japanese American Judge (Judge Ito); the two black lawyers – one "militant"/bad/profane (Johnnie Cochran), and one "unmilitant"/good/sacred (Christopher Darden) (see Cose 1997b).

As illustrated in figures 4.1 and 4.3, for most whites, the dominant theme of the O. J. Simpson ritual media event was a spectacular fall from grace. O. J. Simpson went from being the quintessential "unmilitant" black man and "race-neutral" celebrity athlete, to being "just another violent black male criminal." As Crenshaw (1997, p. 98) states, "the very ideological framework that embraced Simpson as a symbol of a colorblind ideal ... later spat him out as the embodiment of black criminality and irresponsibility."

Specifically, before O. J., no black athlete, no matter how great, had ever "crossed over" with anything like such success. As Johnson and Roediger (1997, p. 202) point out, in the late 1960s, black athletes with far more significant professional accomplishments in their sport than O. J. – including Willie Mays, Hank Aaron, Bill Russell, Oscar Robertson, Wilt Chamberlain, Jimmy Brown, and above all, Muhammad Ali (who was "militant" and therefore "bad") – were still not getting endorsements. So why O.J.? Johnson and Roediger (ibid.) maintain that O.J. became a star not for winning the Heisman Trophy or some other extraordinary professional accomplishment (for after all, then and now, winning the Heisman has had little relation to professional success). Rather, O.J. became a star,

above all, because he was refreshingly "inoffensive". Specifically, O.J. embodied the symbolic opposite of what Harry Edwards called the "revolt of
the black athlete" (see chapter 3). Simpson publicly denounced the protests and raised fists of the American track and field athletes at the 1968
Mexico City Olympic games. O. J. also stood in symbolic contrast to
Muhammad Ali, who faced jail in 1968 and suffered suspension from
boxing for his refusal to be inducted into the military as a draftee. Outside
of the athletic realm, O. J. stood in sharp contrast to the other televised
images of *militant* black men – college protestors and activist rebels (Johnson
and Roediger 1997, p. 202).

Indeed, as early as 1960, O. J. boasted that his triumph lay in being seen
as a "man" and not a black man (Johnson and Roediger 1997, p. 230). In
denouncing not only racial politics but racial identification, O. J. became
the idol for thousands of white males. Since O. J., we have seen an out-
pouring of upper-middle-class, white masculinist fantasies of identification
with black celebrity athletes. In addition, according to Johnson and Roediger
(1997, p. 231), "forging pan-male unities, athletic striving particularly
shores up male dominance in periods of forward political and economic
motion by women so that women's liberation movements as well as Black
Power form a critical context for Simpson's rise in the late 1960's."[36]

Yet, the "unmilitant black man" is not merely a *race* hero and a *gender*
hero but a *class* hero for white America. Like the proverbial "Horatio
Alger," "unmilitant black men" – like Cliff Huxtable/Bill Cosby, as well as
the pre-trial, "race-neutral," assimilated, unmilitant O. J. – "pick themselves up by their bootstraps" from the projects (e.g., of Portrero Hill) to a
beautiful home in the suburbs (e.g., Brentwood). Unmilitant black men,
like Cliff Huxtable and the pre-trial O. J. Simpson, affirm not only the
ability of "anyone" to "have it all"; they help clarify what all of "it" is
(Miller 1986).

In addition, Miller (1986 as cited by Jhally and Lewis 1992, p. 17)
argues that the "unmilitant black man" represents a "threat contained";
Bill Cosby offers "deep solace to a white public terrified that one day
blacks might come with guns to steal the copperware, the juicer, the
microwave, the VCR, even the TV itself", at a time when "American
whites need such reassurance because they are now further removed
than ever, both spatially and psychologically, from the masses of the
black poor".

Once again we see that "racialization" and "classification" are intimately intertwined; we see the symbolic opposition between "white"/"middle-class"/"the suburbs" and "black"/poor/"the projects" or "ghetto". The
point is that in "moving up", the black man not only moves *economically*
but *racially*; the "unmilitant" black man becomes distanced not merely
from his lower *class* position, but from his very *"blackness"*.

After the murders of Ronald Goldman and Nicole Brown, the white obsession with O. J. as the quintessential unmilitant black man gave way to contempt for another common stereotype, the *criminal* black man. The "real" O. J. was revealed; and whites were "betrayed" by their "hero." States Carr (1997, p. 151), "there is a great fear in the White nation of the African American criminal and it is not without some foundation. The census bureau annual survey of crime victimization shows that African Americans commit 55 percent of all murders, 33 percent of all rapes, and 71 percent of all robberies." While most murders and rapes are "black on black," 38 percent of all robberies involved an African American assailant and white victim (Hacker 1995, p. 191).

Most importantly, that whites were "let down" with the exposure of O. J. as a criminal black man (rather than an unmilitant black man) is important because it underscores another basic fear within "white" America: one simply *never knows* whether "assimilation" is "real." As Gillespie (1997, p. 101) states:

> The notion of the lazy, venal, good-for-nothing, hot-blooded, over-sexed, violent, childike, morally loose, criminally inclined Negro [has been] powerfully appealing in white America. And historically the criminal justice system helped reinforce this belief. According to popular lore, we were either good and faithful God-fearing subservients; playful, fun-loving, natural - born entertainers; or "junglebunnies" with voracious sexual appetites, animal cunning, and feral instincts. Uncle Tom and Porgy and Beulah or Bess and Stagger Lee. Always there are the lingering questions. Did Uncle Tom have a heart of darkness; could he be a Bigger Thomas? On Saturday night, did Mammy put on her red petticoat and turn into Carmen Jones? Were all blacks criminally inclined; was it just our nature?

Most interestingly, this insecurity as to whether assimilation can *genuinely* be achieved by "nonwhite" groups is not at all new. On the contrary, it has been a fundamental element of American racial discourse from the beginning. Could Indians *really* be "saved"? Or would an "Indian always be an Indian," even if he wore Western clothing and went to church? Were Japanese Americans *really* loyal to the United States in World War II? Or, as an editorial in the *Los Angeles Times* bluntly put it, was a viper "nonetheless a viper wherever the egg is hatched – so a Japanese American, born of Japanese parents – grows up to be a Japanese, not an American" (cited by Takaki 1993, p. 380)?

Just as fundamental "race" and "class" narratives infused the O. J. spectacle as a whole, "race" and "class" explanations existed for the acquittal of O. J. Simpson in the criminal trial. The dominant *class* narrative (prominent especially, but not exclusively, among whites) was that O. J. attained the "best defense money could buy." The pre-trial image of O. J.

as a "race-neutral" Horatio Alger was replaced by a post-trial image of O.J. as the equally "race-neutral," privileged elite. In either case, the myth of the colorblind society is confirmed: the only color that mattered was "green."

The dominant *racial* narrative for the verdict among whites was the "reverse-discrimination" or "nullification hypothesis": jurors (and especially black female jurors) acquitted O. J. because he was black – period. Whether it was to "get back" at the system that had so abused blacks in previous eras, to "get back" at the white females that "stole" successful black men from black women, or simply because of a blind solidarity with "their own," the trial was a miscarriage of justice. This notion that blacks are now *getting back* at whites is also implicit in many other politically-charged debates today, e.g .the "reverse racism" of affirmative action. As duCille (1997, p. 334) maintains, "Simpson's acquittal confirmed the widely held, though intensely erroneous belief that blacks are getting away with murder in this country: that they are doing as well or better than whites." Moreover,

> while we were preoccupied with the trials of the century . . . while we were sleeping with O. J., and Nicole and Ron and Kato and Chris and Marcia, Marcia, Marcia – reactionary legislation at the federal state and local levels ended "welfare as we know it," rolled back public assistance, Head Start, and affirmative action programs; limited immigration from the third world; and initiated the three strikes law designed to put even more black men permanently behind bars. . . . Once Simpson walks, whites will riot the way we [whites] do: leave the city, go to Idaho, Oregon, or Arizona, vote for Gingrich . . . and punish blacks by closing their day-care programs and cutting off their Medicaid" (duCille 1997, pp. 333–4).

Of course, for many black Americans, the "race"/"class" narratives were quite different from that of whites. First, as indicated previously, the notion of "colorblindness" is by and large a *white* phenomenon. This is readily apparent in Hunt's (1999) audience reception research on the O.J. trial (discussed in chapter 6 of this book). Hunt (1999, p. 204) found not only that black informants viewed race as a pivotal issue in the case, while white informants did not; in addition, he found that "white informants rarely referred to themselves in racial terms when talking about the case, while black informants openly talked about themselves as raced subjects throughout the discussion."

Moreover, what was most obvious about the O. J. case for African Americans (and not for whites) was that it was shot through with major blunders by both the police and the prosecution. As Gillespie (1997, p. 111) states, "It shouldn't take a jury acquittal to make a black district attorney face the fact that . . . an admittedly racist cop is a detriment to your case if the defendant is black." Of course, this divergence in perception of "law and order" goes *hand in hand* with the white/black differences in colorblindness discussed previously. Whites tend to view "law and order" unsuspiciously (i.e., as a racially neutral system of "justice"), while for many African Americans, constitutional government has been so "twisted and perverted in the promotion of [white supremacy] . . . that African-Americans . . . [regard] law and order as an instrument for their repression" (Berry 1994, pp. 240–1, as cited by Hunt 1999, pp. 72–3). Indeed, some black observers refuse to use the term "criminal *justice* system" at all, opting instead for the term "criminal *law* system." Still others underscore the system's propensity to process blacks by sarcastically referring to it as the "Just-Us" (rather than "justice") system (Hunt 1999, p. 74). This perception is not just black "paranoia." Black males face an incredible 28 percent chance of entering state or Federal prisons in their life times, compared to only a 4.4 percent of white males (Hunt 1999, p. 75).

Finally, African Americans (and not "white" Americans) detected a fervent media "pogrom" against O. J. As Morrison (1997, p. xii) eloquently states:

> The narrative of the entertainment media and their "breaking story" confederates was so powerfully insistent on guilt, so uninterested in any other scenario, it began to look like a media pogrom, a lynching with its iconography intact: a chase, a cuffing, a mob, name calling, a white female victim, and most of all the heat, the panting, the flared nostrils of a pack already eager to convict.

Of course, as Hunt (1999, p. 8) points out, this distinction between how blacks and whites perceived the media's coverage of the O. J. case corresponds to the sharp distinctions between how blacks and whites perceive the media coverage of African Americans in general. In answer to the question, "In general, do you think the news media in the United States is biased in favor of blacks, or is it biased against blacks, or does it generally give blacks fair treatment?," blacks were more than three times as likely as whites to respond that the media are biased against blacks (45 percent versus 13 percent), while whites were nearly twice as likely as blacks to view the media as racially neutral (68 percent versus 35 percent). Hunt (1999, p. 214) concludes:

> Whether the issue was the prosecution and defense cases, science and DNA, domestic violence, wealth and celebrity, race, conspiracy, or the *Primetime* text itself, informant stances could be organized along a single dividing line: white investment in official institutions and accounts (e.g., criminal justice system, the media), black suspicion of them.

In sum, for African Americans, no matter how spectacularly the black man *seems* to "make it" in American society (by acquiring a beautiful, white "trophy wife," a Brentwood mansion, and even by "selling out"), he is still a *black* man. The central notion that transcended class lines was that black men are *always* vulnerable to white lynching.

The Other "Others", Part II: "Hybridization" and Racialization

Thus far, we have focussed on a dominant "black"/"white" symbolic *dichotomy* in the United States. But since the 1980s, many cultural analysts have explicitly turned their attention toward the liminal, *border* areas of racialization. Led by lesbian feminists such as Gloria Anzaldúa and Cherríe Moraga (1981), whose work is devoted to analyzing "the mestizo world view" (the term *mestizo* stems from the Latin term "to mix"), these writers emphasize the ambiguous, labyrinthine identity of American Latinos. Quips the Mexican-born writer Ilan Stavans (1995, pp. 17–18, in a chapter called "Life in the Hyphen"): "divided we stand, without a sense of guilt. Gringolandia, after all, is our ambivalent, schizophrenic *hogar*."[37]

On one hand, hybridization is rooted in US history, geography, and demography. As Stavans (1995, p. 13) points out, "We are all to become Latinos *agringados* and/or *gringos hispanizados*; we will never be the owners of a pure, chrystalline collective individuality because we are the product of a five-hundred-year-old fiesta of miscegenation that began with our first encounter with the gringo in 1492." The facts are that "Los Angeles, first visited by Spaniards in 1769 and founded as a town a few years later, is Mexico's second capital, a city with more Mexicans than Guadalajara and Monterrey combined"; Miami has incorporated some 300,000 refugees from Latin America and become the "second Havana"; and since the 1970s, Puerto Rican identity has given way to Nuyoricanness, a unique blend of Puerto Ricanness and New Yorkese (ibid., p. 15).

But *hybridity* is also a *postmodern* phenomenon. Today, not just "Latinos" but all sorts of folks explore their "mixed" or *hyphenated* roots. Today many different writers conceptualize "race" as not an ascribed (or "given") "genetic" disposition, but a voluntary *choice*, much like "religion." Today individuals go to great lengths to *locate* and *fix* their racial and/or ethnic identities, although fluidity may be the best route *out* of unproductive racial dichotomization.

Conclusion

In this chapter, we have seen that "race" is one of our most salient, volatile systems of meaning in the United States today. We have traced this symbolization historically, and seen the complexities of American racial formation. The point is not that we cannot "move beyond" "race," but that, ironically, the goal of "colorblindness" is shot through with racial symbolization. These systems or patterns of meaning about race – *including* the notion of "colorblindness" – were readily apparent in the most spectacular recent media ritual event: the O. J. Simpson trial. Before his abrupt "fall from grace," O. J. was the quintessential "race-neutral" celebrity/athlete; O. J. was *racialized* as an "unmilitant black man," a *hero* for many "white" Americans. However, after the murders of Nicole Simpson and Ron Goldman, white America presumed guilt, and O. J. became a (*still racialized*) "bad" black man – the quintessential dangerous, violent, black male criminal. What is most extraordinary about the O. J. spectacle is that white Americans did not ask jurors (and Americans in general) to not "overcompensate" for America's "past" racial wrongs by judging the "black" defendant too easily. Rather, they asked for "colorblindness" which meant wishing the whole issue of racialization away. Wishing away the issue of race makes sense in a nation in which, indeed, race has histori-cally been an "obsession." But it is not a particularly "realistic" idea. It is like wishing away one's *language* or *culture*. In my view, it makes more sense to try to *understand* this deep symbolic scaffolding, and then to conscientiously try to *change* it. My hope is that this chapter is a first step in that direction.

IMPORTANT CONCEPTS INTRODUCED IN THIS CHAPTER

- Race
- Ethnicity
- Racism
- Racialization
- Stratification
- "Colorblindness"
- "Laissez-faire racism"
- Inferential racism

STUDY QUESTIONS

1   Conduct a mini-survey on "colorblindness" by asking ten people of vary-
    ing "racial" and/or "ethnic" backgrounds the following two questions: "Do
    you think you are "colorblind" when it comes to race? What does being
    "colorblind" mean to you?" Do not simply "report" your results, but try
    to analyze your respondents' answers in terms of the issues discussed in
    this chapter. To what extent do your results confirm Carr's (1997) find-
    ings? In addition, discuss your *relationship* to your respondents (i.e., it is
    quite different to ask these questions of "family members" rather than
    "strangers," especially if racial identities are not the same).

2   Write an autobiographical essay about your own *racial* (not ethnic) iden-
    tity. What does it mean to you to be "white," "black," etc.? Now discuss
    the extent to which these systems of meaning about *race* intersect with
    systems of meaning about *ethnicity*. Do you have a strong "ethnic" (but not
    "racial") identity, or vice versa? How have your racial and ethnic identities
    have been formed *explicitly*? How have they been formed *implicitly*?

3   Pick a favorite television sitcom and videotape five episodes. Now, count,
    and list the characters according to "race." Also note whether they are
    major/minor characters, etc. What are the implicit and explicit racialized
    features that "go" with each character? Who watches this show (if you
    know) – e.g., is it a "white" (or "black") show? What makes this show a
    "black" or "white" (or some other kind of) show?

4   There are many excellent films on the history of race in the United States,
    as well as race and representation. Choose one of the following films, and
    write a one-page response as to how the film reflects, reaffirms, or con-
    tradicts one or more issues introduced in this chapter.
    Eyes on the Prize series, especially *Awakenings*
    In Their Own Image
    Who Killed Vincent Chan

Suggested Further Reading

Cose, Ellis. 1997. *Color-Blind: Seeing Beyond Race in a Race-Obsessed World.* New York:
    HarperCollins.
Du Bois, W. E. B. 1998 [1920]. "The Souls of White Folk," in David Roediger,
    Black on White, pp. 184–203. New York: Schocken.
Gossett, Thomas. 1963. *Race: The History of an Idea.* New York: Schocken..
Hall, Stuart. 1990. "The Whites of their Eyes: Racist Ideologies and the Media," in
    Manuel Alvarado and John O. Thompson, eds., *The Media Reader,* pp. 7–23.
    London: BFI.
hooks, bell. 1992. *Black Looks: Race and Representation.* Boston: South End.
Hunt, Darnell. 1997. *Screening the Los Angeles Riots.* Cambridge: Cambridge Uni-
    versity Press.

——. 1999. *O. J. Simpson Facts and Fictions*. Cambridge: Cambridge University Press.

Jordan, Winthrop. 1968. *White Over Black: American Attitudes Toward the Negro, 1550–1812*. Chapel Hill, NC: Duke University Press.

Lamont, Michèle, ed. 1999. *The Cultural Territories of Race: Black and White Boundaries*. Chicago: University of Chicago Press.

Lott, Tommy L. 1999. *The Invention of Race*. Malden, MA: Blackwell.

Morrison, Toni, and Claudia Brodsky Lacour, eds. 1997. *Birth of a Nation'hood*. New York: Pantheon.

Nelkin, Dorothy, and M. Susan Lindee. 1995. *The DNA Mystique: The Gene as Cultural Icon*. New York: W. H. Freeman.

Omi, Michael and Howard Winant. 1994. *Racial Formation in the United States*, 2nd ed. New York: Routledge.

Ortner, Sherry. 1974. "Is Female to Male as Nature Is to Culture?," in Michelle Rosaldo and Louise Lamphere, eds., *Women, Culture, and Society*. Stanford, CA: Stanford University Press.

Prager, Jeffrey. 1982. "American Racial Ideology as Collective Representation," *Ethnic and Racial Studies* 5: 99–119.

Roediger, David. 1991. *The Wages of Whiteness*. London: Verso.

Spencer, Ranier. 1999. *Spurious Issues: Race and Multiracial Identity Politics in the United States*. Boulder, CO: Westview.

Steinberg, Stephen. 1981. *The Ethnic Myth: Race, Ethnicity, and Class in America*. New York: Atheneum.

Stavans, Ilan. 1995. *The Hispanic Condition*. New York: Harper Collins.

Takaki, Ronald. 1993. *A Different Mirror*. Boston: Little, Brown.

Notes

1 In recent years, scholars such as Niemann (1998, p. 170) have noted that research on race relations and prejudice in the United States has focussed primarily on attitudes and actions between blacks and whites, thereby leaving huge populations out of the equation. Much work remains, for instance, on the concept of "colorblindness" and how it is integrated (or not integrated) into the lives of Asian Americans and Hispanic/Latino Americans (see Edles 2001). However, in this chapter I also focus on the historically volatile "black"– "white" divide *because this is the fundamental binary opposition at the heart of racialization in the United States*. In other words, here I do not seek to illuminate the "experience" and perception of all American racial/ethnic groups; rather, I explore the basic "black/white" symbolic dichotomy that undergirds *all* race/ethnic symbolic configurations.

2 While Holmes's central finding as to the *taken-for-grantedness* of "whiteness" in "white" children, as opposed to the *cognizance* of some sort of "racial" identity in African American children, is both important and consistent with other research, her study is plagued by serious theoretical and empirical problems. As Thorne (1995, p. 602) points out, Holmes pays inadequate attention to the ambiguous, situational, and power-laden nature of racial

and ethnic classifications; she ignores the impact of her own racial identity (white) in the interviews; and most problematically, she insists that she is studying "ethnic" rather than "racial" differences, which, as will shortly see, confuses two different conceptual categories.

3   In the 1960s, the "culture of poverty" thesis, advocated by Oscar Lewis (1959, 1966) and Daniel Moynihan (1965), became a popular explanation of racial/class inequality. The "culture of poverty" thesis emphasized differences in the *"way of life,"* particularly "values and goals," in impoverished (non-white) and middle-class (white) communities. However, Lewis and Moynihan underemphasized the *structural* (i.e., politico-economic) determinants of racial/class inequality, and the media grossly oversimplified and distorted the "culture of poverty" thesis, reducing it to merely "blaming the victim" (i.e., *individual* pathology rather than *cultural* conditions). Sociologists responded by replacing the study of "culture" in the creation and maintenance of poverty with the study of *institutional racism*. This was part and parcel of the structuralist wave of the 1970s (discussed in the introduction of this book). It also led to Wilson's economy-centered approach (explored here), which shares fundamental characteristics with structuralist, economy-centered Marxist perspectives. In recent years, even structuralists, such as Wilson (1996) and Massey and Denton (1993), have turned toward incorporating cultural variables into their arguments; however, they still tend to view culture as secondary and epiphenomenal to *structural* conditions. More generally, the problem is in conceptualizing culture as a "way of life" or static "values," rather than *systems of meaning*. See Roediger (1999 [1991]) and Jung (1999) for two excellent culturalist critiques of structural Marxist approaches to race and class.

4   In *The Bell Curve* (1994), Richard Herrnstein and Charles Murray boldly assert that social achievements are primarily a function of inborn, superior, immutable intelligence, *as measured by IQ tests* (Duster 1995, p. 158). Stephen Jay Gould (1994 as cited by Hauser 1995, p. 149) has summarized *The Bell Curve* as "a rehash of the tenets of social Darwinism" combined with a rehash of scientific racism, the proposal that racial differences in IQ are substantially genetic in origin and cannot be altered by known environmental interventions.

5   It is for this reason that in this chapter, I use both the terms "black" and "African American." Each term has an important component, but does not entirely capture the reality of ethnicity/racialization. Specifically, "black" is a useful term to portray that whether one is Senegalese, Jamaican, Cuban, Nigerian, or Brazilian, or tenth-generation American, people with this particular physical type are classified as "black" and treated accordingly (e.g., by police officers who stop people of this physical type more frequently than those who are "white"). By contrast, the term "African American" is useful in emphasizing a common African heritage, either to distinguish a recent "black" immigrant from a tenth generation "African American"; or to emphasize a common, "pan-African" heritage before involuntary migration.

6   Both because of higher rates of intermarriage and qualitative differences in the *definition* of "white" and "black" that trace back to the "one-drop" rule

(see Omi and Winant 1994, p. 53), more "Asians" and "Latinos" "become white" than do "black" Americans. Indeed, rates of intermarriage are as high as 50 percent for some Asian groups. However, interestingly, today many "multiracial" men and women and couples (including celebrities like Tiger Woods) are resisting the notion that they must choose *one* category to describe their (or their child's) "race"; others are seeking to devise new categories – e.g., "double" rather than "half" – that put a more positive, complex spin on multiracial identity and experience (see Edles 2002).

7   See Karen Brodkin Sacks, "How Did Jews Become White Folks?," James R. Barrett and David Roediger, "How White People Became White," and Kenneth Karst, "Paths to Belonging," in Delgado and Stefancic (1997).

8   This is not to say that the dramatic changes brought about by the civil rights movement came about easily. On the contrary, the racial upsurges of the 1950s and 1960s were among the most tempestuous events in postwar American history (Omi and Winant 1994, p. 95).

9   Interview with the executive director of the Human Relations Commission, Joe Hicks, in the *Los Angeles Times* (May 31, 1998, p. M3). Hicks is a former communist and Black nationalist, who now champions "race neutral" policies. Interestingly, this edition of the *Los Angeles Times* reflects the current media preoccupation with middle-class, black male conservatives. On this day, UC Regent Ward Connerly and the conservative radio show host, Larry Elders, were featured on the covers of the *Parade* and *LA Times Magazine*, respectively.

10   Kinder and Sanders (1996) do not define "symbolic racism" or "racial resentment" as a specifically anti-black phenomenon, but their definition of "symbolic racism" and/or "racial resentment" is also super-individualistic and not cultural. Kinder and Sanders (1996, pp. 36–9) maintain that individual attitudes are shaped by "material interests," "sympathy/ resentment toward social groups," plus "matters of principles."

11   See Gossett (1963) and Lott (1999).

12   Arguments as to the *rationality* of discrimination (e.g., D'Souza 1997) allow "prejudice without guilt" as well.

13   See chapter 6 for more on the concept of "genealogy."

14   Churchill (1998) argues that white colonialists needed to view Indians as *invisible* in order to justify continued occupation of their land.

15   D'Souza (1997, p. 60) argues that Europeans were captivated by the Americas, which they saw as a land largely uninhabited, a land flowing with milk and honey, a land of long beaches, ideal climate, abundant fruits, and singing birds. By contrast, Africa was dark, mysterious, and virtually uninhabitable; Europeans' primary interest in it was confined to gold and slaves. Moreover, in Africa, Europeans suffered from insects and disease, to which Africans had developed immunities. In addition, D'Souza (1997, p. 61) maintains that the "promiscuity" of Africans also confirmed the "link" between animals and Africans for Europeans. Europeans were shocked by African sexual mores (such as the custom for men to show hospitality by offering his wife or daughter for the night). To make matters worse, some African tribes espoused a mythology which traced their own origins to the union of women with animals.

16   D'Souza's history of racialization is at times insightful. However, D'Souza misconstrues both history and motivation by calling these early racist beliefs "rational." Specifically, D'Souza (1997, p. 64) maintains that "whatever its later career, racism began as part of a *rational* project to understand human differences" (emphasis added). But as contemporary culturalists as well as sociologists such as Erving Goffman eloquently show, neither *sincerity* or symbolic *sense* makes actions "rational." "Science" often takes on the role of the *sacred* in modern, western, society – our reliance on "scientific proof" is also a reflection of the "nonrational" cultural realm. For more on culturalist definitions of "rational" and nonrational," see Alexander (1987, p. 10). Relatedly, Cose (1997a, p. 231) points out that, for the most part, slave owners did not "hate" their slaves; they simply did not see them as fully human, let alone consider them equals.

17   These arguments were also reaffirmed by Charles Darwin's notion of "natural selection" in his groundbreaking *Origin of the Species*, first published in 1859.

18   Of course, anti-Asian legislation emerged again in World War II, when more than 100,000 Americans of Japanese ancestry were relocated to internment camps (Espiritu 1999, p. 42).

19   Relatedly, Hodes (1997) found that a white husband who accused his wife of adultery with a black man in the nineteenth century was usually granted a divorce, but she could find no cases in which a white wife whose husband begot "mulattoes" was granted a divorce.

20   Taylor (*Esquire* v. 122, n. 1, July 1994): 46 (viewed on Internet). The Rosewood massacre was the subject of a recent docudrama, called *Rosewood* (1997), directed by John Singleton.

21   Despite preponderant evidence (including one eye-witness), an all-white jury found the white defendants "not guilty". The defendants admitted their guilt to a journalist years later. However, the Emmett Till case turned into an important media ritual event. Till was from Chicago; he had been murdered in Mississippi where he was visiting relatives. From Chicago, Till's mother spoke eloquently and candidly to the media about her son's tragic death; a photo of Till's brutalized face appeared on the cover of *Ebony* magazine. For a most moving account of this tragedy, see volume 1, "Awakenings", of the award-winning *Eyes on the Prize* video series.

22   The "negro-ape" metaphor was also apparent in the 1940s, after the popular childrens' rhyme, "eenie meanie miney mo, catch a nigger by the toe" was deemed "politically incorrect". Then the popular rhyme became, "eenie meanie miney mo, catch a *monkey* by the toe".

23   From a culturalist point of view, whether filmmakers *intended* for "King Kong" to be a metaphor for the black man or not is not the primary issue, for racialization often works at a relatively *unconscious* level.

24   Interestingly, this notion as to the more "primal" nature of "blacks" in symbolic opposition to the more "civilized" nature of "whites" parallels seminal work by Ortner (1974) on the linkage of "women" and "nature" in symbolic opposition to "men" and "culture" (in the "high culture" sense of the term). Ortner [1974 (in Gould 1997, p. 18)] argues that there are three levels in which the physiological fact of women's *bodies* have significance:

(1) woman's *body and its functions*, more involved more of the time with "species life," seem to place her closer to nature, in contrast to man's physiology, which frees him more completely to take up the projects of culture; (2) woman's body and its functions place her in *social roles* that in turn are considered to be at a lower order of the cultural process than man's and (3) woman's traditional social roles, imposed because of her body and its functions, in turn, give her a different *psychic structure*, which like her physiological nature and her social roles is seen as being closer to nature.

25 Ogbu has been criticized for implicitly adopting a "blame the victim/culture of poverty" stance. The "culture of poverty" thesis overemphasized differences in *values* and *goals* in impoverished and middle-class communities (see note 3). However, here the point is that symbolic frameworks create psychological and emotional *risks* for members of extirpated communities. African Americans in certain extirpated communities *quite rightly* comprehend that adopting certain attitudes and behaviors might smack of the "white" "mainstream." Elsewhere (Edles 1999), I make a similar point about the symbolic *risks* Basque nationalists faced in their negotiations with the central government in post-Franco Spain. Ironically, as we will shortly see, "Asian American" teenagers commonly experience the *opposite* problem: getting good grades, spending a lot of time studying, going to the library, etc. does not mean *denouncing* their "Asian" identity; rather, it *constricts* identity to a narrow stereotype.

26 Cose (1993; 1997b) and Feagin and Sikes (1994) find that middle-class blacks often report feeling estranged from the white world even while mastering it.

27 Lott (1999, p. 12) also maintains that the appropriation of the "Negro-ape" metaphor by African Americans pales beside the advertising industry's shameless interpolation of black bodies.

28 Of course, the other central problem with the "model minority" myth is that it lumps 34 different Asian groups together, though they vary tremendously in terms of education, histories, income, wealth, language, traditions, etc. For instance, Japanese Americans are, as a class, one of the United States' richest "non-white" ethnic groups. But 40 percent of Vietnamese and Cambodian families are welfare-dependent, as are 60 percent of the Mien community, a nonliterate, nomadic, mountain tribe from Vietnam recruited to assist the Central Intelligence Agency during the Vietnam War (Kim 1998, p. 188). Relatedly, whereas some 65.7 percent of Asian Indian men and 48.7 percent of Asian Indian women in the United States have at least a bachelor's degree (compared to 2.3 percent of men and 17.6 percent of women in the total population); only 7 percent of Hmong men have at least a bachelor's degree, and only 3 percent of Hmong women (Espiritu 1999, p. 66).

29 To be sure, one could argue that the "model minority" myth *is* an example of "laissez-faire racism" because it *is anti-black*. But this distorts the *symbolic parameters* of the "myth of the model minority." It ignores both the *negative*

impact of the myth on the "model minority" group itself, and it ignores that the same "not model minority" characteristics (lack of discipline, lack of "value" for education, etc.) can be attributed to *any* "not model minority" (not only "blacks"), as is the case for native Hawaiians and Samoans in Hawai'i.

30   Yet, as early as 1870, Chinese laborers were held up as a model for Irish workers; for instance, in 1870, the editor of *The Nation* maintained: "The Chinese . . . show the usual quickness of their race in learning the process of their new business, and already do creditable hand and machine work" (Takaki 1993, p. 148).

31   After his death, Martin Luther King, Jr. became the symbolic epitome of the "unmilitant black man." Today "Dr. King" (the title *Dr.* or *Reverend* also reflects his "safety") represents civil rights and peaceful change, the sacred symbolic opposite of militant, violent "black power" (epitomized by Malcolm X).

32   Following the Italian semioitician Umberto Eco (1976), who uses diagrams to show how metaphors work (see chapter 6 of this book), I use "cultural maps" to illuminate symbolic *patterns* that are commonly intelligible and widely accessible (see also Edles 1998). These cultural maps do not represent individual shared "values" or internalized "ideologies" at the level of personality; rather they exemplify certain elements of the massive conceptual arena we call "culture." Yet, for both Eco and myself, these maps are purely a *heuristic* device: a bidimensional graph cannot wholly reproduce – indeed, it impoverishes – the associations in terms of both number and dimensions. (This fluidity is represented through the use of curved lines, etc.). The idea is that each symbol can and is linked to various other symbolic networks; these maps merely show a rough estimation of one dimension of symbolization at a fixed point in time.

33   See also Steinberg (1999) who shows that Martin Luther King was well aware of – and dismayed by – the "liberal retreat from race." For instance, in *Why We Can't Wait* (1964, p. 147), King maintained: "Whenever this issue of compensatory or preferential treatment for the Negro is raised, some of our friends recoil in horror. The Negro should be granted equality, they agree; but he should ask nothing more."

34   Significantly, the civil rights movement drew on African American, biblical, and international symbols, images, and tools as well. For instance, the movement's "intellectuals" were largely preachers, who infused their activism with images of bondage and liberation – as embodied in the Exodus, or the theology of Christian redemption (Omi and Winant 1994, p. 99). Martin Luther King also used common African American preachers' strategies (such as call and response), and provocatively adapted the Gandhian philosophy of *satyagraha* (the "sit-in") to the African American situation.

35   Similarly Schwartz (1999, p. 2) points out the cynical nature of revisionist historical constructionism: "Constructionists present Columbus's (and the nation's) sins as matters of fact, but define Columbus's (and the nation's) virtues as 'myths', 'meta-narratives' and 'constructions' concocted by a privileged majority determined to secure its domination over marginalized mi-

norities. Constructionist scholars are actually positivists on the vices of American history while they dismiss its virtues as politically mediated 'representations.'"

36 Indeed, many feminists suspected that there was some male bonding going on when, in the first moments of the white Bronco chase, men were cheering and chanting "Go, O. J.!"

37 As Stavans (1995, pp. 24–5) points out, the terms "Hispanic" and "Latino" are often used interchangeably, but the term "Hispanic" has a more conservative bent (emphasizing European Spanish, rather than indigenous, roots), and both are problematic empirically. "Nowadays the general feeling is that one unifying term addressing everybody is better and less confusing; but would anybody refer to Italian, German, French and Spanish writers as a single category of European writers?" (Or would anybody refer to Irish, Australian, British, Canadian, and US writers as a single category of "Anglo writers"?)

38 See also Spencer (1999), who eloquently argues *against* the new "multiracialist" movement. Spencer maintains that multiracialism *reaffirms* rather than "destabilizes" the race construct, for it "requires the explicit acknowledgment of biological race in order to arrive at the alleged existence of multiracial individuals" (p. 193). He takes an "antiracial" rather than "multiracial" position because he considers the assertion of multiracial identity "every bit as untenable and inconsistent as the monoracial myth on which it is founded" (p. 6).

PART TWO

Cultural Methodology: Getting a Handle on Culture

Thus far, we have focussed on what culture is, how culture works, and why understanding culture is important. In chapter 2, we explored religion and ideology; we saw how fundamental processes at the heart of religion (e.g., the dichotomization of the sacred and profane) reflect the workings of culture in general. In chapter 3, we focussed on how the media and popular culture shape and reshape meaning. In chapter 4, we analyzed "race" and representation; we saw how patterns of symbols (or systems of meaning) about "race" subtly (and not so subtly) inform our actions and view of the world.

In the second part of this book, we look at *methods* for studying culture and society. We ask, given that we know what culture *is,* how do we go about identifying and analyzing critical cultural elements? How do we get a handle on culture?

We begin our discussion of cultural methodologies with a look at "naturalistic" research which is rooted in the "ethnographic" conceptualization of culture as an "entire way of life" (see chapter one). The goal in this type of research (which is called "ethnography", "field research", as well as "participant observation") is to *document* the particular "way of life" of a social group as it is "naturally" found. We then explore recent sociological innovations, including dramaturgical theory, ethnomethodology, and conversation analysis, which also seek to "capture" *naturally occurring* social behavior and action in detail.

In chapter 6, we turn toward exciting new ways to explore culture in the *symbolic* rather than *ethnographic* sense (see chapter 1). We explore quantitative and qualitative forms of textual analysis, and various ways to analyze texts/discourse rooted in different disciplinary traditions (e.g.,

Table 5.1 Types and characteristics of qualitative methods

Method	Primary empirical focus	Central realm of analysis	Contemporary exemplar (featured in this book – chapter)	
Traditional ethnography	Entire "way of life" of social group	Cultural (ethnographic)	Bourgois Duneier J.W. Gibson	(5) (5) (7)
Dramaturgical theory	"Interaction order"	Social	Goffman Leidner	(5) (5)
Ethnomethodology/ conversation analysis	"Natural" social order/ conversational interaction	Social mechanisms	Garfinkel Schegloff Weider	(5) (5) (5)
Semiotics/discourse/ narrative analysis	Systems of meaning	Cultural (symbolic)	Carbaugh Hays Hunt Jacobs Wagner-Pacifici Morrison Lipsitz J. Gamson J. W. Gibson	(6) (6) (6) (6) (6) (6) (6) (7) (7)
Frame analysis			Goffman Eliasoph	(7) (7)
Audience/reception studies	Individual interpretation	Cultural (symbolic)	Hays Hunt Radway J. Gamson	(6) (6) (6) (7)
Cultural history	Systems of meaning	Cultural (symbolic)	E. P. Thompson Schmidt J. W. Gibson	(6) (6) (7)
Social history	Social experience	Social	E. P. Thompson Clark-Lewis Schmidt	(6) (6) (7)

linguistics, history). In addition, we will explore audience/reception studies that highlight *individual* interpretation. We will see that, today, many cultural analysts use both discourse analysis and audience/reception research in order to understand processes of "encoding" as well as "decoding" (although they do not necessarily use this terminology, or explore "encoding" and "decoding" to the same degree).

In chapter 7, we explore the discursive approaches of Erving Goffman and Pierre Bourdieu, who explicitly situate culture structures in social frameworks, while accounting for individual experience and interpretation. We conclude this chapter (and this book) by highlighting a few recent exemplars in what I call *comprehensive* cultural sociology. For today cultural sociologists such as J. Gamson (1998) and J. W. Gibson (1994) provide rich, theoretically provocative, methodologically rigorous, empirical accounts of the complex interpenetration of culture and social structures, without undermining individual agency.

Table 5.1 summarizes a few of the basic characteristics of the types of qualitative research discussed in this section.

C H A P T E R   F I V E

Naturalistic Inquiry: Ethnography, Ethnomethodology, and Dramaturgical Research

The oldest and best-known method for getting a handle on "culture" has alternatively been called "fieldwork," "ethnography," or "participant observation." Some analysts use the term "naturalistic" to refer to this type of research, because the basic premise behind it (no matter what the label) is that it is done in a "natural" environment. The idea is for the researcher to observe and engage in a nonmanipulated "natural" environment directly and intensely, over an extended period of time. The assumption is that reality exists in textured and dynamic detail in the "natural" environment of the social world, and that the naturalistic researcher must strive to richly and accurately describe these "dense" realities without unduly disrupting – and thus distorting – them in the process (Gubrium and Holstein 1997, p. 19).

Put in another way, the hallmark of "naturalistic" ethnography/observation studies is "noninterventionism." As veteran ethnographers Patricia and Peter Adler (1998, p. 80) maintain:

> Observers neither stimulate nor manipulate their subjects. They do not ask the subjects research questions, pose tasks for them, or deliberately create new provocations. This stands in marked contrast to researchers using interview questionnaires, who direct the interaction and introduce potentially new ideas into the arena, and to experimental researchers, who often set up structured situations where they can alter certain conditions to measure the covariance of others.

Similarly, Herbert Blumer (1969, p. 46, as cited by Clough 1992, p. 30) maintains that what characterizes the naturalistic method of participant observation is that it "respects and stays close to the empirical domain." Rather than "preset images" becoming a "substitute" for "first hand acquaintance with the sphere of life under study" (p. 37), naturalistic observation permits a "faithful reportorial depiction" of the empirical world (p. 152).

As this last comment makes clear, "naturalistic" observation research also relies on an assumption of *realism*, i.e., the notion that there is a concrete "reality" "out there waiting to be uncovered" and articulated by the researcher. Most significantly, the assumption is that this "reality" precedes and proceeds unimpaired by the ethnographer. As Adler and Adler (1998, p. 81) maintain:

> Observers follow the flow of events. Behavior and interaction continue as they would without the presence of a researcher, uninterrupted by intrusion . . . . Qualitative observation . . . occurs in the natural context of occurrence, among the actors who would naturally be participating in the interaction, and follows the natural stream of everyday life . . . . Qualitative observers are not bound, thus, by predetermined categories of measurement response, but are free to search for concepts or categories that appear meaningful to subjects.

The Origins of Ethnography

Today, many different types of analysts "take to the field" in order to understand a wide variety of phenomena. However, "field research" is most firmly rooted in the discipline of anthropology. Not only does the methodology of fieldwork set anthropology off from other social sciences; "fieldwork," i.e., "a lengthy stay in an 'exotic' culture," "is *the* central *rite of passage* serving to initiate and anoint a newcomer" to the discipline (Van Maanen 1986, p. 14, emphasis added).

Yet, as Van Maanen also notes, anthropology has not always been based on direct observation. Rather, when anthropology first emerged as a discipline in Britain in the nineteenth century, anthropologists were "thinkers" and intellectuals who merely put together slabs of notes gathered by travelers and "men on the spot." The Darwin-like idea was to classify and compare societies and show how a single culture evolved from the savage to the civilized (Stocking 1968, 1987, as cited by Van Maanen 1986, p. 15). Van Maanen (1986, p. 16) states that, far from going "eyeball to eyeball with the 'Bongo Bongo'," ethnography was either a "speculative form of social history carried out by anthropologists who for the most part remained seated in their writing workshops or it was carried out as a canonical count-and-classify social science based on a stiff form of interviewing." In either case, these analyses were shot through with ethnocentric assumptions and imposed categories, and grounded almost entirely on what people said, rather than what they did (ibid.).

The move toward "open-air" ethnography is traced to the Polish anthropologist, Bronislaw Malinowski. Under house arrest by the British for the duration of World War I, Malinowski was forced to live alongside the natives of the Trobriand Islands in the South Pacific for several years. This led to one of the first "modern" ethnographic studies, *Argonauts of the Western Pacific* (1922). In the United States, anthropologists such as Franz Boas also pushed students out of the university and into the daily lives of the people about whom they wrote. "The crucial contribution of both men was to urge students to stop relying on second-hand reports for the analysis of culture (native or pen-pal) and go to the field themselves to collect their own data" (Van Maanen 1986, pp. 16–17). The central methodological premise now was that *only* through living and experiencing what "the natives" are up to in their own natural environment, can a researcher really come to "know" the people and way of life s/he is studying; *only* an eyewitness ethnographic account is a legitimate account of the society in question.

Sociological fieldwork first emerged in the United States and Britain around the turn of the twentieth century. As in anthropology, the purpose of sociological fieldwork was to come to know and document the "way of life" of a particular, geographically bounded social group. However, in contrast to anthropology, sociological ethnography was undertaken in conjunction with social reform movements, and the object of study was not a distant, "primitive," "third- world" "tribe" – but dispossessed and marginalized groups within one's *own* community. Most importantly, British researchers, such as Sidney and Beatrice Webb, sought to document – and thereby help alleviate – the "unseen" conditions of London's urban poor. In a parallel way, the African American sociologist W. E. B. Du Bois wrote a monograph called *The Philadelphia Negro* (1899), in which he called attention to the plight of Philadelphia's urban poor, with whom he lived during his study.[1]

Just before the great Depression, a school of activity which came to be known as the Chicago school of urban ethnography emerged at the University of Chicago. It began when Robert Park and his associates at the university (most importantly, W. I. Thomas and Ernest Burgess) encouraged their students to explore ethnic enclaves, urban communities, and "exotic" urban subcultures, e.g., taxi dancers, urban gang members, and hobos (Cressey 1932, Thrasher 1927, Anderson 1923, as cited by Van Maanen 1986, pp. 16–19).[2] In the 1940s and 1950s, this program expanded, as Chicago students under the direction of C. Everett Hughes began to branch out and study "mainstream" American groups and communities. Public school teachers, funeral directors, policemen, business executives, and machinists now became objects of study (Becker 1951, Habenstein 1954, Westley 1951, Dalton 1951, Roy 1952, as cited by Van Maanen 1986, p. 20).

However, in contrast to anthropology (where fieldwork was understood as the "only" way to document the entire "way of life" of a particular isolated, "primitive" social group or community); in sociology, ethnographers have long been vulnerable to *positivistic* (or "scientific") standards and criteria.[3] Since Durkheim's seminal quantitative study, *Suicide* (1897), sociology has prioritized quantitative over qualitative analysis (although this point is not without debate); and introductory textbooks routinely focus on quantitative rather than qualitative methods (this is rarely contested).[4] In short, in sociology, there are *other*, more "scientific" ways than fieldwork to document the empirical realities of modern, industrial society. From a positivistic point of view, no matter the length of time the author spends getting to "know" an area or subject, ethnographic "data" it is still idiosyncratic, impressionistic, and descriptive. The problem is that "single case studies" – no matter how well researched – do not show *causality*; they do not produce findings that enable *generalization*.

Yet ethnography has long had a "place" in mainstream sociology. Traditionally, ethnography has been construed as most "appropriate" for studying deviant or marginalized groups – i.e., *subcultures* not amenable to "survey" or other statistical (read "real") research methods. That ethnography is especially suitable for specific *types* of inquiries seems clear in exemplary, canonical ethnographic studies, such as Becker's (1953) study of marijuana users, or Humphreys's (1970) analysis of homosexual encounters in public restrooms. These works have become sociological "classics" precisely because they fit into this category; the "data" gathered by the authors about these particular groups and their activities could not be acquired any other ("conventional") way. Once again, the parallel to traditional, "naturalistic" anthropological ethnographies is clear: participant observation is most suitable for projects in which the purpose is to "find out" and "document" the workings of "exotic," relatively unknown, and marginalized social groups.

Relatedly, introductory sociology textbooks often tout ethnography as a handy "preliminary" or "exploratory" tool. They suggest that the central "advantage" of participant observation is that it enables one to come up with the very *categories* with which to use in *future*, more systematic ("real" or "viable") empirical research. However, in either case – whether as an "exploratory tool" or as a tool for studying "exotic" or "marginalized" social groups – the mainstream sociological attitude toward ethnography has been that it is a "last-ditch" methodology. One *resorts* to ethnography *if* one cannot get "scientific" information, i.e., if information cannot be uncovered in any other way.

Yet the problem with this perception is that it unnecessarily restricts ethnography to *descriptive, microscopic* analysis. It confines ethnography to simply identifying and describing the dynamics and characteristics of *particular*, small social groups or communities, many of which were literally "subcultures" or "sub-societies" in that they were subordinate, subaltern, or subterranean (Thornton 1997, p. 4). However, as we will see, implicitly or explicitly, ethnographers often have more *general* concerns.

Ethnography under Fire: The Postcolonial and Feminist Challenge

Thus far we have seen that "ethnography" has traditionally been *the* methodological approach in anthropology (though somewhat marginalized in sociology). However, beginning in the 1970s, the taken-for-granted legitimacy of ethnography as a viable anthropological method – and the very *raison d'être* of cultural anthropology – was challenged. The questions were political, epistemological, and methodological: who gets to say what about whom, and why? What are the interests and motivations behind *alleged* ethnographic "realism"?

Most importantly, as colonized nations gained their independence in the 1970s, anthropology came to be seen as a *colonial* discipline. Recall that anthropology first emerged in the late 1800s when white Western "adventurers" sought to "document" and "place" "primitive," "uncivilized" peoples and tribes within a universalized evolutionary framework in which the epitome was European civilization. The *object* of study was the "primitive Other," while the *audience* and *author* were "Western" Europeans.

Just as damning as the colonial *history* of anthropology was the colonial *attitude* of the Western researcher. Anthropologists imagined themselves as either (1) value-free observers, neutrally "documenting" what was going on; or (2) "helpers" or "advocates" for the "tribe" (for instance, by providing medical and/or other goods and supplies, and serving as a translator or intermediary between the tribe and Western governments and/or international organizations). Ironically, anthropologists warned that "bias" impedes one from "accurately" studying one's *own* group – but they ignored how "biases" impeded them from "accurately" "documenting" "the Other."[5] And even when ethnographers *did* acknowledge their own biases, they tended to construe them as *personal* (rather than political, economic, social, or cultural), i.e., they trivialized their biases by making them *seem* relatively innocuous and idiosyncratic, a matter of *individual* personality and "inspiration."

However, in the 1970s, "postcolonialists" began to view the Western anthropological ethnographer not as a "neutral conduit" (let alone a "helper" or "advocate" on the *same side* as the "tribe") – but as just another *colonizer*. Like the missionaries, industrialists, and militarists that came before them, anthropologists were now seen as arrogant, aggressive, ethnocentric intruders. Most importantly, from this point of view, it was not simply that the Western ethnographer was writing *biased* accounts from a position of "privilege"; s/he was *exploiting*, even *raping* indigenous peoples of their culture, *using* the sacred details of their lives to titillate and entertain Western viewers.

One of the most famous of these postcolonial critics is the esteemed Columbia University professor, Edward Said. Said (1978) maintains that "Orientalism", i.e., the Western obsession with the exotic, non-Western "Other," is a system of *domination*. Orientalism establishes authority over the Other through knowledge of and access to the Other's language, history, and culture as a privilege of the colonial agent. The power of knowledge lies in the authority to define the colonized subject and determine its fate (Lee 1999, p. 114). Said states (1979, p. 32): "to have such knowledge of such a thing is to dominate 'it', to have authority over 'it' . . . . Since we know it and it exists in a sense as we know it" (cited by Lee 1999, p. 114).

In addition, Said (1978) argues that ironically, Orientalism actually tells us more about the white, Western world than it tells us about Eastern and Arab cultures. Western ethnographies articulate and reify European worldviews much more so than they illuminate that of the "natives." The Orient functions "as a theatre, a stage on which a performance is repeated" (Clifford 1986, p. 12). During this narrative performance, Western constructions of reality supplant those of the "natives" they allegedly wish to understand.

So thorough is Said's disdain for "writing the Other" that he rejects "writing culture" altogether. For Said "writing culture" *obscures* more than it clarifies, for writing culture is *necessarily* about *domination*. As he states (1978, p. 325):

> How does one *represent* other cultures? What is *another* culture? Is the notion of a distinct culture (or race, or religion, or civilization) a useful one, or does it always get involved either with self-congratulation (when one discusses one's own) or hostility and aggression (when one discusses the 'other')?

In a similar vein, since the 1970s, feminists have challenged the androcentricity (male- centeredness) of traditional ethnography. Feminists have shown that ethnographies have been conducted mainly by "male fieldworkers concerned mostly with the comings and going of male natives" (Van Maanen 1988, p. 37, fn. 4). Consequently, a great many portrayals of "cultural truths" actually reflect male domains of experience (Clifford 1986, p. 18). Although there are important exceptions (most importantly Margaret Mead's work, which will be discussed shortly), in much ethnographic research, women are simply "there"; it is not seen how women contribute to the social settings of which they are part (Reinharz 1992, p. 51).

Indeed, "androcentricity" is readily apparent not only in classic anthropological books and films (e.g., Evans-Pritchard's *The Nuer*; Chagnon's work on the "fierce" Yanamano), but in classic Chicago school ethnographies. As Lois Easterday and her colleagues (1977, p. 62; see also Reinherz 1992, p. 54) point out, canonized sociological ethnographies, such as Whyte's *Street Corner Society*, Liebow's *Tally's Corner*, and Humphrey's *Tea Room Trade*, basically focus on only three types of settings: primarily male (those dominated in number and power by men), traditional male–female (those dominated in power but not in number by men), and nontraditional male–female (those in which women occupy some positions of power). These studies are male-oriented not only because they were carried out by male researchers, focused on male-dominated settings, and focused on male behavior; but because they pose their methods and findings as generic.

Recently, the psychoanalytic feminist Patricia Clough (1992) has taken the feminist critique of traditional "naturalist" ethnography (and particularly the Chicago school) even further. Clough argues that it is not only the manifest "position of power" and personal "style" of the researcher that lends authority in naturalist ethnography. Rather, Clough (1992, p. 6) maintains that an *Oedipal logic* informs traditional, realist ethnography as well. This invisible force that works to constitute "realist" ethnography is *unconscious"desire"* (Gubrium and Holstein 1997, p. 85). "Realist" ethnography sustains itself by denying what it simultaneously desires, that is, a highly proximate world to penetrate and probe. This is most readily apparent in Herbert Blumer's (1969, p.40) metaphor of "lifting the veil":

> The metaphor that I like is that of lifting the veils that obscure or hide what is going on. The task of scientific study is to lift the veils that cover the area of group life that one proposed to study . . . . The veils are lifted by getting close to the area and by digging deep into it through careful study . . . . This is not a simple matter of just approaching a given area and looking at it. It is a tough job requiring a high order of careful and honest probing.

Clough (1992, p. 6) maintains that this Oedipal logic first developed as a narrative logic of mass media throughout the eighteenth century, culminating in the realist novel. Whether it is found in novels, films, or ethnographies, realist narrativity gives an appearance of wholeness and completeness to the empirical world (Clough 1992, p. 37).[6] In sum, for Clough, "ethnographic authority, and the distinct social worlds ethnographers authoritatively describe, unconsciously stem from (masculine) narratives of separation and identity" (Gubrium and Holstein 1997, p. 85). "Through their methods of inquiry, naturalistic qualitative researchers unconsciously desire the very world they purport to represent" (Gubrium and Holstein 1997, p. 85), though realist narrativity "makes narrative appear as if nearly dead, dead to desire" (Clough 1992, p. 3).

The Margaret Mead Scandal

In the 1980s, the postcolonial challenges to anthropology came to a head in an explosive scandal involving none other than the legendary "Mother-Goddess" of anthropology, Margaret Mead (Freeman 1999, p. 208). Mead, who was the most famous student of the Chicago anthropologist Franz Boas, shot to prominence after the publication of her book, *Coming of Age in Samoa* (1928), which "documented" the sexual promiscuity and "erotic freedom" of young Samoan girls. Based on several months of fieldwork in Samoa (completed in 1925–6), Mead argued that the "smooth," unproblematic sexual transition of Samoan adolescents proved that it was culture, not physiology, which "determined the calmness or explosiveness of adolescence," i.e., that American teenage angst had cultural (rather than physiological) origins.

However, in 1988, the Australian anthropologist Derek Freeman made the astonishing claim that Mead's "exciting revelations about sexual behavior were in some cases merely extrapolations of whispered intimacies, whereas those of greatest consequence were the results of a prankish hoax" (1999, p. 1). In a most damning sworn testimony, Fa'apua'a Fa'amu, one of the adolescents studied by Mead in 1925–6 (and now in her eighties) maintained that "numerous times" she and her friend "just fibbed" to Margaret Mead. Mead "failed to realize that we were just joking" when they said that at night they "go out with boys." "Margaret accepted our trumped up stories as though they were true." Mead failed to realize that "Samoan girls are terrific liars when it comes to joking" (Freeman 1999, p. 3).

The significance of this scandal cannot be overstated. Mead was one of the most celebrated anthropologists of the twentieth century; *Coming of Age in Samoa* was one of the bestselling anthropology texts of all time; and Mead's categorical conclusions (as to the primacy of "nurture" over "nature") were "common knowledge" and went unchallenged for over fifty years. However, even more paradoxically, until as recently as a decade ago, *Coming of Age in Samoa* was unilaterally heralded as a *methodological* exemplar – "a classic scientific study" that set "new standards for anthropological fieldwork."[7]

Clearly the "hoax" on Margaret Mead reaffirms the traditional *positivist* criticisms of ethnography: the problem with Mead's "fieldwork" was that her data were neither "reliable" or "valid." However, in addition, the "hoax" on Margaret Mead reflects the *postcolonial* and *psychoanalytic* objections to "traditional" anthropological fieldwork, i.e., the *Orientalizing* to which Said referred, and the "unconscious desire" to which Clough referred as well. Fa'apua'a Fa'amu simply told Mead what she *quite rightly imagined* that Mead wanted to hear. Moreover, Mead's "fieldwork" was not only steered by – it *canonized* – the symbolic opposition between the non-white Polynesian seductress, and the repressed, white *femme fatale* (i.e., the passionless Victorian True Woman as the moral center of the chaste and obedient social order) (Lee 1999, p. 89).

Sadly, even though Mead mis-celebrated the "freedom" of the "hypersexualized" exotic Other, Polynesian women (and sometimes Asian or Asian American women) are still often portrayed as "hypersexual" (e.g., the Polynesian seductress in tourist advertising – see figure 5.1). Relatedly, Espiritu (1997, p. 13) maintains that Asian men are often portrayed as "asexual" – but both the stereotype of the female Asian "seductress" and the "asexual" Asian man exist to define and confirm the virility and superiority of the white male. For instance, Lee (1999, p. 85) maintains that Oriental sexuality is constructed as a "'third sex'. . . a gender of imagined sexual possibility." "Ambiguous, inscrutable, and hermaphroditic; the Oriental (male or female)" is potentially subversive and disruptive to heterosexual orthodoxy (Lee 1999, p. 88).

Postmodern Ethnography

Thus far we have seen that postcolonialists and feminists both challenge the *privileged* "gaze" of the white, male, Western ethnographer. Yet postmodernists take this criticism one step further. They argue that *no one* writes from a "neutral" position, and thus the problem is not simply one of "setting the record straight." From a postmodern point of view, whether one is an "expert" or a "native," "male" or "female," "insider" or "outsider," etc., culture is inherently "contested, temporal, and emergent"; and representation and explanation is inherently partial (Clifford 1986, pp. 18–19). Postmodernists render problematic any talk of "real" social relations; they doubt the possibility of *any* totalizing or exhaustive theory or explanation.

Figure 5.1   "See the other side of Tahiti!": travel advertisement for Tahiti and the South Pacific, *Los Angeles Times*, June 11, 2000. Reproduced by permission of Renaissance Cruises, Inc.

For instance, James Clifford (1986) emphasizes that *writing* ethnography is an "interpretive" process, far more complex than *either* "documenting" "reality" or "debunking" information. The ethnographer *imposes* a narrative on (rather than merely "documents") "reality" – for "reality" does not exist as a preexisting entity to be "uncovered." Metaphor, figuration, and narrative all "affect the ways cultural phenomena are registered, from the first jotted 'observations', to the complete book, to the ways these configurations 'make sense' in determined acts of reading" (Clifford 1986, p. 4). As Clifford (1986, p. 6) states:

> Ethnographic writing is determined in at least six ways: (1) contextually (it draws from and creates meaningful social milieux); (2) rhetorically (it uses and is used by expressive conventions); (3) institutionally (one writes within, and against, specific traditions, disciplines, audiences); (4) generically (an ethnography is usually distinguishable from a novel or a travel account); politically (the authority to represent cultural realities is unequally shared and at times contested); and (5) historically (all the above conventions and constraints are changing). These determinations govern the inscription of coherent ethnographic fictions.

For radical postmodernists,[8] the very notion of "*genres*," of division between "ethnographic writing," "travel writing," and "journalism" – and even "fiction" and "nonfiction" – are false. The categorization of writing into "literature" (e.g., autobiography, fiction) and the "social sciences" (e.g., "sociology", "ethnography", etc.) is, at best, a distinction in "style," and at worst, an insidious discursive strategy whose underlying purpose is to assert authority, dominate, and maintain privilege. In either case, disciplinary divisions and categories are *myths*; hence, there is no need to sustain them. "Postmodern ethnographers" therefore mix styles and genres; they blend autobiography, biography, and ethnography, and even "fiction" and "nonfiction."

For instance, the postmodern ethnographer (and sociologist) Laurel Richardson pointedly blends literary and "social scientific" "styles" in order to come up with a new, more open mode of representation (which she calls "postmodern ethnography"). Quoting Robert Frost, who first suggested that "the shortest emotional distance between two points" is the poem, Richardson (1992) converts 26 pages of transcribed tape describing the life of an "unwed mother named Louisa" into a three-page poem, called, "Louisa May's Story of her Life" (Denzin 1998, p. 319). Richardson maintains that a poem *better* conveys the life story of her subject than would a traditional documentary-style paragraph. Richardson was particularly concerned that a "transcript" of her interview with Louisa May might not faithfully represent its lived qualities, particularly its "core" tone (Gubrium and Holstein 1997, p. 93). Richardson did not want the reader to view Louisa's life story as simply "data", a search for "background variables", etc., to explain what Louisa May says and does; hence she emphasizes not standard demographic variables (such as race, class, age, etc.), but Louisa's "words, her tone, her diction" (ibid.).

Thus, like the Pulitzer Prize-winning historian, Edmund Morris (who, as we saw in chapter 3, explicitly melded "fact" and "fiction" in his recent autobiography of Ronald Reagan (1999)), Richardson boldly meshes "fictional" and "nonfictional" styles. Moreover, like Morris, who, as we saw, daringly inserted himself as a fictional character in his "biography," Richardson melds her own writing desires and experience *with* that of her respondent. Rather than imagine that her own interests and desires are not reflected in her writing, Richardson admits that she chose poetry as her medium not only in order to better convey *Louisa's* story, but because "a part of me that I had suppressed for more than eight years demanded attention: the part that writes poetry" (Gubrium and Holstein 1997, p. 93). In postmodern parlance, Richardson pointedly collapses "subject" and "object," and writes *herself* along with the "Other."[9]

But, the problem is that even radical postmodernists like Richardson still write "the Other" *as well as* themselves. Richardson heroically attempts to present individual "biographies" of main characters in a "naturalistic" way – by using a *literary* rather than a *social scientific* device – but the problem is that the final "account" is still, in fact, *Richardson's*. Furthermore, though she overtly acknowledges the subjectivity involved, Richardson's poetry is not necessarily a "better" reflection of the "essence" of Louisa's life than a less self-reflexive documentary transcription. As Geertz (1988, as cited by Clandinin and Connelly 1998, p. 173) points out, "being there in the text" is even more difficult than "being there in the field." The dilemma is that too vivid an ethnographic signature runs the risk of obscuring the field and its participants; too subtle a signature runs the risk of deceiving the reader into thinking that the text speaks from the point of view of the participant (Clandinin and Connelly 1998, p. 173).

In sum, postcolonialists and postmodernists have quite rightly criticized traditional "naturalist" ethnography for vicariously reflecting and reaffirming the sensibilities and worldview of the ethnographer (rather than the subject). But ironically, postmodernist ethnography seems to *increase* the centrality of the ethnographer rather than decrease it, i.e., it results in egocentric "navel-gazing."[10] As Best (1995, p. 128, as cited by Gubrium and Holstein 1997, p. 99) cynically states:

> Today, the post-modernist slogan might be: "out of the streets, into the armchairs". After all, if the analyst inevitably shapes the analysis, the reasoning goes, we should focus our attention, not on the subject of analysis,

but on the analytic act. The focus shifts from social life to the analyst's self, a shift which is self-centered, self-congratulatory, and self-indulgent.

Responding to Postmodernist and Postcolonialist Challenges: The Reflexive Turn

Today, most analysts recognize that field research is not a "straightforward, unproblematic descriptive . . . task based on an assumed Doctrine of Immaculate Perception" (Van Maanen 1986, p. 73). But rather than *collapse* subject and object (as do radical postmodernists like Richardson), most ethnographers today take a less drastic approach – and simply *disclose*, to the best of their ability, exactly where they are "coming from." Today's ethnographers routinely "confess" their own "place" in the field, and how their own actions, attitudes, and mere presence *impact* and *shape* "reality."

For instance, in his recent ethnography on "selling crack" in a Harlem barrio, Philippe Bourgois (1995, pp. 19–22) begins with a story (under the heading "Learning Street Smarts") in which he articulates the dilemmas of being a "white middle-class academic researcher" in an inner-city barrio. In this story, Bourgois confesses as to how he unintentionally "disrespected" "Ray", one of his story's main characters. To quote at length from Bourgois (1995, pp. 19–21):

> In retrospect I wince at my lack of street smarts for accidentally humiliating the man who was crucial not only to my continued access to the crack scene, but also to my physical security. Perhaps, despite my two and a half years of crackhouse experience at that point, I was justified in being temporarily seduced by the night's friendly aura . . . . Perhaps it was also only normal for me to want to bask in my increasingly close and privileged relationship with the "main man". Earlier that week Ray had confided to me the intimate details of his stickup artist past . . . . Perhaps my guard was also down because Ray had just made a point in front of everyone of buying me a bottle of Heineken instead of the fifteen-cents-cheaper can of Budweiser that everyone else had received . . . . I felt even more privileged when I saw that he had purchased a Heineken for himself as well, as if to distinguish us from the run-of-the-mill street drinkers by our distinctively green imported bottles.
>
> Surrounded by all this good feeling and security, I thought it might be a good moment to share my minor media coup from earlier that day: a photograph of me on page 4 of the *New York Post* standing next to Phil Donahue following a prime-time television debate on violent crime in East Harlem. I hoped this would impress Ray and his entourage, raising my credibility as a "real professor", capable of accessing the mainstream world of white-dominated daytime television. I was eager to legitimize my presence because

there were still a few people in Ray's network who suspected that I was an imposter – nothing more than a fast-talking closet drug addict, or a pervert – pretending to be a "stuck up professor". Worse yet, my white skin and outsider class background kept some people convinced to the very end of my residence in the neighborhood that I was really a narcotics agent on a long-term undercover assignment.

I noticed Ray stiffen uncharacteristically as I proudly pushed the newspaper into his hands – but it was too late to stop. I had already called out loudly for everyone to hear "Yo big Ray! Check out this picture of me in the papers!" . . . There was an eager silence as he fumbled awkwardly with the newspaper . . . . I tried to help by pointing directly to the lines where the caption began . . . . [Ray] screwed his face into an expression of intense concentration. I suddenly realized what the problem was: Ray did not know how to read.

This compelling, autobiographical story epitomizes the self-reflexive turn in ethnography. Here Bourgois not only explicitly confesses his "place" in the community he is studying (white, male, middle-class academic in a Puerto Rican, inner-city barrio); Bourgois admits and demonstrates that far from being a neutral "fly on the wall," passively *observing* what is going on, Bourgois's actions – specifically his class-centric (or academic-centric) blunders – explicitly shape the events he is "reporting."

However, while Bourgois conscientiously tries to address postcolonial and postmodern concerns – e.g, the "dilemmas" inherent in being a "white, middle-class" researcher, *impacting* the people/culture s/he studies (i.e., when the goal of ethnography is allegedly to capture *naturally occurring* human behavior) – his "gaze" is *still* strikingly familiar. First, though Bourgois acknowledges his "privileged" position and his need for "legitimation" from the people he is studying, his narrative still rests on traditional, naturalistic, experiential ethnographic authority. He *uses* the above story to tell readers that he has "two and a half years of crackhouse experience"; he *uses* the story to "prove" the "genuine closeness" between himself and Ray. Also typical of the traditional, "naturalistic" (or "realist") ethnographic tradition, Bourgois presents his "problem" of access/impact on the situation as a mere "technical hurdle that can be overcome through methodological skill and rigor" (Gubrium and Holstein 1997, p. 106). The implicit *conclusion* behind the narrative is that despite the significant "hurdles" he had to cross, Bourgois *did*, in fact, successfully get inside the "inner realms" of "*their* worlds." Akin to earlier Chicago school works, the narrative "proves" that Bourgois was really *there* ("on the corner"), in that natural habitat "full of life," really "getting to know" those who were "there."

However, the problem is that no matter how "self-reflexive" and "conscientious" he is, no matter how many bottles of beer he consumes, and no matter how many conversations he and Ray have, Bourgois is not – and never will be – a "member" of the group he is studying. In the end, like many of his Chicago school predecessors, Bourgois is still a "white, middle-class academic" studying an "exotic" inner-city world. In fact, the problems of representation are still unresolved – for the story Bourgois tells is very much *his* story (the story of a white academic unexpectedly faced with illiteracy).

Also akin to earlier urban ethnographers, there is a striking androcentricity to Bourgois's account. Parallel to classic Chicago school ethnographies in which the male gaze on male-oriented activities was equated with "life" on "the corner" as a whole; Bourgois moves seamlessly from his focus on a handful of male crack dealers to a discussion of "life" in the barrio. He (1995, p. 19) justifies moving from the lives and worldview of a handful of crack dealers to the barrio as a whole because, he insists, these crack dealers have "managed to set the tone of public life." But the obvious question is, how does he know this? Bourgois relies on a lone female informant (Candy) to explore the "female" perspective on drug dealing, and he presents the worldview of the "non-drug-using public" simply through *ad hoc* anecdotes about his landlord.

Most interestingly, however, Bourgois's account also seems to reflect the same Oedipal tensions as those of his Chicago school predecessors. For instance, Bourgois imagines himself as *"violating* apartheid," which seems analogous to Blumer's metaphor of "lifting the veil." Yet, even more problematic from a psychoanalytic or feminist point of view, is Bourgois's "confessional" account of brutal street rape:

> Despite the almost three years that I had already spent on the street at the time of this particular conversation, I was unprepared to face this dimension of gendered brutality. I kept asking myself how it was possible that I had invested so much energy into taking these "psychopaths" seriously. On a more personal level, I was confused because the rapists had already become my friends. With notable individual exceptions, I had grown to like most of these veteran rapists. I was living with the enemy; it had become my social network. They had engulfed me in the common sense of street culture until their rape accounts forced me to draw the line. (p. 207)

But what does Bourgois mean by "drawing the line"? The fact is that Bourgois covets his "place" in the field as "one of the boys"; he *revels* in calling these rapists not simply his respondents but his *"friends."* This is precisely why Bourgois does *not* "draw the line" (and actually *challenge* misogynist behavior). His only "challenge" to the boys was what he acknowledges as a patently "weak" appeal to "patriarchal logic" – "Do you ever worry about this happening to your sisters?" (p. 211).[11]

Moreover, Bourgois readily admits that "most of the dozens of tape recordings I collected on the subject [of rape] came from the perspectives of the perpetrators" (not the victims), and he confesses that he did not have the "same kinds of long-term relationships with [the few survivors whose accounts he did get] to allow for the detail and confidence of a meaningfully contextualized life-history interview or conversation" (p. 207). Nevertheless, Bourgois cheerily asserts that women "are not paralyzed by terror. On the contrary, they are in the midst of carving greater autonomy and rights for themselves in El Barrio" (p. 213). However, Bourgois provides no evidence to support this assertion. One wonders *how* women are "carving greater autonomy and rights for themselves in El Barrio," given that, as Bourgois also states, "street culture strives to maintain women in subordinated roles as mothers or as dependent girlfriends." Apparently, Bourgois's belief in the increasing autonomy of women in El Barrio is rooted in conversations with "Candy" ("one of only two females in Ray's network"), even though "Ray's network roundly decried her [Candy's] failings as a single mother and head-of household" . . . and that "one of their recurrent criticisms was that Candy needed a strong male figure to discipline her" (p. 216).

Auto-ethnography

Of course, the most obvious way to "resolve" the problem of writing "the Other" is to *abandon* writing the "Other" altogether. This is the central premise behind "insider ethnography" or "auto-ethnography" – in which one writes about one's *"own"* group. Auto-ethnography has several obvious advantages. First, it circumvents traditional logistical problems of "access" and "confidentiality," etc. Writing about one's own group makes ethnographic rhetorical "games" like "proving" that one was really "there" and is *really* "in the know", etc. (à la Bourgois), moot. In addition, auto-ethnographers maintain that writing from the inside out circumvents the elitism of traditional ethnography, i.e., who gets to say what about whom. In auto-ethnography, subjects speak *directly* for themselves, rather than through an "ethnographic fieldworker" (or "conduit" or "intermediary").

Relatedly, some ethnographers have promoted "informants" from invisible, disembodied conduits for information to "joint authors." As Van Maanen (1986, p. 137) notes, this "let-them-speak-for-themselves" approach compares to the sociological "life history" approach in which "history" is told by the actor him/herself. The idea is to break down the boundaries between "researcher" and "researched," and to present "many voices [clamoring] for expression" (Clifford 1986, p. 15).

However, the problem in writing about one's *own* group is that it may impede identification of fundamental, but latent, social processes that are *taken for granted* by group members. As we have seen, ethnographers have traditionally been warned *against* studying one's "own" group for fear of biases, and a lack of "objectivity."[12] In addition, if we take the postmodernist position seriously, the problem is that simply being a *part* of a group does not authorize one to "write" the group as a whole. The "auto-ethnographer" may not understand how the group looks and works from *other* (also "insider") positions. Indeed, one could argue that the "auto-ethnographer" is *doubly* privileged (rather than *un*privileged): ethnographic authority rests on both being an "Insider" *and* being the "Ethnographer."

But if one speaks only for onself (and not for "the group"), the result is not insider ethnography (or auto-ethnography), but simply *autobiography*. The subject is exclusively and candidly the *self*, the individual researcher. While, as we have seen, for radical postmodernists such as Laurel Richardson, this diffusion of ethnography into "autobiography" is not problematic, this is of utmost concern for *cultural* sociologists, for autobiography addresses individual, personal, psychological issues and dynamics much more so than *patterns* of action or *systems* of symbols.

In short, the problem with postmodernist, confessional, autobiographical, and jointly-authored styles is that they have steered ethnographers *away* from the study of *culture* altogether. While this is most evident in auto-ethnography and autobiography – the epitome of individualistic accounts – aculturalism is evident also in "postmodernist" and "jointly-authored" accounts; for no matter how many "voices" are "heard," no one has the "authority" to *transcend* the "many voices" and speak to the more general *systems* of shared meaning, i.e., the *cultural* realm. In other words, while the *raison d'être* of "messy texts" as Marcus (1994) calls them, is to better capture heterogeneity and "polyphony"; "culture" is *not* the result of simply *adding up* individual experiences/interpretations. Cultural analysis involves *transcending* individual experience in order to identify common symbolic patterns and threads of shared meaning.[13]

Formally Theoretical Ethnography

Thus far we have seen that "naturalist" ethnography is pointedly "descriptive" and "atheoretical." The goal is to "abandon" preconceived ideas, simply *observe* a natural situation or environment, and "report" *whatever* is going on. However, as we have also seen, postcolonialists, postmodernists, and feminists have all challenged the *alleged* "atheoretical" attitude of the ethnographer. These analysts have all pointed out that regardless of their intent, ethnographers necessarily write from a specific *subjective* (and thus *quasi-theoretical*) position.

In direct opposition to the atheoretical and descriptive approach for which ethnography is well known, "formally theoretical" (or "theoretically informed") ethnography refers to work that explicitly situates itself within a concrete theoretical framework. "Formally" theoretical ethnographers *choose* the site for their research for explicit theoretical as well as empirical reasons. Negatively stated, formally theoretical ethnographers have a theoretical "agenda."

One of the earliest and most influential formally theoretical ethnographies is Paul Willis's *Learning to Labor* (1977). In this cultural studies classic, Willis provides a "thick description" of the "way of life" of a group of British "working-class" lads, and, at the same time, demonstrates the workings of a central *Marxist* tenet: "the reproduction of labor." Willis maintains that ethnographers who study "marginalized" groups must not ignore the political and economic waters in which these groups swim in order to survive, especially the political economy of capitalist societies (Marcus 1986, Van Maanen 1988, p. 128).

Specifically, Willis carries out "a case study and five comparative case studies" of working-class boys in northern England schools in order to explain the processes by which "working-class kids get working-class jobs." Willis explores the issue of "*how* labor power is reproduced, how it becomes subjectively apprehended" (Aronowitz 1981, p. xi). Willis focussed on "a group of twelve non-academic working-class lads" (Willis 1977, p. 4), whom he studied "intensively by means of observation and participant observation in class, around the school and during leisure activities; regular recorded group discussions; informal interviews and diaries" (p. 5). Willis also taped long conversations with all the parents of the main group of lads, and with the senior masters of the school. In addition, for comparative purposes, Willis studied a few groups of "working-class conformist lads" and "working-class nonconformist lads" in the same and other schools and in nearby towns.

The theoretical and empirical significance of Willis's study is that it illuminates the actual *workings* of the classic Marxist concept of class reproduction *in situ* at the micro-level. Willis shows *how* the strong backs, "weak minds," and submissive spirits that capitalism demands of the working class are produced in working-class secondary schools. Most importantly, Willis rejects the Frankfurt school supposition that the working class is simply *duped* and *manipulated* into a working-class life. As Willis states (1977, p. 12): "people cannot be filled with ideology as a container is filled with water." Rather, he (*Preface*, p. xii) maintains:

> working-class "lads" create their own culture of resistance to school knowledge. Or, to be more exact, truancy, counterculture, and disruption of the intended reproductive outcomes of the curriculum and pedagogy of schools

yield an ironic effect: the "lads" *disqualify* themselves from the opportunity to enter middle-class jobs. They acquire none of the middle class skills that are the intended result of faithful subordination to the three R's (i.e. discipline preparing them for work). Instead, the students produce themselves as rebellious, "uneducated" workers, whose single choice is the unskilled and semi-skilled occupations found in manual labor.[14]

Willis's groundbreaking formally theoretical ethnography has been well received, but it is not without criticism. The central criticism of formally theoretical ethnographies is that the formally theoretical ethnographer wittingly and unwittingly narrows his/her sights according to his/her preconceived ideas/interests. The *theory* is sovereign; it animates the tale (Van Maanen 1988, p. 131). Marxist-inspired ethnographers, such as Willis, especially, are criticized not only because they tend to ignore the tacit, hidden variables that contradict, or are irrelevant to, the theoretical subject at hand, but because of their "crusading" bent (Van Maanen 1988, p. 129). Marcus (1986, p. 184) asks: "does Willis' articulated critical theory of capitalism really come from the lads?" Van Maanen (1988, p. 131) states: "Whether they blame it on the devil, the sign, the id, the universal myth, the low-protein diets, or the running dogs of capitalism, fieldworkers must tread softly when telling formal tales, for in the end, all representations are contestable. Formal tales alone cannot protect us from the wind."

However, that Willis *uses* Marxist theory to illuminate social processes "above and beyond" the words and actions of "the lads" does not necessarily condemn Willis's study as false. Rather, as Morley (1996b, p. 20) maintains:

> The fact that the analyst finally produces an account of his subjects' activities which is not expressed in their own terms, and which may in fact be different from the account they would offer of their own activities, hardly invalidates it, but is perhaps precisely the necessary responsibility of the analyst. Surely it is better that the analyst's role . . . be explicit, rather than obscured in the editing process, while remaining nonetheless, powerful . . . .

Put in another way, the formally theoretical ethnographer does not necessarily "narrow" his/her sights any more (or less) than the allegedly "atheoretical" ethnographer. As we have seen, the traditional ethnographer does *not* approach his/her subject with a "clean" slate, an "empty" head, but with all kinds of complex and far-reaching assumptions and information. From this point of view, the difference between "theoretical" and "atheoretical" ethnographies is simply that only the former *admits* his/her theoretical orientation. From this point of view, the "theoretically informed" ethnography parallels the "confessional" tale.

Nevertheless, it is also true that "formally theoretical" ethnographers run the risk of veering *away* from their empirical site into more "provocative" theoretical arenas. This is precisely the problem in Bourgois's study of "selling crack in the barrio" discussed previously. Akin to earlier urban ethnographers, Bourgois studies a concrete, geographically *bounded* community (to the extent that he even provides a map as to the exact geographic location of "El Barrio"); however, Bourgois (1995, p. 2) does not set out merely to "describe" the "little world" of the barrio. Rather, citing what he calls "cultural production theory" (which is not really a "theory" at all, but a hypothesis), Bourgois sets out to uncover the "deeper dynamics of marginalization and alienation." He seeks to show that "street culture's resistance to social marginalization is the contradictory key to its destructive impetus ... through cultural practices of opposition, individuals shape the oppression that larger forces impose upon them" (p. 17).

But the problem is that (in contrast to Willis) Bourgois's assertions about a "culture of resistance" remain just that – assertions. For feminists, the obvious question is how is brutal street rape "oppositional"? Oppositional to what? In what way? To be sure, on one hand "street rape" is both "illegal" and counter to *certain* "mainstream" values; misogyny and brutal street rape might also be viewed as an assertion of *power*, a direct response to the "de-powering" (and therefore "demasculization") of impoverished, non-white men. However, at the same time, the misogyny of Bourgois's subjects can also be understood as *perfectly contiguous* with the misogyny evident in "mainstream" rock, heavy metal, and rap music, Hollywood films, and "mainstream" American culture. Indeed, as we have seen, both the dominant American racialized framework and the symbolic framework of the barrio rest on the *super-masculinity* of black (and Latino) men. Thus what would be *truly* "oppositional" would be to *reject* this *super-macho misogyny* and replace it with expressions, norms, and rituals that privilege *compassion* (not aggression), and *effeminate* (not super-macho) men; though, theoretically, the point is that symbolic frameworks are far more fluid and multivocal than that, i.e., ideologies are not hegemonically "adopted" or "resisted" at all.[15]

Symbolic Interaction and Dramaturgical Theory

Willis's formal fusion of neo-Marxism and ethnography broke new theoretical and methodological ground. However, this is not to say that earlier Chicago school ethnographies were entirely "atheoretical." Indeed, Willis's work can be seen as directly challenging the "functionalism" *implicit* in many Chicago school accounts. The hallmark of Willis's study was that it melded a neo-Marxist perspective on the importance of the *reproduction of inequality* with "symbolic interactionist" concerns.

"Symbolic interaction" is a theoretical tradition which traces its lineage to the Pragmatists – John Dewey and George Herbert Mead – and to the "Chicago School", and their successors (McCall and Becker 1990, p. 3). The fundamental principle behind symbolic interaction is that:

> Any human event can be understood as the result of the people involved (keeping in mind that that might be a very large number) continually adjusting what they do in the light of what others do, so that each individual's line of action "fits" into what the others do. That can only happen if human beings typically act in a nonautomatic fashion, and instead construct a line of action by taking account of the meaning of what others do in response to their earlier actions. Human beings can only act this way if they can incorporate the responses of others into their own act and thus anticipate what will probably happen, in the process creating a "self" in the Meadian sense. (This emphasis on the way people construct the meaning of others' acts is where the "symbolic" in "symbolic interaction" comes from.) (Adapted from Becker 1988:18, as cited by McCall and Becker 1990, pp. 3–4)

Thus, symbolic interactionists place great emphasis on *individual agency;* they seek to correct the mainstream sociological supposition that culture or social structure determines what people do. In addition, the theoretical tradition of symbolic interaction is highly *empiricist*: it demands using research to give meaning to its abstract propositions (McCall and Becker 1990, p. 4). As McCall and Becker (1990, p. 5) maintain: "The ultimate interactionist test of concepts is whether they make sense of particular situations known in great detail through detailed observation. You answer questions by going to see for yourself, studying the real world, and evaluating the evidence so gathered." This is why, somewhat confusingly, McCall and Becker (1990, p. 4) call symbolic interaction "an empirical research tradition as much or more than a theoretical position."

In short, the Chicago school pragmatists combined a theoretical concern for locating symbols and the production of meaning in the negotiation of social order with an empirical focus on the actual language and gestures used in human interaction. The idea was to reconstruct the social psychological processes of interaction that constitute the detailed texture of social life (Alford 1998, p. 42). For instance, in his seminal observational study of drug use, Howard Becker (1953) does not use ethnography merely to illuminate the "way of life" of a small, bounded group; rather, he uses it to illuminate the complex *social* processes through which a particular group creates and produces *meaning*. Becker focuses on a specific network of individuals who used marijuana in order to show that it is individuals' *participation* in groups of users that taught them how to respond to the drug. He emphasizes that it is only in the context of a social network that people learn *how* to "get high"; without this socialization, i.e., without the teachings (both explicit and implicit) of the group, novices would not understand how to get "high" and would not continue to use marijuana (Silverman 1993, p. 33). Of course, this is a profound theoretical insight relevant to understanding all sorts of social processes, not just this particular group of drug users.

One of the twentieth century's most brilliant sociologists, symbolic interactionists, and "urban ethnographers" was Erving Goffman. Goffman studied anthropology at the University of Toronto, and earned his Ph.D. in sociology from the University of Chicago in 1953 (Collins 1986). Because of his links with social anthropology and the Chicago school, many analysts describe Goffman as a "symbolic interactionist" in the "urban ethnography" tradition.[16] Indeed, Goffman shared the urban ethnographers' penchant for poignantly identifying and articulating the nuanced characteristics of socially situated groups; and he shared the symbolic interactionists' emphasis on the "self" as "a social product." Goffman was a prolific writer, whose works include eight books, three collections of essays, and at least twenty-eight essays, published from 1951 to 1983 (Branaman 1997, p. xlv).

However, Goffman's work far exceeds the confines of the "symbolic interactionist," "urban ethnographer," or "Chicago school" labels. The term "urban ethnographer" is especially misleading. In contrast to the "naturalist" urban ethnographer (but akin to many a contemporary postmodernist), Goffman's methodology was eclectic and *anti*-empiricist. Goffman abjured all the self-authorizing manners of scientists – appeals to proofs, evidence, etc.; he used *whatever it took* to explain the social world. Indeed, in addition to traditional participant observation, Goffman used newspaper clippings, comic strips, scenes from popular films, cartoons, personal observations and anecdotes, "Dear Abby" columns, etiquette manuals such as those by Emily Post, popular fiction, serious novels, autobiographies, the writings of "respectable" researchers, "informal memoirs written by colorful people" (Goffman 1959, p. xi), and contemporary and ancient theatrical writings. In one essay, called "Radio Talk," Goffman (1981) drew on "eight of the LP records and three of the books produced by Kermit Schafer from his recordings of radio bleepers . . . twenty hours of taped programs from two local stations in Philadelphia and one in the San Francisco Bay area; a brief period of observation and interviewing of a classical DJ at work; and informal note-taking from broadcasts over a three-year period" (Ferrante 1998, p. 73).

Also akin to contemporary postmodernists, Goffman took great liberties with his "data." He rarely provided footnotes, and his ethnographic "incidents" often seem hypothetical. As the following comment suggests, Goffman was not overly concerned with methodological criticisms: "The method that is often resorted to here – unsystematic, naturalistic observation – has very serious limitations. I claim as a defense that the traditional research designs thus far employed have considerable limitations of their own" (Goffman 1971, p. xv, as cited by Adler and Adler 1998, p. 92). Quips the British playwright Alan Bennett (as cited by Lemert 1997b, p. xiv): "Much of Goffman could be a commentary on Kafka. One puts it that way round, the artist before the academic, but the truth one finds in Goffman's work is the truth one goes to fiction for."

Goffman used the term "dramaturgical theory" to refer to his unique approach. The term "dramaturgical" emphasizes Goffman's assumption that (1) the self is a product of the *performances* that individuals put on in social situations, and (2) that the self depends upon the validation awarded and withheld by copresent audiences (Branaman 1997, p. xlvi; emphasis added). In other words, the term "dramaturgical theory" reflects that Goffman was particularly concerned with how people construct their self-presentations and manage them in front of others (Adler and Adler 1998, p. 92). As Brissett and Edgley (1990, p. 37, as cited by Adler and Adler 1998, p. 92) describe this perspective: "The theater of performances is not in people's head, it is in their public acts. People encounter each other's minds only by interaction, and the quality and character of these interactions come to constitute the consequential reality of everyday life."

Thus, Goffman's primary goal was not simply to identify and describe the "way of life" of a particular, situated, urban social group. Rather, he sought to illuminate the *basic* elements at the heart of the social world. He set his sights on uncovering the *layers* of "hidden expiatory functions" behind acts that each of us perform daily (Lemert 1997b, p. xi).

For instance, in one of his most famous works, *Asylums* (1961), Goffman does not simply seek to "expose" the reader to the "way of life" of a marginalized social group. Rather, he seeks to demonstrate the basic principles of the "total institution". He shows that total institutions, like asylums, are "forcing houses for changing persons; each is a natural experiment on what can be done to the self" (p. 12). He demonstrates how "the mental patient is identified by the institution, and has little hope of combating the framework by which his experience is interpreted" (ibid.). "The self of the mental patient is defined by institutional conditions to such an extent that there is little room for maneuvers aimed at maintaining a viable self-image in the eyes of others" (Branaman 1997, p. lvii).

Yet even more importantly, Goffman suggests that *society* in general is analogous to a total institution. As in the mental institution, one of the major preoccupations of everyday life is assessing others' and conveying our own moral character (Branaman 1997, pp. lvii–lviii). Wittingly and unwittingly, we use all sorts of resources – clothing, language, body language, etc. – to "figure out" and convey who we "are." Moreover, our social life is so all-encompassing that it persists even when we are "alone." As Goffman (1981, p. 79), states:

> To be alone, to be a "solitary" in the sense of being out of sight and sound of everyone, is not to be alone in another way, namely as a "single", a party of one, a person not in a *with*, a person unaccompanied "socially" by others in some public undertaking (itself often crowded), such as a sidewalk traffic, shopping in stores, and restaurant dining.

However, Goffman is not a social determinist. On the contrary, Goffman emphasizes that the self is a "stance-taking entity," and that even the most marginalized members of society are capable of preserving their "self" by adopting "postures" of resistance. For instance, Goffman describes how patients make adjustments using resources of the institution officially designed for other purposes to reestablish territories of the self, spheres of autonomy, a separate social structure, and a separate system of status (1961a, pp. 201–3, as cited by Branaman 1997, p. lxi). Most importantly, Goffman argues that this practice of reserving something of oneself from the clutch of an institution is not an incidental mechanism of defense, but an essential constituent of the self (1961a, p. 316, as cited by Branaman 1997, p. lxi). As in the asylum, individuals use whatever is at their disposal to fill in the cracks of the institutional framework.

In sum, rather than be a purveyor of "the exotic," Goffman "is the quintessential sociologist of everyday social life" (Branaman 1997, p. xlv). Goffman wittily demonstrates the "ordinary" in the "extraordinary" as well as the "extraordinary" in the "ordinary." Readers of Goffman are "called into a netherworld in which the peculiar and the familiar are perfectly joined" (Lemert 1997b, p. ix). Goffman shows the basic *social principles*, or "interaction rituals," behind and within the most familiar activities (e.g., riding a merry-go-round) and complex, unfamiliar social worlds (e.g., the mental institution).[17]

Interestingly, since the 1980s, sociologists such as Arlie Hochschild (1983) and Robin Leidner (1993) have extended Goffman's dramaturgical approach into a more *systematic* and methodologically *rigorous* direction.[18] For instance, Robin Leidner's, *Fast Food, Fast Talk* (1993) is a wonderful, "theoretically informed" ethnography that tests and develops the theories of Max Weber and Erving Goffman on *routinization* in the workplace. Leidner wants to identify and sort out the "kinds of tensions and problems that routinizing human interactions creates" (p. 15). Thus, in the spirit of the "formally-theoretical" ethnographer," Leidner *chooses* a site for analysis that would illuminate *routinization* in the workplace.

Significantly, she chooses McDonald's, and an insurance agency called "Combined Insurance", as her sites for observation – not because she thought they were "typical" interactive service organizations, but "because both companies take routinization to an extreme" (p. 14). Leidner's goal is to demonstrate *how* routinization *works*, how it is *achieved*.

However, in studying *two* types of routinized service work, Leidner's study is not only explicitly theoretical but also explicitly *comparative*. In contrast to the traditional ethnographic tendency to implicitly and unsystematically supersede the contextual limitations of data, Leidner explicitly selects two sites for analysis based on *how* she wants us to generalize from these two "cases." Leidner studies McDonald's *and* Combined Insurance because "although these two companies both pushed routinization almost to its logical limits, their public-contact employees did very different kinds of work and had different kinds of relations with service-recipients. The companies therefore adopted dissimilar approaches to routinization, with distinctive ramifications for workers and service-recipients" (p. 15). As Leidner (1993, p. 20) states: "the relevant contrasts are not only between these two jobs, but also those between routinized interactive service work and other kinds of routinized work, and those between routinized service interactions and nonroutinized interactions." Leidner (p. 222) finds that while McDonald's and Combined Insurance share appeals to individuality and friendliness, they differ in the values they draw on to support routinization. McDonald's draws on service routines that appeal to American egalitarianism (the idea that everyone will be treated equally), while Combined relies not on submission to corporate rules, but individual commitment to self-reformation, i.e., "The company presents itself as offering the opportunity to succeed to anyone willing to accept the challenge of self-transformation" (pp. 223).

In my view, formally theoretical and explicitly comparative ethnographies, such as Leidner's, are an important response to the postmodern and postcolonial challenge. Rather than situate the ethnographic study *personally* (as do "confessional" or "reflexive" accounts), these ethnographies situate the study in a cogent theoretical and empirical framework – and this allows findings and conclusions to be modified, rejected, or otherwise challenged.

At the same time, however, it is imperative to recognize that dramaturgical analysts such as Leidner (and Hochschild and Goffman) focus on *social* rather than *cultural* realms of experience (see table 5.1). These analysts seek to illuminate the nature of the self, the nature of social interaction, and the organization of the social world. They discuss symbols as they are used in social life, but their goal is not to map out the relations between symbols, or identify symbolic *patterns*. This dramaturgical emphasis on social interaction contrasts significantly with cultural sociologists' concern with systems of meaning – (though as we will see in chapter 7, in his later work Goffman turned from a more concrete analysis of the self in society toward a seemingly more abstract focus on the subjective cultural *schemas* that "frame" social interaction).

However, in the next section, we focus on a relatively new type of naturalistic inquiry, called "ethnomethodology," and particularly the branch of ethnomethodology called "conversation analysis." We will see that, even more so than dramaturgical analysts such as Leidner, ethnomethodologists and conversation analysts seek to ferret out the *most minute, taken-for-granted* details of the *social* world.

Ethnomethodology

Ethnomethodology literally means the methods people use on a daily basis to accomplish their everyday lives (Ritzer 1992, p. 253). It was "founded" by UCLA Professor of Sociology Harold Garfinkel in the 1940s, but it became much more visible and influential with the publication of his *Studies in Ethnomethodology* in 1967 (Ritzer 1992, p. 257). In this book, Garfinkel turned the traditional Parsonian "problem of order" upside down, by asking not how it is that society *creates* order, but how it is that order exists *despite* social action.[19] Garfinkel (1988, p. 104, as cited by Ritzer 1992, p. 254) focused on "immortal, ordinary, society," and sought to identify and understand everyday action as it is – routine and relatively unreflective.

Specifically, in *Studies in Ethnomethodology*, Garfinkel sought to explain not how the so-called social order is *internalized* by actors who then act out those socially prescribed norms and values, but rather how order is produced as the local achievement of those same actors (Boden 1990a, p. 189). Garfinkel rejected the fundamental sociological conceit (especially prevalent in mass culture theory) that actors' views of their social worlds are somehow flawed or marginal to a full understanding of social phenomena (see Cicourel 1964, as cited by Boden 1990a, p. 189). The basic premise of ethnomethodology is that "people do what they do, right there and then, to be reasonable and effective and they do so for pervasively practical reasons and under unavoidably local conditions of knowledge, action and material resources" (Boden 1990a, p. 189).

Symbolic interactionism, "naturalist" ethnography, and ethnomethodology have much in common (Baert 1998, p. 82). They all focus on patterns of everyday interaction; they all are acutely interested in *actually occurring* or *naturally occurring* instances of social interaction or expression. All focus on the organization of life as it is "locally, endogenously produced."

However, there are fundamental differences between symbolic interaction, "naturalist" ethnography, and ethnomethodology as well. Most importantly, in contrast to the "naturalist" ethnographer, who seeks to "discover" new social worlds simply by "being there," ethnomethodologists maintain that "there is no 'there' until it has been constructed" (Gubrium and Holstein 1997, p. 38). "Whereas naturalists want to be there, inside the worlds of their subjects, ethnomethodologists aim to describe the natural as a matter *in the making*" (ibid.). Ethnomethodology provides "a way of questioning which begins to reveal the richly layered skills, assumptions and practices through which the most commonplace (and not so commonplace) activities and experiences are constructed" (Pollner 1987, p. ix). "Worlding, not the world, is the object of ethnomethodological inquiry, shifting the focus from the substance of reality to reality *construction practices*" (Pollner 1987, as cited by Gubrium and Holstein 1997, p. 38).

In other words, the central theoretical assumption in ethnomethology is that *it is in micro-level interaction that (macro-level) social order is produced*. Ethnomethodologists "confer much greater agency and responsibility on society's members by attributing the very existence of an apparently real world to their interactional and interpretive skills" than do ethnographers (Gubrium and Holstein 1997, p. 40). The microsociological theoretical rigor of the ethnomethodologist is quite distinct from the "atheoretical" attitude of the "naturalist" ethnographer – i.e., to simply "document" and "describe" the "world" of a particular social group – though, both ethnographers and ethnomethodologists are firmly rooted in the "empirical" world.

Relatedly, as we have seen, traditional "naturalist" ethnographers and symbolic interactionists seek to completely *immerse* themselves in the communities and/or social groups they are studying. By contrast, ethnomethodologists seek to explain the "extraordinary organization of the ordinary" (Pollner 1987, p. xvii, as cited by Ritzer 1992, p. 254), which requires an epistemological distancing, *not* total immersion. Ethnomethodology involves "stepping back" in order to "gain purchase on just how everyday realities are experienced and conveyed" (Gubrium and Holstein 1997, p. 39). While proximity to the action is still essential, the goal shifts from "describing reality to describing *reality-constituting procedures.*" This means that the researcher must separate him/herself from the "commonsense assumptions that underpin everyday beliefs about the factual character of the lifeworld" (ibid., p. 41; emphasis added).[20]

This difference is most evident in how ethnographers and ethnomethodologists approach "talk." Whereas traditional "naturalist" ethnographers and symbolic interactionists treat "informants'" talk *descriptively*, i.e., as information about an underlying existing (i.e., "real") order, ethnomethodologists see "talk itself is an essential feature of the settings that it describes" (Gubrium and Holstein 1997, p. 53). For ethnomethodologists, what is said and how it is said are *constitutive* of the situation, rather than descriptive. Thus, for instance, ethnomethodologists have shown that no matter how banal it may appear, conversational turn-taking is "a highly precise and predictable system for structuring interpersonal exchange, a kind of driving mechanism for all interaction" (Boden 1990b, p. 250).

D. Lawrence Wieder's *Language and Social Reality* (1974) is an ethnomethodological exemplar that is notable too because it explicitly confronts the differences between ethnography and ethnomethodology (Gubrium and Holstein 1997, p. 45). This book is based on Wieder's participant observation experience as a resident staff member of a halfway house for convicted narcotics offenders. Wieder is especially interested in uncovering why the halfway house – conceived of as a "decompression chamber" that would gradually prepare the ex-prisoner for the pressures of normal life – did not have the intended effect, i.e., why the parolee-addict participants in the halfway house did not seem to abstain from drug use (pp. 132–3, as cited by Gubrium and Holstein 1997, p. 45).

In the first part of his book, Wieder presents a traditional ethnographic account of life in the halfway house; Wieder explains the geographic site of the halfway house, the process by which convicts end up as residents there, the daily routines, and most importantly, the notable *patterns* in resident and staff behavior. Through this participant observation, Wieder concludes that residents' "deviance" was a function of their adherence to an indigenous normative order – i.e., a set of rules, roles, and prescriptions generally known as the "convict code" (Gubrium and Holstein 1997, p. 46). The code acts "like a set of subcultural counterdirectives, compelling residents to defy the objectives of the staff and to violate house rules"; thus, residents' observance of "the code" leads directly to rule violations (ibid.). The code includes maxims like "above all, do not snitch," "do not cop out" (confess one's rule violation), "do not trust staff," etc. (Wieder 1988 [1974], pp. 115–20, as cited by Gubrium and Holstein 1997, p. 47).

However, in the second part of his book, Wieder looks at the same case from an ethnomethodological point of view. Wieder, a student of Harold Garfinkel, treats inmates' accounts, not *naturalistically*, i.e., as informed "reports" from residents about their lives and activities, but as *reality-producing* activities. What became clear to Wieder was that, as Gubrium and Holstein (1997, p. 49) state:

> residents were doing much more than merely reporting on the features of
> their lives when they "told the code." They were trying to accomplish things

in the telling, "doing things with words" to create the very social structures they were otherwise apparently just describing. They were, in practice, actively marking the border between deviance and nondeviance through talk and interaction.

In sum, in the first part of his book, Wieder portrayed "the code" as a *moral* structure that shapes and constrains behavior. However, in the second half of his book, Wieder portrayed "the code" as something else: as a "device for legitimately declining a suggestion or order." As Wieder (1988, p. 175, as cited by Gubrium and Holstein 1997, pp. 51–2) states:

> It [the "code"] was a device for urging or defeating a proposed course of action. It was a device for accounting for why one should feel or act in the way that one did as an expectable, understandable, reasonable, and above all else acceptable way of acting or feeling. It was, therefore, a way of managing a course of conversation in such a way as to present the teller (or his colleague) as a reasonable, moral and competent fellow. The code, then, is much more a *method* of moral persuasion and justification than it is a substantive account of an organized way of life. It is a way, or set of ways, of causing activities to be see as morally, repetitively, and constrainedly organized. (emphasis in original)

Conversation Analysis

In the 1960s, the ethnomethodological emphasis on "talk" as a constituting *practice* (rather than simply a "realist" *source* of data) combined with new technology (audio and videotape), and resulted in a new type of ethnomethodology, called "conversation analysis." Conversation analysts use audio and videotape to catch and reanalyze "natural occurring bits of social action." They infuse the general ethnomethodological interest in the *details of action* and the detailed production of order with an even more rigorous methodology and a focus on *conversation*.

In other words, just as ethnomethodologists seek to explain the background rules and norms that allow interaction to proceed, conversation analysts focus on the stable, orderly properties that do not determine what is said but are used to "accomplish" a conversation. Conversation analysts focus not on the external forces that constrain talk, but on the constraints that are internal to the conversation itself (Ritzer 1992, p. 258). The focus is on the *"technology* of conversation," specifically, on *"find*[ing] this technology out of actual fragments of conversation" (Sacks 1984, p. 413–14; emphasis added).

Yet, as Boden (1990b, p. 248) points out, the name "conversation analysis" is somewhat of a misnomer. For in addition to studying everyday oral communication, such as a conversation between friends, conversation analysts study nonlinguistic forms of expression, such as applause (see Heritage and Greatbatch 1986) and booing (Clayman 1993). "Conversation analysts" also study written communication, such as newspaper editorials, and formal communication, such as presidential speeches or religious tracts. Moreover, even when conversation analysts do study actual oral communications between two people, *everything* in the interaction, "from a quiet in-breath to the entire spatial and temporal organization of the scene, may be subject to analysis" (Boden 1990b, p. 248, emphasis added).

Today, conversation analysis is probably "the most visible and influential form of ethnomethodological research" (Maynard and Clayman 1991, p. 396, as cited by Gubrium and Holstein 1997, p. 55). Conversation analysis is an especially "rigorous" brand of ethnomethodology, as it enables conversation analysts to produce data unimpaired by the presence of the researcher. The *positivistic* nature of conversation analysis distinguishes it both from other types of discourse analysis (to be discussed in the next chapter) as well as ethnographic research. Conversation analysts *directly* observe the social world with fewer mediating and filtering effects than other social scientific methodologies. Conversation analysts literally "catch" discourse on magnetic tape and analyze it in order to uncover its basic properties.

As discussed previously, in traditional naturalist ethnography, informants are used to describe and explain *particular* social and cultural phenomena. "What is said as such, how it is said, and the interactional and other contexts for what is said is [sic] generally disregarded in favor of exclusively examining *what was meant* by some utterance or collection of utterances" (Wieder 1988 [1974], p. 129, as cited by Gubrium and Holstein 1997, p. 54; emphasis in original). By contrast, conversation analysts study such phenomena as turn-taking, telephone openings, and applause not to discover their *particular meaning* for participants; even where cases are very idiosyncratic, they are examined more for their general organizational pattern. The goal of conversation analysis is to uncover the formal organization of talk into which local particularities are infused (Schegloff 1979, p. 71). Put in another way, conversation analysts are interested in actually occurring bits of *social action* that *happen to be* expressive (e.g., applause, booing, openings and closings of conversations). They are not particularly interested in determining the various *meanings* behind and within expression, nor are they interested in *the subject* – the author him/herself. [21] Rather, conversation analysts seek to articulate precisely what the parameters and rules of expression *are*; instances of expression are viewed as *elementary forms of social action* (Clayman 1993, p. 110).

This positivistic emphasis on transpersonal structures has led to some important and provocative cross-national comparisons and collaborative research (Boden 1990b, p. 247). For instance, in their seminal work on the sequential organization of turn-taking in conversation, Sacks and his colleagues (Sacks, Schlegoff, and Jefferson 1974; Jefferson 1978) showed how conversational transitions are recurrently managed with no (or minimal) gap and overlap. In addition, they documented the ritualized respect for the rights of a speaker, having begun an utterance, to bring it to a point of possible completion, as well as occurrences of interruptions and interutterance gaps. In the last several years, Sacks et al.'s findings about the normative organization of conversation (and specifically, "turn-taking") have been shown to hold across *all* languages and cultures studied (Moerman 1977, Boden 1983, Besneir 1989, as cited by Boden 1990a, p. 190); and Schegloff (1982) continued this discussion by focusing on cases of ambiguity in which a question-formed utterance is interpreted initially as a question and subsequently as an instance of showing agreement.

It is precisely for this reason that conversation analysis is well suited for studying contemporary, heterogeneous, postmodern, "global" culture and society. In contrast to traditional "naturalist" fieldwork, which, as we have seen, has traditionally been used to study specific, *geographically bounded* societies or social groups, conversation analysts pointedly seek to illuminate sequences of expression that *supersede* spatial or other specific social boundaries.

But not surprisingly, this very emphasis on "transpersonal normative structures" annoys critics of ethnomethodology. For instance, the existentialist sociologist Jack Douglas (1977, p. 10) harshly criticizes ethnomethodology for ignoring that "unexpressed, even unexpressable" netherworld of experience at the heart of everyday life. Douglas insists that sociologists must address *all* the dimensions of human activity – including the most subjective.[22]

Conclusion

In this chapter, we have seen that ethnography first emerged as a method to capture and illuminate the workings of a *naturally occurring* world (such as a "primitive" tribe, or marginalized social group). However, the basic tenets of "naturalist" ethnography have long been challenged. Ethnography has been criticized by more positivistic analysts as (at best), a useful "background" or "exploratory" tool, and (at worst) unsubstantiated, psuedo-scientific (rather than "scientific") description. In recent years, postmodernists and postcolonialists have even more fervently maintained that "naturalist" ethnography is not as "objective" as its adherents let on. Postmodernists and postcolonialists have criticized the *colonial* history and attitude of ethnography, and they have argued that, ironically, the presence and subjectivity of the ethnographer necessarily *pollutes* the allegedly "naturally occurring" behavior that ethnographers claim to present. Radical postmodernists insist that since there is no way to circumvent the subjectivity and location of the researcher, we might as well *dissolve* the (false) dichotomy between "subject" and "object," and draw on (rather than seek to exclude) one's own emotions and experience.

In my view, postmodernism offers an important *critique* of traditional naturalistic research. Postmodernism and postcolonialism remind us that participant observation is an *interpretive* process that takes place in a specific political and historical context, and that all social scientific writing – especially ethnographic writing – has specific *narrative* dimensions. Thus, for instance, a central (but usually implicit) goal in ethnographic writing is to attain ethnographic "authority" and/or "legitimacy," i.e., to convince the reader that the researcher was really *there*, that s/he s really "in the know," and that his/her interpretations/observations are the "best" and most "insightful" ones. Yet ethnographers must continually ask themselves if the particular story s/he is telling might be told in another way, and wonder about their underlying personal as well as theoretical orientation and interests. Indeed, as Geertz (1973, p. 20) succinctly stated over twenty-five years ago, "Cultural analysis is guessing at meanings, assessing the guesses, and drawing explanatory conclusions."

But that naturalistic research is inherently "interpretive" does not mean that we must succumb to relativism, collapse "fiction" and "nonfiction, and throw out the proverbial "baby" with the "bath water". Again, as Geertz (1973, p. 30) pointed out: "I have never been impressed by the argument that, as complete objectivity is impossible in these matters (as, of course, it is), one might as well let one's sentiments run loose . . . that is like saying that as a perfectly aseptic environment is impossible one might as well conduct surgery in a sewer."

In this chapter, we have also seen that the most common "middle path" between "realism" (or "positivism") and postmodernism – is "reflexivity," i.e., "confessing" the *personal* position and experience of the researcher. But reflexivity is fraught with problems as well. Most importantly, it shifts attention away from *culture*, and back toward the *author* him/herself. In the final section of this chapter, I have suggested that ethnographers might do well to focus less on situating themselves *personally* and more on situating themselves *theoretically*. Formally theoretical ethnography provides "thick description," but it also provides theoretically grounded explanation and analysis, thereby greatly enhancing our understanding of the everyday world. In addition, we have seen that by making her study not only explicitly theoretical but *comparative*, Robin Leidner confronts some of the charges about the "hidden agendas" and "generalizability" of ethnography – and, in my view at least, comes out quite well.

In the final section of this chapter, we explored conversation analysis and the more general field of ethnomethodology, which tend to be "positivistic" explorations of "naturally occurring" talk and behavior. New technology (namely audio and videotape) has enabled conversation analysts to produce data unimpaired by the presence of the researcher. However, ethnomethodologists focus on *social* (not *symbolic*) processes (see table 5.1). These are important types of *naturalistic* inquiry that document the *mechanics* of discourse and interaction, but they are not theoretically or methodologically equipped to discuss *meaning*. Thus, in order to explain *symbolic* systems, we need to turn toward other, more *interpretive* research methods. In the next chapter, we focus on discourse (or textual) analysis. We will see that textual/discourse analysis is one of the most important methods for identifying and sorting out the *symbolic* scaffolding behind and within action, and hence, that textual/discourse analysis is one of the most important ways to illuminate "culture" in the *symbolic* (rather than *ethnographic*) sense of the term (see chapter 1).

IMPORTANT CONCEPTS INTRODUCED IN THIS CHAPTER

- Ethnography
- "Realism"
- "Formally theoretical" ethnography
- Postmodern ethnography
- Dramaturgical theory
- Auto-ethnography
- Ethnomethodology
- Conversation analysis

STUDY QUESTIONS

1 Think of a specific *subculture* of which you are a part. This may be a religious group, a sports team, or a sorority/fraternity. Using a traditional "naturalist" (or "realist") approach, describe the specific *symbols* (including language, dress, etc.) and *norms* (specific, expected behaviors) which characterize this group. In what ways is this group its own "little world"?

1a Now "write" the subculture using a "confessional" approach. In other words, whereas in the "realist" account, the author situates him/herself as a "neutral" "fly on the wall," in the "confessional" account the author situates him/herself somewhere "in the field," and speaks from that position. See Van Maanen (1988) for more on "realist" versus "confessional" narrative traditions.

1b Now write a *postmodern* ethnography of that same subculture. This means you may blend "subject" and "object" and write about yourself in relation to "others" in the group; and/or blend "fictional" and "nonfictional" styles and genres, e.g., poetry and "data" (à la Richardson). Which of the three types of writing – "realist," "confessional," or "postmodern" – do you think best *describes* and best *explains* the "essence" of this subculture? Do you think it is possible to combine the accounts, taking the merits of each position?

1c Thus far you have written "realist," "confessional," and/or "postmodernist" accounts of a subculture in which you are a part. Now write a "constituitive" account of the subculture, i.e., an ethnomethodological account of the process of accounting itself.

2 Find a place on campus to observe how people move through and manage a cafeteria line. Pay particular attention to the symbols (including language) and actions involved in this process of *routinization*. What do people do when "problems" arise? Are there specific points/places where "breaches" tend to occur? How does this simple experiment demonstrate that social order is not a "reality in itself," but an accomplishment?

Suggested Further Reading

Bourgois, Philippe. 1995. *In Search of Respect*. Cambridge: Cambridge University Press.

Clifford, James, and George Marcus, eds. 1986. *Writing Culture*. Berkeley: University of California Press.

Clough, Patricia. 1992. *The End(s) of Ethnography: From Realism to Social Criticism*. Newbury Park, CA: Sage.

Du Bois, W. E. B. 1899. *The Philadelphia Negro*. Philadelphia: University of Pennsylvania Press.

Duneier, Mitchell. 1999. *Sidewalk*. New York: Farrar, Straus, and Giroux.

Freeman, Derek. 1999. *The Fateful Hoaxing of Margaret Mead*. Boulder, CO: Westview.

Geertz, Clifford. 1973. "Thick Description: Toward an Interpretive Theory of Culture," in Geertz, *The Interpretation of Cultures*. New York: Basic Books.

Gubrium, Jaber, and James Holstein. 1997. *The New Language of Qualitative Method*. New York: Oxford University Press.

Hoschchild, Arlie. 1983. *The Managed Heart: Commercialization of Human Feeling*. Berkeley: University of California Press.

Leidner, Robin. 1993. *Fast Food, Fast Talk*. Berkeley: University of California Press.

Lemert, Charles, and Ann Branaman, eds. 1997. *The Goffman* Reader. Oxford: Blackwell.

Sacks, Harvey. 1984. "Notes on Methodology," in J. Maxwell Atkinson and John Heritage, eds., *Structures of Social Action: Studies in Conversation Analysis*, pp. 2–17. Cambridge: Cambridge University Press.

Van Maanen, John. 1988. *Tales of the Field.* Chicago: University of Chicago Press.

Wieder, D. Lawrence. 1988 [1974]. *Language and Social Reality: The Case of Telling the Convict Code.* Lanham, MD: University Press of America.

Willis, Paul. 1977. *Learning to Labor.* New York: Columbia University Press.

Notes

1   Du Bois used surveys and interviews as well as participant observation in his study of the Philadelphia slum; but his work was largely ignored. Ethnographic studies at the turn of the century were few and far between, and racial prejudice muffled what is now heralded as a provocative and eloquent voice (Van Maanen 1988, p. 17).

2   Howard Becker (1999, p. 10) maintains that "the Chicago school, so-called . . . was never the unified chapel of the origin myth, a unified school of thought" that many analysts project. He suggests that the "Chicago school" is better understood as a school of *activity*, rather than a unitary, coherent theoretical tradition. Relatedly, Harvey (1989, p. 50) maintains that "the Chicago school" lacked the analytical component to be truly "ethnographic"; he prefers the term "first-hand descriptive studies."

3   As mentioned previously (see p. 20, n.18), "positivism" refers to the application of the "scientific method" to the social world, or the view that material objects are real and that causal laws can be formulated to state the relationships that exist among them (Orum, Johnston, and Riger 1999, p. 529).

4   Van Maanen (1988, p. 23) maintains that sociological ethnographers have internalized this positivistic bias, such that, in contrast to the more metaphorical anthropological ethnographies, sociological ethnographies tend to be "stiff, dry, and documentary in style," exhibiting little "interpretive nerve." Certainly, some sociologists approach "participant observation" with positivistic disciplinary standards and criteria; sociology has a long tradition of couching unscientific methods in "scientific" discourse (e.g., "convenience sampling": is the term "sampling" supposed to obscure the fact that one's "data" have been cohered *ad hoc*, i.e., according to "convenience")? In a more positive light, one of the more fortunate consequences of the recent cultural/postmodernist turn is that it has led to a decline in this type of quasi- positivistic posturing (since abandoning or taking a less orthodox position regarding "positivistic" standards of validity and reliability are acceptable too).

5   Indeed, even today, methods texts still assert that the "first rule of thumb" of doing fieldwork is: "Try to refrain from studying your own group . . . . As a member of a group, you may be too close to that group to be fair and accurate in your reporting" (Janesick 1998, p. 67). The odd thing about Janesick's traditionalist assertion (that "outsiders" are more "objective" than

"insiders") is that it completely contradicts her self-image as a "critical, post-modern, interpretive interactionist with a feminist artistry" (p. 5). For as we will shortly see, critical postmodernists reject the traditionalist assumption that the *outsider* is likely to be more "objective" and "accurate" than the "insider" on two counts: (1) they assert that "insiders" provide a better understanding of what is going on than "outsiders"; and (2) they reject such notions as "fair and accurate reporting," since, they insist, there *is* no objective "reality" without *subjective* perception, interpretation, etc.

6   Specifically, Clough argues that while Chicago school ethnographers, such as Herbert Blumer, insist that naturalistic observation permits a "faithful reportorial depiction" of the empirical world, "it is realist representation itself that makes what is seen seem real, makes it believable in its opposition to the individual's imaging" (Blumer 1969, p. 252, as cited by Clough 1992, p. 37). "The interchange of individuals' points of view, which Blumer argues constitutes an adequate representation of the empirical world, is understood within feminist criticism to be an effect of realist representation itself – the displacement of subjectivity from producer to receiver only appearing as an interaction of subjective perspectives" (p. 37).

7   *The Dictionary of Cultural Literacy* (1988), as cited by Freeman (1999, p. 1).

8   Following Lemert (1997a), I use the term "radical postmodernism" to refer to a type of postmodernism that takes the notion that "modernity" is a thing of the past at full value. Radical postmodernists tend to believe that "modernity is utterly overthrown by a new social arrangement in which reality is a virtual reality, in which the differences between fact and fiction no longer apply, and in which there is little basis for defending any specific idea or ideal as more real than any other" (Lemert 1997a, pp. 52–3). In short, here I mean epistemologically (having to do with the study of the grounds for knowledge) and not politically "radical."

9   To be sure, as Lemert (1997a, p. 87) points out, writing that is not in any shape or form "postmodern" can also be "personal" and/or "self-referential." For instance, Rousseau's *Confessions* was highly personal and perhaps self-referential; while Kant's famous *Critique of Practical Reason* was self-referential, though not at all personal.

10   This point is expressed in the following joke, first told to me by my research assistant, Ida Yoshinaga: What did the native say to the postmodernist? "Enough about *you* – now let's talk about *me!*"

11   Bourgois also recognizes *"unconscious taboo buttons"* in his *readers* (but not himself). As he (1995, pp. 207–8) maintains:

> Readers in the United States are so unconsciously subjected to the racialized common sense of their society, than many of them are likely to interpret these passages [on street rape] as some kind of a cultural reflection on the Puerto Rican community . . . . Once again, as a white male researcher, to avoid pushing unconscious taboo buttons it would have been easier to eliminate this discussion of gang rape. I feel, however, that a failure to address sexual violence in street culture would be colluding with the sexist status quo.

12 See note 5 above.

13 Of course, some analysts *intentionally* remain at an *individual* level of analysis. Psychoanalysts, such as Prager (1999, p. 3), routinely emphasize that even though belief systems transcend individuals and are of great social import, delineating a "natural history" of these phenomena is problematic: "One person's racial attitudes, let us say, and the meaning they hold for that person, cannot stand in for another person's racial attitudes and their meaning to that person." Similarly, "personal experience" researchers rely on *individualistic* methods, such as life history, oral history, annals, chronicles, and autobiography. The central assumption undergirding "personal experience methods" is that understanding a single, in-depth experience is useful in and of itself, i.e., that "stories . . . lived and told, educate the self and others, including the young and those, such as researchers, who are new to their communities" (Clandinin and Connelly 1998, p. 155).

14 Willis also shows how the reproduction of masculine workplace culture makes the hard, brutal nature of factory life come to be seen as a property of gender, rather than as a dehumanizing product of capitalist production itself (Alexander 1990, p. 22).

15 Similarly, Bourgois collapses rather than sorts out the workings of race, class, and gender in marginalized communities, i.e., he does not explain how gender and ethnicity fit into his study of *economic* (and *social*) marginalization. Thus, for instance, he worries that his accounts of brutal street rape reflect "badly" on *"Puerto Ricans"* – but not the "underclass."

By contrast, in his highly acclaimed *Sidewalk* (1999), Mitchell Duneier provocatively melds insights from symbolic interaction (discussed below) and journalism into a traditional, participant observation study of life on "the sidewalk" at a busy intersection in Greenwich Village. On one hand, in the spirit of traditional urban ethnography and symbolic interactionism, Duneier paid strict attention to the intricate details of the lives of the "poor black men who make their livelihoods . . . by selling second hand goods, panhandling, and scavenging books and magazines left out for recycling" (book flap). He kept a digital tape recorder "running all the time," because he was determined to "get meaning right," and he knew that this meant getting the "exact words right too" (p. 339). However, in contrast to the traditional urban ethnographer and symbolic interactionist, Duneier "followed his nose" and went to great lengths to "check stuff out" to make sure there was "a warrant for believing" what he had been told (p. 345). He sought to "grasp the connections between individual lives and the macroforces at every turn" (p. 344). This meant that Duneier undertook extensive investigative research, and conducted many interviews (with family members, government officials, and others) far removed from Sixth Avenue.

16 Lemert (1997, p. xii) notes that Goffman is claimed by a variety of other traditions and empirical areas as well:

Anthony Giddens, for example, suggests that Goffman, the least systematic of sociologists, was in fact a "systematic social theorist." (What he meant, rather, was that in spite of it all, there is a common thread to Goffman's wild mix of stuff.) William Gamson . . . insists that Goffman's legacy did not exclude political sociology. (This may be, but Gamson strains to demonstrate the point which, in the end, is more that political sociology ought to consider the microevents out of which political action is contrived.) Pierre Bourdieu, a persistent inventor of rare methods, thinks of Goffman as a kin of sorts. (True, but only upon taking "methods" with a grain of salt.)

17   Nevertheless, Goffman was a pragmatist not an idealist (and he was *funny* as well). As Goffman (1974, p. 1; Lemert and Branaman 1997, p. 149) states: "All the world is not a stage – certainly, the theatre isn't entirely. (Whether you organize a theater or an aircraft factory, you need to find places for cars to park and coats to be checked, and these had better be real places, which incidentally, had better carry real insurance against theft.)"

18   In her seminal study, *The Managed Heart* (1983), Hochschild explores how workers' emotions are managed by their employers (e.g., flight attendants have to "smile" and adopt a specific persona as part of their job). Hochschild (as cited by Leidner 1993, p. 12) argues that workers whose emotions are managed by their employers "become alienated from their feelings in a process parallel to that described by Marx of alienation of proletarians from the actions of their bodies and the products of their labor. These workers thus have difficulty experiencing themselves as authentic even off the job, for they lose track of which feelings are their own."

19   In *The Structure of Social Action* (1937), the eminent theorist Talcott Parsons (1902–79) sought to answer Thomas Hobbes's famous "problem of order": how can society persist given that each of its members pursues his/her own goal? Following Durkheim, Parsons maintained that social order is rooted in the internalization of values and norms through socialization. Most importantly, Parsons supposed that in general people are unable to develop an instrumental orientation toward the values and norms which they have internalized (Baert 1998, p. 83).

20   In recent years, analysts such as Miller and McHoul (1998) have attempted to meld ethnomethodology and cultural studies. Quite rightly noting that cultural studies is often based on mere speculation, and that ethnomethodology represents the exact opposite – an obsessively empirical focus on "real," practical "everyday life" – they introduce an "ethnomethodologically inspired cultural studies." They set out to explore "social relations via everyday meaning" (p. 2). However, they speculate about "meaning" ad hoc, following cultural studies far more than ethnomethodology.

21   As we will see in the next chapter, orthodox semiotics shares this same methodological characteristic.

22   See Gubrium and Holstein (1997, ch. 4) for an informative critique of Douglas's existential sociology, or emotionalism.

CHAPTER SIX

Discourse Analysis and Audience/Reception Research: Constructing and Deconstructing Texts, Talk, and Meaning

In the last several years discourse analysis has become increasingly popular in sociology (as well as throughout the social sciences and humanities). By "discourse analysis" (or "textual analysis"), I mean any type of analysis of the *content* of "discourse", from quantitative "content analysis" to the interpretive analysis of abstract symbols.[1] By "discourse" I mean not just oral/written language, but *"symbolic sets* that embody clear references to social system relationships" (Alexander 1998, p. 31; emphasis added).

However, discourse analysis is not new to sociology. On the contrary, discourse analysis has been part and parcel of sociology since the late 1800s, when sociology first emerged as a discipline. Indeed, Weber's canonical *The Protestant Ethic and the Spirit of Capitalism* (first published in 1904–5), can be considered an exemplar in not only interpretive sociology but discourse analysis. In this famous work (discussed in chapter 2), Weber uses *texts*, most importantly, Calvinist doctrines, in order to get a handle on a particular (Protestant) *ethic.* He assumes that systems of *meaning* ("spirits" and "ethics") help explain complex, multivariate relations and historical events – and that these meanings can be located in doctrines. Weber assumes that people have to be *motivated* both to be economically active and not to consume the fruits of their labor; and he uses textual analysis to show what gave people the "idea of the necessity of proving one's faith in worldly activity... [thus creating] a positive incentive to asceticism" (p. 121, as cited by Alford 1998, p. 73).

In addition, some of the first major American empirical studies, most importantly, William I. Thomas and Florian Znaniecki's *The Polish Peasant in Europe and America* (1918), and W. E. B. Du Bois's *The Souls of Black Folk* (1903), relied upon discourse analysis. Thomas and Znaniecki analyzed diaries, letters, and other personal documents in order to illuminate the impact of immigration to the United States upon Polish immigrants (Lemert 1995, p. 268). Even more poignantly, in his long ignored but now widely acclaimed book, *The Souls of Black Folk* (1903), Du Bois used not only surveys, interviews, and ethnography, but autobiography and poetry, to help dispel the dominant image of blacks as different and inferior. He began each essay in *The Souls of Black Folk* with a bar of the Sorrow Songs – "some echo of haunting melody from the only American music which welled up from black souls in the dark past" (p. 2) – because for Du Bois (as for Douglass, fifty years earlier), this is where "the souls of black folk" are most readily revealed. Du Bois had lost his faith in a rational solution to the deeply ossified patterns of racial inequality (Cruz 1997, p. 105); in *Souls*, he suggests that "other elements of personality besides rationality are needed in order to deal reasonably with racial issues" (Gibson 1989, p. x).[2]

Nevertheless, as discussed in the previous chapter, qualitative methods have long been overshadowed by quantitative methods in sociology. Indeed, until the recent "postmodern" and "culturalist" turns, discourse analysis has not been considered a "mainstream" sociological method at all. Weber, Thomas and Znaniecki, and Du Bois were (and are) routinely heralded as great "historical" (not *discursive*) sociologists. Introductory textbooks rarely even *mention* discourse analysis in their sections on "qualitative methodology"; *quantitative* content analysis sometimes appears, but not more qualitative versions.

In the remainder of this chapter, I seek to help correct this lacuna by demonstrating the importance of discourse analysis to sociology. We begin with a brief exploration of the more traditional, quantitative version of discourse analysis (still called "content analysis"); we then turn our attention to more *interpretive* forms of discourse analysis (or "qualitative content analysis") – most importantly, *semiotics*, which is the linguistic exploration of sign systems. We then explore *audience/reception* studies, which, as discussed in chapter 3, focus not on as much on the content of the *texts* themselves, but on the *act* of individual/audience interpretation. We then move to *narrative analysis* and *social and cultural history*, both of which overlap with semiotics in important ways, but have roots in literature and history, rather than linguistics. We conclude this chapter by looking at the *poststructuralist* discourse analysis of Michel Foucault, which first bridged *structuralism* and *history*.

Quantitative Content Analysis

Since the 1950s, "content analysis" has been the most widely accepted method of textual investigation in the social sciences. By "content analysis," I mean the deceptively simple method of establishing categories and then counting the number of instances when those categories are used in a particular text or media (e.g., a television program). Content analysis is widely considered a "viable" social scientific method not merely because it is quantitative, but because it pays attention to, and tries to meet, traditional social scientific standards of "reliability" and "validity" (Silverman 1993). Content analysts examine texts *systematically*, usually over an extended period of time; they do not simply discuss symbols and categories *ad hoc* (as do literary and media critics). In addition, quantitative content analysis is considered "objective" because different analysts are able to apply the same set of categories to the same, or perhaps different, texts.

Content analysis is used in many different disciplines for many different purposes – from coding shifts in dance choreography over time (Bergesen and Jones 1992), to coding the peculiarities of labor unrest (Franzosi 1998). However, content analysis is most prominent in the field of communications, especially the study of television. In communications, numerous television content analysis studies are done every year, in the same style as Gallup surveys. Indeed, the first content analyses of television programs were done in the early 1950s (e.g., Head 1954, Smythe 1954); but by 1975, more than 200 content analysis studies of television had already been conducted (Comstock 1975, as cited by Stroman and Jones 1998, p. 271).

One of the most well-known and influential communications content analysts is George Gerbner. In the 1960s, Gerbner and his associates launched a massive data collection and longitudinal analysis of television violence. They tracked violence programming trends across years and networks, developing both a Violence Index (program rating) and a Violent: Victim Ratio (profiling the aggressor and the victim within violence portrayals) (Palmer 1998, pp. 53–4, Murray 1998, p. 382). Gerbner and his colleagues set the standards for content analysis studies of television violence, and now content analysis studies of television violence are done nearly every year. Television violence studies typically involve thousands of hours of television, and numerous coders. For instance, in one recent, especially comprehensive longitudinal study, the National Television Violence Study (NTVS) (1997), researchers analyzed a total of 3,185 programs across 23 television channels from 6 A.M. until 11 P.M., 7 days a week, for the course of a television season, for 3 years. The researchers found that 57 percent of all programs analyzed had some violence, and that one-third of programs presented nine or more violent interactions.[3] They also found that rarely was the violence punished and rarely were victims shown as suffering any harmful consequences; that 37 percent of the perpetrators of violence were portrayed as being attractive, and that 44 percent of the acts were shown as being justified. These patterns led the researchers to conclude that not only was violence prevalent throughout the entire television landscape, but that it was typically shown as sanitized and glamorized (Potter 1998, p. 166; Grossberg, Nelson, and Treichler 1998, p. 157).

Of course, content analysis can be used to track and analyze all sorts of television images – not just television violence. For instance, content analysis has been used to document the numbers and types of representations of specific ethnic or other social groups (African Americans, women, the elderly, etc.), as well as a variety of social behaviors (e.g., alcohol use, sexual acts) (Stroman and Jones 1998, pp. 271–2). Thus, for example, a recent study of 92 prime-time shows on the six major broadcast networks found that 80 percent of all prime-time characters were white; 13 percent were black; and all other minority groups accounted for 3 percent or less. In terms of the roughly 12 percent of prime-time characters who were younger than eighteen or in high school, African American youths constituted only 7.9 percent, while Latinos represented only 3.7 percent, Asian Pacific Americans only 1.2 percent, and Native Americans only 0.6 percent.[4]

Theoretically, most television content analysis studies rely on the implicit assumption that television is a powerful means of *socialization*. Communications analysts tend to assume, à la "common sense," that people "internalize content from a medium with which they spend so much time" (Shanahan and Morgan 1999, p. 173); television simply *socializes* viewers in its own image. Thus, for instance, the sponsor of one important study on ethnicity and prime-time television maintains that "The absence of cultural images and characters that reflect them . . . is disturbing to kids. It affects their aspirations" (*Los Angeles Times*, January 12, 2000, F12).

Similarly, content analysts have long argued that continuous exposure to violence *desensitizes* us to violence. More than a few researchers have found that children who watch television violence exhibit more aggressive play and behavior (Murray 1998, p. 385). Indeed, it seems that in certain situations even *adults* may *directly* emulate television violence. For instance, Phillips (1982, 1983) found that whenever a major suicide (i.e., that of a main character) occurred in a soap opera in the 1960s, there was a significant increase in the national incidence of suicide by women (a major audience for soap operas in those days) within three days of the telecast. Phillips suggested that television portrayals can stimulate subtle changes in attitudes that might make a particular behavior or course of action (such as suicide) seem more acceptable to viewers (Murray 1998, p. 386).

However, today many analysts take a more nuanced "cultivation" approach to the media. This theoretical approach was first developed by George Gerbner (1958, as cited by Shanahan and Morgan 1999). The basic premise of cultivation theory is that the impact of television is not instantaneous and direct, but *cumulative*. Cultivation theorists hold that "watching a great deal of television" *cultivates* a specific worldview, "specific and distinct conceptions of reality, conceptions that are congruent with the most consistent and pervasive images and values of the medium" (Shanahan and Morgan 1999, p. 3). As Shanahan and Morgan (1999, p. 5) state:

> Cultivation is *not* about how voters' feelings about a political candidate might be affected by some newscast or campaign. Cultivation is *not* about whether a new commercial can make people buy a new toothpaste . . . .
>
> Cultivation *is* about the implications of stable, repetitive, pervasive and virtually inescapable patterns of images and ideologies that television (especially dramatic, fictional entertainment) provides . . . cultivation research approaches television as a *system* of messages . . . . The focus of cultivation analysis is on the correlates and consequences of cumulative exposure to *television in general* over long periods of time.

Thus, for instance, Gerbner and his colleagues have surveyed vast numbers of Americans and found a correlation between the amount of television people watch, and their perceptions as to the *prevalence* of crime and "dangers" in the world. Gerbner et al. call this attitude *cultivated* by the media the "Mean-World Syndrome" (Shanahan and Morgan 1999, p. 55). They maintain that "long-term exposure to television, in which frequent violence is virtually inescapable, tends to cultivate the image of a relatively mean and dangerous world . . . in which greater protection is needed, and most people 'cannot be trusted', and most people are 'just looking out for themselves'" (Murray 1998, p. 387). For instance, when asked if "most people can be trusted," 48 percent of light viewers but 65 percent of heavy viewers responded that "you can't be too careful" (Shanahan and Morgan 1999, p. 55).

In addition, cultivation theory has an explicit *critical* bent. Parallel to cultural Marxists (see chapters 2 and 3), cultivation analysts assume that social and economic elites codify and accent messages in the media that serve their own aims (Shanahan and Morgan 1999, p. 16); consequently, "*audience members more 'committed' to media will have belief structures more consonant with those desired by social elites*" (ibid., p. 18, emphasis in original). Thus, for instance, Gerbner et. al (1984) find that "on variable after variable, heavy viewing indicated deep erosion for classically liberal positions on social issues." Most obviously, the "Mean World Syndrome" cultivated by the media coincides quite nicely with the *socially conservative* idea that we desperately "need" harsher criminal sanctions (e.g., the "Three Strikes Law"), more prisons, and more police. In addition, cultivation theorists emphasize that heavy viewing produces a *mainstreaming* effect – in which the mainstream is bent to the political and economic task of the medium and its client institutions (Shanahan and Morgan 1999, p. 86). In short, for Gerber et al. (1984) the political orientation cultivated by the media is unlikely to produce tolerance or economic austerity – but it *is* "highly congruent with the consumption-oriented demands of commercial media institutions" (Shanahan and Morgan 1999, p. 91).

As discussed in chapter 3, there are significant theoretical problems inherent in the neo-Marxist and communications approaches. Most importantly, these analysts have been criticized for oversimplifying the relationship between the media and the audience, and exaggerating the *control* elites have in the process of making *meaning*.

In addition, there have been important methodological critiques of quantitative content analysis (whether or not it is of a neo-Marxist bent). Critics commonly charge that researchers "count" each "act" of television "violence" as if each incident is of equal dynamic and weight. There is little discussion about different *genres* of violence; each violent "act" is counted in exactly the same way. Thus, for instance, NTVS researchers typically count instances where violent acts are "punished" (or not) to assert that violence is "glamorized" and "sanitized" (or not). But without exploring the context of violence, how do NTVS researchers know what "unpunished" violent acts *mean?* Cartoon violence (e.g., Tom slugging Jerry); slapstick violence (e.g., Moe poking Curly in the eyes); docudramas (e.g., on the Civil War); sensationalistic cable-television movie violence (e.g., about a serial murderer who rapes, slashes, and chops up victims); "real" crime-show violence (*Cops*); and "live" television news violence (e.g., "live" shootouts) tend to be categorized and labeled using the same criteria (number of incidents; "who" does what to "whom," etc.). There is an implicit assumption in quantitative content analysis studies that the meaning *is* the message, and that "significance will be revealed by counting the frequency with which items of manifest content appear" (Bruner and Kelso 1980, p. 240).

Put in another way, the quantitative nature of content analysis at times impedes its usefulness as a *cultural* methodology. The problem is not "counting" or quantification itself, but that quantification is often substituted for analysis of fundamental issues of *context* and *meaning*.[5]

This is precisely why some communications analysts use both quantitative and qualitative techniques to analyze media images. For instance, Rakow and Kranich (1991) use quantitative methods to ascertain the frequency of the appearance of women as sources of information on the CBS, NBC, and ABC evening news programs during the month of July 1986, and categorize the ways in which women appeared. However, noting that "the frequency or infrequency of women's appearance do[es] not give a complete picture of how women are used to carry meaning in news stories" (p. 15), they select 46 news stories for more detailed analysis. From this more interpretive analysis, Rakow and Kranich (1991, p. 14, as cited by Stroman and Jones 1998, pp. 278–9) conclude that women appearing in news stories are not there to speak but rather are there to serve as signs, i.e., they are used to symbolize the consequences of, and emotions underlying, public events, or as anonymous examples of "public opinion." As is typical of neo-Marxist communications researchers, Rakow and Kranich find the *passivity* of women in this ritualized role particularly disturbing. They lament that women are positioned as "passive reactors and witnesses to public events" rather than active participants (ibid.).

Yet, the question remains, *how* do we systematically analyze the *meaning* of images or texts? In the remainder of the chapter, we attend to the *interpretive* analysis of signs – with all its incumbent theoretical, empirical, and methodological complications. We will see that there are various ways that researchers today conceptualize and systematically ferret out the *meaning* of symbols, i.e., the *latent* content behind physically presented data (Berg 1995, p. 176, as cited by Stroman and Jones 1998, p. 275).

Structuralism and Semiotics

"Semiotics" is a term used to refer to a rigorous type of "qualitative content analysis." Semiotics is the analysis of signs or sign systems (e.g., myth, language, fashion) that produce meaning.[6] The basic premise of semiotics is that sign systems must be studied in and of themselves (and not reduced to social organization). In other words, semiotics focuses on the *sign system* itself. Semioticians seek to identify the *relationship* between signs, and to map out symbolic *scaffolding* or *patterns*.

Theoretically, semiotics is rooted in French structuralism. Indeed, "semiotics" is sometimes used synonymously with "structuralism," even though, strictly speaking, "semiotics" refers to a methodological approach, while "structuralism" refers both to a general theoretical perspective as well as a method. The essence of French structuralism/semiotics is that "beneath the surface appearance of an individual-centered world that is contingent and in flux are universal structures that are manifested in the organization of the mind, knowledges, and human behavior" (Baert 1998, p. 10).

Significantly, semiotics has disciplinary roots not in sociology or communications, but in linguistics. Semiotics traces back to the Swiss linguist Ferdinand de Saussure, whose *Course in General Linguistics* (1915) first situated language in a scientific frame. Saussure separated signs into two parts: the signifier and the signified. The signifier is the sound-image or term used to refer to the physical form of the sign: the written work, the lines on the page that form a drawing, a photograph, a sound. The signified is the mental concept referred to by the signifier. Thus, for instance, when we hear the word "tree" (signifier), we realize that it means tree (a plant with a main stem, etc.) (signified) (Alasuutari 1995, p. 100).

Saussure points out that the relationship between the signifier and signified is *arbitrary*. There is no "reason" that the sound-image of a concept *has to* be associated with any particular meaning. The reason we call a "tree" a "tree," and the reason "red" means "stop" and "green" means "go," is not because it *has* to be this way, but because of habit and tradition. To be sure, a few words that describe sounds are onomatopoeic, i.e., formed by copying the sounds (e.g., "hiss"), but even these words are different in different languages, and must be learned. This is most readily apparent in the variety of words in different languages for animals sounds (e.g., "cock-a-doodle-doo" versus "ki-kiki-ri-kiki," etc.).[7] Saussure maintained that meaning arises not from the "sign" itself, but from the *relations* between signs (Leeds-Hurwitz 1993, p. 51). Meanings are the result of the *interplay* of a network of relationships between combination and selection, similarity and difference.

Neo-Marxist semiotics

For many analysts, Roland Barthes is the true founder of semiology because he extended Saussure's ideas to all areas of social life (Ritzer 1997, p. 30). Barthes suggested that just about everything in life can be understood as "signifying practices." For Barthes, the whole of human experience, without exception, is an interpretive structure mediated and sustained by signs (Deely 1990, p. 5); "even the harshest realities of the everyday world only exist to us through meanings" (Alasuutari 1995, p. 29). As Barthes (1967 [1964], as cited by Ritzer 1997, p. 30) states: "Semiology . . . aims to take in any system of signs, whatever their substance and limits; images, gestures, musical sounds, objects, and the complex associations of all these, which form the content of ritual convention, or public entertainment: these constitute if not *languages*, at least systems of signification."

In addition, Barthes infused semiotics with a neo-Marxist bent. He maintained that *all* the apparently spontaneous forms and rituals of contemporary bourgeois societies are subject to a systematic distortion, liable at any moment to be dehistoricized, "naturalized," converted into myth (Hebdige 1993 [1979], p. 360). Indeed, between 1954 and 1956, Barthes wrote a short piece each month on a current aspect of French popular culture, "attacking with all the satiric zest of a Parisian intellectual (and man of the left) the sacred objects of the French petit-bourgeoisie – Persil soap-powder advertising, the design of the latest Citroen, publicity for Garbo's face" (Easthope and McGowan 1992, p. 238).

Thus, akin to the Frankfurt school, Barthes sought to show the *false* and insidious nature of advertising; he demonstrated that popular "desires" are rooted in capitalist ideological hegemony. However, in contrast to the Frankfurt school, Barthes also took a strikingly *anti-elitist* position. For example, in one famous essay on professional wrestling, Barthes suggests that professional wrestling is not a vacuous, vulgar "sport" (as the Frankfurt school would surely attest) – but a "spectacle," analogous to Shakespearian theatre. States Barthes, "it is no more ignoble to attend a wrestled performance of Suffering than a performance of the sorrows of Arnolphe or Andromaque."[8] The wrestlers are simply *signs*; they act out basic elements in a highly structured system of meaning.

Barthes's work on French popular culture has profoundly impacted the contemporary study of culture. Today social scientists, literary critics, historians, and communications analysts (among others) all analyze cultural texts, especially television and movies; and much of this work (especially in British cultural studies) has a strong, populist, neo-Marxist bent. Barthes has been particularly influential in the field of communications – especially the study of advertising. This makes sense because in advertising the relationship between the signifier and signified is consciously thought out and manipulated for the express purpose of inducing consumption (and therefore profit). Advertisers typically deploy a signifier already conventionally related to a mental concept they wish to attach to their product as a means of providing their product with that meaning (Turner 1996 [1990], p. 20; see also Williamson 1978). (This tendency is illustrated in figure 5.1, which builds on the stereotype of the Polynesian "seductress.")

Interestingly, advertising researchers, such as Sut Jhally (1987), infuse Barthes's semiology with a *psychoanalytic* bent, emphasizing, for instance, how sexual titillation in advertisements works in the selling of goods (e.g., subliminal advertising). Similarly, Thorson (1989) and her colleagues show how emotional, "feelgood" advertisements work. They suggest that "emotion adds to the richness of memory traces" as viewers watch emotion-laden advertising, and "when this occurs, counter-arguing and other information from noncommercial sources is eliminated" (p. 403, as cited by Grossberg et al. 1998, p. 252).

Michael Schudson (1984), however, maintains that neo-Marxist communications analysts overestimate the "control" that advertisers have over symbols, imagery, and most importantly, the "audience." Schudson emphasizes that advertisers are "uneasy," because evidence as to the "effectiveness" of advertising to actually get people to buy products is not at all clear (Grossberg et al. 1998, p. 294). While the *goal* in advertising is to *link* two (or more) signifiers in a particular way, every sign is actually multivocal, as meaning is "polysemic." Advertisement campaigns (and cultural products) often fail precisely because advertising executives must navigate complex, often contradictory, sign systems. Even core meanings are never *fixed* (as we saw earlier with "race"), so the intended meanings *encoded* in the text may (or may not) be that *decoded* by the viewer/reader. In other words, advertisers intend for signs (and combinations of signs) to generate particular meaning, but advertisers cannot be sure that the meanings they attempt to create will be the meanings taken (Turner 1996 [1990], pp. 16–17).

Of course, from a more critical perspective, while some signs (and advertisements) are more ambiguous than others, some signs seem virtually immutable.[9] Women's bodies are used to sell all sorts of products precisely because they evoke a narrow, powerful, and predictable response. "Sexy women" are a sure bet. For instance, how many different ways do viewers interpret the "Tahiti" advertisement shown in figure 5.1? Everyone "knows" what constitutes "beautiful" and "sexy," and that "beautiful" and "sexy" are "good" (i.e., "desirable"). By definition, stereotypes (e.g., the "Polynesian seductress," "Willie Horton" images of black male criminality, etc.) are signs that are forceful and dominant, such that "multivocality" is not much of an issue.

NEO-DURKHEIMIAN SEMIOTIC ANALYSIS

In contrast to neo-Marxist semioticians, who focus on how elites strategically manipulate signs for the express purpose of inducing consumption, neo-Durkheimian semioticians emphasize the *all-encompassing* nature of signs. They stress that sign systems are collectively *shared*, such that *no one* – not even the most powerful advertising executive or media mogul – is "above and beyond" the code itself. We necessarily work *within* – rather than invent and reinvent – sign systems.

For instance, in *Sixguns and Society* (1975), Will Wright sees Hollywood Westerns not as an ideological, alienating, pernicious product of the American culture industry (as cultural Marxists would assert), but as "a symbolically simple but remarkably deep conceptualization of American social beliefs" (p. 23, as cited by Storey 1996, p. 57). Drawing on Saussure as well as the French anthropologist Claude Lévi-Strauss, Wright analyzes the structure and meaning of Hollywood Western films, because "the myths of a society, through their structure, *communicate a conceptual order* to the members of that society" (p. 17; emphasis added). For instance, Wright finds that there are 16 functions to the narrative structure of the classical Western, which correspond to different types of people inherent in our conceptualization of society, and four basic symbolic oppositions (inside / outside society; good/bad; strong/weak, and wilderness/civilization) that comprise the basic classification of people in the Western myth.[10]

Similarly, rather than perceive *The Phil Donahue Show* as artificial and manipulated (à la neo-Marxist semiotics), Donal Carbaugh (1989 [1994]) sees *Donahue* as a vibrant, *American* text. He is particularly interested in the *political code* contained within the show's discourse on the "self"; as Carbaugh (1989 [1994], p. 21) maintains:

> My initial purpose is to describe a spoken system of symbols that is used on "Donahue" to construct a sense of the person as "an individual." The symbols I will be considering are "the individual," "rights" and "choice." . . . I call this system of symbols a political code, since it involves expressions that derive from the principles of the Constitution and the Bill of Rights.

Interestingly, Carbaugh describes his project as an "*ethnographic* interpretation of linguistic communication" (p. 6; emphasis added). He conceptualizes the show as a "natural" and "meaningful resource for the conduct of *everyday discourse*" (pp. 21–2; emphasis added). He methodically analyzes the discourse "heard to operate" on the *Donahue Show*. Thus, like the traditional, "naturalist" ethnographer as well as the conversation analyst (see chapter 5), Carbaugh seeks to *document* "naturally" occurring phenomena, although, in contrast to the traditional "naturalist" ethnographer and conversation analyst, Carbaugh seeks to document and analyze naturally-occurring *symbolic* phenomena (rather than social behavior).

Moreover, like the conversation analyst (see chapter 5), Carbaugh is not interested in the *individual speaker* behind the sign. Rather, Carbaugh sets out to interpret "some of the common meanings that recur prominently when Americans use this discourse" *regardless* of the position and intention of the speaker. As Carbaugh (1989 [1994], p. 21) states:

> My task here is not to treat the individual as an abstract objective construct, but to explore an intersubjective cultural category, the individual, that is used when Americans speak. Similarly, I am not describing particular persons or specific individuals. What I am describing are the meanings and forms of speech that provide a cultural model of and for the person.

Carbaugh maintains that while "no one speaks in sole terms of the following symbolic system . . . such a system can be *heard* to operate in the
"Donahue" context, and in other scenes of similar design" (p. 14, emphasis in original).

In addition, akin to the conversation analyst (as well as the quantitative content analyst), but in contrast to both the traditional ethnographer
and the interpretive narrative analyst within the tradition of humanities
(to be discussed shortly), Carbaugh documents the symbols "heard" on
Donahue systematically. Carbaugh illuminates the "political code" of American individualism by coding every single reference to the "self" on every
single episode of the *Donahue* show for a full year. Moreover, in the spirit
of "objective" social science (and conversation analysis), Carbaugh then
watched new *Donahue* shows in order to further "test and revise" his
tentative formulations about communication patterns.

In sum, neo-Durkheimian semiotics shares important characteristics
with "conversation analysis" (discussed in chapter 5): most importantly,
both envision codes as "a shared plurisituational, constraining, and
transpersonal normative order" (Zimmerman 1974 [1981], p. 16). Both
are concerned not with the *individual* speech-act; but with the overarching
structure (whether *symbolic* or *social*) within which action/speech takes
place. In other words, both semioticians and conversation analysts assume that linguistic units exceed the limits of a single sentence; both look
beyond the *particular* use of language/ discourse/ conversation, and focus
on the extended *sequences* of expression (Thompson 1984, p. 8).

As in conversation analysis, this emphasis on *transpersonal* normative
order lends itself to interesting cross-national research. For instance, in
her semiotic analysis of national flags and anthems, Karen Cerulo (1989)
does not focus on the *particular, historically specific*, meaning of national
flags and songs. Rather, Cerulo systematically measures "objective" aspects of musical elements such as melody, phrasing, harmony, form, dynamics, rhythm, and instrumentation; for visual materials she measures
contrasts in hue, value, and chroma as well as geometric patternings.
Cerulo argues that in both musical and graphical arts, symbols vary in
their complexity along a "basic-embellished continuum," and that variations in national flags and national anthems reflect the historical circumstances of their adoption. She finds, for instance, that politically turbulent
regimes opt for unencumbered symbolic simplicity (e.g., Libya's monotone
green flag), whereas more stable polities generate much busier symbolic
representations (Shapiro and Markoff 1997, p. 16).

Yet, not surprisingly, it is precisely this rigorous focus on "transpersonal"
structures that annoys critics of both semiotics and conversation analysis.
Persons are not seen as bundles of sentiments or investigated "with reference to inner subjective and cultural meanings" (Lemert 1979, p. 100, as

cited by Manning and Cullum-Swan 1998, p. 255). The speaker is merely the "speaking object," a user of codes and symbols who selects among *preconstituted* options, voices and programs (Manning and Cullum-Swan 1998, p. 255; emphasis added). The problem is that both orthodox semiotics and conversation analysis are "dehumanizing" and "deterministic" in their drift and implications. In elevating social elements to sign systems, "cultural structures are not only said to inform social patterns but are held to determine them" (Alexander 1990, p. 13). As Alexander (1998, p. 31) states: "Even at its most socially embedded, semiotics can never be enough. By definition, it abstracts from the social world, taking organized symbolic sets as psychologically unmotivated and as socially uncaused. By contrast, for the purposes of cultural sociology, semiotic codes must be tied into both social and psychological environments and into action itself."

INDIVIDUAL AGENCY AND CULTURAL CODES: THE SEMIOTICS OF UMBERTO ECO

One of the most important semioticians to explicitly confront the issue of symbolic determinism is Umberto Eco. Eco envisions culture not as a static set of values that prescribes specific behaviors, but rather, as a system of "multicontiguous" representations, which frees a series of possible readings. For Eco, just as a speaker unknowingly draws upon a range of syntactical and other rules in order to utter a sentence, and in the process of drawing upon those rules, reproduces the overall totality which is the language, so is there a massive conceptual arena geared into the continuities of day-to-day social life and whose knowledgeability is expressed in practice. Just as speakers or writers of a language are often unaware of the underlying grammatical structures and rules that guide his/her speech, so too are human beings often unaware of the rules and parameters behind systems of meaning.

In other words, Eco maintains that, like linguistic systems, cultural systems are commonly *intelligible* and widely *accessible*, and that they work at a relatively unconscious (or "prediscursive") level. Moreover, symbols are "multivocal" (not univocal); they are not all of the same logical order, but are drawn from many domains of experience and ethical evaluation. Components of meaning are not closed in number, or frozen into a system of relevant units, but form an open series. Thus the existence of, and our reliance on, cultural codes does not at all make us "cultural dopes"; on the contrary, it enables the generation of both "factual" messages which refer to original experiences, and messages which place in doubt the very structure of the code itself. Indeed, an aesthetic function of art as well as language is to create connections which do not yet exist, which thus enriches the code's possibilities. And original interaction and experience create unique configurations in the formation of a complex conceptual arena. At the level of the individual, a certain symbol (and/or meaning) can be shared across a cross-section of groups, and at the same time, be intertwined in other, less consensual representations. This allows for (micro-level) rational action and individual agency, without undermining the collective structure of systems of meaning.

Eco explains how culture works by showing that apparent leaps of metaphoric substitution are in fact short circuits of a preestablished path. A "long white neck," being a property of both a beautiful woman and a swan, means that a woman can be metaphorically substituted for by the swan.[11] As Eco states:

> A metaphor can be invented because language, in its process of unlimited semiosis, constitutes a multidimensional network of metonymies, each of which is explained by a cultural convention rather than by an original resemblance . . . the imagination is nothing other than a ratiocination that traverses the paths of the semantic labyrinth in a hurry and, in its haste, loses the sense of their rigid structure.

In other words, metaphors exemplify the *cultural* process; metaphors rely on symbolic connections, and these symbolic connections enable both individual creativity and collective understanding. According to Eco (1976, p. 124), the cultural system may be likened to an enormous box of marbles, in which shaking the box forms different connections and affinities among the marbles. However, the cultural system is more analogous to a box of magnetized marbles which establish a system of attraction and repulsion, so that some are drawn to one another and others are not. Better yet, we could imagine that every marble emits given wave- lengths, which put it in tune with a limited (though possibly very large) number of other marbles. But these wavelengths can change according to new messages emitted; therefore, the possibilities of attraction and repulsion change over time.

Eco uses diagrams to illustrate the "real linguistic mechanisms" behind poetic metaphors. These diagrams show how metaphor itself is a process of unlimited semiosis, or the continual generation of signs. In my own work, I use the same type of map to illuminate complex cultural codes. For instance, in chapter 4, I used cultural maps to illuminate the symbolic linkages behind and within such notions as the "unmilitant black man" and the "model minority" myth.[12] Yet, for both Eco and myself, these diagrams have a purely "orientative" value: a bidimensional graph cannot wholly reproduce – indeed, it impoverishes – the associations in terms of both number and dimensions. Each symbol is linked to various other symbolic networks; these maps merely show a rough estimation of *one* dimension of symbolization at a fixed point in time. (This fluidity and multivocality is illustrated in the maps by curved lines and few fixed points.)

Audience/Reception Studies

As discussed in chapter 3, "audience" or "reception" analysis first emerged in direct response to the elitism and "interpretive omnipotence" of semiotics as well as mass culture theory. Audience/reception analysts focus on how readers/viewers *interpret* texts (rather than on the "texts" themselves). Like postmodern critics of traditional ethnography, audience/reception analysts celebrate *agency* – the freedom of readers/viewers to pick and choose which parts of texts to attend, and thereby create their own meaning. As communications researcher Lawrence Grossberg (1992, pp. 52–3) maintains:

> We have to acknowledge that, for the most part, the relationship between the audience and popular texts is an active and productive one. The meaning of a text is not given in some independently available set of codes which we can consult at our own convenience. A text does not carry its own meaning or politics already inside of itself ; no text is able to guarantee what its effects will be. People are constantly struggling, not merely to figure out what a text means, but to make it mean something that connects to their own lives, experiences, needs and desires. The same text will mean different things to different people, depending on how it is interpreted. And different people have different interpretive resources, just as they have different needs. A text can only mean something in the context of the experience and situation of its particular audience. Equally important, texts do not define ahead of time how they are to be used or what functions they can serve. They can have different uses for different people in different contexts. (cited in Storey 1996, pp. 6–7)

As also indicated in chapter 3, following Radway's (1984) seminal study on how women actually *read* romance novels, audience/reception studies have grown very popular, especially in the field of communications. Feminist cultural sociologists, such as Press (1991), argue that television may fill important individual needs, hence they warn against demeaning female viewers/readers as hopeless consumerists and doormats. However, in addition we have seen that critics such as Gitlin (1997), Garnham (1997), and Roach (1997) criticize audience/reception analysis for its implicitly conservative (naïve, "pluralistic") stance. From this point of view, audience/reception analysts *overestimate* agency; they take an *overly* individualistic stance.

In recent years, many audience/reception analysts have turned toward using "focus groups" rather than individual one-on-one interviews to assess "meaning." Commonly used in marketing, focus groups typically bring together four to twelve people to discuss a specific issue or product. The basic idea behind focus groups is that group discussions emulate "natural" conversation more than a "one-on-one" interview; in a group dynamic, people feed off one another's comments, talk, listen, and respond naturally, rather than merely self-consciously "answer" questions.

Theoretically, the central premise behind focus groups is that *interpretation* takes place in a *social* context. People construct meaning not individually, but through their interactions with other people. The problem with in-depth interviews (and surveys) is that the "topics" for discussion are prefabricated, the participants take on the role of "interviewer" and "interviewee," thus answers and opinions sound stronger than they really are. The stage is set for stock answers. By contrast, in focus group interviews, individuals view and discuss a cultural product (e.g., a television show) *together*. Thus, advocates insist, focus groups illuminate the *process* of understanding or "decoding" a text (rather than a static "meaning"). Individuals construe meaning as they "normally" would (in a social context), without the "pressure" of a one-on-one interview with a researcher. Ideally, the focus group becomes so "informal" that it is somewhat akin to a "natural" discussion or conversation.

For instance, in *The Export of Meaning* (1990), Tamar Liebes and Elihu Katz sought to explain how people in different countries *viewed* the Hollywood hit television show *Dallas* (a 1980s "soap opera" chronicling the lives of a wealthy Texas oil family). *Dallas* was extremely popular worldwide, but Liebes and Katz wanted to find out if different national audiences *interpreted* the show in similar or different ways. Liebes and Katz conducted focus groups in three countries (with individuals of six different ethnic groups), and found that different national audiences "decoded" the show using different interpretive strategies. For instance, Arab audiences tended to place the show in the context of a serious *morality* play; they understood the show as reflective of the rampant *immorality* in the United States. By contrast, Americans were playful and detached in their reading of the program; they saw the show as nothing more than "entertainment" (Croteau and Hoynes 1997, p. 246).

However, interestingly, what Liebes and Katz's study explicitly demonstrates is that audience/reception analysts must turn their individual level data (on experience/interpretation) into *texts* (e.g., interview transcripts) in order to do *cultural* analysis. Parallel to social historians, who, as we will see, must generalize beyond individual experience in order to identify

Table 6.1 Levels and realms of analysis of various qualitative methods

	Social	*Cultural*
Individual	oral history/"personal experience" methods	audience/reception studies
	focus: individual experience	*focus*: individual interpretation
Collective	social history	semiotics/discourse analysis
	focus: historical patterns	*focus*: symbolic patterns

historical processes; audience/reception analysts *use* "individual" interpretation in order to explain *systems* of meaning. But, significantly, at this point the audience/reception researcher is *not* focused exclusively on "individual" acts of meaning-making anymore; s/he is focused on the larger symbolic scaffolding *behind* and *within* individual interpretation. As shown in table 6.1, at this point, audience/reception analysis *becomes* semiotic/discursive analysis. It is no longer *merely* a study of *individual* experience/interpretation. In sum, audience/reception researchers must *shift* from an individual to a collective level of analysis to order to explain *cultural* codes. This point is most obvious in that Liebes and Katz describe their work as an exploration of "interpretive communities."

MULTIPLE METHODOLOGIES: EXPLORING MEANING FROM BOTH THE "BOTTOM UP" AND "TOP DOWN"

Today a few cultural analysts face debates about (collective) *ideology* versus (individual) *interpretation* head-on by engaging in *both* systematic discourse analysis and audience/ reception research. These analysts formally investigate the making of meaning from the "bottom up" *and* the "top down."

For instance, in her well-researched book, *The Cultural Contradictions of Motherhood* (1996), Sharon Hays uses both systematic discourse analysis and in-depth interviews in order to illuminate the cultual codes that give shape to contemporary American childrearing. Hays is particularly interested in the cultural contradictions behind "intensive mothering" – the idea that women are to be nurturing and unselfish in their role as mothers, but competitive and even ruthless as paid workers. Thus, in the first part of her book, Hays systematically analyzes the works of the three bestselling authors on childrearing: Dr. Spock, Penelope Leach, and T. Berry Brazelton. Hays (1996, p. 286) notes the amazing popularity of these three authors: Brazelton's two most famous books (*Toddlers and Parents*, and *Infants and Mothers*) have sold some 715,000 copies; Leach's most popular book, *Your Baby and Child*, has sold 1.5 million copies; while "Dr. Spock's *Baby and Child Care* (1992) has outsold all other books in the history of publishing with the single exception of the Bible." Hays unpacks, decodes, and deconstructs "the implicit rules for social behavior and the underlying images of social life that are found in these particular symbolic products," precisely because "these bestselling advice books remain an important source of information in and of themselves" (Hays 1996, p. 287). Hays assumes that "the popularity of these particular manuals, rather than others, indicates they struck a chord with readers, and evidently supply what many parents perceive as the necessary and appropriate information and guidance" (ibid., p. 289).

However, Hays does not stop with a discourse analysis of these popular parenting texts. Rather, she uses in-depth interviews and a 13-page questionnaire in order to explore the relation between the *encoded* dominant ideologies found in the books and the way women actually *interpreted* (or decoded) them. Specifically, Hays interviewed 38 mothers in order to see whether and to what extent mothers adopt, modify, or eschew the experts' advice. Hays found that, "despite the diverse backgrounds of these women they tended to share a specific set of ideas about good child rearing" (p. xvii). "Working-class, poor, professional-class, and affluent mothers alike nearly all believe that child rearing is appropriately child-centered and emotionally absorbing" (p. 113).[13]

Similarly, in *Screening the Los Angeles "Riots"* (1997), Darnell Hunt identifies 14 "assumptions" *encoded* in a 17-minute extract from one news operation's coverage of the first night of the Los Angeles "riots." But Hunt spends the bulk of his analysis explaining how this extract was actually viewed (or "decoded") by differently "raced" viewers. Not surprisingly, Hunt found that "black-raced" and "white-raced" informants decoded the video clip in quite different ways. Specifically, "black-raced" informants "understood themselves first and foremost as '*black*' subjects *vis-à-vis* the events and KTTV text . . . . Accordingly, black-raced informants . . . used the interviews as an opportunity to take oppositional stands and, in the process, (re)affirm their own raced subjectivities" (p. 167). By contrast, "white-raced" viewers tended to focus not on "race" (let alone their *own* race), but on the "brutality of the mob" – as did the incumbent President George Bush, "who stood firm in his early denouncement of the rebellion as 'the brutality of a mob, pure and simple'" (pp. 167–8).[14]

In his recent book on the O. J. trial, Hunt (1999) provides an even more thorough analysis of the processes of *encoding* and *decoding*. First, he ex-

plores "news construction," i.e., the journalistic, organizational, and bureaucratic parameters behind the *production* of O. J. images and stories –
both television and print, and both "black" and "white" media. He explicitly ferrets out the "narratives that have been privileged by mass-circula-
tion" (p. 89). However, in addition to exploring the *symbolic content encoded*
in texts, he also analyzes "the other side of the meaning-negotiation process": audience reception (p. 182). Specifically, Hunt selects "two ten- member
Los Angeles-based groups" – one "black", one "white" – that enable him
"to simulate in the study environment the meaning-negotiation processes
that undoubtedly influenced most observers of the case" (ibid.).

Most interestingly, Hunt's focus groups echoed the "black–white divide" so prevalent in mainstream news media accounts (p. 213). "Whether
the issue was the prosecution and the defense cases, science and DNA,
domestic violence, wealth and celebrity, race, conspiracy, or the *Primetime*
text itself, informant stances could be organized along a single dividing
line: white investment in official institutions and accounts (e.g., criminal
justice system, media) and black suspicion of them."

MEDIA ETHNOGRAPHY

In contrast to corporate focus group researchers, who typically bring together strangers and have them discuss an advertisement or product in
an artificial (or official) environment, audience/reception researchers seek
to uncover how viewers actually "read" or interpret a text in as "natural"
an environment as possible. Liebes and Katz (1990), and Hunt (1997)
seek to transcend simple, "normative" answers that might result from a
formal questionnaire or a one-on- one interview, in order to get a handle
on *genuine* experience and meaning. Thus, they use focus groups made up
of family and friends who meet in their own homes, and they go to great
lengths to minimize the impact and role of the focus group leader.

However, the fact remains that focus groups are *not* natural. Rather,
they are one step *away* from "real life" as it is endogenously produced.
Indeed, one could argue that focus groups are *contrived*, almost "experi-
mental" in form. Thus, critics charge, focus group interviews may not
reveal so much the "natural" process of "decoding," but the quirks and
idiosyncracies of *small group interaction*, which may have only a tangen-
tial relation to the text, and which may shift and slide according to the
dynamics of the group itself.

In recent years, a new type of analysis, called "media ethnography,"
has emerged that takes these concerns seriously. Combining audience/
reception analysis with "naturalistic" field research, media ethnographers
actually go *into* viewers' homes, in order to observe the "watching" of

television in its "natural" setting. The idea is to attend not solely to the interpretation of isolated texts (à la Hunt, and Liebes and Katz), but the entire *practice* of watching television in its natural environment. Media ethnographers shift the focus from the interpretation of the *text* to "the domestic viewing context itself" (Morley 1986, p. 14, as cited by Turner 1996 [1990], p. 134).

One of the earliest and most important of these ethnographic audience analyses is Dorothy Hobson's, *Crossroads: the Drama of a Soap Opera* (1982). In contrast to previously heralded audience/reception studies which relied on formal discussions and/or focus groups, Hobson analyzed the entire *world* of the popular British soap opera *Crossroads*. She attended production meetings, rehearsals, and taping sessions of the show; she talked to those involved about what she observed. Most importantly, she *watched* the show *with* viewers *in their own homes*, at the time they were aired. She had long, unstructured conversations with her subjects about the programs after they were finished. Hobson concludes that "a television program is a three part development – the production process, the program, and the understanding of that program by the audience or consumer – and it is false and elitist criticism to ignore what any member of the audience thinks or feels about the program" (p. 136, as cited by Turner 1996 [1990], p. 132).

Nevertheless, audience/reception researchers and media ethnographers are still vulnerable to the same *realist* criticisms as ethnographers. The danger is in erroneously assuming that there is a single, interpretive "reality" to be "told," and/or in inflating inherently partial "data" into an all too "complete" *narrative*. The final result of audience/reception research is "a particular reconstruction of an individual's narrative, and there could be other reconstructions" (Clandinin and Connelly 1988, p. 39). There are always a rich array of possible field texts (Clandinin and Connelly 1998, p. 167).

Indeed, radical postmodernists not only reject "fixating" meaning in a single *text* (à la orthodox semiotics), but they reject "fixating" meaning in a single discursive *act* as well. Radical postmodernists insist that the reader *continuously* reworks the text as s/he reflects on and recalls the text, and integrates it into new contexts and experiences. How a conversation about a video clip plays itself out today may be totally different from how the discussion plays out tomorrow – even with the same people. The whole notion of *an* "audience" is itself a *fiction* (Hartley 1992). As Hartley (1992, p. 105) maintains: "audiences are not just constructs; they are the invisible fictions that are produced institutionally in order for various institutions to take charge of the mechanisms of their own survival. Audiences may be imagined empirically, theoretically or politically, but in all cases the product is a fiction that serves the need of the imagining institution."

Thus, from a postmodern point of view, meaning is always in process, a momentary stop in a continuous flow of possibilities, a very *un*stable thing, always in a sense both present and absent. This is why the famous French postmodernist Jacques Derrida (1973) invented a new word to describe the divided nature of the sign: *différance* – meaning both to defer and to differ (Storey 1996, p. 60). The idea is that in contrast to "logocentrism," which posits the existence of fixed *meanings*, *différance* sees meaning as permanently *deferred*, always produced by and continuously subject to its difference from other meanings, and thus volatile and unstable. From this perspective, "meaning is always relational, never self-present or self-constituted" (Hawthorn 1994, p. 45). Whether one uses semiotics or audience/reception research, meaning can *never* be completely ascertained.

But of course, the notion that "reality" is completely idiosyncratic and fluid, and that interpretation is completely open, undermines the very idea of doing cultural analysis. It ignores that it is *culture* that enables people to "communicate, perpetuate and develop their knowledge about and attitude toward life" (Griswold 1994, p. 86). Radical postmodernism implies that there are no *patterns* of interpretation or meaning. Indeed, radical postmodernism denies that there are concrete differences between cultural products: we cannot say that some cultural products are "better" or "worse" than others of the same genre, nor can we even describe a cultural product as "inspirational" or "depressing," "happy" or "sad," etc. From this point of view, even individual attitudes and opinions – e.g., whether one *likes* a cultural product or not – are unstable, i.e., depending upon the particular "moment" and context. There are only different people experiencing different cultural products at different moments. Meaning becomes entirely a function of the receiver's mind (Griswold 1994, p. 86). In sum, radical postmodernism denies the very *existence* of the cultural realm, i.e., that the creation and interpretation of texts relies not just on "subjectivity" but *inter*subjectivity.

Narrative Analysis

Anyone who watches a lot of television knows that the media tells the same stories over and over. Television programs rely on a blend of predictability and surprise (Real 1996, p. 124). Television's themes, plots, and characters are new, but familiar. "Narrative analysis" is a general term that refers to the study of *narratives*, i.e., structured stories with a *plot* (or "message"), *setting*, and *characters*, as found in texts, discourse, or events (e.g., a film, a social debate, or a spectacle, such as the O. J. Simpson trial). "Narrative analysis" includes both "rigorous" semiotic analysis (e.g., Wright

1975), systematic cultural sociology (e.g., Jacobs 2000), and literary/ postmodern essays (Morrison 1997).

The central distinguishing characteristic of a "narrative" is that it *organizes* information. Without narrative, there is only a jumble of disconnected "facts." One of the basic ways that narratives are organized is chronologically, i.e., in time. This is most readily apparent in the type of narrative we call "history" (discussed shortly), but *all* narratives, by definition, construe "a chain of events in cause-effect relationship occurring in time and space" (Bordwell and Thompson 1993, p. 65, as cited by Real 1996, p. 125).

Another way that narratives are organized is via *plot* – the events that are selected for narration. Narratives are also organized by their cast of *characters*, most importantly "heroes" and "anti-heroes" (see Alexander and Smith 1993; Jacobs 2000; Wright 1975). Finally, narratives come to us in recognizable groupings – Westerns, science fiction, comedies, and so forth – for which the French word for type of kind, *genre*, has become the label. The value and power of genre is efficacy. "With a few brush strokes directors create and we recognize a western – horses, open range, cowboy hats, six-guns, lawmen, outlaws, and simple codes of force and honor" (Real 1996, p. 130).

Most importantly, it is this organization that drives a text forward. It is the *narrative* that powerfully attracts and holds our attention, that compels us to finish even a lousy book or film (i.e., we want to know how the darn thing will end!) In other words, "the narrative progressively chooses one option and closes off other options . . . the anxiety of the narrative uncertainty is resolved in an experience of psychological and dramatic closure, or resolution, satisfaction, and peace" (Real 1996, pp. 128–9).

Today cultural sociologists, such as Jacobs (2000) and Wagner-Pacifici (2000), are rigorously and *systematically* analyzing the *narratives* behind and within texts. For instance, in his recent *Race, Media, and the Crisis of Civil Society* (2000), Ron Jacobs compares African American and "mainstream" media coverage (in Chicago, New York, and Los Angeles newspapers) of some of the most memorable racial crises since the 1960s. He seeks to show not only how narratives diverge along racial lines, but how race crises are inserted into other, ongoing public narratives about race, nation, and civil society. Jacobs (p. 141) maintains:

> while the black press has introduced new narratives and new points of difference to the interpretation and discussion of public events . . . there are three factors which have prevented it from having a more significant impact on American civil society: (1) the place-bound nature of news media; (2) the racial stratification of the public sphere; and (3) the rise of tragic discourse as the dominant cultural form for discussing race and racial crisis.

Similarly, Robin Wagner-Pacifici (1986; 1994; 2000) systematically and comparatively explores the *narrative* dimensions of social *dramas* (e.g., the kidnapping of the Italian political leader Aldo Moro in 1978 by the Italian terrorist group, the Red Brigades; and contemporary "standoffs", such as Wounded Knee in 1973, MOVE in Philadelphia in 1985, and the Branch Davidians in Waco, Texas in 1993). As Wagner-Pacifici (ibid.) maintains:

> A paradox of the stand-off is that while all participants have committed themselves to the situation . . . they have, in a profound sense, committed themselves to *different* situations. They have taken their "stands," that is positioned themselves around some set of issues. And their definitions of the situation are usually diametrically opposed. Institutions of law and politics and organizations of law enforcement attempt to appropriate the standoff with preferred categories of assessment and control. The antagonist is alternatively terrorist, cultist, fanatic, fundamentalist, or . . . just plain old serial killer. Antistate groups, as well, have their own rigid and reified categories of identity within which they operate.

Within cultural studies, analysts such as Morrison (1997) and Lipsitz (1997a) take a less systematic, more *literary* approach to ferreting out the *narratives* behind and within texts and events. For instance, as discussed in chapter 3, Toni Morrison (1997) points out that the central *setting, plot,* and *characters* of the O. J. spectacle are strikingly familiar:

> A best-seller story requires the familiar ingredients of 'a good read': fame, death, money, sex, villains, and, of course, race, and in this regard Mr. Simpson is ideal – already an entertainer with a surfeit of the talents successful entertainers have. Also, he is black. When race culpability or pathology is added to this market brew, profits soar and the narrative coalesces quickly, takes on another form and moves from commodity to lore. In short to an official story.

According to Morrison (1997, pp. xii; xxvii), the "official story" enlisted not only a protagonist that *epitomized* that "perfect marriage of Jekyll and Hyde," but the *plot* of "*A Birth of a Nation*" writ large. Similarly Lipsitz (1997a, p. 9) maintains:

> The Simpson trial became a story that was easy to sell, in part, because it seemed to replicate so perfectly the world of commercial television and its generic conventions. The athlete/actor/celebrity defendant charged with murder could have come from *Murder, She Wrote* or *Columbo* while the details about his residence and vehicles might fit easily into segments of *Dallas, Dynasty,* or *Life Styles of the Rich and Famous.* For experienced television viewers, courtroom confrontations enacted half-remembered episodes

of *L.A. Law*, *Perry Mason*, and *Quincy*, while the history of unheeded claims of spousal abuse evoked the concerns and conflicts often aired in the movie-of-the-week. The search for justice by grieving relatives and the short, glamorous lives of the victims sparked associations with daily soap operas or weekly serial dramas.

Most importantly, whether done in a "systematic" or "literary" way, contemporary narrative analysts (e.g., Jacobs 2000; Wagner-Pacifici 2000; Morrison 1997; Lipsitz 1997a) emphasize that "real life" is given meaning through acts of narration. As Ricoeur (1971) first pointed out, social action can be read like a *text*; we "read" "real" life using familiar narratives. Similarly, Barthes (1977 [1966], p. 79 as cited by Franzosi 1998, p. 517) maintains:

> Narrative is present in myth, legend, fable, tale, novella, epic, history, tragedy, drama, comedy, mime, painting (think of Carpaccio's Saint Ursula), stained glass windows, cinema, comics, news items, conversations. Moreover, underneath this almost infinite diversity of forms, narrative is present in every age, in every place, in every society; it begins with the very history of mankind and therefore nowhere is nor has been a people without narrative. All classes, all human groups, have their narratives . . . narrative is international, transhistorical, transcultural: It is simply there, like life itself
> . . . .

The fusion of "narrativity" and "real life" is most readily apparent at Disneyland. Walt Disney instilled *narrative* into the park by dividing it into distinctly themed "lands" (Tomorrowland; Fantasyland, etc.). Disney borrowed from his cinematic background and designed each land like a movie lot, so that the visitor experiences a "narrativized space" broken into micronarratives. Thus, as the visitor moves about the park, he or she experiences "thematic coherence" (Willis 1991, p. 57, as cited by Real 1996, p. 129). In addition, the park's moving vehicles (e.g., It's A Small World, the Haunted Mansion, Pirates of the Caribbean, etc.) "carry the viewer through the plot like a movie camera" (Finch 1973, p. 415, as cited by Real 1996, p. 129).

Yet, paradoxically, cultural analysts not only study narratives – they *create* them as well; they do not merely "uncover" preexisting narratives "in" events, but *impose* them. For example, in illuminating the *story, plot* and *characters* of the O. J. spectacle, Lipsitz and Morrison create their *own* stories. Morrison points out the similarities between the O. J. spectacle, Melville's story "Benito Cereno," and the infamous film, *Birth of a Nation*, while Lipsitz draws the comparison between the O. J. spectacle and *Life Styles of the Rich and Famous*, etc. We do not simply "retell" but *create* events through their "retelling," turning selected "facts" into coherent

Figure 6.1 Wiley, *Non Sequitur*: "Realityland," *Los Angeles Times*, August 2, 2000. © 2000 Wiley Miller. Distributed by Universal Press Syndicate. Reprinted with permission. All Rights Reserved.

stories (e.g., "So how did you and John meet?"). "In telling a story, the author attempts to weave a text that re-creates for the reader the real world that was studied" (Denzin 1998, p. 328).

Interestingly, some narrative analysts resolve this confusion between the narrative "studied" and the narrative "constructed" by using the term "story" to refer to the phenomena to be studied and "narrative" to refer to the method or "patterns of inquiry for its study" (Clandinin and Connelly 1998, p. 155). In short, people "lead storied lives and tell stories of those lives, whereas narrative researchers describe such lives, collect and tell stories of them, and write narratives of experience" (Clandinin and Connelly 1998, p. 155). Thus, Morrison titles her narrative on the O. J. spectacle, "The Official *Story*: Dead Man Golfing"; while George Lipsitz titles his narrative on the O. J. spectacle (in the same book), "The Greatest *Story* Ever Sold" (emphasis added).

However, as postmodernists such as Denzin quite rightly point out, this naming *legitimates* and "privileges" academic "stories." Denzin (1998) rejects the distinction between "narrative" and "story," and refers to them all as "storytelling." As Denzin (1998, p. 313) states: "In the social sciences, there is only interpretation. Nothing speaks for itself. Confronted with a mountain of impressions, documents, and field notes, the qualitative researcher faces the difficult and challenging task of making sense of what has been learned" (p. 313). In short, for Denzin (as for most postmodernists), *all* storytelling (whether "sociological," "autobiographical," "historical," "semiotic," "narrative," etc.) is necessarily *partial*, and therefore suspect.

"Hermeneutics" and Social and Cultural History

Though many people conceive of "history" as simply "true" – as opposed to "fiction" which is conceived of as "false" (because it *invents* reality) – historians have long recognized that writing history involves not simply relaying "the facts," but placing them in a *narrative* framework. Historians call this the "problem of selection," i.e., deciding *what* will be told. In the nineteenth century, German historiographer Leopold von Ranke solved "the problem of selection" (how to define his subject matter), with a neat (but wrong-minded) realist elitism. He proposed a "scientific" history that focused on political and religious elites, whom, he supposed, represented the "cutting edge" of history, and defined the overall pattern (J. Hall 1990, p. 18). Even today, historians sometimes *implicitly* adopt this realist, elitist solution (although, like traditional "naturalist" ethnographers, they purport to be simply "reporting" the "facts" as they are "found"). For instance, American grade-school history textbooks still tend to emphasize dates and military leaders/battles/treaties, and imply that these "facts" *are* "history" itself (see Schwartz 1998).

Yet, even in the late nineteenth and early twentieth centuries, the "objectivity" and elitism of Rankean history was called into question. On the one hand, the now-famed French *Annales* school, which first emerged in the 1930s, injected relativity into the historical equation by placing all events on multiple scales of objective time: short-term history (history of the specific event in question), medium-term history (the slower moving time of social forces and economic systems and cycles), and long-term history (the very slow moving history of the physical environment – a level of time which historians had rarely considered before) (J. Hall 1990, p. 18; Fairburn 1999, pp. 35–6). *Annales* adherents advocated interdisciplinary research, and they used quantitative data to address issues such as demography, class, diet, health, and hygiene, though they addressed problems of ideology, collective systems of belief, and worldviews as well.

On the other hand, interpretive historians – including Wilhelm Dilthey, Georg Simmel, Max Weber, and Herbert Mead – focused on reconciling historical causation and action. These latter "subjectivists" argued that meaningful action and interaction gave time its shape, i.e., that "time is subjectively and socially constructed" (J. Hall 1990, p. 19). They sought to show "which events, when their connections are shown, bring to light the patterns of history that are otherwise lost in the detail" (J. Hall 1990, p. 18).

"Social history" has existed since the formation of the *Annales* school, but it gained new impetus in the 1960s and 1970s. Social historians explicitly reject the *elitism* of Rankean history; they make a concerted effort to tell the story of "the people," rather than that simply of "elites." The idea is to include "everyone's past, humble as well as mighty, colonized as well as colonizer, children as well as adults, women as well as men" (Davidoff 1995, p. 14). Toward this end, social historians analyze not only "major" events (e.g., military battles and treaties) reflected in "official" documents and archives; they rely on *popular* documents and texts (e.g., diaries and letters) in order to sort out the experience of "common" folk as well.

Theoretically, social history tends to exhibit an underlying neo-Marxist bent. This is most evident in E. P. Thompson's *The Making of the English Working Class* (1963), which highlights working-class *agency* and resistance to exploitation. Specifically, in this social history (as well as cultural studies) classic, Thompson attacks orthodox labor history for obscuring "the agency of working people, the degree to which they contributed, by conscious efforts, to the making of history" (p. 12). He rejects too the academic tendency to read history "in the light of subsequent preoccupations, and not as in fact it occurred" (ibid.). Thompson sets out to rescue the casualties of ruling class history, "the poor stockinger, the Luddite cropper, the 'obsolete' handloom weaver, the 'utopian' artisan, and even the deluded follower of Joanna Southcott, from the enormous condescension of prosperity" (ibid.). As he maintains: "We cannot understand class unless we see it as a social and cultural formation, arising from processes which can only be studied as they work themselves out over a considerable historical period. This book can be seen as a *biography* of the English working class from its adolescence until its early manhood" (ibid., p.11; emphasis added).

Since E. P. Thompson's seminal study of the English working class, social historians have sought to tell the "untold" story of not only the working class – but underprivileged, or otherwise marginalized groups (i.e., racial/ethnic minorities, women).[15] In addition, social historians have turned toward using oral history (or "life history") in order to get "first-hand" accounts of the past. Oral histories typically consist of a series of "in-depth" (or "depth") interviews – "quality," one-on-one interviews in which a researcher digs deep in conversation with a respondent in a relatively informal way over a long period of time (minimally, two or three hours). The goal in "depth" interviews is to transcend the simple "normative" answers that might result from a questionnaire or formal interview situation, in order to get a handle on *genuine* experience and meaning. Ideally, the interview becomes so "informal" that it is somewhat akin to a "natural" conversation.

Of course the central advantage of oral history over archival sources is that the traditional reliance on *documents* is itself *elitist* – for not everyone (and certainly not illiterate or semiliterate folks) writes letters or keeps diaries, etc, or is officially "tabulated." However, the shift toward oral methods reflects, too, the rejection of not only the *elitism* – but the univocal *realism* – of Rankeian history. The idea is to move beyond demographic and socioeconomic analyses of working-class life to exploring "popular cultural *perceptions*" (Desan 1989, p. 47; emphasis added) as well.

Thus, akin to "personal experience" researchers and "joint-author" ethnographers (see chapter 5), oral historians seek to illuminate the "experience" of their subjects using the subjects' *own voices*.[16] They seek to tell the story of previously ignored or marginalized folks using *their* own words. The goal is to rid history of its traditional academic, *authorial* (as well as historiographical) privilege and elitism – the idea is that if you want to understand the experience of heretofore marginalized individuals, you must simply *ask* them and *listen* to their answers.[17] Oral history also reflects the turn toward interdisciplinarity in recent years, concretely, the *merging* of the social sciences and the humanities (and vice versa).

For instance, in *Living In, Living Out* (1994), Elizabeth Clark-Lewis uses oral history to bring to light the experience of African American women who migrated from the rural South to work as domestic servants in Washington, DC in the early decades of the twentieth century. Clark-Lewis interviews 81 African American women who worked for wealthy white families, telling their stories, because, as Clark-Lewis (1994, p. viii) maintains, history teaches us about "well known names ... but not about women like my ancestors, living relatives, and neighbors. Where were they in the books, where were their voices? This book tries to recover those voices."[18]

This *interpretive* approach to social history is often called "hermeneutic." For instance, Fairburn (1999, p. 31) maintains that E. P. Thompson "self-consciously operates within the *hermeneutic* genre," for Thompson aspires to explain events "by referring to the motives, reasoning, meanings and intentions of the actors" themselves (Fairburn 1999, p. 31; emphasis added). However, "hermeneutics" is much more than simply presenting the "voices" of historical subjects. Thompson takes a hermeneutic approach not because he illuminates the "experience" of the English working class – but because he seeks to *understand* and *explain* this experience, by situating it in a social, cultural, and historical framework. In Alexander's (1987) terminology, the hermeneutic approach resolves the "individual" versus "collective" dilemma – hermeneutics is the *bridge* between *individual* "voices"/interpretations/experiences and symbolic/historical *patterns* (see table 6.1).[19]

Specifically, as the eminent philosopher and historian Wilhelm Dilthey (1833–1911) first maintained, the central feature of hermeneutic analysis is a shifting back and forth from the whole to the part: a whole can only be comprehended in terms of its parts, while the latter acquire their proper meaning within the whole. Dilthey called this process of understanding complex wholes and their parts "the hermeneutic circle." The hermeneutic circle is most readily apparent in terms of words and sentences. For instance, we understand "hand me my clubs" (the whole) by grasping the meaning of the individual words, but we can only select the proper meaning of the word "club" and discard the other meaning of the word "hand" (noun) when we have an idea of what the whole sentence means (Rickman 1976, pp. 9–10). As Rickman (ibid., p. 11) states:

> The hermeneutic circle is so important because the part–whole relationship is, according to Dilthey, pervasive in the human world ... to interpret a culture we must treat it as a system in which art, literature and science are related to each other and in which each fulfills a function ....
>
> Put negatively, this principle means that there are no absolute starting-points, no self- evident, self-contained certainties on which we can build, because we always find ourselves in the middle of complex situations which we try to disentangle by making, then revising, provisional assumptions. This circularity – or perhaps one might call it a spiral approximation towards greater accuracy and knowledge – pervades our whole intellectual life.

More generally, Dilthey defined "hermeneutics" as the "systematic coordination of elementary acts of understanding in order to comprehend the meaning of a complex, permanent expression" (Rickman 1976, pp. 9–10). For "what is usually separated into physical and mental is vitally linked in mankind .... Human beings are unique in their tendency to reflect and comment on their actions. They also convey meaning ... [thus] a proper study of mankind [sic] must emphasize, not obliterate, these features" (Dilthey, in Rickman 1976, p. 170; Rickman 1976, p.8).

In other words, the human studies involves the study of *meanings* and *values*, not just physical objects or overt behaviors; hence the human sciences must be based on a mode of knowledge that goes beyond "perception." As Rickman (1976, p. 9) states:

> Both processes [perception and understanding] are taken for granted in everyday life; we perceive houses or cars and understand (as well as perceive) the smiles of friends or the signals of policemen. Both processes are fallible but also fundamental because we cannot correct mistakes by appealing to another form of cognition. We can only *look* again or try, once more, to *understand.*

Dilthey insisted that "if we are to follow the example of the great pioneers of science such as Galileo, we must (like them) intelligently adjust the methods to our subject matter rather than imitate without regard to the subject matter, the methods they had actually used" (Rickman 1988, p. 58).[20]

Since E. P. Thompson's seminal, *interpretive* study of the English working class, cultural sociologists and cultural historians have used just this type of *hermeneutic* approach to *understand* and *explain* historical processes of *symbolization.* One recent exemplar in this regard is cultural sociologist Barry Schwartz's (2000) examination of the national *memory* of Abraham Lincoln. Drawing on a wide variety of sources (art and statuary, schoolbooks and speeches, surveys, etc.), Schwartz tracks the steady, relentless evolution of the *image* of Lincoln in our national consciousness. Schwartz argues that Abraham Lincoln came to be revered as he was as much on account of the needs of particular historical moments and groups in the population as because of his own deeds and words.[21]

Similarly, in *Consumer Rites* (1995), cultural historian Leigh Eric Schmidt thoroughly explores the historical importance and *meaning* of American holidays. Borrowing from the anthropology of festival and celebration, the sociology of consumption and gift exchange, as well as the history of popular culture and religion, Schmidt points out that it is not simply an issue of commercialization and secularization – but "devout consumption" (to use Veblen's sardonic phrase[22]). People construct, design, and order their physical world through goods and gifts. States Schmidt (1995, p. 9), "social critics have all too often succumbed to the temptation of seeing gifts and goods in terms of simplicities: hierarchic display, status competition, consumer manipulation, capitalist hegemony, mass-cultural banality, and the like. Lost in such interpretations are the miscellany of cultural meanings and the array of intimate relationships that various possessions and presents embody".

In sum, the works of Schwartz (2000) and Schmidt (1995) are exemplary because they do not merely seek to "document" – but to *understand* and *explain* – *cultural* phenomena (historical "memories" and holidays); they are interested in *understanding* and *explaining* not only "events" and/or "products", but *systems of meaning.* This brings us to the work of the late French theorist (and historian) Michel Foucault, who first forged the links between "history" and "structuralism", i.e. who first called our attention to discursive *genealogy*.

From Structuralism to Poststructuralism: Historicizing Discourse

As discussed previously, for Saussure, the relation between the signifier (e.g., the symbol "tree") and the signified (e.g., the concept or image in our heads conjured up by the symbol "tree") is arbitrary. Signs do not possess a fixed or essential meaning. Thus, for instance, we could just as well use "blue" to *mean* "stop" (e.g., in a stoplight), and "pink" to *mean* "go." Similarly, we could just as well call the four-legged animal "sheet" rather than "sheep" (and the rectangular bedding item "sheep"), or we could call it "dog" or "cat." The relation between the signifier and the signified is fixed only by habit and tradition.

Most importantly, this means that the relation between the signifier and the signified is never *permanently* fixed. Words shift in their meaning (the term "gay" is a good example). The relation between the signifier and the signified changes, historically, "and every shift alters the conceptual map of the culture, leading different cultures, at different historical moments, to classify and think about the world different" (Hall 1997, p. 32). "Because it is arbitrary, the sign is totally subject to history and the combination at the particular moment of a given signifier and signified is a contingent result of the historical process" (Culler 1976, p. 36, as cited by Hall 1997, p. 32).

In the 1970s, the late French theorist Michel Foucault (1926–84), invented a new historical, poststructuralist type of discourse analysis. Foucault, who was trained as an historian but particularly influenced by linguistics and structuralism, sought not to simply identify the discursive structures at the heart of a society or social group at a specific point in time (à la semiotics/structuralism), but to situate them in a *social* and *historical* framework. Foucault makes us aware that *the present has not always been* (Baert 1998, p. 121). Foucault showed that every historical *period* has its own discourse and therefore knowledge practices; he set out to illuminate what he calls the *genealogy* of discourse, or the *archeology* of knowledge (Hall 1997, p. 46). For Foucault, the goal of discourse analysis is not merely to demonstrate that symbolic elements exist, but to show *why* it is "that one particular statement appeared rather than another in a field of discourse" (Foucault 1969, p. 27).

For instance, in his famous historical study of human sexuality (1978) Foucault maintains that while sexual relations have always existed, "sexuality," i.e., a specific way of talking about, studying, and regulating sexual desire, its secrets, and its fantasies, only appeared in Western societies at a particular historical moment. Thus, while there may always have been homosexual forms of behavior, "the homosexual" as "a specific kind of social subject, was *produced*, and could only make its appearance within the moral, legal, medical and psychiatric discourses, practices and institutional apparatuses of the late nineteenth century, with their particular theories of sexual perversity" (Weeks 1981, 1985, as cited by Hall 1997, p. 46).

Similarly, Foucault (1961) argues that it was only *within* a definite discursive formation that the object "madness" could appear at all as a meaningful or intelligible construct, and that it was only after a certain definition of "madness" was put into practice, that the appropriate subject – "the madman" – could appear (Hall 1997, p. 46). As Foucault (1961, p. 32) states: "Madness was constituted by all that was said, in all the statements that named it, divided it up, described it, explained it, traced its development, indicated its various correlations, judged it, and possibly gave it speech by articulating, in its name, discourses that were to be taken as its own."

Specifically, until the seventeenth century, persons and actions considered to be evil were dealt with in public, and madness and reason were not separated. But in the seventeenth century, shame became associated with that which was considered "inhuman," and confinement became the standard means for dealing with those who were considered morally or spiritually "evil" (Ritzer 1997, p. 48). In the nineteenth century, the discourse of scientific psychology and psychiatry further *separated* the "mad" from the "sane." But, rather than see this development as a scientific "advance," Foucault sees it as a conversion of "therapeutics into repression" (Foucault 1961, p. 266). Now the madman was constantly being watched, judged, and condemned; he was "imprisoned in a moral world" (Foucault 1961, p. 269).

Most importantly, as a poststructuralist, Foucault does not see the development of "madness" as an isolated process. Rather, Foucault sees a *discursive relationship* between the founding of houses of confinement, e.g., hospitals, asylums, workhouses, and prisons. In his later work, especially, Foucault focused on how *power* operated within what he called the institutional *apparatus* and its *technologies* (techniques), i.e., that *knowledge* was put to work through discursive practices in specific institutional settings to regulate the conduct of others. Foucualt's conception of the *apparatus* of punishment included a variety of diverse elements, linguistic and non-linguistic – discourses, institutions, architectural arrangements, regulations, laws, administrative measures, scientific statements, philosophic propositions, morality, philanthropy, etc. (Hall 1997, p. 47). As Foucault (1980, p. 131, as cited by Hall 1997, p. 49) states:

> Each society has its regime of truth, its "general politics" of truth; that is, the types of discourse which it accepts and makes function as true, the mechanisms and instances which enable one to distinguish true and false statements, the means by which each is sanctioned ... the status of those who are charged with saying what counts as true.

On one hand, Foucault's conceptualization of power and knowledge is similar to the neo-Marxist notion of "ideology": both emphasize the intertwined power relation between ideology/knowledge and structures/institutions. In expressing a way of seeing, knowledge/power simultaneously expresses a way of *not* seeing. Knowledge/power is *exclusionary*: it silences alternative understandings. However, Foucault rejected the neo-Marxist image of power as always radiating in a single direction – from top to bottom – and coming from a specific source (e.g., the sovereignty, the state, the ruling class, etc.) (Hall 1997, p. 49). Rather, Foucault (1980, p. 119, as cited by Hall 1997, p. 50) thought of power as "deployed and exercised through a net-like organization." For Foucault, power *circulates* rather than functions "in the form of a chain." It is never monopolized by one center (Hall 1997, p. 49). Thus, Foucault insists that power relations permeate all levels of social life, and are therefore to be found operating at every site of social life – in the private spheres of the family and sexuality as much as in the public spheres of politics and the law (Hall 1997, p.50).

In addition, Foucault rejected the traditional Marxist dichotomy (most readily apparent in the Frankfurt school) between "true" (i.e., class) and "false consciousness." Foucault maintained that *no* form of thought could claim an absolute hold on "truth." Foucault believed that all political and social forms of thought were inevitably caught up in the interplay of knowledge and power (Hall 1997, p. 48). As Foucault states:

> There is not, on the one side, a discourse of power, and opposite, another discourse that runs counter to it. Discourses are tactical elements or blocks operating in the field of force relations; there can exist different and contradictory discourses within the same strategy; they can, on the contrary, circulate without changing their form from one strategy to another, opposing strategy.

In other words, for Foucault, there is no privileged standpoint (like that asserted for the working class by Marxists). We are all trapped within culturally constructed standpoints that imprison our reasoning (Hall and Neitz 1993, pp. 149–50). Thus for instance, Foucault does not cast blame on doctors for the medicalization of madness, sexuality, etc., for they, like patients, are governed by the categories that discipline their thinking.

In this respect, Foucault's approach can be considered somewhat "neo-Durkheimian." Both Durkheim and Foucault assume an *overarching* symbolic framework, i.e., they both see elites as "victims" of systems of knowledge/power (though, in contrast to Durkheim, Foucault shows that when elites operationalize power/knowledge, the societal *impact* is great). Foucault maintains that resistance cannot emerge in *exteriority* to (or in the absence of) power. Foucault sees power as not only repressive or as an impediment – but as also constitutive. Foucault maintains that rather than simply label discourse "hegemonic" or "resistant," we must consider them as *interlinking* parts of the same system. As Foucault (1978) states:

> We must conceive of discourse as a series of discontinuous segments whose tactical function is neither uniform nor stable. To be more precise, we must not imagine a world of discourse divided between accepted discourse and excluded discourse, or between the dominant discourse and the dominated one; but as a multiplicity of discursive elements that can come into play in various strategies.

Yet it is precisely this ambiguity that annoys Foucault's critics. They think that Foucault's emphasis on "fluidity" and "contradiction" merely reflects fuzzy thinking, and avoidance of responsibility. Neo-Marxists have been especially concerned about Foucault's redefinition of "power" as not merely "negative." As Baert (1998, p. 130) states:

> A concept which hardly excludes anything is a highly suspect one. Why stretch the concept of power beyond the boundaries of our daily use of the concept, and why neglect fine distinctions drawn by other theorists? Concepts, such as the Parsonian concepts of influence, socialization, and internalization, suddenly fall under the imperialist heading of the catch-all Foucauldian concept of power or domination.

Nevertheless, Foucault's discursive approach has been extraordinarily influential. Today all sorts of analysts are investigating the social construction of, and meanings behind and within, *discourse*, in the spirit of Foucault, often in rich detail.

Conclusion

In this chapter we have seen that there are many different ways to analyze discourse. We have explored both quantitative and qualitative versions of discourse analysis (e.g., Gerbner's studies of television violence; Carbaugh's analysis of *Donahue*). We have seen that quantitative content analysis studies are useful in specifying the *prevalence* of and *correlations* between specific media images, but that qualitative discourse or textual analysis may be better attuned to sorting out what specific images *mean*. In terms of "qualitative content analysis," we have focused especially on "semiotics," i.e., the formal study of sign *systems* or patterns of meaning. We have seen that semioticians illuminate the *meaning* of symbols by showing how symbols are *interrelated*; they focus on symbolic *organization*. However, orthodox semiotics tends to be deterministic as well as ahistorical; it illuminates *systems* of symbols, but leaves out the specific idiosyncratic and historical conditions behind and within individual interpretation. Audience/reception analysis emerged as a direct challenge to the symbolic determinism of semiotics (and mass culture theory). In contrast to semioticians, audience/reception analysts focus on how specific individuals/groups *read* and *interpret* texts. Today contemporary cultural analysts, such as Hunt (1997; 1999) and Hays (1996), use both discourse analysis and audience/reception studies in order to illuminate how culture works from both the "bottom up" as well as the "top down."

Theoretically, Hays and Hunt seek to insert *contingency* and individual *agency* into qualitative discourse analysis. Similarly, semioticians such as Umberto Eco, narrative analysts such as Jacobs (2000) and Morrison (1997), and poststructuralists such as Foucault all attempt to highlight the *structure* of codes, but without eliminating individual interpretation and the potential for *change*. These more multidimensional approaches to culture are intimately related to an "hermeneutic" approach, i.e., ferreting out the "part" and the "whole," in order to *understand* as well as *explain* individual experience/agency as well as larger historical and symbolic patterns. In the next chapter, we continue our exploration of methodologically multifaceted, theoretically multidimensional approaches to culture and society, focusing on what I call "comprehensive" cultural sociology.

IMPORTANT CONCEPTS INTRODUCED IN THIS CHAPTER

- Content analysis
- Structuralism
- Semiotics
- Audience/reception studies
- Focus groups
- Media ethnography
- Narrative analysis
- Social history
- Oral history
- Hermeneutics
- Cultural history
- Discourse analysis (Foucault)
- Genealogy (Foucault)

214 *Discourse Analysis and Audience/Reception Research*

STUDY QUESTIONS

1 Videotape three episodes of a sitcom that you like, or that you regularly watch. Now, do a quantitative content analysis of some concrete behavior on, or element of, the show, such as (1) acts of violence, (2) alcohol or drug use, or (2) the ethnic/racial, class, or gender distribution of the show's characters. Are the categories and numbers you found interesting? Do they succinctly and accurately capture some basic elements of the show? Why or why not?

2 Do a *qualitative* discourse analysis based on your findings in question 1. Assess, for instance, what the most prominent incidents of violence *mean* on this show, or the *representations behind* specific gendered, classed, and raced characters. Can you combine quantitative and qualitative analysis in a fruitful way? In other words, do the two types of analysis *together* provide a better understanding of "what is going on" on this show than either one alone?

3 Do a systematic discourse analysis of a volatile social debate of particular concern to you (e.g., affirmative action, abortion). Specifically, find and analyze each and every article, editorial, etc., in a specific media (e.g., *The New York Times, The Nation*) over a specific time period concerning this particular issue. You may choose one source (e.g., *The New York Times*) or several (e.g., *Newsweek, The Nation*), but it is imperative to include in your analysis each and every article about your subject for a clearly specified time period. Identify the *core symbols* at the heart of the debate, i.e., explain *what* the core symbols are, and *how* the symbols are used (e.g., by different people in different situations). Are the core symbols the same over time and between social groups (e.g., men and women, etc.)? Are the *meanings* of the symbols the same over time? How so? If you wish, you can discuss the possible resolutions to this conflict. See Edles (1998), Luker (1991), and Binder (1993) for models and examples.

4 Do an *historical* discourse analysis of a particular issue (e.g., "family values"), or cultural product (e.g., *Pokémon*), i.e., using as many materials about the issue/product as you can find. The goal is to explain (1) what the salient symbols and features of this issue/product are, and (2) how and why these symbols and features have (and have not) changed over time.

5 Conduct an *oral history* in which you interview a family member or close friend about a significant historical moment in their lives. The goal in this project is to simply "report" the "voice" and "experience" of your subject, as accurately as you can. Be sure to *tape record* and transcribe your interview; you also may want to conduct the interview in more than one segment (e.g., two one-hour interviews) so your subject does lose his/her interest/concentration. Write a two- to five-page paper on what you found. Remember, the goal is to *describe* in as rich detail as possible, the *particular* experience of your interviewee, without unnecessary abstraction. See Rubin

and Rubin (1995) for nuts-and-bolts information about doing interview research; see Clark-Lewis (1994) and Weitz (1992) for two excellent empirical models.

6   Conduct two (or more) one-on-one interpretive interviews or conduct a focus group interview (or two or three) about a specific social issue (e.g., abortion, body piercing) or cultural product (e.g., a television show, like *Survivor*). Be sure to *tape record* your interviews; you'll need to transcribe them, and listen to them again and again. Write a two- to five-page essay on the *symbolic scaffolding* behind and within this issue/product. Your goal is to identify core symbols and what they mean to specific individuals, i.e., how they are used.

7   Conduct a focus group (or two or three) regarding a specific "ritual media event" or a popular television show (use a video clip). The purpose of this project is to find out what makes the show or event *appealing* or *intriguing*. Begin by asking the group to "summarize" the video clip and then move on to specific issues (which will depend on the specific clip at hand). See Morgan (1988) for methodological guidance on how to do focus groups. See also Liebes and Katz (1990) and Hunt (1997, 1999) for excellent models.

8   Conduct a media ethnography in your own home. Describe in detail *how* your household uses television, i.e., exactly when the television is on, who watches and how (e.g., attentively or in passing). Do different members of the household "view" shows differently? How so? Can you identify any *temporal, gender,* or other patterns?

Suggested Further Reading

Carbaugh, Donal. 1989 [1994]. *Talking American: Cultural Discourses on DONAHUE.* Norwood, NJ: Ablex Publishing.

Clark-Lewis, Elizabeth. 1994. *Living In, Living Out: African American Domestics in Washington, D.C., 1910-1940.* Washington, DC: Smithsonian.

Edles, Laura Desfor. 1998. *Symbol and Ritual in the New Spain: The Transition to Democracy After Franco.* Cambridge: Cambridge University Press.

Foucault, Michel. 1973. [1966]. *The Order of Things: An Archaeology of the Human Sciences.* New York: Vintage.

——. 1978. *The History of Sexuality*, vol. 1. New York: Vintage.

Hays, Sharon. 1996. *The Cultural Contradictions of Motherhood.* New Haven, CT: Yale University Press.

Hunt, Darnell. 1997. *Screening the Los Angeles Riots.* Cambridge: Cambridge University Press.

——. 1999. *O. J. Simpson Facts and Fictions.* Cambridge: Cambridge University Press.

Jacobs, Ronald N.. 2000. *Race, Media and the Crisis of Civil Society.* Cambridge:

Cambridge University Press.

Liebes, Tamar, and Elihu Katz. 1990. *The Export of Meaning*. Oxford: Oxford University Press.

Schmidt, Leigh Eric. 1995. *Consumer Rites*. Princeton, NJ: Princeton University Press.

Schwartz, Barry. 2000. *Abraham Lincoln and the Forge of National Memory*. Chicago: University of Chicago Press.

Schwartz, Barry and Todd Bayma. 1999. "Commemoration and the Politics of Recognition: The Korean War Veterans Memorial," *American Behavioral Scientist* 42 (6): 946–67.

Thompson, E. P. 1963. *The Making of the English Working Class*. New York: Random House.

Wagner-Pacifici, Robin. 1986. *The Moro Morality Play: Terrorism as Social Drama*. Chicago: University of Chicago Press.

———. 2000. *Theorizing the Standoff: Contingency and Action*. Cambridge: Cambridge University Press.

Wagner-Pacifici, Robin, and Barry Schwartz. 1991. "The Vietnam Veterans Memorial: Commemorating a Difficult Past," *American Journal of Sociology* 97: 376–420.

Notes

1   Though quantitative content analysis can be considered a type of discourse analysis, in the remainder of this chapter I use the term "content analysis" (or "quantitative content analysis") to refer to the traditional, quantitative type of textual inquiry, and I use the terms "textual analysis" and "discourse analysis" synonymously to refer to a broad range of qualitative discursive approaches.

2   Today intellectual historians identify Du Bois as one of the founders of American empirical sociology, a characterization based on his book *The Philadelphia Negro* (1899) – the first major empirical sociological study of Negro life in the United States (Cruz 1997, p. 104). However in addition, as discussed in chapter 5, Du Bois was one of the first American sociologists to use ethnography to study a marginalized urban social group, and as discussed in chapter 4, Du Bois was one of the first to study race and representation. See Cruz (1997) for more on how Du Bois's work fits within historical, interpretive, cultural, and sociological traditions.

3   The analysts defined violence as "any overt depiction of a credible threat of physical force or the actual use of such force intended to physically harm an animate being or groups of beings" (p. 41, as cited by Grossberg et al. 1998).

4   *Los Angeles Times* (January 12, 2000, p. F1).

5   Stinchcombe (1978, p. 6) makes a similar point regarding quantitative history:

The problem of quantitative history is not, then, that numbers cannot be illuminating. The problem is instead that if a scholar is going to select only one aspect of an instance (say of a proletarian) to make him comparable to the next proletarian, in preparation for counting, that scholar better have hold of the causally relevant aspect of the instances before counting.

6   While today many cultural analysts use the terms "symbol" and "sign" interchangeably, historically semioticians have used these terms in a more precise way. Following C. S. Peirce (1839–1914), semioticians have tended to distinguish three basic types of "signs": (1) images or *icons*, which are more or less graphic representations, more or less faithful to the object; (2) *indices*, i.e., beings or objects linked to the symbolized object and necessary to its existence, for example, smoke is an *index* of fire; and (3) *symbols*, which concern an *arbitrary* form of signification, which arises from a social convention of limited validity in space and time (e.g., a word) (Thom 1985, p. 275).

7   Similarly, even though early language systems and Eastern characters were/ are pictographic–ideographic (drawn to resemble the object at hand), there are still a variety of ways any particular object can be drawn, such that even ideographic language systems rely on habit and tradition.

8   In Molière's *L'Ecole des Femmes* and Racine's *Andromaque*.

9   As indicated in note 6 above, this is the crux of semioticans'distinction between "symbol" and "sign." For Saussure (1915) (reprinted in Innis 1985, p. 38), in *symbols*, "there is a rudiment of a natural bond between the signifier and the signified. The symbol of justice, a pair of scales, could not be replaced by just any other symbol, such as a chariot."

10   See Shively (1992) for an interesting audience/reception study that both expands on and challenges Wright's thesis. See Berger (1995) for a criticism of Wright from a "production of culture" point of view. However, to me, Berger's critique (e.g., that Wright does not attend "to the fact that the cowboy is a 'farm worker' to the Bureau of Labor Statistics" – p. 63) simply reflects a misunderstanding as to what structuralists do.

11   Interestingly, Eco does not discuss the extraordinary racialization in his example (beautiful, long, *white* neck). But clearly, the "swan" metaphor above both reflects and reaffirms the existence of a "white" standard of beauty, a predominant, often hegemonic cultural pattern. In other words, Eco further demonstrates that "race" is more akin to *language* than *biology*. "Race" is a cultural *code*, with specific symbolic parameters, although, as Eco pointedly states, the symbols that make up codes are far from stagnant; they shift and slide. Thus, the existence of a cultural code, such as the swan/beauty metaphor or the Negro/ape metaphor (see chapter 4), does not mean that this metaphor is unilaterally internalized as a static "value" for any particular person or group. Rather, it means that this symbolization is *recognized*. Hence, ironically, even in its very reversal, the original cultural pattern is thereby oftentimes reaffirmed. Thus for instance, it is an open question whether the appropriation of the "Negro-ape" metaphor by black artists, such as Da Lench Mob – whose recent works include *Guerrillas in the Mist* (1992) and *Planet of the Apes* (1995) – successfully *subverts* and *challenges*, or further reaffirms, the symbolic patterns upon which *they themselves* rely.

12   See Edles (1998) for another example of this same type of semiotic analysis. I use systematic discourse analysis to show how a new symbolic framework emerged in post-Franco Spain which enabled the resolution of specific events critical to the success of the Spanish democratic transition.

13   Though Hays's book is an excellent methodological exemplar – demonstrating the merits of combining textual analysis and audience/reception research – Hays does not discuss the "white," middle-class origins and dimensions of the ideology of intensive mothering. *All* the experts (both British and American) were "white"; 28 out of 38 mothers that Hays interviewed were "white," 6 were Latinas, 2 were Asian American, and two were African American. Thus the question remains, to what extent does this discourse, prominent (or dominant) in the United States, compare to the discourse about mothering in communities in which women have *always* "worked" outside the home (i.e., African American communities)? Put in another way, it is interesting to compare Hays's thesis with the ideas about mothering revealed in Clark-Lewis's study of African American women who worked as "live-in" and "live-out" domestics. Many of Clark-Lewis's subjects spent an extraordinary amount of time away from their *own* children. More positively, a comparison of mothering ideology in African American and predominantly "white" communities would be an excellent topic for future research (as would cross-national research of this kind).

14   In *Screening the L.A. Riots*, Hunt quite rightly problematizes traditional racial categories; "to proceed as if 'race'-per-se explains differences in the television experience essentializes 'race' and explains nothing . . . . The real question . . . is . . . how does raced subjectivity influence the television decoding process, and how does this process, in turn influence the construction and reproduction or raced subjectivities?" (1997, p. 217). However, Hunt labels his focus groups according to the "race" of each group *leader* (rather than the self-identity of each informant). Consequently, in one "Latino-raced" group, three out of four of his informants identified themselves as "white" or "Caucasian"; while in one "white-raced" group, half of the "white-raced" informants identified themselves as "Asian." The latter phenomenon is most problematic because Hunt had no "Asian" focus group leader, thus the "Asian" voices were completely wiped out in Hunt's qualitative analysis, and implicitly subsumed as "white-raced." Ironically, this phenomenon coincides with the current trend, discussed in chapter 4, of pitting "whites" and "Asians" together *against* blacks (and to a lesser extent, Latinos) in our contemporary system of racialization.

15   Indeed, in the last several years, feminists have criticized Thompson for assuming that the experience of exploitation and struggle by English working-class women was the same as it was for working-class men.

16   Rose Weitz's thoughtful book, *Living with AIDS* (1992), demonstrates the virtues of personal experience methods. Weitz interviewed 37 men and women with HIV in order to find out what "living with AIDS" is like, especially "how the lives of persons with HIV disease change as a result of their illness and how they cope with these changes" (1992, p. 3). Most importantly, Weitz places the voices and concerns of her *subjects* (rather than herself or

"academia") at the forefront of her analysis. In stark contrast to either the conversation analyst or semiotician, Weitz seeks to present "a *holistic* picture of the experiences of persons with HIV disease, using their own words wherever appropriate and focusing on the issues that they consider important in the experience of living with AIDS" (ibid; emphasis added).

17 Morley (1996b, pp. 20–1) warns that providing "voice" to a "marginalized" people may not necessarily have the "ends" that politically liberal analysts might hope, for "it can also produce a disempowering incoherence, even if the analyst, in disburdening him or herself of the responsibility of producing an explicit meta-narrative, is able to step more lightly the while."

However, for folks who have long been ignored, or who are just beginning to speak in their own name and to develop their own past and future, locating "voice" is not at all inconsequential. "Who speaks and who is heard are political questions, a fact that is especially apparent when people in positions of low status and power find their voice" (McCall and Wittner 1990, pp. 46–7).

18 Also parallel to Thompson, Clark-Lewis emphasizes not only the unique experience of her subjects, but their *resistance* to exploitation. She maintains that the women she interviewed "encountered – but never accepted – the master–servant relationship," and she recounts "the strategies they used to change their status from 'live-in' servants to daily paid workers who 'lived out'" (book flap).

19 See Winthrop Jordan, *White Over Black* (1968) and David Roediger, *The Wages of Whiteness* (1991) (discussed in chapter 4) for two excellent "hermeneutic" social historical analyses of "race."

20 See also Alexander and Smith (1993); and "Dilthey, Wilhelm," *Microsoft7 Encarta7 98 Encyclopedia* © 1993–7 Microsoft Corporation.

21 See Schwartz (1987); Wagner-Pacifici and Schwartz (1991); and Schwartz and Bayma (1999) for equally insightful, well-researched, historical, interpretive work.

22 Thorstein Veblen's *The Theory of the Leisure Class* (1899), is a now classic account of the status struggle of the *nouveaux riches* in the United States in the latter half of the nineteenth century. Veblen shows how the new upper class sought to translate its money into symbols of status. He coined such terms as "devout consumption" and "conspicuous waste."

CHAPTER SEVEN

Structure, Agency, and "Comprehensive" Cultural Sociology

In this final chapter, we focus on "comprehensive" cultural sociology – i.e., theoretically multidimensional, methodologically multifaceted, "hermeneutic" explorations of culture. We begin by looking at the work of two very important, multidimensional social and cultural analysts: Erving Goffman and Pierre Bourdieu. We will see that Goffman (whose dramaturgical approach was discussed in chapter 5) was interested not only in interaction, but in the subjective cultural schemas behind social organization; while Bourdieu confronts issues of "culture," "structure," and "agency" head-on by creating new concepts that explicitly integrate both the constraints and the contingencies of our everyday world.

Frame Analysis

In his later work, Erving Goffman turned from a more concrete analysis of the self in society to a seemingly more abstract analysis of the principles that organize our experience (Branaman 1997, p. lxxiv). In his quest to illuminate the implicit expectations for civil behavior, Goffman turned toward explaining the *subjective cultural schemas* behind social organization. He pointed out that social experience is organized in *frames*, which he defined as principles of organization which govern the subjective meaning we assign to social events. Goffman (1997, p. 155) used the term "*frame analysis*" to refer to the "examination in these terms of the organization of experience," i.e., how symbolic representations and messages are selectively conveyed to persuade an audience (Gusfield 1989, pp. 8–10).

Yet, despite his developing interest in schemas, Goffman never abandoned his focus on *social interaction.* He continually emphasized that "people encounter each other's minds only by interaction, and the quality and character of these interactions come to constitute the consequential reality of everyday life" (Brissett and Edgley 1990, p. 37, as cited by Adler and Adler 1998, p. 92). Goffman emphasized that individual participants in social encounters do not usually create the frames that determine the meaning of their experience (1974, p. 11, as cited by Branaman 1997, p. lxxiv); but he sought "to isolate some of the basic frameworks of understanding available in our society for making sense out of events and to analyze the special vulnerabilities to which these frames of reference are subject" (Goffman 1974, p. 11; 1997, p. 155).

Most importantly, Goffman's dual emphasis on cultural and social structures (or cognition and behavior) reflects his acknowledgment of both "structure" and "agency." As William Gamson et al. (1992, p. 384, as cited by Sasson 1995, p. 10) quite rightly point out, this is precisely the strength of Goffman's concept of "frame":

> On one hand, events and experiences are framed; on the other hand, we frame events and experiences. Goffman warns us that "organizational premises are involved, and those are something cognition arrives at, not something cognition creates or generates." At the same time, he calls attention to the fragility of frames in use and their vulnerability to tampering. This underlines the usefulness of framing as a bridging concept between cognition and culture. A cultural level analysis tells us that our political world is framed, that reported events are pre-organized and do not come to us in raw form. But we are active processors and however encoded our received reality, we may decode it in different ways.

Since the 1980s, sociologists have developed Goffman's work on framing and applied it empirically. "Frame analysis" has become particularly prominent in the study of social movement organizations. Social movement researchers argue that "frames" are what make "facts" intelligible, and that political conflicts are, in part, symbolic contests between contesting frames (Sasson 1995, p. 10). They show how politicians, grassroots activists, journalists and other claimsmakers vie with one another to get their definition of the situation before the public and to rebut those of their rivals. They measure their own success . . . by the degree of visibility they win for their preferred frames" (Gamson et al. 1992, as cited by Sasson 1995, p. 10).[1]

Though there are important exceptions, social movement researchers tend to stress the *rationalistic* dimensions of framing, i.e., how individuals actively and *strategically use* frames in mobilization (Snow and Benford 1988).[2] This *rationalistic* approach to framing is rooted in an "action-centered" conceptualization of culture as "a *'tool-kit'* of symbols, stories rituals and worldviews, which people may *use* in varying configurations to solve different kinds of problems" (Swidler 1986, p. 273; emphasis added). As Ann Swidler (1995, p. 34) states:

> Since social movements lack political power . . . they can reshape the world more effectively through redefining its terms rather than rearranging its sanctions. And of course opponents employ the giant machinery of publicity that defines antiwar activists as unpatriotic, feminists as man haters, and the wealthy as beleaguered taxpayers to subvert social movements and their goals, precisely by winning the battle for symbolic encoding.

To be sure, social movement researchers acknowledge that "not all symbols are equally potent" (W. A. Gamson 1998, p. 202). They emphasize that certain frames resonate with "cultural narrations, that is with the stories, myths, and folk tales that are part and parcel of one's cultural heritage" (Snow and Benford 1988, as cited by W. A. Gamson 1998, p. 203). However, rather than explore the subconscious, historical, and/or cultural reasons behind and within a frame's "success," social movements researchers emphasize how activists *mold* "symbols, values, meanings, icons, and beliefs . . . to suit the movement's aims" (ibid.). Social movement frame analysts stress "the intentional assembly of frame packages" (Gamson 1988, as cited by Johnston 1995, p. 217), and how frames are "injected into the broader culture via institutionalization and routinization" (Johnston and Klandermans 1995, p. 9).

This *rationalistic* approach to framing contrasts significantly with Goffman's more multidimensional approach. Goffman never lost sight of the *interpenetration* of collective structures and individual agency. This is most evident in "Felicity's Condition," one of Goffman's final essays; as Goffman (1983a, pp. 50–1, as cited by Lemert 1997b, p. xvi) states:

> The general constraint that an utterance must satisfy, namely, that it connects acceptably with what the recipient has in, or can bring to, mind, applies in a manner to nonlinguistic acts in wordless contexts . . . . Whenever we come in contact with another through the mails, over the telephone, in face-to-face talk, or even merely through immediate co-presence, we find ourselves with one central obligation: to render our behavior understandably relevant to what the other can come to perceive is going on. Whatever else, our activity must be addressed to the other's mind, that is, to the other's capacity to read our words and actions for evidence of our feelings, thoughts, and intent. This confines what we say and do, but it also allows us to bring to bear all the world to which the other can catch allusions.

In other words, the problem with "action-centered" approaches to culture is that they disregard the intersubjective cultural "field" on which discursive interaction "games" are played, the symbolic dimensions *not amenable* to conscious manipulation (Alexander and Smith 1993, p. 159). But as T. S. Eliot (1948, pp. 94, 107, as cited by Eagleton 2000, p. 113) eloquently points out, "culture cannot altogether be brought to consciousness; and the culture of which we are wholly conscious is never the whole of culture."

Nina Eliasoph (1999) takes a less rationalistic, more "Goffmanian" approach to discourse and interaction. She uses participant observation to uncover the "everyday" racial discourse of a country-western dance club. She wants to know "how people talk about race in conversations that are not exclusively devoted to talking about race" (p. 479). As she (ibid.) maintains: "we have not yet examined how people talk about race in everyday life, in natural settings, where race is but one of many topics of conversation, to hear how the topic of race flows in and out of speech, and how speech about race circulates through the body politic. This exploration is an attempt to remedy that gap."

Interestingly, Eliasoph found that "politically incorrect" race talk was *normative* in the all-white country-western dance group. But Eliasoph maintains that this "compulsory racism" was more of "a move in a game" (Goffman 1981), than an expression of deeply held beliefs or ideas. It was part and parcel of a "strenuous effort at appearing unconstrained." As Eliasoph (ibid., p. 487) states:

> Common sense among country-western dancers held that the goal for fun, free time was to avoid constraint. Conversation – of which there was very little to begin with – was devoted to demonstrating energetically how free and unconstrained speakers felt. In practice, that meant searching very hard for things to say that would violate some taboo that "everyone knew" was out there. In this strenuous, mandatory effort at appearing unconstrained, most conversation had to take the form of racist, sexist, homophobic, and scatological jokes. Group conversation was almost never serious.

Thus, Eliasoph concludes that the *interactional* reasons for appearing racist (or complacent about racism) were far more important than inner "beliefs." "The beliefs that mattered most were beliefs about talk itself: about how talk matters, about where to talk, about what is polite to say where" (p. 499). What this research demonstrates is that "race talk" is far more complex than many analysts let on. "Race talk" is a flexible system of meaning that individuals bring with them into all sorts of interactions, in all sorts of ways. In my view, this indicates that eliminating racism in the United States necessitates not only establishing new, antiracist *institutional* structures, but new *symbolic* structures as well. For however ironic and benign the country-western dancers' "race talk" may appear, it is based on, and it reaffirms, the same old (same old) racist symbolic framework.[3]

Structure and Agency in Cultural Analysis: The Sociology of Pierre Bourdieu

One of the most important culturalists to explicitly address the issue of the relationship between social structures, culture structures, and individual agency is the French theorist, Pierre Bourdieu. Indeed, Bourdieu is also arguably *the* most influential cultural theorist in the world today: a prolific writer and researcher, he has published some 35 books and 350 articles since the 1960s.[4] Bourdieu is also the founder and director of his own research center (the Centre de Sociologie Euopéenne), and he directs his own sociological journal (*Actes de la Recherche en Sciences Sociales*) (Swartz 1997, pp. 1–2).

Bourdieu's work is difficult to summarize – empirically, methodologically, and theoretically, it is complex and far-ranging.[5] Empirically, Bourdieu's projects range from "ethnography among peasant in Algeria, to sociological analysis of nineteenth-century artists and writers, education, language, consumer and cultural tastes, religion, and science in modern French society" (Swartz 1997, p.2). Methodologically, Bourdieu relies on all sorts of qualitative and quantitative data – ranging from ethnographic observation, literary texts, photographs, and interviews, to statistical tables, questionnaire surveys, and census reports. As Swartz (1997, p. 143) states, "it is quintessential Bourdieu to find in a single paragraph literary and philosophical references interspersed with percentages of a survey." Theoretically, Bourdieu forges his concepts as correctives to opposing viewpoints; thus his work reflects an ongoing polemic against positivism, empiricism, structuralism, and Marxism, among other things, although he also continues some aspects of each of these traditions (Swartz 1997, p. 5).[6]

While Bourdieu's work is difficult to categorize, clearly, one of Bourdieu's central concerns is the relationship between culture and power. Bourdieu combines a Goffmanian concern with people's improvisational, *practical mastery* over the complex logic of everyday life; with a *neo-Marxist* concern for the reproduction of inequality. As Swartz (1997, p. 6) maintains, "Whether he is studying Algerian peasants, university professors and students, writers and artists, or the church," Bourdieu is most concerned with "how stratified social systems of hierarchy and domination persist and reproduce intergenerationally without powerful resistance and without the conscious recognition of their members."

Specifically, Bourdieu extends Goffman's focus on the practicalities of the everyday world, by devising a new term – *habitus* – which means "cultural know-how" (Taylor and Whittier 1995, p. 168). *Habitus* provides a "feeling for the game" or "practical sense," allowing people to develop an infinite number of strategies to cope with an infinite number of situations (Baert 1998, p. 31). *Habitus* is a generative scheme of dispositions, tacitly acquired through early childhood, that generate people's practices, improvisations, attitudes, or bodily movements.

However, in contrast to Goffman, Bourdieu is primarily concerned with showing how *habitus* is central to the reproduction of *inequality*. Bourdieu emphasizes that dispositions are adjusted to the constraints of the social surroundings in which they emerge; thus, *habitus* differs according to background. Once members of the less privileged classes enter the struggle for status, the differences in *habitus* make for an unequal fight and hence for the reproduction of inequality (Baert 1998, pp. 31–2). In an analogy with financial capital (which gives a person economic security and status), Bourdieu uses the term *cultural capital* to refer to the practical competencies and tastes which underpin our status and position, and help us differentiate ourselves from those who are less well "culturally endowed" (Hall 1997, p. 376). Bourdieu devotes much of his work to examining the various forms economic and cultural capital can assume. As a general rule, Bourdieu finds that "the greater the difference in asset structure of these two types of capital, the more likely it is that individuals and groups will be opposed in their power struggle for domination" (Swartz 1997, p. 137).

In other words, Bourdieu argues that the primary business of class is to *stratify* tastes in such a way as to construct and reinforce differentiations of social status which correspond, in historically variable and often highly mediated ways, to achieved or aspired-to class position. Thus for instance, tastes in food (e.g.,whether we drink imported or domestic beer) are not direct "functions of income but of inherited life-style" (1984, p. 130). "Cultural discrimination involves a constant negotiation of position with the aim of naturalizing one's own set of values, distinguishing them from the values of others, and attempting more or less forcefully to impose one's values on others. It is thus not just a matter of self-definition but also a struggle for social legitimation" (Frow 1995, p. 85). As Bourdieu (1984, p. 2) maintains:

> A work of art has meaning and interest only for someone who possesses the cultural competence, that is, the code, into which it is encoded. The conscious or unconscious implementation of explicit or implicit schemes of perception and appreciation which constitutes pictorial or musical culture is the hidden condition for recognizing the styles characteristic of a period, a school or an author, and more generally, for the familiarity with the internal logic works that aesthetic enjoyment presupposes. A beholder who lacks the specific code feels lost in a chaos of sounds and rhythm, color and lines, without rhyme or reason.

In exactly the same way, upper-middle-class children come to school with "cultural capital" in the form of knowledge and skill in the symbolic manipulation of language and figures. Purportedly "meritocratic" testing relies precisely on those skills which "cultural capital" provides. Hence seemingly "fair" testing helps ensure the success of dominant groups, and hence the reproduction of class position and privilege. To be sure, a few working-class students can and do overcome the built-in disadvantage of possessing the "wrong" class culture; but this simply legitimates the system as a whole – the entire "working class" can never follow. "The middle and upper-middle class enjoys its privilege not by virtue of inheritance or birth, but by virtue of an apparently proven greater competence and merit" (Willis 1977, p. 128).

Thus, Bourdieu shows that behind/within such *seemingly* individualistic phenomena as *"taste"* are complex symbolic structures and patterns. Indeed, in *Distinction*, Bourdieu (1984, p. 468) defines his research objective as identifying "the cognitive structures which social agents implement in their practical knowledge of the world [and which] are internalized" (cited by Swartz 1997, p. 48). On one hand, this assumption that the symbolic world is *internalized* by individuals parallels Durkheim's emphasis on a shared collective consciousness. However, in contrast to Durkheim, Bourdieu is most concerned with uncovering the symbolic structures that create and sustain social *differentiation* rather than social integration. Bourdieu develops a theory of symbolic *power*, which "stresses the active role played by taken-for-granted assumptions in the constitution and maintenance of power relations" (Swartz 1997, p. 43).

Yet, it is precisely this goal of *exposing* the power relations *embodied* in "taste" that disturbs Bourdieu's critics. As Alexander and Smith (1993, p. 152) maintain: "Although *habitus* enables actors to construct their actions as meaningful, it is itself described as the product of underlying social structural conditions." As a result, in practice, Bourdieu makes action either strategic or totally unreflexive. "Because the actual ideational content of the cultural capital cannot vary independently of objective position, culture and habitus are, in a causal sense, irrelevant to the structuring of action and the shaping of institutional forms" (Alexander and Smith 1993, p. 152–3).

In addition, in recent years cultural sociologists such as Lamont (1992) and Halle (1991, 1994) have questioned the extent to which Bourdieu's insights apply to *American* society. For instance, in her cross-cultural study of upper-middle-class managers in France and the United States, Michèle Lamont (1992, p. 127) finds that too much involvement with "high culture" can be a distinct liability in American corporations, labelling the individual an egghead or outsider. There is a significant strain of anti-intellectualism in the United States, such that people are "more likely to use their knowledge of baseball or other popular cultural forms to gain status and make valuable contacts and alliances" rather than "high culture" (Press 1994, p. 225). Similarly, David Halle (1991, 1992, 1994) uses audience/reception methods to compare differences in how three American class groups discuss the landscape paintings, family photographs, and abstract art in their homes. While Halle does find significant class differences (for instance, upper-middle-class residents are more likely to be able to name the artists of their paintings and speak about their value); he nevertheless concludes that culture and power in the United States are not neatly consonant. "Reception becomes a complicated process involving not only the existence of powerful cultural authority but a complex and sometimes oppositional reaction to it as well" (Press 1994, p. 225). In sum, as Alexander (1995, p. 194) maintains, Bourdieu's social theory is not analytically differentiated enough to "come to grips with the empirical differentiation of the societies in which we live today, with the new possibilities for freedom and solidarity these societies offer, and with the gut-wrenching social conflicts and new forms of domination that are so often its result." [7]

Comprehensive Cultural Sociology: Making Sense of – and Gathering Data about – Culture and Society without Festishizing – or Ignoring – the "Real"

In recent years, many analysts have turned toward using several different methodological tools in order to thoroughly *understand* and *explain* complex social and cultural phenomena. Thus, for instance, in the last chapter we saw that cultural sociologists such as Hunt (1997; 1999) and Hays (1996) use both discourse analysis and audience/reception research to illuminate specific systems of meaning from the "bottom up" as well as "top down." Most importantly, utilizing multiple methods – especially when they work at different levels of analysis – abets an *hermeneutic* approach – the interpretive shifting back and forth between the "part" and the "whole."

In my view, one of the most important recent examples of the new, methodologically and theoretically multifaceted, cultural sociology is James William Gibson's *Warrior Dreams* (1994). In this extraordinarily well-researched book, Gibson uses participant observation, interviews, discourse analysis, as well as historical analysis to in order to *understand* as well as *explain* "paramilitary" culture in the post-Vietnam United States. Specifically, Gibson combines participant observation in a combat training school, paintball games, and at paramilitary and gun-oriented conferences; with interviews with leaders and members in gun and paramilitary organizations; and historical, discursive analysis of warrior mythology, as evident in films, books, and magazines (but especially post-Vietnam films), and even the lives of serial killers. Gibson "deconstructs" America's post-Vietnam "cult of the warrior," illuminating especially the relationship between America's long history of violence and post-Vietnam paramilitary subcultures. Thus, Gibson emphasizes both the historical continuities and changes in American paramilitary culture over the course of 30 years.[8]

Most interestingly, Gibson maintains that the 1980s saw a new fascination with warriors and weapons (e.g,. the *Rambo* films, paintball, etc.); and that this highly energized, "New War" culture was not so much "military" as "paramilitary" (e.g., the new warrior hero typically fought alone or with a small elite group of fellow warriors rather than as part of a conventional military or law enforcement unit). Gibson argues that the New War culture can only be understood in the context of the United States' defeat in Vietnam – which disrupted American cultural identity – as well as other social and economic transformations (e.g., ethnic pride movements, feminist movements, budget deficits, etc.). With defeat in Vietnam, the archetypical pattern that Slotkin (1973) called "regeneration through violence" – the notion that we win our wars because, morally we deserve to win – was broken, and previously taken-for-granted assumptions about customary male behavior (i.e., what it meant to be a "good" man) were challenged. Not surprisingly, then, "American men – lacking confidence in the government and the economy, troubled by the changing relations between the sexes, uncertain of their identity or their future – began to *dream*, to fantasize about the powers and features of another kind of man who could retake and reorder the world. And the hero of all these dreams was the paramilitary warrior" (Gibson 1994, p. 11).

Another important exemplar of hermeneutic, methodologically multifaceted – i.e., *comprehensive* – cultural analysis is Joshua Gamson's *Freaks Talk Back* (1998). In this book, Gamson uses all sorts of methodological tools – ethnography, interviews, textual analysis, etc. – in order to understand "what is going on" with "trash talk" television (i.e., the "illegitimate children" of *Donahue* – such as *Geraldo, Sally Jesse Raphael,* and the infamous *Jerry Springer Show*). As Joshua Gamson (1998, p. 227) states:

> I set out . . . to find out as much as I could about the way talk shows are put together, the pattern of content they contain, and the way they are understood by those viewing them. . . I was particularly interested in what was said through shows with lesbian, gay, bisexual, and transgender topics, how those involved in the production of them behaved and thought, and how audiences saw these particular kinds of shows.

In technical terms, Gamson (1998, p. 227) takes a "three-pronged" approach to understanding "trash talk" television: he analyzes (1) the *production* of daytime television talk shows ("activities through which it is created"); (2) their "thematic, narrative, visual or textual content (what is being said in and through it)"; and (3) their reception (how those encountering it use and interpret it).[9]

Most interestingly, akin to popular reception analysts, such as Radway (see chapter 3) – who showed that romance novels were not just "trash" for empty-headed females (as mass culture theorists would suppose), but that "romance reading is oppositional because it allowed the women to refuse momentarily their self-abnegating social role" (p. 210) – Gamson finds *value* in "trash talk" television shows. In direct contrast to the elitism of mass culture theorists and the Frankfurt school – who would surely have lambasted "trash talk shows" as the epitome of vacant, stupified mass culture – Gamson provocatively "confesses" that, as a gay man, he actually "loves trash talk television," especially the display of so many "transgendered" and "transsexual" guests. As he states (1998, p. 5): "For people whose life experience is so heavily tilted toward invisibility, whose nonconformity, even when it looks very much like conformity, discredits them and disenfranchises them, daytime TV talk shows are a big shot of visibility and media accreditation. It looks, for a moment, like you own this place."

This is not to say that Gamson *blindly* revels in popular culture (as do some contemporary popular culture analysts – see chapter 3). Rather, Gamson readily acknowledges the profoundly exploitative and manipulative dimensions of trash talk TV.[10] (Indeed, it is Gamson's provocative statement that he "loves" trash talk TV that is exaggerated). However, in conjunction with the recent populist and multiculturalist turn, Gamson points out that while the earlier *Donahue Show* targeted and reflected a white, middle-class culture and audience, trash talk television targets and reflects more working class, more ethnically diverse, and more marginalized communities. Trash talk television reflects an immediacy, spontaneity, emotional expressiveness, humor, quick beat, and impatience with "respectable" etiquette rooted in working-class culture (J. Gamson 1998, p. 65). Gamson maintains that *The Donahue Show* reflected a tight and direct "symbiosis between mainstream movement organizations and talk show production . . . . Producers wanted [white middle-class] viewers to identify with and respect guests" (p. 53). But the "second generation" talk shows reflect a grass-roots experience often far removed from formal, middle-class, social movement organizations. As Gamson (1998, p. 47) states:

> In an unspoken, pragmatic way, the code of liberal individualism . . . was a built-in requirement of the *Donahue*-created talk show mix. And for a while

the code would also serve to put a cork in the mouth of the unruly, emotion-driven, gallery-sitting twin, invited to feed on sensational social conflict while sucking on the pacifiers of tolerance and respect for individuals.

Theoretically, Gamson takes an eclectic approach, but he borrows heavily from postmodernism. In a chapter tellingly titled "Truths Told in Lies," Gamson (1998, p. 88) suggests that whereas the undercurrent of *The Donahue Show* was "real folks" telling "the truth"; today in "trash talk" shows, "guests and audiences are mostly playing some exaggerated or truncated version of themselves, not unreal, but not real either. They play themselves as they might be if they were one of those people on a talk show." Moreover, talk show producers today "seek out *unforeseeable* moments of *emotional truth*, even more than the canned mimicry of talk show behavior . . . . Especially when it is fresh, when a new truth is being uncovered, it can be gripping to watch . . . . For a moment, there's a sense that *anything might happen*, that *something really real is going on here*" (p. 91). As Gamson (1998, p. 166) states:

> The shows freakify to get viewers in the door; they humanize to keep them there. This combination makes them scarily intriguing enough to glue people to the TV set. And the "freaks" don't just sit there on the stage looking pretty and bearded. They talk about childhoods, about fears, or about how bad you look in that outfit. They are strange and not-strange, you and not-you, inside and outside of recognizable categories. Talk shows love them for that reason, although not for that reason alone.

Most significantly, the postmodern idea that people are "playing some exaggerated or truncated version of themselves, not unreal, but not real either" seems an apt portrayal not only of the "self" seen on television talk shows, but in chat rooms, and Internet sites like voyeurdorm.com. Indeed, one might argue that all that is left today *are* "truncated" versions of the "self," as, for instance, "real" folks "play" "bride," "groom," "guest," etc. at full service resorts; and "real" folks "play" "mom," "dad," and "neighbor" in "pioneer" towns like Disney's Celebration – as well as in hyperreal suburbs everywhere (see chapter 3).

However, once again the question arises: is this "new" postmodern moment in fact really new? Hasn't rendering the "self" *always* been complex, and to some extent artificial? Over thirty years ago, Goffman described the public self as "*simultaneously* a product of dramatic performance, an object of social ritual, and a field of strategic gamesmanship" (Branaman 1997, p. lxiii; emphasis added). Goffman showed that (1) the self is a product of performances in social life; (2) that the self that an individual is able to perform, and have accepted by others, is in large part determined by the social status and resources to which an individual has access; and

(3) thus, the self "is not a property of the person to whom it is attributed, but dwells rather in the pattern of social control that is exerted in connection with the person by himself and those around him (Goffman 1961a, p. 168, as cited by Lemert 1997b, p. xiii). As Goffman (1961b, p. 87, emphasis added) states:

> In performing a role the individual must see to it that the impressions of him that are conveyed in the situation are compatible with role-appropriate personal qualities, effectively imputed to him: a judge is supposed to be deliberate and sober; a pilot, in a cockpit, to be cool; a bookkeeper to be accurate and neat in doing his work. These personal qualities, effectively imputed and effectively claimed, combine with a position's title, when there is one, to provide a basis of *self-image* for the incumbent and a basis for the image that his role others will have of him. *A self, then, virtually awaits the individual entering a position.*[11]

In sum, the works of J. Gamson and J. W. Gibson are exemplary because they combine thick and thorough empirical analysis with a multidimensional understanding of culture and society. These analysts do not simply identify deep symbolic structures; they show how cultural variables work, and how culture is part and parcel of concrete social debates and concerns. Moreover, these analysts explain how preexisting symbolic and cultural systems take new guises and forms in different historical moments. These analysts provide methodical, well-researched books on popular American culture, without "fetishizing" – or ignoring – "the Real" (Seidman 1997, p. 55 – see chapter 1).[12] They exemplify how one *does* cultural sociology: by thoroughly investigating the complex interpenetration of the social and cultural realms, while fully accounting for the level of the individual.[13]

To be sure, one need not be a social scientist or historian to take a methodologically multifaceted, "hermeneutic" approach. For instance, political satirist M. G. Lord (1994) uses all sorts of methodological tools – social and cultural history, interviews, autobiography, and participant observation – in order to *understand* as well as *explain* the "Barbie" phenomenon. Lord begins with an historical analysis of the emergence of the Barbie doll; then, like Radway (and Gibson and Gamson), Lord explores the multiple levels and meanings in Barbie – through interviews with the founder of Barbie, interviews with the "Living Barbie" herself (see below), autobiographical reflections, and participant observation.

Most interestingly, Lord points out that, on one hand, "Barbie" is *the* cultural icon of a *hyper-sexualized* body; Barbie not only helps perpetuate – Barbie *is* – the beauty myth, the white standard of beauty, with what would be in real-life, a 36-inch bust and a 20-inch waist. Moreover, Barbie is quintessentially a reflection and embodiment of our materialistic

Figure 7.1   Wiley, *Non Sequitur:* "... Survivor Barbies ...," *Los Angeles Times,* July 27, 2000. © 2000 Wiley Miller. Distributed by Universal Press Syndicate. Reprinted with permission. All rights reserved.

consumerist society; she is obsessed with outfits and accessories; she *lives in a super- materialistic world.* Nevertheless, Lord notes that, in contrast to the baby doll, Barbie can be "whatever she wants to be" (so long as she has the right outfit); and when little girls play with Barbie, *Ken* is the "accessory," found "face down on the floor," or relegated to "bringing around the car." For this is a *girls'* world.[14]

Moreover, akin to Gamson, Lord emphasizes the *postmodern* ironies of the Barbie phenomena. While, as most everyone knows, Barbie has long reflected *the* (white) "standard of beauty"; Lord emphasizes that today, this beauty is *simulated,* not "real." Barbie imagery has replaced "genuine" "beauty" to such an extent that not only models and actresses (whose livelihoods arguably rest on such perfection) are routinely surgically "enhanced" – and even still, their photographs are routinely "touched up";

"real" women are having surgery in order to look like a plastic doll. As Lord (1994, p. 244) states: "In Barbie's early years, Mattel struggled to make its doll look like a real-life movie star. Today, however, real-life celebrities – as well as common folk – are emulating her. The postsurgical Dolly Parton looks like the postsurgical Ivana Trump looks like the postsurgical Michael Jackson looks like the postsurgical Joan Rivers looks like . . . Barbie."

Former factory worker Cindy Jackson of Fremont, Ohio is the unabashed world champion of cosmetic surgery; she has had "had more than twenty operations and spent $55,000 to turn herself into a *living doll*" (ibid.; emphasis added). Yet, Jackson confesses, "I don't even want to walk down the street in California . . . . They've all done what I've done. Over there I'm just another Barbie doll" (Lord 1994, p. 251).

To be sure, as Goffman pointed out nearly twenty years ago, it is "engagingly optimistic" to imagine that we could actually wrap our hands around what Dilthey called "human-social- historical-reality." Shortly before his death in 1982, Goffman (1983b, p. 2, as cited by Lemert 1997b, p. xvii) quipped:

> I have no universal cure for the ills of sociology. A multitude of myopias limit the glimpse we get of our subject matter. To define one source of blindness and bias as central is engagingly optimistic. Whatever our substantive focus and whatever our methodological persuasion, all we can do I believe is to keep faith with the spirit of natural science, and lurch along, seriously kidding ourselves that our rut has a forward direction.

However, in my view, the best way we can "lurch along" is by openmindedly and humbly asserting that after extensive (even exhaustive), methodical, diligent, research, analysis, and reflection, we have provided the best explanation and interpretation of "human-historical-reality" that we can, despite our social structural, cultural, and historical limitations. Cultural analysts such as Gamson, Gibson, and Lord, demonstrate that more is gained if, rather than assert "objectivity" or retreat to "subjectivity," we *intensify* our systematic, *interpretive* search for the "real" – or hyperreal (while maintaining our sense of irony and humor).

IMPORTANT CONCEPTS INTRODUCED IN THIS CHAPTER

- Frame (Goffman)
- Frame analysis (Goffman)
- Habitus (Bourdieu)
- Cultural capital (Bourdieu)

STUDY QUESTIONS

1 Visit a museum and discuss the organization and *framing* of specific exhibits and displays. Can you think of any other possible way the objects in the museum could be classified or organized? Why do you think that the exhibit was organized in this way? See Hall (1997, pp. 170–2) for more on how museum exhibitions establish *preferred readings*.

2 Combine a study of "framing" at the museum with an *ethnographic* analysis, i.e., combine an analysis as to how exhibits are *framed* by museum curators, with a participant observation study of how the exhibits are "viewed" or "received." Does the ethnographic analysis enhance your textual research? Or do the two methods address different issues?

3 Use *both* an ethnographic and historical discursive approach to explore a particular issue or cultural product. For instance, investigate *how* children *wield* and *play* with *Pokémon* cards, while, at the same time, investigating how this crosscultural fad came into being. (See Gibson 1994; Lord 1994, for examples.)

Selected Further Reading

Binder, Amy. 1993. "Constructing Racial Rhetoric: Media Depictions of Harm in Heavy Metal and Rap Music," *American Sociological Review* 58 (December): 753–67.

Bourdieu, Pierre. 1984. *Distinction: A Social Critique of the Judgement of Taste.* Cambridge, MA: Harvard University Press.

Eliasoph, Nina. 1999. "'Everyday Racism' in a Culture of Political Avoidance: Civil Society, Speech, and Taboo," *Social Problems* 46 (4): 479–502.

Gamson, Joshua. 1998. *Freaks Talk Back: Tabloid Talk Shows and Sexual Nonconformity.* Chicago: University of Chicago Press.

Gibson, James William. 1994. *Warrior Dreams: Violence and Manhood in Post-Vietnam America.* New York: Hill and Wang.

Goffman, Erving. 1974. *Frame Analysis: An Essay on the Organization of Experience.* New York: Harper and Row.

——. 1979. *Gender Advertisements.* New York: Harper and Row.

——. 1981. *Forms of Talk.* Philadelphia: University of Pennsylvania Press.

——. 1983. "Felicity's Condition," *American Journal of Sociology* 89 (1): 1–53.

Lord, M.G. 1994. *Forever Barbie.* New York: Avon Books.

Swartz, David. 1997. *Culture and Power: The Sociology of Pierre Bourdieu.* Chicago: University of Chicago Press.

Notes

1 The turn toward culture and "framing" in social movement research was in large part a response to the highly empirical and rationalistic "resource mobilization" approach, dominant in the 1970s and early 1980s. The resource mobilization perspective emphasized the pragmatic, *material resources* of social movement organizations, critical to political mobilization. Significantly, the resource mobilization perspective was itself a reaction to the dominant functionalist and modernization approaches, dominant in the 1950s. Functionalists emphasized the *irrational* and *ideological* dimensions of what was called, significantly, not "social movements," but "collective behavior." They focused not on material and political resources, but on emotional *grievances*.

2 For "exceptions" to this trend, see Billig (1995), who champions an "anti-cognitivist" approach, and Eyerman (1999), who explicitly rejects the overly rationalistic approach to "framing."

3 In a parallel way, Binder (1993) explores media depictions of "harm" in heavy metal and rap music and finds that it is the racial backdrop to this discourse that makes these media explanations of harm comprehensible.

4 Much of this work is collaborative, however (Swartz 1997, pp. 1–2).

5 See Swartz (1997, p. 4), Miller and Branson (1987, p. 214), and Calhoun, LiPuma, and Postone (1993, p. 12), all of whom note the difficulty in summarizing Bourdieu's work.

6 Unfortunately, Bourdieu's work is also dense and difficult to read. Bourdieu creates his own terms (e.g.,"habitus" and "field"), but the similarity and overlaps in his use of these terms is confusing. Swartz (1997) provides an excellent explanation and analysis of Bourdieu. This section relies heavily on Swartz's work.

7 Moreover, it is ironic that Bourdieu's work on the *elitism* of French culture would be so, well, *elitist*. Bourdieu's dense, convoluted writing seems to reflect, above all, the appropriating practices and properties of academia.

8 Unfortunately, like Goffman (as well as many cultural historians), Gibson does not provide a methodological section or appendix in his book. Gibson describes his methods as he goes along, only in order to explain the empirical issue at hand.

9 Significantly, Gamson relegates this methodological discussion to the *appendix* of his book, which situates his work on the interpretive, postmodern side of the theoretical and methodological pendulum. In other words, in more traditional "social scientific" accounts, methodological discussions are both lengthy and central to the analysis (hence they appear at a book's beginning). By contrast, in literary cultural studies, there is often no methodological discussion at all (since there is nothing to "discuss"); the author discusses symbols and meaning ad hoc, i.e., unsystematically.

10 The most dangerous and dysfunctional aspects of trash TV came to light in 1995, with the tragic murder of Scott Amedure. Amedure had admitted his "secret crush" on Jonathan Schmitz on a never-aired *Jenny Jones Show*. Schmitz retaliated by going to his admirer's trailer home near Detroit several days

later and murdering him with a 12-gauge shotgun at close range. Schmitz complained that the show had set him up to be humiliated, and that Amedure had "fucked me on national TV" (J. Gamson 1998, p. 6).

11   In addition, Goffman points out that rendering the self is complex because "we do not take on items of conduct one at a time but rather a whole harness load of them and may anticipatorily learn to be a horse even while being pulled like a wagon" (Goffman 1961b, p. 87). Society "forces us to switch back and forth between many complicated roles, thus making us always somewhat untruthful, inconsistent, and dishonorable" (Ritzer 1992, p. 218).

12   Of course, while here I advocate the use of "multiple" methodologies, the radical postmodernist Laurel Richardson (1998, pp. 357–8) maintains that the notion of "multiple methodologies" is quixotic – for no matter how many methods sociologists use and cross- tabulations they generate, our insights and conclusions are necessarily incomplete and illusive. Richardson favors "crystallization" over "triangulation" (using three or more methods to "validate" findings) in order to acknowledge the partiality, variability, and illusiveness of our work. As Richardson (1998, p. 357) states: "Crystals are prisms that reflect externalities and refract within themselves, creating different colors, patterns, arrays, casting off in different directions. What we see depends upon our angle of repose. Not triangulation, crystallization."

13   In Dilthey's terms, these analysts provide a rich and systematic explanation and understanding of "human-social-historical reality." In Alexander's (1987) terms, they demonstrate the rational and nonrational dimensions of action, at both the individual and collective level.

14   To me one of the most interesting aspects of the Barbie phenomenon is that it exposes a dichotomous *choice* that permeates "girl culture" as well as American society: girls can *either* play at being the *mom* (i.e., when playing with baby dolls); or at *displaying themselves* (when playing with Barbie), which is, not coincidentally, the central categories within which women are viewed in society in general. In other words, the same symbolic dichotomy at the heart of the baby dolls vs. Barbie dolls phenomenon is at the heart of the "Madonna"/ "whore" complex (in which women are both loved and hated for their purity and impurity); which is, I would venture, the same dichotomy at the heart of the "stay-at-home" versus "working" mom debates, and other social concerns. These symbols are operationalized differently in different situations – from sacralizing "stay-at-home" moms and demonizing selfish "career moms," to celebrating feminine freedom and sexuality, and disrespecting "stay-at-home" moms. But the same *symbolic framework transcends* these idiosyncratic and varied meanings and expressions – which is exactly what we mean by "ferreting out the workings of culture."

References

Abramson, Jeffrey F., Christopher Arterton, and Gary Orren. 1988. *The Electronic Commonwealth: The Impact of New Media Technologies on Democratic Politics*. New York: Basic Books.

Abelman, Nancy, and John Lie. 1995. *Blue Dreams: Korean Americans and the Los Angeles Riots*. Cambridge, MA: Harvard University Press.

Adler, Patricia, and Peter Adler. 1998. "Observational Techniques," in Norman Denzin and Yvonna Lincoln, eds., *Collecting and Interpreting Qualitative Materials*, pp. 79–109. Thousand Oaks, CA: Sage.

Adorno, Theodor. 1992 [1941]. "On Popular Music," in A. Easthope and K. McGowan, eds., *A Critical and Cultural Theory Reader*. Toronto: University of Toronto Press.

Agger, Ben. 1998. *Critical Social Theories*. Boulder, CO: Westview.

Alasuutari, Pertti. 1995. *Researching Culture: Qualitative Method and Cultural Studies*. Thousand Oaks, CA: Sage.

Alba, Richard. 1992. "Ethnicity," in Edgar F. Borgatta and Mary L. Borgatta, eds., *Encyclopedia of Sociology*, vol. 2, pp. 575–84. New York: Macmillan.

Alexander, Jeffrey C. 1987. *Twenty Lectures in Sociology*. New York: Columbia University Press.

——. 1988. "Introduction: Durkheimian Sociology and Cultural Studies Today," in Jeffrey C. Alexander, ed., *Durkheimian Sociology: Cultural Studies*. Cambridge: Cambridge University Press.

——. 1990. "Analytic Debates: Understanding the Relative Autonomy of Culture," in J. Alexander and S. Seidman, eds., *Culture and Society: Contemporary Debates*, pp. 1–27 Cambridge: Cambridge University Press.

——. 1998. *Real Civil Societies: Dilemmas of Institutionalization*. Thousand Oaks, CA: Sage.

Alexander, Jeffrey C., and Philip Smith. 1993. "The Discourse of American Civil Society: A New Proposal for Cultural Studies," *Theory and Society* 22: 151–207.

Alexander, Jeffrey C. 1995. *Fin de Siècle Social Theory*. London: Verso.

Alexander, Jeffrey C., and Ronald N. Jacobs. 1998. "Mass Communication, Ritual, and Civil Society," in T. Liebes and J. Curran, eds., *Media, Ritual, and Identity*, pp. 23–41. London: Routledge.

Alford, Robert R. 1998. *The Craft of Inquiry*. Oxford: Oxford University Press.

Anderson, Benedict. 1983. *Imagined Communities: Reflections on the Origin and Speed of Nationalism*. London: Verso.

Anderson, Elijah. 1976. *A Place on the Corner*. Chicago: University of Chicago Press.

Anderson, Nels. 1923. *The Hobo*. Chicago: University of Chicago Press.

Ang, Ien. 1990. *Desperately Seeking the Audience*. London: Routledge.

Angus, Ian. 1994. "Democracy and the Constitution of Audiences: A Comparative Media Theory Perspective," in Jon Cruz and Justin Lewis, eds., *Viewing, Reading, Listening*, pp. 233–52. Boulder, CO: Westview.

Ansell, Amy. 1997. *New Right, New Racism*. New York: New York University Press.

Anthias, Floya, and Nira Yuval-Davis. 1992. *Racialized Boundaries: Race, Nation, Gender, Color, and Class and the Anti-racist Struggle*. London: Routledge.

Anzaldúa, Gloria, and Cherrié Moraga. 1981. *This Bridge Called My Back: Writings by Radical Women of Color*. Watertown, MA: Persephone Press.

Appelbaum, Herbert, ed. 1987. *Perspectives in Cultural Anthropology*. Albany: State University of New York Press.

Appelrouth, Scott. 1999. "Jazz: The Symbolic Meaning of an Emerging Music." Unpublished Ph.D. dissertation, New York University.

Arendt, Hannah. 1958. *The Human Condition*. Chicago: University of Chicago Press.

Aronowitz, Stanley. 1981. "Preface" to Paul Willis, *Learning to Labor*. New York: Columbia University Press.

Arrington, Leonard. 1958. *Great Basin Kingdom: Economic History of the Latter-Day Saints, 1830–1900*. Lincoln: University of Nebraska Press.

Asamen, Joy Keiko, and Gordon L. Berry, eds., *Research Paradigms, Television, and Social Behavior*. Thousand Oaks, CA: Sage.

Baert, Patrick. 1998. *Social Theory in the Twentieth Century*. New York: New York University Press.

Bagdikian, Ben. 1992. *The Media Monopoly*, 4th ed. Boston: Beacon.

——. 1996. "Brave New World Minus 400," in George Gerbner, Hamid Mowlana, and Herbert Schiller, eds., *Invisible Crises*, pp. 7–14. Boulder, CO: Westview.

Baldwin, James. 1985. "The Fire Next Time," in *The Price of the Ticket: Collected Nonfiction, 1948–1985*, 1st ed. New York: St. Martin's Press.

Baran, Paul, and Paul Sweezy. 1966. *Monopoly Capital: An Essay on the American Economic and Social Order*. New York: Monthly Review Press.

Barber, Benjamin. 1995. *Jihad vs. McWorld*. New York: Times Books.

Barlow, Philip. 1999. "Shifting Ground and the Third Transformation of Mormonism," in Peter W. Williams, ed., *Perspectives in American Religion and Culture*, pp. 140–53. Oxford and Malden, MA: Blackwell.

Barnet, Richard J., and John Cavenagh. 1994. *Global Dreams: Imperial Corporations and the New World Order*. New York: Simon and Schuster.

Barrett, James R., and David Roediger. 1997. "How White People Became White," in Richard Delgado and Jean Stefancic, eds., *Critical White Studies: Looking Behind the Mirror*, pp. 402–6. Philadelphia, PA: Temple University Press.

Barthes, Roland. 1964 [1967]. *Elements of Semiology*. Trans. Annette Lavers and Colin Smith. London: Jonathan Cape.

——. 1972. *Mythologies*. New York: Hill and Wang.

——. 1977 [1966]. "Introduction to the Structural Analysis of Narratives," in Stephen Heath, ed., *Image, Music, Text*, pp. 79–124. London: Cape.

Baudrillard, Jean. 1988 [1983]. "Simulacra and Simulation," in Mark Poster, ed., *Jean Baudrillard: Selected Writings*. Stanford, CA: Stanford University Press.

——. 1993 [1976]. *Symbolic Exchange and Death*. London: Sage.

——. 1995. *The Gulf War Did Not Take Place*. Bloomington: Indiana University Press.

Becker, Howard. 1951. "Role and Career Problems of the Chicago Public School Teacher." Ph.D. dissertation, University of Chicago.

——. 1953. "Becoming a Marijuana User," *American Journal of Sociology* 59: 235–42.

——. 1982. *Art Worlds*. Berkeley: University of California Press.

——. 1988. "Herbert Blumer's Conceptual Impact," *Symbolic Interaction* 11 (Spring): 13–21.

——. 1999. "The Chicago-School, So-Called," *Qualitative Sociology* 22 (1): 3–11.

Berbrier, Mitch. 1999. "Impression Management for the Thinking Racist," *Sociological Quarterly* 40 (3): 411–33.

Berezin, Mabel. 1994. "Fissured Terrain: Methodological Approaches and Research Styles in Culture and Politics," in Diana Crane, ed., *The Sociology of Culture*, pp. 91–116. Oxford and Cambridge, MA: Blackwell.

Berg, B. L. 1995. *Qualitative Research Methods for the Social Sciences*, 2nd ed. Boston: Allyn and Bacon.

Berger, Bennett. 1995. *An Essay on Culture*. Berkeley: University of California Press.

Berger, Peter. 1967. *The Sacred Canopy*. Garden City, NY: Doubleday.

Bergesen, Albert, and Allison Jones. 1992. "Decoding the Syntax of Modern Dance," in Robert Wuthnow, ed., *Vocabularies of Public Life*, pp. 169–81. London: Routledge.

Berliner, Paul. 1994. *Thinking in Jazz: The Infinite Art of Improvisation*. Chicago: University of Chicago Press.

Berry, Mary Frances. 1994. *Black Resistance, White Law: A History of Constitutional Racism in America*. New York: Penguin.

Besneir, Niko. 1989. "Information Withholding as a Manipulative and Collusive Strategy in Nukulaelae Gossip," *Language and Society* 18: 315–41.

Best, Joel. 1995. "Lost in the Ozone Again: The Postmodernist Fad and Interactionist Foibles," *Studies in Symbolic Interaction* 17: 125–30.

Billig, Michael. 1995. "Rhetorical Psychology, Ideological Thinking, and Imagining Nationhood," in Hank Johnston and Bert Klandermans, eds., *Social Movements and Culture*, pp. 64–81. Minneapolis: University of Minnesota Press.

Binder, Amy. 1993. "Constructing Racial Rhetoric: Media Depictions of Harm in Heavy Metal and Rap Music," *American Sociological Review* 58 (December): 753–67.

Blauner, Bob, ed. 1989. *Black Lives, White Lives*. Berkeley: University of California Press.

Blumer, Herbert. 1969. *Symbolic Interactionism.* Englewood Cliffs, NJ: Prentice Hall.

Bobo, Lawrence, James Kluegel, and Ryan Smith. 1997. "Laissez-Faire Racism: the Crystallization of a Kinder, Gentler, Anti-black Ideology," in Steven Tuch and Jack Martin, eds., *Racial Attitudes in the 1990s: Continuity and Change,* pp. 15–44. Greenwood, CT: Praeger.

Boden, Deirdre. 1983. "Talk International: An Analysis of Conversational Turn-Taking and Related Phenomena in Seven Indo-European Languages." Unpublished paper.

———. 1990a. "The World As It Happens: Ethnomethodology and Conversation Analysis," in George Ritzer, ed., *Frontiers of Social Theory,* pp. 185–213. New York: Columbia University Press.

———. 1990b. "People are Talking: Conversation Analysis and Symbolic Interaction," in Howard Becker and Michal McCall, eds., *Symbolic Interaction and Cultural Studies,* pp. 244–74. Chicago: University of Chicago Press.

Bonilla-Silva, Eduardo. 1997. "Rethinking Racism: Toward a Structural Interpretation," *American Sociological Review* 62: 465–80.

Bordwell, David, and Kristen Thompson. 1993. *Film Art: An Introduction,* 4th ed. New York: McGraw-Hill.

Borgatta, Edgar F., and Mary L. Borgatta, eds. 1992. *Encyclopedia of Sociology,* vol. 2. New York: Macmillan.

Boswell, Terry E. 1986. "A Split Labor Market Analysis of Discrimination against Chinese Immigrants, 1850–1882," *American Sociological Review* 51: 352–71.

Bourdieu, Pierre. 1984. *Distinction: A Social Critique of the Judgement of Taste.* Cambridge, MA: Harvard University Press.

——— 1990. *The Logic of Practice.* Cambridge: Polity Press.

Bourgois, Philippe. 1995. *In Search of Respect.* Cambridge: Cambridge University Press.

Branaman, Ann. 1997. "Goffman's Social Theory," in Charles Lemert and Ann Branaman, eds., *The Goffman Reader,* pp. xlv–lxxxii. Oxford and Cambridge, MA: Blackwell.

Brissett, D. and Edgley, C. 1990. *Life as Theatre,* 2nd ed. New York: Aldine de Gruyter.

Britsch, R. Lanier. 1986. *Unto the Islands of the Sea: A History of the Latter-Day Saints in the Pacific.* Salt Lake City, UT: Deseret.

Bruce, Steve. 1995. "The Truth about Religion in Britain," *Journal for the Social Scientific Study of Religion* 34: 417–31.

———. 1996. *Religion in the Modern World: From Cathedrals to Cults.* New York: Oxford University Press.

Bruner, Edward, and Jane Paige Kelso. 1980. "Gender Differences in Graffiti: A Semiotic Perspective," *Women's Studies International Quarterly* 3: 239–52.

Brunsdon, Charlotte. 1991. "Pedagogies of the Feminine: Feminist Teaching and Women's Genres," *Screen* 32 (4): 372.

Calhoun, Craig. 1993. "Nationalism and Ethnicity," *Annual Review of Sociology* 19: 211–39.

———. 1997. *Habermas and the Public Sphere,* 5th ed. Cambridge, MA: MIT Press.

Calhoun, Craig, Edward LiPuma, and Moishe Postone, eds, 1993. *Bourdieu: Critical Perspectives.* Chicago: University of Chicago Press.

Callois, Roger. 1959. *Man and the Sacred.* New York: The Free Press.

Campbell, James, and James Oakes, 1997. "The Invention of Race," in Richard Delgado and Jean Stefancic, eds., *Critical White Studies: Looking Behind the Mirror,* pp. 145–51. Philadelphia, PA: Temple University Press.

Caplow, Theodore. 1998. "The Case of the Phantom Episcopalians," *American Sociological Review* 63: 112–13.

Carbaugh, Donal. 1989 [1994]. *Talking American: Cultural Discourses on DONAHUE.* Norwood, NJ: Ablex Publishing.

Carr, Leslie G. 1997. *"Color-Blind" Racism.* Thousand Oaks, CA: Sage.

Cerulo, Karen. 1989. "Sociopolitical Control and the Structure of National Symbols: an Empirical Analysis of National Anthems," *Social Forces* 68 (1): 76–100.

Chagnon, Napoleon. 1977. *The Yanomamö: The Fierce People,* 2nd ed. New York: Holt, Rinehart, and Winston.

Chodorow, Nancy. 1974. "Family Structure and Feminine Personality," in Michelle Rosaldo and Louise Lamphere, eds., *Women, Culture and Society,* pp. 43–66. Stanford, CA: Stanford University Press.

——. 1978. *The Reproduction of Mothering: Psychoanalysis and the Sociology of Gender.* Berkeley: University of California Press.

Churchill, Ward. 1998. *Fantasies of the Master Race: Literature, Cinema, and the Colonization of American Indians.* San Francisco, CA: City Lights Books.

Cicourel, Aaron. 1964. *Method and Measurement in Sociology.* New York: The Free Press.

Clandinin, D. Jean, and F. Michael Connelly. 1998. "Personal Experience Methods," in Norman Denzin and Yvonna Lincoln, eds., *Collecting and Interpreting Qualitative Materials,* pp. 150–78. Thousand Oaks, CA: Sage.

Clark-Lewis, Elizabeth. 1994. *Living In, Living Out: African American Domestics in Washington, D.C., 1910–1940.* Washington, DC: Smithsonian.

Clayman, Steven. 1993. "Booing: The Anatomy of a Disaffiliative Response," *American Journal of Sociology* 58: 110–30.

Clifford, James. 1986. "Introduction: Partial Truths," in James Clifford and George Marcus, eds., *Writing Culture,* pp. 1–26. Berkeley: University of California Press.

Clifford, James, and George Marcus. 1986. *Writing Culture.* Berkeley: University of California Press.

Clough, Patricia. 1992. *The End(s) of Ethnography: From Realism to Social Criticism.* Newbury Park, CA: Sage.

Collier, John. 1934. *Memorandum.* Hearings on HR 7902 before the House Committee on Indian Affairs, 73rd Congress, 2nd Session. US Department of the Interior, Washington, DC.

Collins, Randall. 1986. "The Passing of Intellectual Generations: Reflections on the Death of Erving Goffman," *Sociological Theory* 4 (1): 106–13.

——. 1996. "Introduction" to *The Protestant Ethic and the Spirit of Capitalism.* Los Angeles: Roxbury.

Colombo, Gary et al., eds. 1992. *Rereading America: Cultural Contexts for Critical Thinking and Writing,* 2nd ed. Boston: St. Martin's Press.

Comstock, George, A. 1975. *Television and Human Behavior.* Santa Monica, CA: Rand Corporation.

Corsi, C. 1975. [Text of] Department of the Treasury, Internal Revenue Service.

Report of Examination-Exempt Organization: Polynesian Cultural Center, Key District Office–Los Angeles, July 7.

Cose, Ellis. 1993. *The Rage of a Privileged Class.* New York: HarperCollins.

———. 1997a. *Color-Blind: Seeing Beyond Race in a Race-Obsessed World.* New York: HarperCollins.

———, ed. 1997b. *The Darden Dilemma.* NewYork: HarperCollins.

Crane, Diana, ed. 1994. *The Sociology of Culture.* Oxford and Cambridge, MA: Blackwell.

Crenshaw, Kimberlé Williams. 1997. "Color-blind Dreams and Racial Nightmares," in Toni Morrison and Claudia Bordsky Lacour, eds., *Birth of a Nation'hood,* pp. 97–168. New York: Pantheon.

Cressey, Paul G. 1932. *The Taxi-Dance Hall.* Chicago: University of Chicago Press.

Croteau, David, and William Hoynes. 1997. *Media/Society: Industries, Images, and Audiences.* Thousand Oaks, CA: Pine Forge.

Cruz, Jon D. 1997. "Subject Crises and Subject Work: Repositioning W. E. B. Du Bois," in Elizabeth Long, ed., *From Sociology to Cultural Studies,* pp. 92–122. Oxford and Malden, MA: Blackwell.

Cruz, Jon D., and Justin Lewis, eds. 1994. "Introduction," in Cruz and Lewis, eds., *Viewing, Reading, and Listening: Audiences and Cultural Reception.* Boulder, CO: Westview.

Culler, Jonathan D. 1976. *Saussure.* Glasgow: Fontana.

Curran, James, and Tamar Liebes. 1998. "Introduction: The Intellectual Legacy of Elihu Katz," in T. Liebes and J. Curran, eds., *Media, Ritual, and Identity,* pp. 3–20. London: Routledge.

Curran, James, David Morley, and Valerie Walkerdine, eds. 1996. *Cultural Studies and Communications.* London: Arnold.

Dalton, M. 1951. "Informal Factors in Career Achievement," *American Journal of Sociology* 61: 407–15.

Davidman, Lynn. 1997. "Tradition in a Rootless World: Women Turn to Orthodox Judaism," in Thomas Dowdy and Patrick McNamara, eds., *Religion: North American Style,* 3rd ed., pp. 141–6, New Brunswick, NJ: Rutgers University Press.

Davidoff, Leonore. 1995. *Worlds Between: Historical Perspectives on Gender and Class.* Cambridge: Cambridge University Press.

Davis, James, A., and Tom W. Smith. 1991. *General Social Surveys, 1972–1991: A Cumulative Codebook.* National Opinion Research Center, Chicago: Distributed by Roper Public Opinion Research Center, Storrs, CT.

Davis, Kingsley. 1947. "Final Note on a Case of Extreme Isolation," *American Journal of Sociology,* 3 (5): 432–7.

Daws, Gavan. 1968. *Shoal of Time.* Honolulu: University of Hawai i.

Dayan, Daniel, and Elihu Katz. 1988. "Articulating Consensus: The Ritual and Rhetoric of Media Events," in Jeffrey C. Alexander, ed., *Durkheimian Sociology: Cultural Studies,* pp. 161–86. Cambridge: Cambridge University Press.

———. 1992. *Media Events: The Live Broadcasting of History.* Cambridge, MA: Harvard University Press.

Deeley, John N. 1990. *Basics of Semiotics.* Bloomington: Indiana University Press.

Delgado, Richard, and Jean Stefancic, eds. 1997. *Critical White Studies: Looking Behind the Mirror.* Philadelphia, PA: Temple University Press.

Deloria, Vine, Jr., and Clifford M. Lytle. 1983. *American Indians, American Justice.* Austin: University of Texas Press.

De Mooij, Marieke, and Warren Keegan. 1991. *Advertising Worldwide.* New York: Prentice Hall.

Denzin, Norman. 1998. "The Art and Politics of Interpretation," in Norman Denzin and Yvonna Lincoln, eds., *Collecting and Interpreting Qualitative Materials,* pp. 313–44. Thousand Oaks, CA: Sage.

Desan, Suzanne. 1989. "Crowds, Community, and Ritual in the Work of E. P. Thompson and Natalie Davis," in Lynn Hunt, ed., *The New Cultural History,* pp. 47–71. Berkeley: University of California Press.

Dillon, Michèle. 1999. *Catholic Identity.* Cambridge: Cambridge University Press.

Dilthey, Wilhelm. 1976. Ed. H. P. Rickman. *Selected Writings.* Cambridge: Cambridge University Press.

Dixon, Wheeler Winston. 1997. Review of *The Gulf War Did Not Take Place,* by Jean Baudrillard, *Film Quarterly* 50 (4): 54–6.

Douglas, Jack. 1977. "Existential Sociology," in J. D. Douglas and J. M. Johnson, eds., *Existential Sociology,* pp. 3–73. New York: Cambridge University Press.

Douglas, Mary. 1966. *Purity and Danger.* London: Penguin.

Dowdy, Thomas and Patrick McNamara, eds. 1997. *Religion: North American Style,* 3rd ed. New Brunswick, NJ: Rutgers University Press.

D'Souza, Dinesh. 1997. "Ignoble Savages," in Richard Delgado and Jean Stefancic, eds., *Critical White Studies: Looking Behind the Mirror,* pp. 55–65. Philadelphia, PA: Temple University Press.

Du Bois, W. E. B. 1899. *The Philadelphia Negro.* Philadelphia: University of Pennsylvania Press.

——. 1903 [1989]. *The Souls of Black Folk.* New York: Bantam.

——. 1998 [1920]. "The Souls of White Folk," in David Roediger, *Black on White,* pp. 184–204. New York: Schocken.

duCille, Ann. 1997. "The Unbearable Darkness of Being," in Toni Morrison and Claudia Bordsky Lacour, eds., *Birth of a Nation'hood,* pp. 293–338. New York: Pantheon.

Duneier, Mitchell. 1999. *Sidewalk.* New York: Farrar, Straus, and Giroux.

Durkheim, Emile. 1997. [1897]. *Suicide.* New York: Free Press.

——. 1965 [1912]. *The Elementary Forms of Religious Life.* New York: Free Press.

Duster, Troy. 1995. "Symposium on *The Bell Curve,*" *Contemporary Sociology* 24: 158–61.

Eagleton, Terry. 2000. *The Idea of Culture.* Oxford and Malden, MA: Blackwell.

Easterday, Lois, Diana Papademas, Laura Schorr, and Catherine Valentine. 1977. "The Making of a Female Researcher: Role Problems in Fieldwork," *Urban Life* 6: 333–48.

Easthope, Antony, and Kate McGowan. 1992. *A Critical and Cultural Theory Reader.* Toronto: University of Toronto Press.

Eco, Umberto. 1976. *A Theory of Semiotics.* Bloomington: Indiana University Press.

Edles, Laura Desfor. 1995. "Rethinking Democratic Transition: A Culturalist Critique and the Spanish Case," *Theory and Society* 24: 355–84.

——. 1998. *Symbol and Ritual in the New Spain: The Transition to Democracy After Franco.* Cambridge: Cambridge University Press.

———. 1999. "A Culturalist Approach to Ethnic Nationalist Movements: Symbolization and Basque and Catalan Nationalism in Spain," *Social Science History* 23: 311–55.

———. 2001. "What Color *Is* Your Parachute? A Study of Racialization and Symbolization." Unpublished paper.

———. 2002 (forthcoming). "The Experience and Perception of 'Race' and 'Ethnicity' in Hawai'i: The Myth of the 'Model Minority' State," in Herman DeBose and Loretta Winters, eds., *New Faces in a Changing America: Multiracial Identity in the 21st Century*. Thousand Oaks, CA: Sage.

Edwards, Harry. 1969. *The Revolt of the Black Athlete*. New York: Free Press.

Ehrenhalt, Alan. 1999. "Because We Like You." Review of *Celebration USA*, by Douglas Frantz and Catherine Collins, and *The Celebration Chronicles*, by Andrew Ross. *Los Angeles Times Book Review*, September 12, p. 8.

Eliade, Mircea, and Ioan P. Couliano. 1991. *The Eliade Guide to World Religions*. New York: HarperCollins.

Eliasoph, Nina. 1999. "'Everyday Racism' in a Culture of Political Avoidance: Civil Society, Speech, and Taboo," *Social Problems* 46 (4): 479–502.

Eliot, T. S. 1948. *Notes Toward the Definition of Culture*. London: Faber and Faber.

Enzensberger, Hans Magnus. 1974. *The Consciousness Industry*. New York: Seabury.

Espiritu, Yen Le. 1997. *Asian American Women and Men*. Thousand Oaks, CA: Sage.

Eyerman, Ron. 1999. "Moving Culture," in Mike Featherstone and Scott Lash, eds., *Spaces of Culture*, pp. 116–37. Thousand Oaks, CA: Sage.

Fairburn, Miles. 1999. *Social History: Problems, Strategies, and Methods*. New York: St. Martin's Press.

Fanon, Franz. 1968 [1963]. *The Wretched of the Earth*. New York: Grove Press.

Feagin, Joe. 1997. "Old Poison in New Bottles: The Deep Roots of Modern Nativism," in R. Delgado and J. Stefancic, eds., *Critical White Studies: Looking Behind the Mirror*, pp. 348–53. Philadelphia, PA: Temple University Press.

Feagin, Joe, and Melvin Sikes. 1994. *Living with Racism: The Black Middle-Class Experience*. Boston: Beacon.

Ferguson, Marjorie, and Peter Golding, eds. 1997. *Cultural Studies in Question*. Thousand Oaks, CA: Sage.

Ferrante, Joan. 1998. *Sociology: A Global Perspective*. Belmont, CA: Wadsworth.

Ferre, Craig. 1988. "A History of the Polynesian Cultural Center's Night Show: 1963–1983." Ph.D. dissertation, Department of Theater and Film, Brigham Young University, Provo, UT.

Ferree, Myra Marx, and Elaine J. Hall. 1996. "Rethinking Stratification from a Feminist Perspective: Gender, Race, and Class in Mainstream Textbooks," *American Sociological Review* 61 (Dec.): 929–50.

Fieldhouse, D. K. 1973. *Economics and Empire, 1830–1914*. Ithaca, NY: Cornell University Press.

Finch, Christopher. 1973. *The Art of Walt Disney: From Mickey Mouse to the Magic Kingdom*. New York: Harry N. Abrams.

Fine, Gary Alan. 1992. "The Culture of Production: Aesthetic Choices and Constraints in Culinary Work," *American Journal of Sociology* 97 (1): 1268–94.

Finke, Roger, and Laurence R. Iannacconne. 1993. "Supply-side Explanations for

Religious Change," *Annals of the American Academy of Political and Social Science* 527: 609–26.

Finke, Roger, and Rodney Stark. 1992. *The Churching of America, 1776–1990.* New Brunswick, NJ: Rutgers University Press.

——. 1997. "The Churching of America," in Thomas Dowdy and Patrick McNamara, eds., *Religion: North American Style,* 3rd ed., pp. 43–9. New Brunswick, NJ: Rutgers University Press.

Fiske, David. 1996. [1994]. *Media Matters: Race and Gender in U.S. Politics.* Minneapolis: University of Minnesota Press.

Ford, Andrea. 1997. "Black Challenge/White Justice," in Ellis Cose, ed., *The Darden Dilemma,* pp. 133–53. New York: HarperCollins.

Foucault, Michel. 1961. *Madness and Civilization.* London: Tavistock.

——. 1969. *The Archeology of Knowledge and the Discourse of Language.* New York: Pantheon.

——. 1978. *The History of Sexuality,* vol. 1. New York: Vintage.

——. 1980. *Power/Knowledge: Selected Interviews and Other Writings, 1972–1977,* ed. Colin Gordon. New York: Pantheon.

Frank, Andre Gunder. 1967. *Capitalism and Underdevelopment in Latin America: Historical Studies of Chile and Brazil.* New York: Monthly Review Press.

Franzosi, Roberto. 1998. "Narrative Analysis–Or Why (and How) Sociologists Should Be Interested in Narrative," *Annual Review of Sociology* 24 (1): 517–45.

Freeman, Derek. 1999. *The Fateful Hoaxing of Margaret Mead.* Boulder, CO: Westview.

Frow, John. 1995. *Cultural Studies and Cultural Value.* Oxford: Clarendon Press.

Gallup, George, Jr., and D. Michael Lindsay. 1999. *Surveying the Religious Landscape: Trends in U.S. Beliefs.* Harrisburg, PA: Morehouse Publishing.

Gamson, Joshua. 1998. *Freaks Talk Back: Tabloid Talk Shows and Sexual Nonconformity.* Chicago: University of Chicago Press.

Gamson, William. 1988. "Political Discourse and Collective Action," in Bert Klandermans, Hanspeter Kriesi, and Sidney Tarrow, eds., *International Social Movement Research: From Structure to Action.* Greenwich, CT: JAI Press.

——. 1995. "Constructing Social Protest," in Hank Johnston and Bert Klandermans, eds., *Social Movements and Culture,* pp. 85–106. Minneapolis: University of Minnesota Press.

——. 1998. "Discourse, Nuclear Power, and Collective Action," in Philip Smith, ed., *The New American Cultural Sociology,* pp. 202–16. Cambridge: Cambridge University Press.

Gamson, William A., David Croteau, William Hoynes, and Theodore Sasson. 1992. "Media Images and the Social Construction of Reality," *Annual Review of Sociology* 18: 373–93.

Gane, Mike, ed. 1993. *Baudrillard Live. Selected Interviews.* London: Routledge.

Garfinkel, Harold. 1967. *Studies in Ethnomethodology.* Englewood Cliffs, NJ: Prentice-Hall.

——. 1988. "Evidence for Locally Produced, Naturally Accountable Phenomena of Order, Logic, Reason, Meaning, Method, etc., in and as of the Essential Quiddity of Immortal Ordinary Society," *Sociological Theory* 6: 103–9.

Garnham, Nicholas. 1997. "Political Economy and the Practice of Cultural Studies," in Marjorie Ferguson and Peter Golding, eds., *Cultural Studies in Question*, pp. 56–73. Thousand Oaks, CA: Sage.

Geertz, Clifford. 1973. *The Interpretation of Cultures*. New York: Basic Books.

——. 1988. *Works and Lives: The Anthropologist as Author*. Stanford, CA: Stanford University Press.

Gerbner, George. 1958. "On Content Analysis and Critical Research in Mass Communication," *AV Communication Review* 17: 137–48.

Gerbner, George, L. Gross, M. Morgan, and N. Signorelli. 1984. "The Political Correlates of Television Viewing," *Public Opinion Quarterly* 48: 283–300.

——. 1994. "Growing Up With Television: the Cultivation Perspective," in J. Bryant and D. Zillman, eds., *Media Effects: Advances in Theory and Research*, pp. 17–41. Hillsdale, NJ: Lawrence Erlbaum.

Getlin, Josh. 1999. "Reagan Biographer Makes Himself Historical Figure–Literally," *Los Angeles Times*, Sept. 3, p. A5.

Gibson, Donald B. 1989. "Introduction," in W. E. B. Du Bois, *The Souls of Black Folk*, pp. vii–xxxv. New York: Penguin.

Gibson, James William. 1994. *Warrior Dreams: Violence and Manhood in Post-Vietnam America*. New York: Hill and Wang.

Giddens, Anthony. 1990. *Consequences of Modernity*. Stanford, CA: Stanford University Press.

Gilens, Martin. 1999. "Race and Poverty in America: Public Perceptions and the American News Media," in Turner C. Lomand, ed., *Social Science Research*, 2nd ed., pp. 53–64. Los Angeles, CA: Pryczak Publishing.

Gillespie, Marcia Ann. 1997. "Reasonable Doubt," in Ellis Cose, ed., *The Darden Dilemma*, pp. 100–13. New York: HarperCollins.

Gilmore, Samuel. 1992. "Culture," in Edgar F. Borgatta and Mary L. Borgatta, eds., *Encyclopedia of Sociology*, vol. 2, pp. 408–9. New York: Macmillan.

Gitlin, Todd. 1997. "The Anti–political Populism of Cultural Studies," in Marjorie Ferguson and Peter Golding, eds., *Cultural Studies in Question*, pp. 25–38. Thousand Oaks, CA: Sage.

——, ed. 1986. *Watching Television*. New York: Pantheon.

Gladden, R. M. 1993. "Call of the Wild: Animal Fashions and the Dehumanization of Women." Honors thesis, Wesleyan University, Middletown, CT.

Goffman, Erving. 1959. *The Presentation of Self in Everyday Life*. Garden City, NY: Anchor Books.

——. 1961a. *Asylums*. Garden City, NY: Anchor Books.

——. 1961b. *Encounters: Two Studies in the Sociology of Interaction*. Indianapolis: Bobbs-Merrill.

——. 1971. *Relations in Public*. New York: Basic Books.

——. 1974. *Frame Analysis: An Essay on the Organization of Experience*. New York: Harper and Row.

——. 1979. *Gender Advertisements*. New York: Harper and Row.

——. 1981. *Forms of Talk*. Philadelphia: University of Pennsylvania Press.

——. 1983a. "Felicity's Condition," *American Journal of Sociology* 89 (1): 1–53.

——. 1983b. "The Interaction Order," *American Sociological Review* 48: 1–17.

——. 1997. "Frame Analysis," in C. Lemert and A. Branaman, eds., *The Goffman Reader*, pp. 149–66. Oxford and Malden, MA: Blackwell.

Goldscheider, Calvin, and Alan S. Zuckerman. 1984. *The Transformation of the Jews.* Chicago: University of Chicago Press.

Gordon, Dan. 1999. "Nothing but 'Net'," *UCLA Magazine* (Fall), p. 49.

Gossett, Thomas. 1963. *Race: The History of an Idea* (2nd ed. 1989, 3rd ed. 1997). New York: Schocken.

Gould, Carol C., ed. 1997. *Gender.* Atlantic Highlands, NJ: Humanities Press International.

Gould, Stephen Jay. 1994. "Curveball," *The New Yorker,* Sept. 28, pp. 139–49.

Gramsci, Antonio. 1971. *Selections from the Prison Notebooks.* New York: International Publishers.

Gray, Herman. 1997. "Jazz Tradition, Institutional Formation, and Cultural Practice: The Canon and the Street as Frameworks for Oppositional Black Cultural Politics," in Elizabeth Long, ed., *From Sociology to Cultural Studies,* pp. 351–73. Oxford and Malden, MA: Blackwell.

Greenwood, M. R. C., Karen Kovacs North, and Judith Dollenmayer. 1999. "Whose Millennium?," *American Behavioral Scientist* 42 (6): 1041–51.

Griswold, Wendy. 1994. *Cultures and Societies in a Changing World.* Thousand Oaks, CA: Pine Forge.

Grossberg, Lawrence. 1992. *We Gotta Get Out of This Place: Popular Conservatism and Postmodern Culture.* London: Routledge.

Grossberg, Lawrence, C. Nelson, and P. Treichler, eds. 1992. *Cultural Studies.* London: Routledge.

Grossberg, Lawrence, Ellen Wartella, and D. Charles Whitney. 1998. *Media-Making: Mass Media in a Popular Culture.* Thousand Oaks, CA: Sage.

Gubrium, Jaber, and James Holstein. 1997. *The New Language of Qualitative Method.* New York: Oxford University Press.

Gusfield, Joseph. 1989. "Constructing the Ownership of Social Problems: Fun and Profit in the Welfare State," *Social Problems* 36: 431–41.

Habenstein, R.W. 1954. "The Career of the Funeral Director." Ph.D dissertation, University of Chicago.

Habermas, Jürgen. 1997. "Further Reflections on the Public Sphere," in Craig Calhoun, ed., *Habermas and the Public Sphere,* pp. 421–61. Cambridge, MA: MIT Press.

Hadaway, C. Kirk, Penny Long Marler, and Mark Chaves. 1993. "What the Polls Don't Show: A Closer Look At U.S. Church Attendance," *American Sociological Review* 56: 741–52.

——. 1998. "Overreporting Church Attendance in America: Evidence that Demands the Same Verdict," *American Sociological Review* 63: 122–30.

Hall, John. 1990. "Social Interaction, Culture, and Historical Studies," in Howard Becker and Michal McCall, eds., *Symbolic Interaction and Cultural Studies,* pp. 26–45. Chicago: University of Chicago Press.

Hall, John, and Mary Jo Neitz. 1993. *Culture: Sociological Perspectives.* Englewood Cliffs, NJ: Prentice-Hall.

Hall, Stuart. 1980 [1973]. "Encoding and Decoding in the Television Discourse," in Hall et. al., eds., *Culture, Media, Language.* London: Hutchinson.

——. 1990. "The Whites of their Eyes: Racist Ideologies and the Media," in Manuel Alvarado and John O. Thompson, eds., *The Media Reader,* pp. 7–23. London: BFI.

——. 1995. "The Whites of their Eyes: Racist Ideologies and the Media," in Gail Dines and Jean Humez, eds., *Gender, Race, and Class in the Media*, pp. 18–22. Thousand Oaks, CA: Sage.

——. 1997. *Representation: Cultural Representations and Signifying Practices*. London: Sage.

Halle, David. 1991. "Displaying the Dream: the Visual Presentation of Family and Self in the Modern American Household," *Journal of Comparative Family Studies* 22 (2): 217–29.

——. 1992. "The Audience for Abstract Art: Class, Culture, and Power," in Michèle Lamont and Michael Fournier, eds., *Cultivating Differences: Symbolic Boundaries and the Making of Inequality*, pp. 131–51. Chicago: University of Chicago Press.

——. 1994. *Inside Culture: Class, Culture, and Everyday Life in Modern America*. Chicago: University of Chicago Press.

Hansen, Klaus, J. 1981. *Mormonism and the American Experience*. Chicago: University of Chicago Press.

Hartley, John. 1992. *Tele-ology: Studies in Television*. London: Routledge.

Harvey, David. 1989. *The Condition of Postmodernity: An Inquiry into the Origins of Cultural Change*. Oxford and Cambridge, MA: Blackwell.

Hauser, Robert. 1995. "Symposium on *The Bell Curve*," *Contemporary Sociology* 24: 149–53.

Hawkins, Robert J. 1995. "Rock 'n' Roll is Here to Stay," *San Diego Union-Tribune*, April 5, p. E7.

Hawthorn, Jeremy. 1994. *A Concise Glossary of Contemporary Literary Theory*. 2nd ed. London: Edward Arnold.

Hay, James, Lawrence Grossberg, and Ellen Wartella, eds. 1996. *The Audience and Its Landscape*. Boulder, CO: Westview.

Hayes, Sharon. 1996. *The Cultural Contradictions of Motherhood*. New Haven, CT: Yale University Press.

Head, S. W. 1954. "Content Analysis of Television Drama Programs," *Quarterly Journal of Film, Radio, and Television* 9: 175–94.

Hebdige, Dick. 1993 [1979]. *Subculture: the Meaning of Style*. London: Routledge.

Herberg, Will. 1967. "Religion in a Secularized Society: the New Shape of Religion in America," in Richard O. Knudten, ed., *The Sociology of Religion: An Anthology*, pp. 470–81. New York: Appleton-Century-Crofts.

Heritage, John, and David Greatbatch. 1986. "Generating Applause: A Study of Rhetoric and Response at Party Conferences," *American Journal of Sociology* 92: 110–57.

Herrnstein, Richard, and Charles Murray. 1994. *The Bell Curve*. New York: Free Press.

Hobson, Dorothy. 1982. *Crossroads: The Drama of a Soap Opera*. London: Methuen.

Hochschild, Arlie. 1983. *The Managed Heart: Commercialization of Human Feeling*. Berkeley: University of California Press.

Hodes, Martha. 1997. *White Women, Black Men: Illicit Sex in the Nineteenth Century South*. New Haven, CT: Yale University Press.

Holmes, Robyn. 1995. *How Young Children Perceive Race*. Thousand Oaks, CA: Sage.

hooks, bell. 1991. *Black Looks: Race and Representation*. Boston: South End.

Hoover, Stewart, and Douglas Wagner. 1997. "History and Policy in American Broadcast Treatment of Religion," *Media, Culture and Society* 19: 7–27.

Hout, Michael and Andrew Greeley. 1998. "What Church Officials' Reports Don't Show: Another Look at Church Attendance," *American Sociological Review* 63: 113–19.

Humphreys, Laud. 1970. *Tearoom Trade*. Chicago: Aldine.

Hunt, Darnell. 1997. *Screening the Los Angeles Riots*. Cambridge: Cambridge University Press.

——. 1999. *O. J. Simpson Facts and Fictions*. Cambridge: Cambridge University Press.

Iannaccone, Laurence. 1997. "Why Strict Churches are Strong," in Thomas Dowdy and Patrick McNamara, eds., *Religion: North American Style*, 3rd ed., pp. 50–65. New Brunswick, NJ: Rutgers.

Ivins, Stanley. 1972. "Notes on Mormon Polygamy," in Marvin Hill and James Allen, eds., *Mormonism and American Culture*, pp. 101–11. New York: Harper and Row.

Jacobs, Ronald N. 1996. "Civil Society and Crisis: Culture, Discourse, and the Rodney King Beating," *American Journal of Sociology* 101 (March): 1238–76.

——. 2000. *Race, Media and the Crisis of Civil Society*. Cambridge: Cambridge University Press.

Jaeger, Gertude, and Philip Selznick. 1964. "A Normative Theory of Culture," *American Sociological Review* 29: 653–89.

Jaimes, M. Annette. 1992. "Federal Indian Identification Policy: A Usurpation of Indigenous Sovereignty in North America," in Fremont J. Lyden and L. Legters, eds., *Native Americans and Public Policy*, pp. 113–35. Pittsburgh, PA: University of Pittsburgh Press.

Janesick, Valerie. 1998. *"Stretching" Exercises for Qualitative Researchers*. Newbury Park, CA: Sage.

Jay, Martin. 1973. *The Dialectical Imagination*. Boston: Little, Brown.

Jefferson, Gail. 1978. "Sequential Aspects of Storytelling in Conversation," in Jim Schenkein, ed., *Studies in the Organization of Conversational Interaction*, pp. 219–48. New York: Academic Press.

Jhally, Sut. 1987. *The Codes of Advertising: Fetishism and the Political Economy of Meaning in Consumer Society*. New York: St. Martin's Press.

Jhally, Sut, and Justin Lewis. 1992. *Enlightened Racism: The Cosby Show, Audiences, and the Myth of the American Dream*. Boulder, CO: Westview.

Jhally, Sut, Justin Lewis, and Michael Morgan. 1991. *The Gulf War: A Study of the Media, Public Opinion, and Public Knowledge*. Amherst, MA: University of Massachusetts, Amherst, Center for Studies in Communication (Feb. 2–4).

Johnson, Leola, and David Roediger. 1997. "Hertz, Don't It?," in Toni Morrison and Claudia Bordsky Lacour, eds., *Birth of a Nation'hood*, pp. 197–239. New York: Pantheon.

Johnston, Hank. 1995. "A Methodology for Frame Analysis: From Discourse to Cognitive Schema," in Hank Johnston and Bert Klandermans, eds., *Social Movements and Culture*, pp. 217–46. Minneapolis: University of Minnesota Press.

Johnston, Hank, and Bert Klandermans. 1995. "The Cultural Analysis of Social Movements," in Johnston and Klandermans, eds., *Social Movements and Culture*, pp. 3–24. Minneapolis: University of Minnesota Press.

Jordan, Winthrop. 1968. *White Over Black: American Attitudes Toward the Negro, 1550–1812.* Chapel Hill, NC: Duke University Press.

Jung, Moon-Kie. 1999. "No Whites, No Asians: Race, Marxism, and Hawai'i's Preemergent Working Class," *Social Science History* 23 (3): 357–93.

Karst, Kenneth. 1997. "Paths to Belonging: the Constitution and Cultural Identity," in R. Delgado and J. Stefancic, eds., *Critical White Studies: Looking Behind the Mirror,* pp. 407–13. Philadelphia, PA: Temple University Press.

Kellner, Douglas. 1984. *Herbert Marcuse and the Crisis of Marxism.* Berkeley: University of California Press.

Kertzer, David. 1988. *Ritual, Politics, and Power.* New Haven, CT: Yale University Press.

Kim, Bong Hwan. 1998. "Stereotyping by Politicians," in Coramae Richey Mann and Marjorie Zatz, eds., *Images of Color, Images of Crime,* pp. 188–94. Los Angeles: Roxbury.

Kinder, Donald, and Lynn Sanders. 1996. *Divided by Color.* Chicago: University of Chicago Press.

Kinder, Donald, and David Sears. 1981. "Prejudice and Politics: Symbolic Racism versus Racial Threats to the Good Life," *Journal of Personality and Social Psychology* 40: 414–31.

King, Martin Luther, Jr. 1964. *Why We Can't Wait.* New York: Signet Books.

——. 1967. *Where Do We Go From Here: Chaos or Community?* New York: Harper & Row.

Kline, Stephen, and William Leiss. 1978. "Advertising, Needs, and Commodity Fetishism," *Canadian Journal of Political and Social Theory* 2 (1).

Kubey, Robert, and Csikszentmihalyi, Mihaly. 1990. *Television and Quality of Life: How Viewing Shapes Everyday Experience.* Hillsdale, NJ: Laurence Erlbaum.

Kundnani, Arun. 1998. "Where Do You Want To Go Today? The Rise of Info Capital," *Race and Class* (Oct.): 49.

Kuper, Adam. 1996. *Anthropology and Anthropologists,* 3rd ed. London: Routledge.

Lamont, Michèle. 1999. "Introduction: Beyond Taking Culture Seriously," in Lamont, ed., *The Cultural Territories of Race: Black and White Boundaries,* pp. ix–xx. Chicago: University of Chicago Press.

Lazère, Donald. 1987. *American Mass Media and Mass Culture.* Berkeley: University of California Press.

Legters, Lyman H. 1992. "The American Genocide" and "Federal Indian Identification Policy: A Usurpation of Indigenous Sovereignty in North America," in Fremont J. Lyden and L. Legters, eds., *Native Americans and Public Policy,* pp. 101–12. Pittsburgh, PA: University of Pittsburgh Press.

Lee, Robert G. 1999. *Orientals: Asian Americans in Popular Culture.* Philadelphia, PA: Temple University Press.

Leeds-Hurwitz, Wendy. 1993. *Semiotics and Communication: Signs, Codes, and Cultures.* Hillsdale, NJ: Laurence Erlbaum.

Leidner, Robin. 1993. *Fast Food, Fast Talk.* Berkeley: University of California Press.

Leiss, William, Stephen Kline, and Sut Jhally, eds. 1990. *Social Communication in Advertising: Persons, Products and Images of Well-being,* 2nd ed. London: Routledge.

Lemert, Charles. 1979. "Structuralist Semiotics," in S. McNall, ed., *Theoretical*

Perspectives in Sociology, pp. 96–111. New York: St. Martin's Press.

——. 1997a. *Postmodernism Is Not What You Think.* Oxford and Malden, MA: Blackwell.

——. 1997b. "Goffman," in Charles Lemert and Ann Branaman, eds., *The Goffman Reader.* Oxford and Malden, MA: Blackwell.

Lemert, Charles, ed. 1993. *Social Theory: the Multicultural and Classic Readings.* Boulder, CO: Westview.

Lemmen, M. M. W. 1990. *Max Weber's Sociology of Religion.* Heerlen, The Netherlands: Gooi en Sticht.

Lenin, Vladimir Ilich. 1917. *Imperialism: The Higher Stage of Capitalism.* London: International Publishers.

Lévi-Strauss, Claude. 1963. *Structural Anthropology.* Trans. Claire Jacobson and Brooke Grundfest Schoepf. New York: Basic Books.

Levine, Lawrence. 1988. *Highbrow/Lowbrow: The Emergence of Cultural Hierarchy in America.* Cambridge, MA: Harvard University Press.

Levine, Rhonda. 1998. "The Souls of Elite White Men: White Racial Identity and the Logic of Thinking of Race." Unpublished paper prepared for Hawai'i Sociological Association meeting.

Lewis, Oscar. 1959. *Five Families: Mexican Case Studies in the Culture of Poverty.* New York: New American Library.

——. 1966. *La Vida: A Puerto Rican Family in the Culture of Poverty–San Juan and New York.* New York: Random House.

Liebes, Tamar. 1998. "Television's Disaster Marathons," in Tamar Liebes and James Curran, eds. *Media, Ritual, and Identity*, pp. 71–85. London: Routledge.

Liebes, Tamar, and Elihu Katz. 1990. *The Export of Meaning.* Oxford: Oxford University Press.

Liebow, Elliot. 1967. *Tally's Corner.* Boston: Little, Brown.

Lippy, Charles H. 1999. "Pluralism and American Religious Life in the Later Twentieth Century," in *Perspectives on American Religion and Culture*, pp. 48–60. Oxford and Malden, MA: Blackwell.

Lipset, Seymour Martin. 1963. *The First New Nation.* New York: Basic Books.

Lipsitz, George. 1990. *Time Passages: Collective Memory and American Popular Culture.* Minneapolis: University of Minnesota Press.

——. 1994. *Dangerous Crossroads: Popular Music, Postmodernism, and the Poetics of Place.* New York: Verso.

——. 1997a. "The Greatest Story Ever Told," in Toni Morrison and Claudia Brodsky Lacour, eds., *Birth of a Nation'hood*, pp. 3–29. New York: Pantheon.

——. 1997b. "Facing Up to What's Killing Us," in Elizabeth Long, ed., *From Sociology to Cultural Studies*, pp. 234–61. Oxford and Malden, MA: Blackwell.

Long, Elizabeth, ed. 1997. *From Sociology to Cultural Studies.* Oxford and Cambridge, MA: Blackwell.

Lord, M. G. 1994. *Forever Barbie.* New York: Avon Books.

Lott, Tommy L. 1999. *The Invention of Race.* Oxford and Malden, MA: Blackwell.

Lukács, Georg. 1968 [1922]. *History and Class Consciousness.* Cambridge, MA: MIT Press.

Luker, Kristin. 1991. "Dubious Conceptions: The Controversy Over Teen Pregnancy," *The American Prospect* 5 (Spring): 73–83.

252 References

Lull, James. 1995. *Media, Communication, Culture: A Global Approach*. Cambridge: Polity.

Malinowski, Bronislaw. 1961 [1922]. *Argonauts of the Western Pacific*. New York: E. P. Dutton.

Manning, Peter K., and Betsy Cullum-Swan. 1998. "Narrative, Content, and Semiotic Analysis," in Norman Denzin and Yvonna Lincoln, eds., *Collecting and Interpreting Qualitative Materials*, pp. 246–73. Thousand Oaks, CA: Sage.

Marcus, George. 1986. "Contemporary Problems of Ethnography in the Modern World System," in James Clifford and George Marcus, eds., *Writing Culture*, pp. 165–93. Berkeley: University of California Press.

——. 1994. "What Comes (Just) After 'Post'?: The Case of Ethnography," in N. Denzin and Y. Lincoln, eds., *Handbook of Qualitative Research*, pp. 563–74. Thousand Oaks, CA: Sage.

Marcuse, Herbert. 1964. *One-Dimensional Man*. Boston: Beacon.

——. 1969 [1989, 1994]. "Repressive Tolerance," in R. Wolff, B. Moore, and H. Marcuse, eds., *A Critique of Pure Tolerance*. Boston: Beacon.

Marger, Martin. 1997. *Race and Ethnic Relations: Global Perspectives*, 4th ed. Belmont, CA: Wadsworth.

Marx, Karl, and Friedrich Engels. 1970 [1848]. "The Communist Manifesto," in Robert Tucker, ed., *The Marx–Engels Reader*. New York: Norton.

Massey, Douglas, and Nancy Denton. 1993. *American Apartheid*. Cambridge, MA: Harvard University Press.

Maynard, Douglas, and Steven Clayman. 1991. "The Diversity of Ethnomethodology," *Annual Review of Sociology* 17: 385–418.

McCall, Michal M., and Howard S. Becker. 1990. "Introduction," in *Symbolic Interaction and Cultural Studies*, pp. 1–15. Chicago: University of Chicago Press.

McCall, Michal M., and Judith Wittner. 1990. "The Good News about Life History," in *Symbolic Interaction and Cultural Studies*, pp. 46–89. Chicago: University of Chicago Press.

McGuigan, Jim. 1992. *Cultural Populism*. London: Routledge.

——. 1997. "Cultural Populism Revisited," in Marjorie Ferguson and Peter Golding, eds., *Cultural Studies in Question*, pp. 138–54. Thousand Oaks, CA: Sage.

McGuire, Meredith. 1997. *Religion: the Social Context*, 4th ed. Belmont, CA: Wadsworth.

McRobbie, Angela. 1978. *Jackie: An Ideology of Adolescent Femininity*. Birmingham: Centre for Contemporary Cultural Studies, University of Birmingham.

Mead, Margaret. 1928. *Coming of Age in Samoa*. New York: Morrow.

Meertens, Roel W., and Thomas F. Pettigrew. 1997. "Is Subtle Prejudice Really Prejudice?," *Public Opinion Quarterly* 61 (1): 54–72.

Merry, Sally Engle. 2000. *Colonizing Hawai i: The Cultural Power of Law*. Princeton, NJ: Princeton University Press.

Meyer, Michael. 1994. "Fight to the Finish–Video Wars: The World's Electronic-game Makers Battle for Ascendancy," *Newsweek*, Dec. 12, pp. 56–7.

Miller, Mark Crispin. 1986. "Deride and Conquer," in Todd Gitlin, ed., *Watching Television*. New York: Pantheon.

——. 1990. "Introduction: The Big Picture," in M. Miller, ed., *Seeing Through the Movies*. New York: Pantheon.

——. 1992. "The Cosby Show," in Gary Colombo et al., *Rereading America: Cultural Contexts for Critical Thinking and Writing*, 2nd ed., pp. 645–52. Boston: St. Martin's Press.

Miller, Toby, and Alec McHoul. 1998. *Culture and Everyday Life*. Thousand Oaks, CA: Sage.

Moerman, Michael. 1977. "The Preference for Self–Correction in a Tai Conversational Corpus," *Language* 53 (4): 872–82.

Montgomery, Kathryn. 1996. "Children in the Digital Age," *American Prospect* 27: 69–75.

Moore, R. Laurence. 1986. *Religious Outsiders and the Making of Americans*. New York: Oxford University Press.

Morgan, David. 1988. *Focus Groups as Qualitative Research*. Thousand Oaks, CA: Sage.

Morley, David. 1986. *Family Television: Cultural Power and Domestic Leisure*. London: Comedia Publishing Group.

——. 1996a. "Populism, Revisionism and the 'New' Audience Research," in James Curran, David Morley, and Valerie Walkerdine, eds., *Cultural Studies and Communications*, pp. 279–305. London: St. Martin's Press.

——. 1996b. "The Audience, the Ethnographer, the Postmodernist, and their Problems," in Peter Crawford and Sigurjon Hafsteinsson, eds., *The Construction of the Viewer*, pp. 11–27. Højbjerg, Denmark: Intervention Press.

Morris, Edmund. 1999. *Dutch: A Memoir of Ronald Reagan*. New York: Random House.

Morrison, Toni. 1997. "The Official Story: Dead Man Golfing," in Toni Morrison and Claudia Lacour, eds., *Birth of a Nation'hood*, pp. vii–xxviii. New York: Pantheon Books.

Moynihan, Daniel. 1965. *The Negro Family*. Washington, DC: Office of Policy Planning and Research, US Department of Labor.

Murdock, Graham. 1997a. "Cultural Studies at the Crossroads," in Angela McRobbie, ed., *Back to Reality?*, pp. 58–73. Manchester: Manchester University Press.

——. 1997b. "Base Notes: The Conditions of Cultural Practice," in Marjorie Ferguson and Peter Golding, eds., *Cultural Studies in Question*, pp. 86–101. Thousand Oaks, CA: Sage.

Murray, John. 1998. "Studying Television Violence: A Research Agenda for the 21st Century," in Joy Keiko Asamen and Gordon L. Berry, eds., *Research Paradigms, Television, and Social Behavior*, pp. 369–410. Thousand Oaks, CA: Sage.

Nakayama, Thomas. 1998. "Stereotyping in the Media: Framing Asian Americans," in Coramae Richey Mann and Marjorie Zatz, eds., *Images of Color, Images of Crime*, pp.179–87. Los Angeles: Roxbury.

Nelkin, Dorothy, and M. Susan Lindee. 1995. *The DNA Mystique: The Gene as Cultural Icon*. New York: W. H. Freeman.

Neuman, W. Russell. 1991. *The Future of the Mass Audience*. Cambridge: Cambridge University Press.

Niemann, Yolanda Flores. 1998. "Social Ecological Contexts of Prejudice Between Hispanics and Blacks," in Paul Wong, ed., *Race, Ethnicity, and Nationality in the United States*, pp. 170–90. Boulder, CO: Westview.

Ogbu, John. 1978. *Minority Education and Caste: The American System in Cross-Cultural Perspective.* New York: Academic Press.

Okihiro, Gary. 1991. *Cane Fires.* Philadelphia, PA: Temple University Press.

Oliver, Melvin, and Thomas Shapiro. 1995. *Black Wealth, White Wealth: A New Perspective on Racial Inequality.* London: Routledge.

Omi, Michael, and Howard Winant. 1994. *Racial Formation in the United States*, 2nd ed. London: Routledge.

Ortner, Sherry. 1974. "Is Female to Male as Nature is to Culture?," in Michelle Rosaldo and Louise Lamphere, eds., *Women, Culture, and Society,* pp. 67–88. Stanford, CA: Stanford University Press.

——. 1996. *Making Gender: The Politics and Erotics of Culture.* Boston: Beacon.

Orum, Anthony, John Johnston, and Stephanie Riger. 1999. *Changing Societies.* Lanham, MD: Rowman and Littlefield.

Palmer, Edward L. 1998. "Major Paradigms and Issues in Television Research: Field of Dreams, World of Realities," in Joy Keiko Asamen and Gordon L. Berry, eds., *Research Paradigms, Television, and Social Behavior,* pp. 39–66. Thousand Oaks, CA: Sage.

Parenti, Michael. 1993. *Inventing Reality.* New York: St. Martin's Press.

Parsons, Talcott. 1937. *The Structure of Social Action: A Study in Social Theory with Special Reference to a Group of Recent European Writers.* New York: McGraw Hill.

——. 1951. *The Social System.* Glencoe, IL: The Free Press.

Peterson, Richard, ed. 1976. *The Production of Culture.* Beverly Hills, CA: Sage.

——. 1978. "The Production of Cultural Change: The Case of Contemporary Country Music," *Social Research* 45: 292–314.

——. 1994. "Culture Studies Through the Production Perspective: Progress and Prospects," in Diana Crane, ed., *The Sociology of Culture,* pp. 163–89. Oxford and Cambridge, MA: Blackwell.

Pfohl, Stephen. 1997. Review of *The Gulf War Did Not Take Place,* by Jean Baudrillard. *Contemporary Sociology* (March): 138–41.

Phillips, D. P. 1982. "The Impact of Fictional Television Stories on U.S. Adult Fatalities: New Evidence on the Effect of the Mass Media on Violence," *American Journal of Sociology* 87: 1340–59.

——. 1983. "The Impact of Mass Media Violence on U.S. Homicides," *American Sociological Review* 48: 560–8.

Plous, S., and Dominique Neptune. 1999. "Racial and Gender Biases in Magazine Advertising: A Content-Analytic Study," in Turner C. Lomand, ed., *Social Science Research,* 2nd ed., pp. 38–46. Los Angeles, CA: Pyrczak Publishing.

Pollner, Melvin. 1987. *Mundane Reason.* Cambridge: Cambridge University Press.

Potter, W. James. 1998. *Media Literacy.* Thousand Oaks, CA: Sage.

Poulantzas, Nicos. 1982. *Political Power and Social Classes.* London: Verso.

Powell, Walter. 1978. "Publishers' Decision Making: What Criteria Do They Use In Deciding Which Books To Publish?" *Social Research* 45: 227–52.

Prager, Jeffrey. 1982. "American Racial Ideology as Collective Representation," *Ethnic and Racial Studies* 5: 99–119.

——. 1999. *Presenting the Past: Psychoanalysis and the Sociology of Misremembering.* Cambridge, MA: Harvard University Press.

Press, Andrea. 1991. *Women Watching Television: Gender, Class, and Generation in the American Television Experience*. Philadelphia: University of Pennsylvania Press.

———. 1994. "The Sociology of Cultural Reception: Notes Toward an Emerging Paradigm," in Diane Crane, ed., *The Sociology of Culture*, pp. 221–45. Oxford and Malden, MA: Blackwell.

Przeworski, Adam. 1991. *Democracy and the Market*. Cambridge: Cambridge University Press.

Pye, Lucian, and Sidney Verba. 1965. *Political Culture and Political Development*. Princeton, NJ: Princeton University Press.

Rabinow, Paul, and William M. Sullivan. 1979. *Interpretive Social Science: A Reader*. Berkeley: University of California Press.

Radcliffe-Brown, Alfred. 1957. *A Natural Science of Society*, with a foreword by Fred Eggan. Glencoe, IL: The Free Press.

———. 1987 [1940]. "On Social Structure," in Herbert Applebaum, ed., *Perspectives in Cultural Anthropology*, pp. 121–35. Albany: State University of New York Press.

Radway, Janice. 1991 [1984]. *Reading the Romance*. Chapel Hill: University of North Carolina Press.

Ragin, Charles, and Howard Becker. 1992. *What is a Case?* Cambridge: Cambridge University Press.

Rakow, Lana F., and Kimberlie Kranich. 1991. "Women as Sign in Television News," *Journal of Communication* 41 (1): 8–24.

Real, Michael. 1996. *Exploring Media Culture*. Thousand Oaks, CA: Sage.

Reinharz, Shulamit. 1992. *Feminist Methods in Social Research*. New York: Oxford University Press.

Richardson, Laurel. 1992. "The Consequences of Poetic Representation: Writing the Other, Writing the Self," in C. Ellis and M.G. Flaherty, eds., *Investigating Subjectivity: Research on Lived Experience*, pp. 125–37. Newbury Park: Sage.

———. 1998. "Writing: A Method of Inquiry," in Norman Denzin and Yvonna Lincoln, eds., *Collecting and Interpreting Qualitative Materials*, pp. 345–71. Thousand Oaks, CA: Sage.

Rickman, H. P. 1976. "Introduction," in H. P. Rickman, ed., *W. Dilthey: Selected Writings*. Cambridge: Cambridge University Press.

———. 1988. *Dilthey Today: A Critical Appraisal of the Contemporary Relevance of His Work*. New York: Greenwood.

Ricoeur, Paul. 1971. "The Model of the Text," *Social Research* 38: 549–57.

Ritzer, George. 1992. *Contemporary Sociological Theory*, 3rd ed. New York: McGraw-Hill.

———. 1997. *Postmodern Social Theory*. New York: McGraw-Hill.

Roach, Colleen. 1997. "Cultural Imperialism and Resistance in Media Theory and Literary Theory," *Media, Culture, and Society* 19: 47–66.

Robertson, Roland. 1970. *The Sociological Interpretation of Religion*. New York: Schocken.

Roediger, David. 1999 [1991]. *The Wages of Whiteness*. London: Verso.

———, ed. 1998. "Introduction," in Roediger, ed., *Black on White*. New York: Schocken.

Roof, Wade Clark, and William McKinney. 1997. "American Mainline Religion: Its Changing Shape and Future," in Thomas Dowdy and Patrick McNamara, eds., *Religion North American Style*, 3rd ed., pp. 66–80. New Brunswick, NJ: Rutgers.

Rose, Anne. 1999. "Religious Individualism in American Families," in Peter W. Williams, ed., *Perspectives on American Religion and Culture*, pp. 319–30. Malden, MA: Blackwell.

Rosenau, Pauline Marie. 1992. *Postmodernism and the Social Sciences*. Princeton, NJ: Princeton University Press.

Ross, Andrew. 1999. *The Celebration Chronicles*. New York: Ballantine Books.

Roy, D. 1952. "Restriction of Output in a Piecework Machine Shop." Ph.D. dissertation, University of Chicago.

Rubin, Herbert J., and Irene S. Rubin. 1995. *Qualitative Interviewing: the Art of Hearing Data*. Thousand Oaks, CA: Sage.

Sacks, Harvey. 1984. "Notes on Methodology," in J. Maxwell Atkinson and John Heritage, eds., *Structures of Social Action: Studies in Conversation Analysis*, pp. 2–17. Cambridge: Cambridge University Press.

Sacks, Harvey, Emmanuel Schegloff, and Gail Jefferson. 1974. "A Simplest Systematics for the Organization of Turn-taking in Conversation," *Language* 50: 696–735.

Sacks, Karen Brodkin. 1994. *How Jews Became White Folks*. New Brunswick, NJ: Rutgers University Press.

——. 1997. "How Did Jews Become White Folks?," in Delgado and Stefancie, eds., *Critical White Studies*.

Said, Edward. 1978. *Orientalism*. London: Routledge.

——. 1993. *Culture and Imperialism*. New York: Knopf.

Sasson, Theodore. 1995. *Crime Talk: How Citizens Construct a Social Problem*. New York: Aldine de Gruyter.

Saussure, Ferdinand de. 1974 [1915]. *Course in General Linguistics*. London: Fontana.

——. 1985. "The Linguistic Sign," in Robert E. Innis, ed., *Semiotics: An Introductory Anthology*, pp. 28–46. Bloomington: University of Indiana Press.

Schegloff, Emanuel. 1979. "Identification and Recognition in Telephone Openings," in George Pasathas, ed., *Everyday Language: Studies in Ethnomethodology*, pp. 23–78. New York: Irvington.

——. 1982. "Discourse as an Interactional Achievement: Some Uses of 'Uh Huh' and Other Things That Come Between Sentences," in Deborah Tannen, ed., *Analyzing Discourse: Text and Talk*, pp. 71–93. Washington, DC: Georgetown University Press.

Schmidt, Leigh Eric. 1995. *Consumer Rites*. Princeton, NJ: Princeton University Press.

Schudson, Michael. 1984. *Advertising, the Uneasy Persuasion: Its Dubious Impact on American Society*. New York: Basic Books.

——. 1994. "Culture and the Integration of National Societies," in Diana Crane, ed., *The Sociology of Culture*, pp. 21–43. Oxford and Cambridge, MA: Blackwell.

Schumpeter, Joseph. 1951. "The Sociology of Imperialism," in *Imperialism and Social Classes*. New York: Kelley.

Schwartz, Barry. 1987. *George Washington: The Making of An American Symbol*. Ithaca,

NY: Cornell University Press.

——. 1998. "Postmodernity and Historical Reputation: Abraham Lincoln in Late Twentieth-Century Memory," *Social Forces* 77 (1): 63–101.

——. 1999. "Message from the Chair," *Newsletter of the Culture Section of the American Sociological Association* 14 (Fall): 1–2.

——. 2000. *Abraham Lincoln and the Forge of National Memory.* Chicago: University of Chicago Press.

Schwartz, Barry, and Todd Bayma. 1999. "Commemoration and the Politics of Recognition: The Korean War Veterans Memorial," *American Behavioral Scientist* 42 (6): 946–67.

Seidman, Steve. 1990. "Substantive Debates: Moral Order and Social Crisis–Perspectives on Modern Culture," in Jeffrey Alexander and Steve Seidman, eds., *Culture and Society: Contemporary Debates,* pp. 217–35. Cambridge: Cambridge University Press.

——. 1994. *Contested Knowledge: Social Theory in the Postmodern Era.* Oxford and Malden, MA: Blackwell.

——. 1997. "Relativizing Sociology: the Challenge of Cultural Studies," in Elizabeth Long, ed., *From Sociology to Cultural Studies,* pp. 37–61. Oxford and Malden, MA: Blackwell.

Shanahan, James, and Michael Morgan. 1999. *Television and its Viewers: Cultivation Theory and Research.* Cambridge: Cambridge University Press.

Shapiro, Gilbert, and John Markoff. 1997. "A Matter of Definition," in Carl W. Roberts, ed., *Text Analysis for the Social Sciences: Methods for Drawing Statistical Inferences from Texts and Transcripts,* pp. 9–34. Hillsdale, NJ: Lawrence Erlbaum.

Sharma, Miriam. 1980. "Pinoy in Paradise: Environment and Adaptation of Filipinos in Hawai'i, 1906–1946,"*Amerasia Journal* 7: 91–117.

Shively, JoEllen. 1992. "Cowboys and Indians: Perceptions of Western Films Among American Indians and Anglos," *American Sociological Review* 57 (Dec.): 725–34.

Silverman, David. 1993. *Interpreting Qualitative Data.* London: Sage.

Simon, David, and Edward Burns. 1997. *The Corner: A Year in the Life of an Inner-City Neighborhood.* New York: Broadway Books.

Singer, Jerome, and Dorothy G. Singer. 1998. "*Barney and Friends* as Entertainment and Education: Evaluating the Quality and Effectiveness of a Television Series for Preschool Children," in Joy Keiko Asamen and Gordon L. Berry, eds., *Research Paradigms, Television, and Social Behavior,* pp. 305–67. Thousand Oaks, CA: Sage.

Skocpol, Theda. 1979. *States and Social Revolutions.* Cambridge: Cambridge University Press.

Slotkin, Richard. 1973. *Regeneration Through Violence: The Mythology of the American Frontier, 1660–1880.* Middletown, CT: Wesleyan University Press.

Smart, Ninian. 1995. *Choosing a Faith.* London/New York: Boyars/Bowerdean.

Smith, Christian. 1998. *American Evangelicalism: Embattled and Thriving.* Chicago: University of Chicago Press.

Smith, Philip, ed. 1998. *The New American Cultural Sociology.* Cambridge: Cambridge University Press.

Smythe, Dallas W. 1954. "Reality as Presented by Television," *Public Opinion Quarterly* 18: 143–56.

Snow, David A., and Robert D. Benford. 1988. "Ideology, Frame Resonance, and Participant Mobilization," *Interactional Social Movement Research* 1: 197–217.

——. 1992. "Master Frames and Cycles of Protest," in Aldon Morris and Carol McClurg Mueller, eds., *Frontiers in Social Movement Theory*. New Haven, CT: Yale University Press.

Snow, David A., E. Burke Rochford, Steven Worden, and Robert D. Benford. 1986. "Frame Alignment Processes, Mobilization, and Movement Participation," *American Sociological Review* 51: 464–81.

Solomon, Jack. 1988. *The Signs of our Time*. New York: St. Martin's Press.

Spencer, Ranier. 1999. *Spurious Issues: Race and Multiracial Identity Politics in the United States*. Boulder, CO: Westview.

Spurrier, Joseph. 1978. *The Church of Jesus Christ of Latter-day Saints in the Hawaiian Islands*. Honolulu: Honolulu Mission of the Church of Jesus Christ of Latter-day Saints.

Stark, Rodney, and Laurence Iannaccone. 1992. "Religion," in Edgar F. and Mary L. Borgatta, eds., *Encyclopedia of Sociology*, vol. 2, pp. 2031–3. New York: Macmillan.

Starr, Paul. "Computing Our Way to Educational Reform," *American Prospect* 27: 50–60.

Stavans, Ilan. 1995. *The Hispanic Condition*. New York: HarperCollins.

Stein, Stephen. 1999. "Religious Innovation at the Edge," in Peter Williams, ed., *Perspectives on American Religion and Culture*, pp. 22–33. Oxford and Malden, MA: Blackwell.

Steinberg, Laurence. 1996 . *Beyond the Classroom*. New York: Simon and Schuster.

Steinberg, Stephen. 1981. *The Ethnic Myth: Race, Ethnicity, and Class in America*. New York: Atheneum.

——. 1999. "The Liberal Retreat from Race," in Steinberg, ed., *Race and Ethnicity in the United States: Issues and Debates*, pp. 37–54. Malden, MA: Cambridge University Press.

Stinchcombe, Arthur. 1978. *Theoretical Methods in Social History*. New York: Academic Press. Stocking, G. W. 1968. *Race, Culture, and Evolution*. Chicago: University of Chicago Press.

——. 1987. *Victorian Anthropology*. New York: The Free Press.

Storey, John. 1993. *An Introductory Guide to Cultural Theory and Popular Culture*. New York: Wheatsheaf.

——. 1996. *Cultural Studies and the Study of Popular Cultures*. Athens: University of Georgia Press.

——. 1998. *Cultural Theory and Popular Culture*, 2nd ed. Athens: University of Georgia Press.

Strinati, Dominic. 1995. *An Introduction to Theories of Popular Culture*. London: Routledge.

Stroman, Carolyn, and Kenneth E. Jones. 1998. "The Analysis of Television Content," in Joy Keiko Asamen and Gordon L. Berry, eds., *Research Paradigms, Television, and Social Behavior*, pp. 271–85. Thousand Oaks, CA: Sage.

Swartz, David. 1997. *Culture and Power: The Sociology of Pierre Bourdieu*. Chicago: University of Chicago Press.

Swidler, Ann. 1986. "Culture in Action: Symbols and Strategies,"*American Socio-

logical Review 51(3): 273–86.

——. 1995. "Cultural Power and Social Movements," in Hank Johnston and Bert Klandermans, eds., *Social Movements and Culture*, pp. 3–24. Minneapolis: University of Minnesota Press.

Szasz, Ferenc. 1993. "Religion in America," in Mick Gidley, ed., *Modern American Culture: An Introduction*, pp. 23–44. London: Longman.

Takaki, Ronald. 1993. *A Different Mirror*. Boston: Little, Brown.

Taylor, John. 1994. "The Rosewood Massacre," *Esquire* 122 (1): 46.

Taylor, Verta, and Nancy Whittier. 1995. "The Culture of the Women's Movement," in Hank Johnston and Bert Kandermans, eds., *Social Movements and Culture*, pp. 163–87. Minneapolis: University of Minnesota Press.

Thom, René. 1985. "From the Icon to the Symbol," in Robert E. Innis, ed., *Semiotics: An Introductory Anthology*, pp. 275–91. Bloomington: Indiana University Press.

Thompson, E. P. 1963. *The Making of the English Working Class*. New York: Random House.

Thompson, John B. 1984. *Studies in the Theory of Ideology*. Berkeley: University of California Press.

Thorne, Barrie. 1995. Review of Robyn Holmes, *How Young Children Perceive Race*. *Contemporary Sociology* 24 (5): 602–3.

Thornton, Sarah. 1997. "Introduction," in K. Gelder and S. Thornton, eds., *The Subcultures Reader*. London: Routledge.

Thorson, Esther. 1989. "Processing Television Commercials," in B. Dervin et al., *Rethinking Communication: Paradigm Exemplars*. Newbury Park, CA: Sage.

Thrasher, Frederic Milton. 1927. *The Gang*. Chicago: University of Chicago Press.

Tilly, Charles. 1978. *From Mobilization to Revolution*. Reading, MA: Addison-Wesley.

Tiryakian, Edward. 1993. "American Religious Exceptionalism," *Annals of the American Academy of Political and Social Science* 527 (May): 40–83.

——. 1996. "Three Metacultures of Modernity: Christian, Gnostic, Chthonic," *Theory, Culture, and Society* 13 (1): 99–118.

Torpey, John. 1998. "Coming and Going: On the State Monopolization of the Legitimate Means of Movement," *Sociological Theory* 16 (Nov.): 239–59.

Trask, Huanani Kay. 1999 [1993]. *From a Native Daughter: Colonialism and Sovereignty in Hawaiʻi*. Honolulu: University of Hawaiʻi Press.

Trueheart, Charles. 1996. "Welcome to the Next Church," *The Atlantic Monthly* (Aug.) (as copied from internet).

Turner, Graeme. 1996 [1990]. *British Cultural Studies*, 2nd ed. London: Routledge.

Tyack, David. 1999. "The Politics of Textbooks," *American Behavioral Scientist* 42 (6): 922-32.

Tylor, Edward B. 1958. [1871]. *Primitive Culture: Researches Into the Development of Mythology, Philosophy, Religion, Art, and Custom*. Gloucester, MA: Smith.

Updike, John. 1999. "The Future of Faith," *The New Yorker*, Nov. 29, pp. 84–91.

Van Biema, David. 1997. "Kingdom Come: Salt Lake City Was Just For Starters," *Time* 150 (5) (Aug. 4) (via http://www.california.com/`rpcman/TIME.HTM).

Van Maanen, John. 1988. *Tales of the Field*. Chicago: University of Chicago Press.

Veblen, Thorstein. 1953 [1899]. *The Theory of the Leisure Class*. New York: New American Library.

Wagner-Pacifici, Robin. 1986. *The Moro Morality Play: Terrorism as Social Drama.* Chicago: University of Chicago Press.

———. 1994. *Discourse and Destruction: The City of Philadelpha vs. MOVE.* Chicago: University of Chicago Press.

———. 2000. *Theorizing the Standoff: Contingency and Action.* Cambridge: Cambridge University Press.

Wagner-Pacifici, Robin, and Barry Schwartz. 1991. "The Vietnam Veterans Memorial: Commemorating a Difficult Past," *American Journal of Sociology* 97: 376–420.

Wallerstein, Immanuel. 1974. *The Modern World System*, 3 vols. Cambridge: Cambridge University Press.

Walters, Suzanna. 1995. *Material Girls.* Berkeley: University of California Press.

Warner, R. Stephen. 1993. "Work in Progress towards a New Paradigm for the Sociological Study of Religion in the United States," *American Journal of Sociology* 98: 1044–93.

Waters, Mary. 1999. "Explaining the Comfort Factor: West Indian Immigrants Confront American Race Relations," in Michèle Lamont, ed., *The Cultural Territories of Race: Black and White Boundaries*, pp. 63–96. Chicago: University of Chicago Press.

Webb, T. D. 1994. "Missionaries, Polynesians and Tourists: Mormonism and Tourism in La'ie, Hawai'i," *Social Process in Hawai'i* 35: 195–212.

Weber, Max. 1968 [1922]. *Economy and Society*, vol. 1. Berkeley: University of California Press.

———. 1974 [1946]. *From Max Weber: Essays in Sociology.* Trans. and ed. H. H. Gerth and C. W. Mills. New York: Oxford University Press.

———. 1996 [1904–5]. *The Protestant Ethic and the Spirit of Capitalism.* Los Angeles: Roxbury.

Weeks, Jeffrey. 1981. *Sex, Politics, and Society.* London: Longman.

———. 1985. *Sexuality and its Discontents.* London: Routledge.

Weitz, Rose. 1992. *Life with AIDS.* New Brunswick, NJ: Rutgers University Press.

Westley, W.A. 1951. "Violence and the Police" Ph.D. dissertation, University of Chicago.

White, Armond. 1997. "Eye, the Jury," in Toni Morrison and Claudia Bordsky Lacour, eds., *Birth of a Nation'hood*, pp. 339–66. New York: Pantheon.

Whyte, William Foote. 1943. *Street Corner Society.* Chicago: University of Chicago Press.

Wieder, D. Lawrence. 1988 [1974]. *Language and Social Reality: The Case of Telling the Convict Code.* Lanham, MD: University Press of America.

Williams, Raymond. 1977. *Marxism and Literature.* Oxford: Oxford University Press.

Williamson, Judith. 1978. *Decoding Advertisements: Ideology and Meaning in Advertising.* London: Marion Boyars.

Willis, Paul. 1977. *Learning to Labor.* New York: Columbia University Press.

Willis, Susan. 1991. *A Primer for Daily Life.* London: Routledge.

Wilson, William Julius. 1978. *The Declining Significance of Race.* Chicago: University of Chicago Press.

———. 1987. *The Truly Disadvantaged.* Chicago: University of Chicago Press.

———. 1996. *When Work Disappears.* New York: Knopf.

Winant, Howard. 1994. *Racial Conditions*. Minneapolis: University of Minnesota Press.

Wong, Paul, Chienping Faith Lai, Richard Nagasawa and Tieming Lin. 1998. "Asian Americans as a Model Minority: Self -Perceptions and Perceptions by Other Racial Groups," *Sociological Perspectives* 4l: 95–118.

Wood, Houston. 1999. *Displacing Natives*. Lanham, MD: Rowman and Littlefield.

Woodward, C. Vann. 1998. "Dangerous Liaisons." Review of Martha Hodes, *White Women, Black Men: Iillicit Sex in the Nineteenth-Century South. New York Review*, Feb.19, pp. 14–16.

Worsley, Peter. 1997. *Knowledges*. New York: The New Press.

Wright, Will. 1975. *Sixguns and Society: A Structural Study of the Western*. Berkeley: University of California Press.

Wurfel, David. 1988. *Filipino Politics: Development and Decay*. Ithaca, NY: Cornell University Press.

Wuthnow, Robert. 1988. *The Restructuring of American Religion: Society and Faith Since World War II*. Princeton, NJ: Princeton University Press.

——. 1994. *Producing the Sacred: An Essay on Public Religion*. Champaign: University of Illinois Press.

——. 1998. *After Heaven: Spirituality in America Since the 1950s*. Berkeley: University of California Press.

Yang, J. E., and A. Devroy. 1992. "Quayle: 'Hollywood Doesn't Get It,'" *Washington Post*, May 10, p. 19.

Zerubavel, Eviatar. 1997. *Social Mindscapes: An Invitation to Cognitive Sociology*. Cambridge, MA: Harvard University Press.

Zimmerman, Don. 1988 [1974]. "Preface," in D. L. Wieder, *Language and Social Reality*, pp. 9–26. Lanham, MD: University Press of America.

Index

CPSIA information can be obtained
at www.ICGtesting.com
Printed in the USA
JSHW010942160723
44675JS00009B/98

9 780631 210900